Islam and the Political

DECOLONIAL STUDIES, POSTCOLONIAL HORIZONS

General editors:
Barnor Hesse (Northwestern University) and S. Sayyid (University of Leeds)

Since the end of the Cold War, unresolved conjunctures and crises of race, ethnicity, religion, diversity, diaspora, globalization, the West and the non-West, have radically projected the meaning of the political and the cultural beyond the traditional verities of Left and Right. Throughout this period, Western developments in "international relations" have become increasingly defined as corollaries to national "race-relations" across both the European Union and the United States, where the reformation of Western imperial discourses and practices has been given particular impetus by the "war against terror." At the same time hegemonic Western continuities of racial profiling and colonial innovations have attested to the incomplete and interrupted institutions of the postcolonial era. Today we are witnessing renewed critiques of these postcolonial horizons at the threshold of attempts to inaugurate the political and cultural forms that decolonization now needs to take within and between the West and the "non-West." This book series explores and discusses radical ideas that open up and advance understandings of these politically multicultural issues and theoretically interdisciplinary questions.

Islam and the Political

Theory, Governance and
International Relations

AMR G. E. SABET

Pluto Press

LONDON • ANN ARBOR, MI

First published 2008 by Pluto Press
345 Archway Road, London N6 5AA
and 839 Greene Street, Ann Arbor, MI 48106

www.plutobooks.com

British Library Cataloguing in Publication Data
A catalogue record for this book is available from the British Library

ISBN   978 0 7453 2720 4   hardback
ISBN   978 0 7453 2719 8   paperback

Library of Congress Cataloging in Publication Data applied for

10   9   8   7   6   5   4   3   2   1

Designed and produced for Pluto Press by
Chase Publishing Services Ltd, Fortescue, Sidmouth, EX10 9QG, England
Typeset from disk by Stanford DTP Services, Northampton, England
Printed and bound in the European Union by
CPI Antony Rowe, Chippenham and Eastbourne

Contents

Acknowledgements

This book is mostly a compilation of versions of articles which have been published earlier in English. Exceptions are the Introduction, the final chapter—which has been translated and published in Turkish but has not appeared in English—and the interview.

Chapter 1 was published in *Religion, State and Society*, vol. 24 (2/3) (September 1996). Chapter 2 in *Orient*, vol. 38/1 (March 1997). Chapter 3 was also published in *Orient*, vol. 35/4 (December 1994). Chapter 4 was published twice in different academic journals, *Peace and Conflict Studies*, vol. 8/2 (November 2001) and *Religion, State and Society*, vol. 31/2 (June 2003). Chapter 5 was published with minor modification to the title in *Amsterdam Middle East Papers (AMEP)*, Amsterdam: Research Center for International Political Economy and Foreign Policy Analysis, no. 1 (July 1995). Chapter 6 was published in *The Emirates Occasional Papers* as a monograph (Emirates Center for Strategic Studies and Research [ECSSR], vol. 52, 2003). Finally, Chapter 7 on "Human Rights" was published in Turkish, in *Human Rights Review*, Turkey 4/7 2007). I wish to thank all the editors of the above journals for granting permission to republish these articles.

In addition, I owe a debt of gratitude to friends and colleagues who have helped so much in making this work a reality, in particular to the Decolonial Studies series general editors Barnor Hesse and S. Sayyid. Special thanks to S. Sayyid (University of Leeds, UK), who suggested the idea for the book, made valuable comments, and to whom I am much indebted for all his help and encouragement in bringing this project to fruition. The same of course goes for Barnor Hesse (Northwestern University, USA).

I would also like to extend my thanks to David Castle, Commissioning Editor at Pluto Press, for supporting this perhaps challenging project, and for his willingness to accommodate "alternative perspectives."

The interview that closes the book would not have been possible without the sincere and tireless efforts of—in alphabetical order—Cemalettin Hashimi, Shehla Khan, and Nuh Yilmaz to whom I express my deep appreciation for their collaboration and help in conducting the interview.

The anonymous reviewers who supported the publication of this work deserve a good part of my gratitude, particularly for their positive and helpful comments which I have attempted to address wherever possible in the book. Any shortcomings, however, remain the sole responsibility of the author.

Last but not least, I wish to convey my indebtedness to the Department of Public Administration, Vaasa University, Finland, and to all my friends and colleagues there, who have made my visit most enjoyable and productive. My stay at the Department during the 2006–2007 academic year was instrumental in accomplishing the writing of the book.

Introduction

ISLAMIC POLITICS OR POLITICS OF ISLAM: SOME CONCEPTUAL ISSUES

Tenuous differences between terms such as Islamic politics and politics of Islam frequently lead to conceptual confusion. Discerning the relationship between both, therefore, is a matter of complexity and subtlety as well as of risk and intrigue. It is complex and subtle because in many cases the two are organically linked and intertwined. Islamic politics by necessity if not by definition incorporates politics of Islam. Risk and intrigue, however, emanate from the fact that the opposite does not necessarily hold true. Politics of Islam do not inevitably reflect Islamic politics. Mixing up both is a major source of confusion, uncertainty, and disorientation. In many ways, the problem is similar to mystification of ontology and epistemology on the methodological level, strategy and tactics in political and military decision-making, constant values and changing circumstances or conditions on the level of parameters and variables, and consistency and discrepancy at the operational level. While all may be organically linked, inherent in their relationships are potential contradictions. When epistemology for instance always falls back on its ontology dialectically or otherwise, this is a case for a consistent *self-referential* method of thinking. In the different case where epistemology refers to an alien ontology, such as, for example, when Islamic values are justified in terms of an external knowledge system, the outcome is very different and likely to be *other-referential*. The same holds true when we talk about strategy and tactics. The best of strategies could be supported or undermined by consistent or discrepant tactics, respectively. By the same line of reasoning, politics of Islam may consolidate Islamic politics, or in some cases may go so far so as to undermine it. Involved of course are issues of methodological performance, but also of credibility in the light of which micro politics, i.e. the details, the trees, are tested against the macro politics, i.e. the broad picture, the forest. Clarifying differences between Islamic politics and politics of Islam, therefore, is not simply a matter of definitions or of posing comparative distinctions, but also involves a process of conceptual *construction*. This requires creative and mutually buttressing theoretical conceptualization and understanding competencies and capabilities, linking the abstract and the concrete.

Theories, as Kenneth Waltz has observed, are made "creatively" (Waltz 1979:9). "The paradox of creativity," however, "is that it requires both great familiarity with a subject matter, *and* the ability to approach it from a fresh angle" (Kleindorfer et al. 1993:55). By the same token, it must follow a "due process of inquiry" which relates the logic, procedures, and choice of appropriate approaches, to the relevant subject matter (Landau 1972:219–21; quoted by Waltz 1979:13). The process of creativity is thus strongly correlated with the problematization of issues and the search for alternatives; in Islamic parlance, to *ijtihad*. Limitations caused by self-imposed constraints, connected to feelings of "self-discouragement" that a particular course of theoretical creativity or action policy is not possible, will not work, or cannot be done (Kleindorfer et al. 1993:55), are in many instances both constituted by and constitutive of ideological perceptions. An interrelated system of preferences is at play which connects intellectual creativity to ideology. A relationship that is particularly tenuous when a religious worldview limits the horizons of preferences or adaptations that can be made with respect to an opposing worldview or an order, domestic or global, not of its own making.

To theorize is at the same time to conceptualize, and to conceptualize is to understand. "'Understanding' ... means ... having whatever ideas and concepts are needed to recognize that a great many different phenomena are part of a coherent whole" (Heisenberg 1971:33). While a total agreement on the truth-value of subsumed propositions or assumptions may remain wanting, a frame of reference nevertheless exists which informs an intellectual structure of themes developed. This involves a series of processes by which theoretical matrices achieve a significant measure of relative *consensus* and comprehension in any particular community. Conceptualization, in other words, allows for undergoing the theoretical process by which advancement from the level of abstract ideas or constructs toward policy development and application can be made. It guards against confusion and *ad hoc* decision-making, and serves to set and sustain subsequent policies within a coherent strategic framework. It follows, therefore, that a lack of conception or of a conceptual reference entails a lack of and inability to understand or comprehend. It further means that the ability to tackle the flow of information becomes acutely diminished, as is the capacity to judge or make decisions of a strategic nature. Failing to conceptualize and/ or process information preempts the competence to act.

Conceptualization and intellectual sophistication are necessary conditions for understanding and action, yet their effectiveness lies essentially in the ability of ideas and beliefs to create or construct a corresponding reality. Mental structures or imagery may or may not correspond to objective material conditions. They cannot be assumed as intertwined or directly correlated. Where self-conception or identity *dialectically* coincides with structural reality, satisfaction may ensue and the *status quo* be safeguarded. Where this is not the case, and a wide discrepancy exists between the two constitutive dimensions, a sense of crisis develops which is detrimental to a culture or a civilization's strength of character, equanimity, and consistency. This makes the issue of identity, or "what makes *us* believe we are the same and *them* different ... inseparable from security" (Booth 1997:6) and this is essentially a religio-political issue.

Islam in contemporary times has been facing real and serious challenges to its identity structure from a rapidly transforming world and a concomitantly changing order of values. The resulting imbalances and confusion that have afflicted Muslims in effectively all their social, political, economic, strategic, and religious domains, have imposed on them soul-searching questions of existential significance about *what has gone wrong and, what is to be done*. These questions have been wrestled with by many Muslims, scholars as well as laymen, in their different ways, largely from the nineteenth century to the present. Yet no clear consensus has been reached or unambiguous answers finalized. These seemingly perennial questions continue to impose themselves, calling for additional efforts which can help in systematizing a way of thinking that has so far remained incoherent, apologetic, and abstract. This way of thinking was problematic in the fashion it sought to link social theory with Islamic thought, or in its attempt to tackle modern as well as post-modern concerns from a supposedly Islamic perspective. It has not been uncommon for example—depending on circumstances, background, or predispositions—for socialist or liberal-democratic ideas to be re-packaged as basically Islamic principles: it was Islam which had always called for social justice, and it was Islam which had always upheld democracy and freedom. Much in this work attempts to challenge and contest such defensive and apologetic approaches. Mechanisms in general are intertwined with the values upholding them, and democracy whether it be a concept or a sheer procedure can not be separated from its liberal, and therefore secular, umbilical cord and all the power relations which ensue therefrom.

"The high points of politics" as Carl Schmitt has put it, "are simultaneously the moments in which the enemy is, in concrete clarity, recognized as the enemy" (Schmitt 1976:67). By enemy here is not necessarily meant a sole relationship of hostility, but, as significantly, of *demarcation*. It becomes a high point of politics therefore to illustrate how and why Islamic values, principles of governance, and global relations must be differentiated from those of liberal and democratic notions, if they are to remain as *necessary* parameters, not merely as contingent variables. On one level the purpose is to question Western concepts, which have come to occupy a position of "Truth," and emphasize the need to rethink narratives of triumphant secularism and its liberal assumptions about what is politically and morally essential to modern life. The constraints of so-called "political correctness" are thus contested. On another level, the purpose is to expand Islamic theoretical frameworks, to revitalize Islamic thought, and to suggest possible alternatives, using analytical and empirical tools. For, as Abdul-Hamid Abu-Sulayman has observed, the main faults of Islamic classical thought, as well as some contemporary views informed by it, are located not in content but in methodology. Those faults were linked to the absence of a clear conceptualization of the space-time dimension, lack of empiricism (with the notable exception of Ibn Khaldun), and of a rigorous systematic approach to the development of Islamic social and human sciences (Abu-Sulayman 1993:87–94). This book is an attempt at providing a methodological and constructive input toward addressing these issues.

I wish to stress here, however, that this study is not an attempt to make any claims for some form of "Islamization of knowledge" or for that matter, its secularization—claims which I believe harbor more problems than they resolve. Rather it aims toward the *integration* of knowledge, whether secular or religious, through a measure of *intersubjectivity*. In addition to attempting to integrate Islamic thought and social theory, this study seeks to link the former with *decolonization* in order to underscore Islam's liberating commitment not only toward Muslims but toward humanity at large. The decolonization process that had taken place during the post World War II era remains, unfortunately, an unfinished, and even a regressing, project. It could no longer be simply reduced to nominal political independence of the colonized, when in fact colonialism is well and thriving, consolidated by full-fledged alliances with ruling domestic "fifth columns."

In addition to political, as well as economic, independence there is the essential need for the independence of thought, of the mental, the psychological, and the spiritual; for the exorcising of souls and liberating of minds. While *"exorcising"* may constitute the most difficult and tormenting phase of decolonization, it is at this level nevertheless that the ambiguities and ambivalences of incomplete and partial forms of decolonization must be addressed. This can be performed through the development of an anti-imperialist multicultural reformation of knowledge, of polities, economies, and societies, which Islam is eminently qualified to support and sustain. Exorcising, therefore, necessitates never losing sight of preserving and maintaining independence of the ontological and epistemological foundations of Islam, as well as its spirit and universality. It perhaps also involves an acknowledgment that it may still be too early to talk about a "post-colonial" phase.

ON THE INTERNAL CONDITION OF THE MUSLIM WORLD

At this historical juncture, much of the Muslim world is in a state of disarray. There appears to be no clear vision as to where it stands, what determining role its faith should play, and what, as a community of God (*Umma*), is the horizon of its action and position among nations. As a matter of faith, Muslims believe they are entitled to a leading position, not simply as a role but as a mission and obligation (Qur'an 2:143; 22:78; 48:28). Evading such responsibilities carries its own penalties, both worldly and beyond.[1] As far as this world is concerned, strategically speaking, "[e]ligible states [and nations] that fail to attain [their worthy] status are predictably punished" (Layne 1995:134). This maxim is taken as a matter of starting point. Yet other consequences follow—political, military, social, and economic—all merging into the crucible of cultural domination and identity formation. The first step of persuading the Muslim community to undercut its own eligibility is followed by means and methods aiming at throwing it back on the defensive, leveling accusations against it such as "fundamentalism," "terrorism," "extremism," among a range of other possibilities. The idea is to make an opponent or adversary, in this case the Muslims, "uneasy and apologetic" about any objective or objectives it may have or wish to pursue. This would constitute "a first small step in the process of those objectives," *"erosion"* inducing a dynamic through which the adversary would start discarding them (Harkabi 1977:88).[2] This then allows for a continuous process of chipping away at the *will* and resistance of the antagonist, creating new space for the hegemonic induction of new ideas and identity-altering structures associated with claims of superiority and universality. As former US national security advisor Zbigniew Brzezinski pointed out, "cultural superiority, successfully asserted and quietly conceded," has the effect of "reducing the need to rely on large military forces to maintain the power of the imperial center" (Brzezinski 1997:21). The purpose is to generate a good degree of compliance among members of a targeted group, as "the successful state, like the successful criminal, wishes to enjoy [the] spoils in peace and this requires a measure of consent ... from the victims ..." (Reynolds 1989:5).

Such dynamics call for an engaging ability to observe, to conceptualize, to understand, and to theorize, as a prerequisite, most importantly, to planning, organizing, and acting. This is a protracted, risky and arduous *process*. Yet as challenging as it may be, it has been facilitated by the fact that a religio-historical experience, represented by the Iranian Islamic revolution, is actually unfolding on the global landscape in the realm of *praxis*. The dialectics of theory and praxis may thus be "at hand." Such *dialectics* propose the Iranian Islamic revolutionary experience as a model to be studied and evaluated based largely on self-referential Islamic standards. Secondly, they link and embed this experience's unfolding religious, theoretical, and practical manifestations into the dynamics of Islamic history as a means of contributing to a possible intellectual reorientation in the field of social theory, as well as in that of *mazhabi* or Islamic paradigmatic communities. Thirdly, they help identify certain processes and structural distinctions between a case that actually constitutes an Islamic system or regime (i.e. practices Islamic politics), and one that makes a claim to be one (i.e. practices politics of Islam).

A brief comparison of approaches to the nature of systems in the two countries of Iran and Saudi Arabia may help underscore the significance of dialectical distinctions, and provide justifications for theoretical and/or empirical choices made in this study. Both countries harbor systems which present themselves as Islamic.[3] Consequently, Lawrence Davidson (1998) set both Iran and Saudi Arabia in a common Islamic "fundamentalist" framework. In many ways, this is problematic and disinforming. Structurally speaking, Saudi Arabia is a feudal dynastic and absolute monarchy ruling by the right of conquest (Nehme 1998:278, 286, 287). It bears many of the negative characteristics of the historical Umayyad dynasty

(661–750 CE), whose founding ruling figures continue to occupy a seminal position in Wahhabism, the Saudi official school of thought. Ibn Taymiyya (1263–1328 CE), the school's precursor, was a staunch sympathizer of the corrupt and transgressing (*bughat*) Umayyads, at times even against the house of the Prophet (*Al al-Bayt*). The Umayyad dynasty was also considered, even if retrospectively, to be the "Sunni" state par excellence, as opposed to Shi'ite partisans of Ali and the Prophetic household. Yet, it was never perceived as "fundamentalist." Furthermore, the Umayyad state is acknowledged in significantly large and influential Muslim quarters to have brought about the historical shift away from Islamic Caliphate (*Khilafa*) to the corrupt form of tyrannical and hereditary kingship (*al-mulk al-adud*). If the Saudi–Umayyad analogy stands, then one may conclude that Saudi Arabia, notwithstanding its extensive ritualistic trappings, is neither "fundamentalist" nor Islamic, whether structurally or in the basic thrust of its policies and attitudes (process).[4] In terms of structure, it is "*mulk adud.*" In terms of process, as Naveed Sheikh has perceptively observed, "division [of Arabs and Muslims] rather than unification, had always been the preferred way" of the Saudi regime "to maintain leverage" (Sheikh 2003:34). With American help, this regime's perpetual policy of opposing the rise of any Arab or Islamic regional power—be it Egypt, during President Gamal Abdel Nasser's days (1954–70), or current Islamic Iran—essentially served to render Israel the real and sole regional power. It constituted the real foundation of the *de facto* complicity between Israel and the Saudi regime. This anachronistic feudal hypocrisy is then equated with the Iranian Islamic regime, a system based on the principal structural components of *allegiance* (*baya'a*/stem = *Wilayat al-Faqih*) and *choice* (*ikhtiar*/branch = presidency), and whose general religio-political thrust is legitimate in terms of its independence, self-reliance, credible respect, and preservation of Islamic dignity and values internally and *vis-à-vis* the external world. If this assessment stands, why then is Iran designated as "fundamentalist" and not just as Islamic? What purpose does a "fundamentalist" qualification serve? More importantly, what justification is there in the first place to include both regimes in a common framework?

This raises serious questions about the viability of studies which adopt such undiscriminating approaches. By attributing an Islamic character to both regimes one of which is not Islamic, and a "fundamentalist" label to both when neither is, one can imagine the amount and extent of confusion that such a framework of conflicting logics may generate. It provides an opportunity for what may be termed *intellectual strategic deception*. The whole idea behind such deception is to get an opposite party to confuse its purpose and understanding, and/or to do what one wants, consciously, or better yet unconsciously. Essentially that is, to get that opponent to lose his/her sense of self-conception. This would serve two main purposes. First, by subtly and deceptively equating an Islamic regime with a non-Islamic one it creates confusion—throwing the needle into the haystack so to speak. Second, it *liberates* any presumably hostile policy toward Islam, separating religious from political targeting theoretically, while targeting both practically. Consequently Davidson, for instance, can make the claim that American hostility to one "variant" of Islamic interpretation is not to be perceived as targeting Islam but only one policy behavior, or merely one "interpretation." "Friendly" American–Saudi relations are then introduced as an alibi and a confirmation (Davidson 1998:xiii–xiv). King Abdullah of Saudi Arabia, for example, appears to be in the process of being built-up by American media as a "Saudi Desert Fox" who seeks to "take the lead in a strife-torn Middle East," "brushing aside" the United States. This polishing-up process sounds eerily similar to the one in the early 1980s when, shortly before attacking Iran, Saddam Hussain was hailed by the same media as the "Bismarck of the Arabs." In case there are any doubts, *Newsweek* Magazine sought to remind the King of Plato's saying: "He who refuses to rule is liable to be ruled by one worse than himself [read Iran]" (*Newsweek*, April 9, 2007:20–1). The underlying message or subtle threat seems to be, either you lead against Iran, or Iran will lead instead. No wonder that at the Riyadh 19th Arab Summit held on March 28–29, 2007, the King ironically adopted Arab nationalist jargon, so unbefitting of Saudi Arabia. In addition, the conference's final statement, the "Riyadh Declaration," reiterated peace with Israel to be a "strategic choice"—a choice that seems to be reasserted every time some form of aggression against an Arab or Islamic country is in the offing.

Some Muslim intellectuals therefore, including prominent figures such as Hasan al-Banna and Sayyed Qutb, tended to step into murky waters when they claimed that as long as the *Shari'ah* (Islamic Law) is implemented, an Islamic regime could take any form. While there is always room for *differentiation*, this is very different from making imprecise statements of this kind. The actual and *bona fide* application of the Shari'ah as a matter of fact would prohibit this. Moreover, not-withstanding variations, there must be some predominantly common features and idiosyncrasies so that a regime may be defined as Islamic or, more significantly, as non-Islamic, even if it purports to apply the Shari'ah or its pretenses. This is a most important intellectual challenge, which demands the setting of parameters and constraints on the instrumental manipulation of religion. Precise standards of religio-intellectual *falsification* and *affirmation* are required in order to avoid capricious and uninformed judgments about what constitutes Islamic politics as opposed to politics of Islam or sheer opportunism. After all Saudi Arabia claims to "apply" the Shari'ah. Would not this therefore justify a monarchic hereditary system as well as its policies? Inadvertently, some Islamists have provided the intellectual cover for such discrepancies.

The first two chapters that follow attempt to challenge the above assertions while providing for theoretical and methodological alternatives. Chapter 1 examines the dynamic relationship between religion and social change within a theoretical framework that links elements of liberation theology with the revolutionary work of the Iranian intellectual Ali Shari'ati. Chapter 2 attempts to develop a methodology of *appropriation of modernity* that may help "Islamic thought" in a broad sense to interact positively and pro-actively, rather than adaptively or re-actively, with the imperatives of modernity and/or post-modernity, while preserving its sense of integrity. Further elaborations for the choice of the Iranian revolution as an authentic Islamic manifestation are made more apparent in chapters 3 and 4. Chapter 3 elaborates Abd al-Rahman Ibn Khaldun's (1332–1406 AD) concept of *assabiyya* (solidarity) as an *Islamic* concept, and is linked with the principle of Wilayat al-Faqih.

Some ambiguities have been associated with the use of assabiyya and thus some additional reasons and clarifications may be needed regarding its designation as an Islamic concept. Ibn Khaldun's notion of assabiyya has been largely understood and judged by contemporary scholars in the very terms that the great historian had used, over six centuries ago, to refer to tribal solidarities. No serious attempts have been made to expand it or to re-infuse the concept so as to render it more relevant to contemporary forms of solidarities, linking it for instance to socio-political theories of hegemony (à la Gramsci), elites (Pareto, Mosca, Michels), vanguards (Lenin), or Wilayat al-Faqih (Ayatollah Khomeini), among other possibilities. Furthermore, claims that the Khaldunian concept, approach and methodology were *Islamic* are further met with skepticism, as not particularly linked to the ways of "real" Islamic thought, and as being closer instead to the presumably "universal" aspects of social theory. In this study I attempt to expand and reconstruct the concept of assabiyya beyond its conventional and narrow Khaldunian meaning in order to apply it to contemporary structures and contingencies. This requires further exposition.

First, as one of the two pillars of a possible theory and principle of hegemonic leadership, it is significant to note that assabiyya comes from the root Arabic word 'ASB, which means the nerve or the command center of something. It refers, that is, to the ability to exercise *will* power, the foundation of any genuine Islamic politics. To say for instance that Arab will has collapsed, at least at the regime level, or that they are incapable of exercising it, is to say they cannot by definition practice such politics and that, therefore, the assabiyya of Islam cannot be invested in them. They are neither politically nor Islamically viable. More recently, a Turkish "model" under the Justice and Development Party (AKP) has been introduced as an "enlightened" alternative of Islamic politics. This has been so even though it may still be too early to depict Turkey as a model, which at best is simply practicing a form of politics of Islam. The real threat to Islamic politics is that Turkey would be pushed to perform the same manipulative role that countries like Saudi Arabia and Pakistan played during the Cold War against the Communist bloc and the forces of Arab Nationalism, but this time against Islam. The idea would be to present it as an alternative and rival model of the Iranian experience—an American Islam or politics of Islam in a new guise so to speak. As a matter of fact, as far back as 1998, the *Economist* suggested the strategy to be pursued toward Turkey. It described that country as NATO's "front line" state against the spread of Islamic fundamentalism, to be fashioned as the model of a "moderate secular" Muslim state and "an example of how it is possible to be Muslim and democratic at the same time" (*Economist*, August 1, 1998:14). By way of strategic deception, Arab, American, and Turkish politics of Islam is confused with Islamic politics in order to confound the reality of the situation away from where the assabiyya of Islam (Wilayat al-Faqih) should be invested and recognized.

The AKP faces three main options and challenges: 1—If its performance eventually crystallizes into a form of genuine Islamic politics, the risk factor and external as well as internal pressures will multiply and all the contradictions which it had sought to resolve between secularism, liberalism and democracy on the one hand and Islam on the other will most likely burst out into the open. The country will be in for a rough ride. 2—If on the other hand the AKP simply chooses to practice Islamic politics within the context of the strategy suggested by the *Economist*, it is likely to become just another Islamic façade rather than a model of any kind. As a matter of fact the first and major challenge that the AKP will have to face in order to establish its genuine Islamic credentials is to undermine and demolish external hegemonic and penetrating infrastructures in the country. This is a foremost prerequisite, for if Turkey is to institute itself as an Islamic model, it has to acquire a credible assabiyya. Something no superimposed Western value system, even if disguised in the form of politics of Islam, can provide. 3—If in contradistinction one may take at face value the proclamations by the Turkish leaders that their party is committed to the secular values of the Turkish State, then the AKP may turn out to be something akin to the Christian Democratic parties of Europe. It may simply be a reflection of a new, perhaps evolving, case of a liberal democratic system, which may attempt to moderate the radical secularism of post-Ottoman Turkey, but is essentially a continuation of its path. That is, more of the same. In this case any talk about Islamic politics, politics of Islam, or assabiyya becomes largely irrelevant. In the face of such choices, employing all the political skills that served to bring the AKP to power may turn out to have been the easy part. For

as long as a people exists in the political sphere this people must, even if only in the most extreme case ... determine by itself the distinction of friend and enemy. Therein resides the essence of its [religio-]political existence. When it no longer possesses the capacity or the will to make this distinction, it ceases to exist politically [and religiously]. If it permits this decision to be made by another, then it is no longer a politically free people and is absorbed into another political system. (Schmitt 1976:49)

This is what happens when, for instance, the US defines for Arab regimes their own people and their own faith, as well as Islamic Iran, as the enemy, in the process introducing Israel as a friend. Once absorbed into this "other" political system, any form of Islamic politics ceases to *be*, irrespective of any fidelity claims to the Shari'ah, and transforms into a form of politics of Islam or mere politics. Thus, when Ayatollah Khomeini branded the United States as the "Great Satan," apart from simply being a hostile characterization of that country, he was setting boundaries of demarcation and determination, against being absorbed in another political system. Insofar as the branding identified the friend/enemy grouping in an Islamic image and established an autonomous focus of legitimacy, it constituted a high point of Islamic politics, which rearmed, focused, mobilized, and freed. In this sense it is possible to conclude that assabiyyat al-Islam resides today with the "Persians." This has much less to do with the labels of moderation or extremism than with a clear understanding and conceptualization of both politics and Islam.

Second, there have been rather negative religious connotations associated with the concept of assabiyya as a reflection of chauvinism and/or nepotism—characteristics Prophet Muhammad is reported to have condemned. It is reported that he said, regarding assabiyya, "forsake it for it is rotten" (author's translation). Imam Ali, the Prophet's cousin and son-in-law, when asked whether loving one's own kinfolk constituted assabiyya, elaborated that the assabiyya to be condemned was that by which one perceives the wicked of one's own kinfolk, tribe or group to be better than the virtuous of others. What we have here of course are religio-moral statements. They are about a particular form that assabiyya might become a potential source of prejudice and injustice, or a cause of action or attitude not constrained or subsumed under an Islamic hierarchy of meaning or sanction.

The positive significance of the consolidating and organizational aspects of assabiyya however, was not lost on early Muslims. Despite Islam's call for transcending structures and affiliations based on such an organizing principle, this was meant in a *reductive* rather than in a *negating* sense. When early Muslim armies prepared to engage in battle, they sought to *capitalize* on such feelings of assabiyya by positioning members of tribes together, rather than diffusing them as individuals in the mass of the Islamic army. This had been the case long before Ibn Khaldun developed his theory, a fact he, as a Muslim historian, must have been well aware of. His usage of the concept, therefore, does not refer to its negative aspects but to the general sentiments of solidarity, which bring people together in order to create a society, the foundation of any eventual good. Assabiyya in this sense refers not only to those primordial feelings which are embedded in the natural ties of kinship and blood relations, but also to the broader context of group cohesion, affiliation, and common concerns—an *esprit de corps* of sorts. It embodies the moral, natural, and functional purposes of human social and political existence organized around those who lead and those who are led. While Ibn Khaldun stresses the concept in its tribal/nomadic "sociological" aspect, and is thus perceived to be making some "truth" statements/

assumptions about human nature, this does not deprive assabiyya of its Islamic character but rather *affirms* it. Islamic concepts incorporate the universal and the relative, the abstract and the concrete. Ibn Khaldun simply adopted assabiyya in its reductive form informed by Islamic history and conditions. After all, if knowledge is perceived as socially constructed, or society as constructed by "knowledgeable practices" (Wendt 1992:392), in either or both cases Ibn Khaldun was the product of Islamic society and Islamic knowledge. His conceptual framework therefore, remains *embedded* and *grounded*. Even as he attempted to identify the historical causes behind the rise and fall of nations or civilizations, he did not isolate such developments from God's design and unfolding plan. Ibn Khaldun made it clear that God's will, as *primary* cause pertaining to the rise or fall of a nation, a ruling dynasty, or a regime, worked through the *secondary* cause of an opposing assabiyya; a feeling or a condition which God bestows, in His mercy and wisdom, and as a matter of will, on a selected or chosen people, in and for a specified time. In other words, Ibn Khaldun did not separate the sociological aspects of assabiyya from the unfolding Divine laws or *sunnan* of *circulation* (*tadawul* = rise and fall of nations at the *reduced* social theory level), *substitution* (*istibdal/ haymanah* = domination or hegemony at the *reduced* social theory level) of nations, and/or *checking* one nation against another (*tadafu'* = action-reaction, stimulus-response, or balance of power at the *reduced* social theory level).[5] His effort constitutes the foundational meaning of an Islamic philosophy of history and empowerment which, by including God "among the dramatis personae of history ... gives history itself a new dimension" (Toynbee 1972:492).

Such a hierarchy of meaning is inherent in Ibn Khaldun's approach. He in fact observed that the assabiyya of Islam was being invested in the Turks of his time. This was consistent with the Prophetic tradition that had heralded the eventual conquest of Constantinople and praised the conquering army and its Prince (although there was no mention of who the people or the Prince might be, this was nevertheless an event that took place at a later date in 1453 CE by an Ottoman army led by Muhammad the Conqueror. The Turks are universally understood to be the subject of this hadith). If, by the same line of reasoning, Prophet Muhammad had heralded the "resurgence" of Islam at the hands of the Persians some time in the future, one may *understand* this to intimate the endowment of the Persians with assabiyya—an additional "Islamic" justification for the choice of the Iranian case and its linking with Ibn Khaldun's theory within a common Islamic framework.[6]

ON THE EXTERNAL CONDITION OF THE MUSLIM WORLD

The above approach proposes a theory of state or governance, based on the concepts of assabiyya, and of Wilayat al-Faqih, and is a prerequisite to chapter 4 on the Islamic theory of international relations. The conceptual reconstruction and expansion developed here allows for an Islamic approach that connects the internal/domestic and external/international imperatives of religious values, and sets a framework within which Islamic–non-Islamic relations are conducted. By overriding the internal–external separating boundaries of the domestic and the international, the theory of the internal or domestic becomes at the same time a theory of the external—a potentially *global* Islamic alternative.

Breaking down such boundaries opens the door and justifies the Islamic theory or paradigm of nations even if in a modified fashion. This stands in contrast to Sulayman's assertion that the classical Islamic theory is no longer relevant and his attempt to *adaptively* "reconstruct" Islamic history in order to fit it into some form of a nation-state framework. Essentially, his approach is not far from others who call for historicizing Islam, some of whom will be further discussed in later chapters (5, 6, and 7). Starting from the low position that Muslims are intellectually, politically, and technologically weak and backward (Abu-Sulayman 1993:61, 97–8), the thrust of Sulayman's effort pertains to a pragmatic interpretive framework which sets causal beliefs in conflict with both the Islamic worldview and its principled values. Nowhere is this clearer than when he attempts to justify and explain early Muslim battles with the pagans of Mecca and the Jews, and the rules determining conduct with regard to protected religious minorities (*people of the Book*) (Abu-Sulayman 1993:97ff). He stumbles into two main pitfalls. First, he gives precedence to causal factors over the totalizing signification of Islamic events. Instead of being part of a religious history, they are contextualized and historicized. This is not problematic in and of itself provided the hierarchy of meaning is maintained. There may have been immediate reasons behind many of the military and political decisions made by Prophet Muhammad, yet irrespective of these, they were and always will be embedded in the ordained teleology of the Islamic worldview and principled beliefs. The Arabs had to become Muslims, and there was to be only one religion in Arabia.[7] Whether this was achieved peacefully or by war was a contingent matter. The second pitfall, which follows from the first, occurs when Qur'anic verses are also contextualized and thus relativized and historicized, set apart from their absolute standards (Abu-Sulayman 1993:112). The purpose here is by no means to go through the details of Sulayman's approach or to offer an exhaustive critique, but to show what happens when calls for *historicizing* Islam are heeded. How a historicized approach to understanding the Islamic theory of nations reduces it to a mere ideological framework. Rather than exploring or searching for a possible dialectical link between theory and the modern global condition, Sulayman simply claims that the modern world cannot be explained in terms of the classical concepts and frame of mind (1993:61). Yet, an Islamic social or international theory must always maintain the dialectical relation between the absolute and the relative otherwise the theory, even if labeled Islamic, will end up as a reductive secularization of religion. Historicizing effectively secularizes and undermines a whole religious and intellectual edifice instead of expanding its horizons.

Several factors nevertheless account for the contemporary strength and continued relevance of this very same classical theory. First, it is embedded in the Islamic worldview, which endows it with both legitimacy and a good measure of longevity if not permanence. While it may have developed over an extended period of time into a theoretical framework, the fact that it is part of the Shari'ah and is in principle based on the same sources and maintained by the same sanctions situates it in the overlapping realm of theory and law. It was concerned with external relations as well as with Islamic "truth." While the former sets the classical approach in the domain of theory and conception, the latter dimension situates it in the realm of law (Waltz 1979:9), and together in their unity they constitute a paradigm. This is why the classical framework can be referred to as an Islamic *theory* and as an Islamic *law* of nations interchangeably. While its classical formulation as an interpretive theory is such that it does not allow for inferences about concrete events and hence it may be subject to legitimate critique in this respect (as theory), this is no justification for disposing with it (as law). By consistently incorporating the dimensions of worldview, principled beliefs and causal beliefs the theory *integrates* the subject matter and falls within the domain of what might be termed "taxonomico-reductive" theories (Collin 1985:187). In the field of principled action or praxis, these theories record the "dynamic factors behind action, but without specifying these, or the conditions under which they are activated, in such detail that inferential power ensues" (Collin 1985:187). The Islamic theory's abode of War versus the abode of Peace structure simply illustrates two opposing blocs in constant conflict without providing for the possibility of additional inferences, contingencies, or outcomes. Yet its integrative power reigns as the "smallest common denominator between theories which employ the same theoretical vocabulary, but diverge in inferential power." This means that results arrived at for taxonomico-reductive theories are valid for theories of higher inferential power as well (Collin 1985:188)—a strong measure of theoretical consistency. This, and the fact that the classical framework integrated both theory and "law/truth," render it a metatheory—one that theorizes about theories and reinstates Islam as a collective consciousness above that of the modern state. In this sense, it is a "form of preanalysis that disturbs the complacency of received knowledge, its self-evident relations to events, and the 'naturalness' of its language" (Der Derian 1989:7).

Secondly, Islamic theory stands the test of generality and parsimony. It reduces the number of laws and principles needed to account for the data, by replacing a large class of "narrow-scope" principles with a smaller class of more general ones with equal or superior explanatory power (Collin 1985:61). In this Islamic framework, the abode of Islam and the abode of War corresponded to the "*self*" and "*other*" respectively. From thereon developed a whole corpus of scholarly work incorporating narrower principles yet subjecting them to broader autonomous, self-referential constraints. In contrast, Sulayman attempts to present an alternative "dynamic" approach. His is based on the assumptions that decision-makers in Muslim states cannot afford to obey the anachronistic and rigid legal provisions of past ages, and that the value of a foreign policy undertaken by a Muslim state cannot be assessed by traditional legalistic means (Abu-Sulayman 1993:147). In a roundabout way, these assumptions start off by constituting a secularized approach to politics, separating foreign policy decision-making from religious underpinnings and constraints. From the outset an ideological position is adopted which magnificently fits the interests of largely illegitimate regimes in the Muslim states, particularly those which seek to project an Islamic façade devoid of substance. His framework basically proposes that any policy devised to address certain circumstances must be decided upon in the light of five conditions. Those ranged from: 1—the basic principles and values of Islam; 2—the character of threats to and the opportunities for the pursuit of Islamic goals; 3—the strengths and limitations of Muslim societies; to 4—the resources of adversaries and allies; and 5—the limitations of the world environment (Abu-Sulayman 1993:147). Yet in a seemingly contradictory stance he concludes that, "the nature of policies professed in the Muslim state depends, in the last analysis, on the particular situation at hand" (Abu-Sulayman 1993:147). But if such is the case, why is Islam of any significance or importance? It all turns out to be a matter of sheer pragmatism if not outright opportunism. What if the systemic factors (conditions 4 and 5 above) function in such a way so as not to allow space for Islamic values and principled beliefs?

A crucial issue that Islamic theory must deal with is what is to be done so as to change or influence the global environment in a fashion that would serve Islamic values, the latter being set *a priori*, as the classical theory does. Yet instead of setting Islamic standards (*worldview*) which are to be determined based on principled convictions (*fiqh*), and then pursued through causal beliefs (*fatawa*), Sulayman simply takes the global system as a given and then seeks to "adapt" Islam to it. While some may agree with such an ordering, the question remains as to why he labels his theoretical focus as "Islamic," especially when Muslim structures are constituted rather than constitutive. Sulayman's approach makes a choice of a particular theory of state—that of the modern state. This choice determined his external international approach. And since the state "unit" as a product of Western history undermines Islamic premises, the systemic whole can only arrive at a "non-Islamic" conclusion. In adapting to external "imperatives," epistemology is inevitably determined by the totally opposing "ontology" of globalization and systemic inequality, becoming open both to their information and control. Sulayman's pursuit of epistemology undermines Islamic ontology. This is what allows him to conclude that the conditional framework which he proposes could accommodate every shade of political strategy from that applied in the established international community to the radicalism of policies used in Algeria during the struggle for independence (1954–62) (Abu-Sulayman 1993:147). Such a framework, which he claims can be used to explain everything, ultimately explains little. Basically any policy pursued by any Muslim (not necessarily Islamic) country is justifiable in its own right rather than in light of Islamic principled beliefs. His exhortations that regimes should respect the moral dimensions of Islam simply fall in the realm of preaching rather than of policy action or inference.

Values, ideas, and beliefs matter not only as moral guidelines, but also as road maps, particularly when institutionalized as a decision-making determinant in the absence of a unique equilibrium. In an anarchic and in many ways hostile external environment, Islamic theory and action is not solely guided by objective constraints and opportunities but also where selection from a range of viable outcomes is based on beliefs and expectations (Goldstein and Keohane 1993:17). Otherwise *unwillingness* to pursue a particular Islamic course of action or policy could be easily confused with *"inability,"* an example of which could be unity among two or more Muslim states entailing surrender of political incumbency. Thus, in addition to failing the explanatory test, Sulayman fails the parsimony test. In contrast to Prophet Muhammad, who is reported to have stated "I have been given the *parsimony* of words (*ouwtitu jawami' ul-kalim*)," or to Ibn Khaldun and his concept of assabiyya, or more recently to Grand Ayatollah Khomeini and his principle of Wilayat al-Faqih, Sulayman's framework provides no equivalents. Whereas the classical theory explains parsimoniously, that of Sulayman basically dis-integrates the whole subject matter.

Thirdly, the structure of the Islamic theory of nations reflected an "intersubjective conception" in which normative identities and cognitive interests were determined by processes *endogenous* to interaction, rather than exogenous as modern realism and institutionalism assume (Wendt 1992:391–2). At the same time, it incorporated a good measure of concern with issues of actor power and capabilities. However, it sought primarily to "maximize" the "spread" of the message of Islam as a religious "given" rather than the "self-interested utility" of power or material welfare as a modern rationalist argument would suggest. The latter were considered contingent to the necessary former. Unlike functional approaches, religious beliefs offer crucial guidelines even though actions based on their provisions may lead to no perceived gain in efficiency or material benefits for society at large (Goldstein and Keohane 1993:17). This is particularly true in cases where material losses constitute the price of spiritual and/or long run, sometimes unobservable, gain. The Islamic Republic of Iran for instance, would perhaps be better off, from a rational self-interested point of view, if it were to support the Middle East "peace" process and recognize Israel, instead of bringing upon itself the enmity of the United States with all that this entails. In reordering the elements of contingency and necessity, classical Islamic conceptions of world order cut across much of modern Western theoretical assumptions. In their *autonomous* capacity, they incorporated constants and continuities, though much less so change, which respectively and by extension combined the self-referential mechanisms of *retention* and *selection*, but much less so *variation* (Teubner 1993:49, 56). Despite the relative lack of dynamism due to the absence of change and variation—both hindered by the regression in the talents of ijtihad—it was *autonomy* and *self-referentiality* which embedded the theory in the Shari'ah, as well as the intrinsic structure of the theory itself. In other words, while the theory may not be identical with the Shari'ah as revelation, it cannot be separated from it as root and source.

Fourthly, the classical theory's binary opposition between the two abodes is methodologically consistent with corresponding and replete Islamic/Qur'anic binary categories.[8] Dispensing with it chips away at, and bears a negative impact on, the Shari'ah, unless an alternative theoretical binary relationship can be constructed. One that is capable of isolating the normative boundaries within which ethical, religious, and political discourses are reasoned (Graham 1984:103). Furthermore, the principle of *reciprocity* makes up an integral component of the Islamic law of nations. It remains relevant particularly when under globalization, perceived by many to be overtaking the world, the Muslim Umma is not a constitutive but rather constituted part of it, and perhaps much more so, its victim. This renders the external environment one of (neo)realism and anarchy, and not of interdependence, while necessitating a new kind of organic relationship among Muslim states. Given current global conditions, a conflictive state of affairs does in fact exist between two binary *abodes*. In contemporary parlance they are termed the North and the South, and described in terms of a "Clash of Civilizations" (Huntington 1993), or as "zones of peace" versus "zones of turmoil" (Singer and Wildavsky 1993:3). The dual categories exhibit an asymmetrical power relationship of durable inequality, between two worlds, that governs their interaction. A conflictive state in other words, is not necessarily one of hostility or antagonism *per se*, but the actual condition of structuration and asymmetry. Altering such conditions requires a transformation in self-conception, which is no longer restricted by state boundaries, but transcended by universal Islamic values. The structure of the classical theory provides a relevant explanatory and potentially inferential framework, and a correspondence to an increasingly non-territorial world. In many ways in fact, it reflects reality and reciprocity.

Change in "state" and concomitant self-conception, while not sufficient, remains a necessary condition for addressing the systemic durable inequality the modern state has come to entrench. This is a problematic that Sulayman's adaptive approach does not seem able to tackle. It fails to deal with the fact that any system which situates Muslims in a framework of durable inequality, directly opposes Islamic injunctions.[9] Values and beliefs must therefore focus the research agenda on how to reduce or eliminate this condition not how to adapt to it. Only subsequently are opportunities and constraints evaluated. Put differently, in an Islamic approach ontology precedes and guides epistemology not the other way round, or alternatively, as the classical Islamic theory has superbly done, sustains an enduring dialectical relationship between the two. When Sulayman attempted to separate the political aspects of the Islamic revelatory period (seventh century CE) from the legal aspects (1993:97ff), he basically unraveled this connection. This was evident when he attempted to formulate the issue of the legitimacy of the existence of diverse Muslim states under the rule of different rulers rather than just one "Imam," seeking justification in references to some Muslim jurists (Abu-Sulayman 1993:37). Interpretive questions as to whether the "oneness" of the Muslim Umma, as referred to in the Qur'an, is spiritual or also political, is one example of how the manipulative formulation of a question could be such so as to invite polemical divergences and a breakdown in consensus. The Qur'anic verses making a reference to such unity (21:92; 23:52)[10] bear metaphorical/contingent meanings (mutashabeh), which require explanation by a higher categorical/necessary principle (muhkam). Yet Sulayman misses the point. The question is not whether it is permissible to have only one or more Caliphs, rulers, or states, but whether or not the Muslim pseudo-states as they stand are sources of durable inequality. The former is a contingent question, the latter requires a necessary resolution. Any doubts about the allegorical verse regarding the oneness of the Muslim Umma may be resolved by the categorical Qur'anic principle "honor belongs to Allah and His Messenger, and to the Believers" (63:8). Many Muslims may seek to engage in opposing arguments regarding the spiritual or political unity of the Umma. Few though would dissent as to whether a structure or system of "durable inequality" (Tilly 1999) is compatible with the situation of honor that the Qur'an entitles Muslims to. The polemics that the allegorical verse could give rise to are hence resolved by a categorical principle. Such a "hermeneutic" understanding would help in creating a good measure of consensus and in reformulating policy and structural issues in different and perhaps more productive, less polemical directions. The question is no longer the number of rulers but the *optimal* change in state structure, nature and content, which would allow for at least one Islamic *essential* actor capable of reciprocally influencing, participating and, if need be, vetoing in the international and global system. Optimality and essentiality imply that while the bordered state and its colonial formative legacy must be transcended, it is not necessary that there be only one Islamic state. This should not be perceived in any way as contradicting the basic Islamic principles of singularity, as too large a state could otherwise, and depending on contingencies, prove more of a security burden contributing to more rather than less inequality. This is so since variation in form, content, and durability will depend on the nature of the resources involved, the previous political locations of the categories (formal status of state), the nature of the organizational problems, and the relative power and capability configurations of the actors involved (Tilly 1999:8). No longer then, is it merely a question of having a democratically elected representative government with (neo)liberal commitments, but one of reformulating the meaning and horizons of the "state." Substantive issues of the kind pose both theoretical and practical revisionist challenges to the status quo, particularly so as issues of identity come to the forefront.

Abstract proclamations for Islamic "unity" and cooperation nevertheless continue to be made essentially to cover up the need for actual policy guidelines, or to obscure the logical conclusions one must arrive at. Sulayman's de-politicizing approach contributes no inferential or predictive power in this respect. His call for Muslim "unity" (1993:161) does not go much beyond everyday rhetoric (politics of Islam). Yet in examining the empirical cases of some policies such as the abandonment of war as the basis of foreign relations, adoption of diplomatic reciprocity and alliances with non-Muslim countries, and policies of neutrality, all are considered as legitimate even when contradictory (Abu-Sulayman 1993:147ff). How can the war option, for instance, be dropped by an Umma living in an anarchic-realist world and invaded right in its heartland (for example Palestine, Iraq, Afghanistan, Somalia, and the deployment of forces in the Arabian Peninsula)? How could a policy, which effectively leads to the occupation of the Arabian Peninsula by American forces under the guise of "alliance," be equated with that of positive nonalignment? What are the standards, what are the constraints? As things stand in the Muslim world, *outside* systemic goals and objectives are being matched by the *inside* in an unbroken and undivided continuum of *interests*, *ideas*, and *structures*. Breaking this continuum in any one or all three is the challenge that the Muslim states will have to confront.

The crucial and central issue is thus to recognize and acknowledge *where*, in Khaldunian parlance, lies the assabiyya of Islam, who is most capable of reflecting it, and to coalesce around its representative, transcending territorial and vested or so-called "modern" state interests. It is the rational and the reasoned tackling of primarily political and strategic questions of this kind that will determine answers in light of which categorical provisions of the Shari'ah and determination of Islamic interests could be made. This requires an autonomous and self-referential re-conception of the highest intellectual and political magnitude. Policy decisions could then be set accordingly, and human and resource mobilization undertaken in a focused direction. Of all the states, Iran appears to be the sole credible "nucleus" state that holds out for such a prospect, and where a theory and structure of authority does exist.[11] It is more than a coincidence that the only time and place where Israel has been forced to withdraw unconditionally—from the Arab territory of South Lebanon in May 2000, and again bloodied militarily in July 2006 in its attempt to destroy the Lebanese Hezbollah—is where the Iranian Islamic revolution has been relatively successfully exported. In light of the above, the Islamic theory or law of nations continues to play a positive religious and scholarly role in shaping and focusing Islamic consciousness. It further offers a new challenge to the intellectual capacities of Muslims and non-Muslims alike striving in a sincere effort not only to reconcile differences, but perhaps as importantly to explain them. The theory's contemporary relevance must therefore not be underestimated.

REFLECTIONS ON THE SUNNI–SHI'ITE CONTROVERSY

The above begs the question of intra-Islamic relations, particularly those between the Sunnis and Shi'ites. What follows does not attempt to dwell on Sunni–Shi'ite polemics, political or *mazhabi*, or try to resolve and reconcile their differences. Rather it endeavors to raise some points for brainstorming and heuristic purposes. Some may raise the issue that Iran is mainly a Shi'ite country and that it would be difficult therefore to garner needed support for its leadership of a majority Sunni Islamic world. To start with, it is worthwhile to refer to the famous fatwa made by former head of al-Azhar University Shaikh

Mahmoud Shaltout in 1959, that Shi'ism is a *mazhab* as legitimate as its Sunni counterpart.[12] While not all Sunnis have embraced this fatwa wholeheartedly, the barriers between both *mazhabs* seem to be slowly yet steadily breaking down despite attempts by some parties (Salafi groups, the US, some Arab regimes) to continue to instigate sensitivities and rivalries for purposes of their own. This is in addition to the fact that more information about Shi'ism has been made available, particularly after the Iranian revolution's triumph and the, sometimes grudging, admiration in which both Iran and Hezbollah are held.

Secondly, there tends to be a deep-seated disposition toward pointing fingers at the other side at the expense of self-reflection. A point which Sunnis strongly fault the Shi'a for, and to a great measure rightly so, is their sometimes offensive and critical language about some of the companions of the Prophet. However, it is also important to acknowledge that it was the Sunni Umayyad dynasty that had "innovated" (*ibtada'at*) the habit of cursing Imam Ali and other members of the Prophet's household, as well as killing them. Yet they are rarely condemned as vociferously by the Sunnis, as the Shi'a have been. Granted this may be part of the past, but an awareness of such historical facts may help dispose Muslims to put contemporary matters into *perspective*. Change and betterment remains always possible and preferable to futile mutual accusations. *Mazaheb* after all, are derivatives (*branches*) from revelation and cannot therefore make claims to being intrinsic sources of ultimate truth. Otherwise, they would be making the same claim as the origin and source revelation (*stem*), which would put them in a contradictory rather than consistent relationship. While most Muslims may be willing to concede this point, many of their actions belie their claims. Moreover, where a *mazhab* might err in one point, it may show rectitude and insight in another, and vice versa. This is the case for example, when Sunnis have largely invested authority and legitimacy in *political* power, even though they like to deny it, while the Shi'a invested both in *moral* power. By justifying the corrupt state and its tyranny, or at best making peace with it, the Sunni *mazhab* undermined the principle of *Justice* and, over time, its *ulama*, deservedly so, lost much of their credibility, unlike their Shi'ite counterparts (more is said about this in chapter 7 on human rights).[13] This set the Shi'ite *ulama* up as better qualified to lead than the Sunni, since the Sunni clerics tended to lack the knowledge, aptitude, aura or respectability which rendered their Shi'ite opposite numbers more dynamic, authoritative, and capable of transcending emulative tradition. In other words, the Sunni *mazhabi* field appears to be only capable of producing *pseudo-ulama* not only due to the former shortcomings, but, as significantly, due to their lack of independence, both as emulators and as state as well as foreign instruments.[14] Independence is a *necessary* condition of knowledge (*ilm*). Where there is no independence or freedom, there is no *ilm*, in the same vein of the principle: there is "no authority for a prisoner" (*la wilayat li 'aseer*). One may also add, and *no ijtihad for a hired hand* (*la ijtihad li 'ajeer*), at least in general and broad terms, not precluding exceptions.

The point here is not to deny that there have been worthy Sunni scholars. Rather, it is to focus attention on the outcome of the general interaction between the state and the *ulama*, over time and space, which came to be embedded in Sunni Muslims' consciousness; on how this impacted on the Muslim and Islamic condition, notwithstanding some figure or *'alim* here or there making a firm stand against state injustices; and on what implications this had for the Sunni *mazhab* and its *fiqh sultani*—the Islamic jurisprudence or discourse justifying state power. Was *fiqh sultani* the indirect means by which *al-mulk al-adud*, failing to present itself in a positive light, yet seriously concerned about Shi'ite opposition, manipulated both faith and *ulama* to divide the Umma so as to safeguard itself against unified opposition? Aware that mere *political* accusations and repression of the Shi'a might not garner necessary resonance among the masses at large, was a *mazhabi* twist using religious sentiments— which finds its contemporary most radical manifestation among *salafi* groups—perhaps the state's answer? Was it a matter, that is, of formulating the problematic in a particular conceptual framework rather than another? These points are not to be taken lightly nor are they simply rhetorical questions. For when the principle of Justice, in all its aspects and dimensions, had been forsaken, Muslims sought refuge elsewhere in secular codes, which undermined Islamic values. In the barrenness and desolation of their condition, they became susceptible to the combined assault of democracy, (neo)liberalism, and human rights, the three-pronged components of secularism (all three constitute the focus of the critical content of chapters 5, 6, and 7). The net effect has been something similar to what an Arab poet once said about wine: "Heal me with what has been the malady"; wine being the source of both his depressing hang-over, as well as his exuberant high. One recurring state invited the other, entrapping him in the vicious circle of mental and psychological dependency, the same dependency which secularism imposed on Muslim societies, adding to it the cultural component.[15] In both cases, the alcoholic does not transform his reality, though his high may make him feel so transformed for a time until reality sets in again. On a broader scale, neither does the Muslim Umma. It is of concern therefore that, despite the strong resurgence in Islamic religious sentiments, Sunni *pseudo-ulama* and movements, instead of having learned their lessons, end up making a comeback with the same loaded baggage of historical disappointments. This time additionally vindicated by what they perceive to be the failure of the modern secular project in the Arab world. Hopefully this does not turn out to be a situation where nothing has been learned and nothing has been forgotten.

Alternatively, *knowledgeable* Muslims on both sides of the Sunni–Shi'ite divide may consider some form of *mazhabi synthesis* in order to attain a higher level of Islamic consciousness capable of saving the "baby," so to speak, while doing away with the dirty water. This ought to constitute a different and future looking *strategic* project that avoids the burdens of historical grievances, biases, and prejudices, actual or perceived. These reflections, which I pose heuristically and as potential road maps for further examination, call as well for collective archeological excavation of the real nature and dynamics of the historical relationship between Islamic *mazaheb*, *politics*, and the *state*. This could be done by constructing a common Sunni–Shi'ite framework within which such a relationship may be examined and the process of excavation undertaken.

A second set of heuristic reflections relates to the religio-philosophical meaning of change *within* "family" branches. This is particularly significant as symbolized by the historical shift in the prophethood lineage from that of the Israelites to that of the Ismaelites (the Arabs). The Israelites were the chosen people of God (Qur'an 2:47; 2:122), yet, when their work proved them unworthy (Qur'an 2:83), the kingdom of God was taken from them and given to another people or nation, to use biblical language (Matthew 21:43).[16] When Prophet Muhammad declared the message of Islam (610 CE), and called also upon the Jews of Medina to believe in the new faith, he was essentially calling upon them—using social theory's non-religious language—to "reconceptualize" (read both *renounce* and *confirm*) their long-held beliefs in favor of an Islam that would bring them back to their own pristine message. The moral of this *analogical* historical experience may be relevant today, although on a reduced dimension.[17] Whereas Jews of the time were presented with the stark choice of having to change their religion, Muslims, mercifully, need only "reconceptualize" interpretations, opinions, methodologies, nuances, as well as prejudices—the constructing elements of *mazaheb* as they have come to stand. Sunni Muslims need to develop a reflexive mind-set regarding some of their long-cherished opinions and their attitudes *vis-à-vis* the *mazhabi* branch of their Shi'ite brethren. For resting content in their "orthodoxy" is a luxury they can no longer afford. The point here is not to be construed as some call for a collective *mazhabi* change. Rather it is an appeal for self-reflection among the Sunni majority, as to what their *mazhab*, apart of mere ritualism, could still offer—whether it has reached some kind of an impasse or dead end and whether it has become a burden on Islam instead of the facilitator it was supposed to be. What does it have to offer socially, politically, institutionally, and from thereon morally? It is also a call for pondering Iranian leadership of the Umma, notwithstanding *mazhabi* considerations. Especially so, when the Arab state itself has reached a parallel impasse and dead end, not only as a corrupt and tyrannical regime structure, but, taking matters a step further, as a *corruptor* state and a destroyer of values, deprived essentially of its *raison d'être*.

Al-*mulk al-adud* and *fiqh sultani*, the two components of the historical ideology of *sunn-ism*—the ideological aspect of the broader Sunni *mazhab*—or any of their variations (for example *hukm jabri* or rule by force), are unlikely to have the means, methods, will or capacity to remedy or address these problems. In addition, by continuously reproducing, on the one hand, a class of religious sycophants and emulators (*muqallidin*) lacking in *praxis* knowledge, and a dogmatic *salafi* mentality on the other—with a forlorn majority in between infused with a spirit of submissiveness to ruling power whatever its nature, as a matter of "religious" obligation—*sunnism* effected a pathological Islamic condition which permeated all levels of Muslim society. Perhaps this "empirical" observation is consistent with and a sound hint toward understanding the Qur'anic and Prophetic tradition concerning "Divine substitution" (*istibdal*) (Qur'an 47:39; see also note 5). In fact, it might very well be the case that in order for Sunnis to ensure the effective survival of their *mazhab*, they capitalize on the burst of energy and dynamism of their *Ja'fari* Shi'ite counterpart, as well as on that of the Iranian revolutionary experience, instead of conspiring against it. When Abdullah II of Jordan made his alarmist statement in 2005 about a "Shi'ite Crescent" threat to the region, and with King Abdullah of Saudi Arabia being groomed for an "ambiguous" role as leader of the American-sponsored *unholy* alliance of "Sunni moderates," comprising the former two countries plus Egypt, the foreboding signs are there to see. It is perhaps this reality which prompted the leading Egyptian journalist and political analyst Muhammad Hasanein Heikal, commenting on the historical pattern of American–Arab relations, to indicate that this "game" between the "swindler and the buffoons" has gone on way too long (Heikal April 26, 2007). It further raised the fundamental and existential question about who and "what saved the state when the ruler offered catastrophic leadership or none at all" (Knox 1996:616).

Even when Arab regimes claim that they are concerned about the "political" not the *mazhabi* project of Iran, and that Iran has a nationalist agenda involved, it is important to note that Islam does not mean the absence of strategy, politics or interests. One does not negate the others. As a matter of fact, it is a reflection of the genius of a people or a civilization when it is capable of either reconciling or *appropriating* otherwise potentially conflicting values. For instance, the zeal of early Muslim armies to spread the faith did not prohibit taking spoils, nor did the religious duty of pilgrimage proscribe engagement at the same time in legitimate worldly concerns or benefits (Qur'an 22:27–8). Compare this with the unfortunate and largely unnecessary conflicts that occurred, in the contemporary Arab world, between nationalist and religious currents, and then within each current itself. Arabs may also recall that they had once been "substituted" by the Sunni Ottoman Turks, in terms of loss of political power. If they ally themselves with the US or Israel in order to *allegedly* protect both their *interests* and *mazhab*, they may effectively lose their soul as well as end up wasting both of the former objectives[18] and deserving of "*substitution*." For in the end it is not *mazhabi constructions* which matter most when the ultimate Islamic criterion of judgment is clear: "Verily the most honoured of you in the sight of Allah is (he who is) righteous of you. And Allah has full knowledge and is well acquainted (with all things)" (Qur'an 49:13).

1
Religion, Politics, and Social Change: A Theoretical Framework

RELIGION VERSUS SECULARISM: TENSIONS WITHIN MODERNITY

Social change in contemporary political jargon has conventionally come to mean the natural evolution of all members of the global village toward a *modern* state of existence. Modernity was both ontologically and teleologically subsumed in this process of change as the inevitable goal. It therefore became the banner of secular salvation in countries with recent colonial experiences, especially during the 1950s and through the 1970s. Having achieved their independence from colonial powers, the leaders of those newly emerging nations made it their paramount objective to undergo a rapid process of modernization in order to improve their peoples' and nations' material well-being.

In many cases, however, and despite the best of intentions, the modernization process produced less than the expected results. Attempts at modernization brought with them new kinds of problems and raised new issues which had not previously been perceived or encountered. In most cases these countries had to deal with the destructive as well as the constructive dimensions of this complex process. Old traditions and institutions were broken down, family ties of kinship were loosened, and cities had to absorb the population migrating from rural to urban centers. Ties with the past were weakened, yet nations experiencing profound change failed to become part of the modern "present" or an aspiring part of the future. These profound changes had serious effects on the social relations and structures of societies undergoing the modernization experience.

This situation called for a reassessment on the part of an increasing number of developing nations of the basic premises of modernity and its impact on indigenous cultures in which religion formed a major component. Knowledge, technology, and modernity have so far proved to constitute a complex and value-laden package which involves not just industrialization and material improvement, but a whole array of profound attitudinal and cultural transformations pertaining to and concomitant with a relevant value structure reflective of the undertaking.[1] This chapter aims at proposing a theoretical frame within which the nature of the conflictive relationship between religious and modern regimes in religiously mediated societies may be analyzed. It further attempts to investigate the autonomous role that religion plays within its social context. The underlying discourse of the Iranian Islamic revolution is then conceptualized at the ideational/epistemological level as a case in point.

MODERN CULTURE AS SOURCE OF HUMAN DISENCHANTMENT

Modernity as the symbiotic offspring of technological innovation effects a most profound transformation in the basic foundations of human subjective and objective consciousness. While it carries different meanings, modernity as a general concept reflects a commonality of salient features. One becomes modern

when one sheds the substantive limitation imposed by traditional values and ways of life. Substantive values limit one's access to a wider field of possibilities; the widest field of possibilities is correlated to an "empty" self, defined by its formal role of maximizing chosen satisfactions or attaining its goals with greatest efficiency. (Kolb 1986:xii)

In light of the criteria of efficiency an intrinsic value is perceived in modernity which is independent of any other virtues. Modern *existence* means

being "advanced" and being advanced means being rich, free of the encumbrances of familial authority, religious authority, and deferentiality. It means being rational and being "rationalized". ... If such rationalization were achieved, all traditions except the traditions of secularity, scientism, and hedonism would be overpowered. (Shils 1981:288–90)

Mankind in its modern dimension becomes in effect the primary determinate cause not only of new instruments of production, but also of all social, political, cultural, and religious modes of existence contrived by its subjective and objective exertions. In this capacity, individuals become the masters of nature and therefore external to and independent of it. In the words of Kant, "in all creation everything one may want or may have in one's power can indeed be used *only as means*; only man, and with him every rational creature, is an end in himself" (Kohanski 1977:xii).

Under this anthropocentric rubric, typologies of human relationships become confined to a relative existence independent of "real knowledge" or the "Truth" as epitomized by the intrinsic nature of revelation. Modernity acquires a dynamism of its own which recognizes no rigorous moral boundaries to its field of action. It leads an autonomous objective material life of scientific discovery which eschews pondering on the spiritual implications. In modernity, "the give-and-take that has always existed between man and the rest of his environment and the constant dialogue that is so necessary both for self-knowledge and social cooperation have no place" (Mumford 1976:29). Its "irresistible inner dynamics," as Jürgen Habermas puts it (1989:v.2, 331), constrain revelation by the dictates of reason as a "religion of culture" (Habermas 1987:86). This culture, through its theoretical capacity to colonize religious life-worlds, opens the previously sealed-off collective religious convictions to the "influx of dissonant experiences" and disseminates them through the structural instruments of rationality and efficiency (Habermas 1989:v.2, 353). As a result it has failed to develop "any synthetic forces that could renew the unifying power of traditional religion" (Habermas 1987:86).

While it is not the purpose here to present a comprehensive or detailed philosophical critique of modernity, underscoring its major shortcomings as a process of social change remains vital in explaining the increasing role that religion has come to play in the last two decades or so. Human self-knowledge, as far as religion is concerned, cannot be achieved in isolation from the "man–society–God" meaning of existence. Mankind's ordered, purposeful, and *a priori* concerns with the issues of truth, certainty, finitude, and infinity cannot be addressed independently of the absolutist criterion of the *Divine*. Incessant strife for mastery over nature which is understood as a reflection of the divine cosmos ultimately puts individuals in conflict with their own selves and their own essence. In the modern project of conquering the environment the real loser, from a religio-philosophical standpoint, has been man, who "through his technological proliferation, has alienated himself from nature as well as from his fellow man" (Kohanski 1977:178–9). In other words, by attempting an autonomous existence from the cosmos, man loses his essence and thus commits the ultimate sacrilege against God. By shedding his responsibility as a reflection of the divine image and as a receiver of his beatitude, mankind ultimately suffers from a "loss of meaning" (Habermas 1989:v.2, 351).

A fundamental problem with modernity is, thus, its externality to restraining boundaries and to the absolute standards of a religio-ethical foundation. Though perceived by many as an unqualified blessing for mankind in the light of its astounding scientific achievements, its subjective costs remain pervasive, subtle and un-quantified. Modernity as a reflection of man's striving for freedom through mastery over his own environment has in effect substituted his harmonious bondage with nature for that of discordant automated alienation.

Observing the impact of modern scientific and technological achievements on human existence, Lewis Mumford comments:

By attempting to eliminate the human factor, by reducing all experience to supposedly ultimate atomic components describable in terms of mass and motion, science discarded mankind's cumulative knowledge of history and biography and paid attention only to discrete passing events. The typical vice of this ideology accordingly, is to overvalue the contemporary, the dynamic and the novel and to neglect stability, continuity, and the time-seasoned values of both collective history and individual human experience. The scientific intelligence, however magnified by its capacity to handle abstractions, is only a partial expression of the fully dimensional personality, not a substitute for it. (Mumford 1976:30)

Modernity thus far has failed to achieve the multi-dimensional fulfillment required by human society. Its alluring promise of a better life has masked a dwindling concern with human self-realization through spiritual as well as material development. The internal dimension of the human essence has been externalized, and this has induced an unprecedented chaotic and conflictive relationship between body and spirit. To restore order and harmony between the two it is necessary, as Jacques Ellul put it, "to question all the basis of that society—its social and political structure, its arts, and its way of life, its commercial system" (Ellul 1972:88). What is required, then, is nothing short of a total discursive-structural transforma-tion which radically opposes the fundamental identifications of modern secularism in both its liberal and historicist manifestations. This reaction to the dilemmas of modern culture, in the words of Manfred Stanley, "is not congruent with longer-standing Western ideals of freedom and personal responsibility, so that all who still care about such traditions are morally obliged to oppose it" (1976:24).

Any fundamental proposed resolution to problems of modernity, in other words, can only be violently anti-modern, anti-secular, anti-democratic, and therefore anti-Western.

That this may eventually prove to be tidings of what is yet to come is echoed by Mumford:

People in contemporary democracies can no longer take for granted the notion that their immediate conceptions of individual and group interests are the best measuring rod for public policy. In complex modern societies, simple conceptions of self-interest may be spurious and potentially harmful to the operation of a genuinely democratic society. Failure to recognize this possibility is at the root of polarizations—such as that between "elitism" and "participation"—that can easily turn into abstract, irrational, and dangerous bifurcations. (Stanley 1976:24)

Ultimately such expectations, which recognize, directly or indirectly, the fallibility of individual and collective choice, may serve as a justification for the rationalization of theocratic regimes or at least of organic religious influences on future human exertions. Most certainly this is expected to provoke a violent discourse between modernists and their opponents regarding the morally and ethically determinate and causal foundations of human social and political organization.

ERRORS OF OMISSION: RELIGION REINSTATED

Observations by two Western scholars, Max Weber and Robert Wuthnow, contribute to justifying the introduction of religion as a rejuvenated, relatively independent and explanatory variable in the field of social sciences. Weber recognized that,

certain conceptions of ideal values, grown out of a world of definite religious ideas, have stamped the ethical peculiarity and cultural values of modern mankind. They have done so by working with numerous political constellations, themselves quite unique, and with the material preconditions of early capitalism. One need merely ask whether any material development or even any development of the high capitalism of today could maintain or create again these unique historical conditions of freedom and democracy in order to know the answer. No shadow of probability speaks for the fact that economic "socialization" as such must harbor in its lap either the development of inwardly "free" personalities or "altruistic" ideals. (Gerth and Mills 1958:71–2)

Reasons and explanations for such conditions are not difficult to discern. Celso Furtado, for example, notes that the dilemmas facing many countries in their attempts to develop arise basically from the fact that these attempts have evolved from a process of grafting onto their pre-capitalist economies "one or more enterprises connected with the commercial activity of industrialized economies in a state of expansion." In this respect, social and political changes in these nations have been exogenously imposed and as such constitute a totally different inductive phenomenon from the classic formation process of the European capitalistic economies (Furtado 1967:142). Even the concomitant modern values of freedom and democracy have failed to be reflected in institutional structures and political processes. Many developing nations, as a consequence, have come to realize after agonizing experiences that the historical origin of modernity had certain unique preconditions which are unlikely to repeat themselves. The superimposition of modernity on societies with very different cultural and historical experiences has underscored the essential biases inherent in Western *ethnocentricity*.

Robert Wuthnow in turn has stated that social theory prevents us from understanding what it means to be an "infidel" civilization. To understand requires abandoning social science as a privileged framework and shifting toward a view of "multiple discourses," each illuminating the meaning of events in different ways. For this shift to occur, religion has to be taken seriously by "granting it parity as an interpretive framework" (Wuthnow 1991:14). Such errors of omission in Western social theory have become the focus of much criticism by non-Western scholars and intellectuals (Hanafi 1991). Though not new, these critiques "are spreading and becoming universal, the common elements are being analyzed, and they are increasingly informed by solid facts and arguments" (Wiarda 1985a:134). Most of them call for a duly accorded respect for indigenous tradition as an organic and instrumental vehicle of progress (Randall and Theobold 1985).

Reflection on such critiques underscores the situational influence which conditions an investigator's definition of *what* should be investigated, *how* the investigation should proceed, and the *purpose* that such an investigation would serve. All of this takes place within the context of a dynamic relationship that synthesizes the socio-religious environment with new directions in theological innovation in order to arrive at a different and healthier plane of social existence

(Maduro 1982:3–38; Sanks and Smith 1977). This synthesis is not to be confined to economic and material indices. It is to incorporate a socio-religious analysis of reality in order to establish social justice and the liberation of mankind from all hindrances to its spiritual, as well as material, well-being. Religion has thus come to represent an alternative vehicle of reintegration capable of challenging modern culture which separates objective material and subjective aesthetic harmony so vital to human fulfillment and wholeness. In addition to bridging the gap between the two, it contributes to the reordering of priorities of socio-political and religious means and ends along transcendentally justified and rationalized foundations.

RELIGION AND SOCIAL CHANGE: A RESEARCH AGENDA

The Iranian Islamic revolution of 1979 was a major event which introduced a new religious dimension into the realm of politics and social change. It represented the culmination of a long-evolving process of criticism in many developing countries of the Western capitalist and socialist models. In addition to carrying this process to its logical objective conclusion and presenting itself as a potential alternative model, the Islamic revolution raised serious questions regarding the nature of religio-political dynamics. For example, what role does religion play in social change? Why have certain revolutionary movements come to be based on or orientated toward religion? What *form* does religion have to take to become an instrument of social change? Why has religion failed at one historical epoch to satisfy the demands of its followers, and why do those same followers at another historical juncture perceive it as an alternative to the status quo? Is there something lacking in secular movements which only religion can rectify? Or are there objective and subjective factors which render religion much more than merely the refuge of the desperate?

In many cases tensions within the modernization process create a social and political vacuum which gives religious forces a new chance to reassert themselves. For some analysts, this phenomenon has created the perception that religiously inspired political movements are simply a reaction to modernization, and are therefore reactionary and anti-progressive. This view tends to be reinforced by the traditional Western analysis of religion as an impediment to change and a relic of ancient irrationalism (Comte 1957; Feuerbach 1957; Marx and Engels 1964; Saint Simon 1964;

Spencer 1961). Such an outlook, unfortunately, is both simplistic and uni-dimensional. It fails to come to grips with the different facets of religio-political dynamics. To be confined to a one-dimensional explanation of a complex phenomenon frequently generates both superficiality and bias which go against the basic principles of "objective" social science research. To adopt such a deterministic approach regarding the emergence of religio-political movements is to ignore the internal dynamics of religion itself.

These theoretical and methodological problems have been the focus of scholarly analytical scrutiny. In order to be able to understand how religion and politics interact and change, Daniel Levine for example has stressed that

analysis must accept the logic of religious belief and practice. This requires a conscious effort to hear it as expressed, to see it as practised, and to construct or reconstruct the context in which these religious ideas resonate. Only then is it possible to see how and why religion helps people to make sense of the world and to organize themselves and others to deal with it. (1986:99)

Levine proposed an agenda for future research which goes beyond the conventional categorization of religious movements along the traditional range of political criteria from radicalism to conservatism (1986:99; 1981). Such classifications render religion a secondary variable, dependent on the contingent definition of varying designations. The first task for the researcher is therefore to identify the sources of transformation in religious ideas, together with the underlying causes which give rise to different interpretations. These sources could be either internal or external, or a combination of both. What one should be looking for, then, is a clarification of how religion itself, together with its interaction with other social variables, explains the phenomenon of religio-political movements. Consequently,

the first step to greater knowledge (of the mutual impact of religion and politics) is to see that influence runs both ways. Political action and commitment grow from religious motives and structures; politics gives models and provides pressures which spur reflection, organization, and action. The whole process spills over formal ideological and institutional limits, shaping and drawing strength from the everyday experience of meaning and power. A second step comes with realization that all this operates not only through the pursuit of short term goals, but also through building languages, universes of discourse, and expectations. These create "spaces" which in the long run can be filled with different ideological contents. (Levine 1986:119)

This process requires one to address the autonomous role that religion plays as a source and agent of change. It also involves identifying the structural factors which provide religion with its prominence and resilience. The ultimate outcome would be a series of comparative generalizations helpful in making deductions and producing theories. In this context one must deal with issues of social and political change, symbols of legitimacy and authority, elite–mass relations, and other historical configurations of power. One must also deal with the centers of religious organization such as churches, mosques, and grassroots organizations, class formations including the clergy, political institutions (executive, legislative, judicial), hierarchies, and religious divisions. Only by undertaking such an exercise can one understand why religious groups turn political or vice versa.

The second task for the researcher is to specify the relationship between changing ideas and existing social groups. In a developing society characterized by a sharp dichotomy between the elites and the masses, what does religion represent for both? What aspects of religion are emphasized by the establishment on the one hand and by the masses on the other? Such questions oblige us to submit to careful examination the social and political environment in the context of which these ideas emerge. Even if it is derived from a revealed scriptural text, religion remains partly situational-contextual in character and partly normative-metaphysical (Engineer 1980:25). A very important distinction therefore has to be made between religion as a universal creed which transcends borders, classes, and races, and ideology, which, according to Marx, constitutes vested interests aiming at perpetuating and justifying the status quo.

The third task for the researcher is to identify any attempts to shape and re-politicize religion and to relate these to an identifiable power base. Organic connections between the leadership, the cadres, and the popular base have to be closely scrutinized in order to be able to identify who determines the program of action, along what lines, and toward what outcome. In the realm of Islam, for example, structural mediations and concepts of legitimacy are most likely to differ depending on whether a Shi'ite or a Sunni leadership is setting the political agenda, notwithstanding those salient features of Islam which remain the same in both cases.

The final task for the researcher is to determine how religious principles and structures exhibit flexibility or rigidity in the face of changing times and demands. Under normal circumstances of stability this task may be of no urgency since continuity is the norm. In times of crises, however, the issue becomes of utmost importance since it is the ability of religion to withstand challenge and attack that will determine the outcome of a conflict. If religious institutions and structures fail to offer answers to newly emerging problems, and instead confine their efforts to protecting and preserving their inherited privileges, the result will be either schism or the disenchantment of the masses. Religion can therefore survive only if it perceives itself as functioning in a specific social context by which it is affected and which it attempts to shape or reconstruct. To be able to do that, religious planning has to exhibit social relevance in order to endow its efforts with legitimacy and authority. People will ultimately commit their convictions not only to that which promises them salvation in the hereafter, but to that which also contributes to their survival in the here and now.

This proposed research agenda may be summarized as shown in Figure 1. The diagram's point of departure is an examination of the interaction of ideas and social structures which are eventually translated into action. The broad concern behind such an exercise

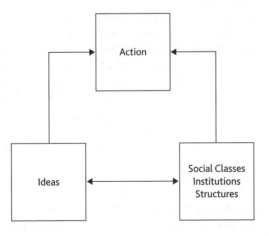

Figure 1

is to be able to form "packages" or "clusters" of elements that lead to or consolidate comprehension. The result of all this "would be work focused less on 'Catholic radicalism,' 'Islamic fundamentalism,' millenarian movements, and the like, as on the clustering of ideas, leadership, followers, resources, and opportunities which make these [movements] emerge and give them enduring impact" (Levine 1981:120–1).

RELIGION AND THE SOCIAL ORDER: A PARADIGMATIC SHIFT

The research agenda proposed by Levine involves a substantial amount of abstraction and generalization which makes it difficult to focus on the more concrete aspects of religion and social change in modern times. Levine's plan in fact attempts to develop a new paradigm for research which deals with the dynamic relationship between religion and politics, a relationship to which earlier works on social change have paid negligible attention (Appelbaum 1970; Black 1966; Finkle and Gable 1963; Huntington 1968; Weiner 1966). In most of the modernization and social change literature, religious influences have frequently been assumed to be epiphenomenal, pre-political, or survivors from the past destined to insignificance by the awesome progression of secularism. Such assumptions—which at best perceive religion merely as a function of socio-historical need, to be cast aside once it has served its purpose—ignore the ontologically causal and transformative potential of supernatural or metaphysical beliefs.

Otto Maduro developed a synthesized neo-Marxist/Weberian model which accepts the economic modes of production as a determining social factor but which nevertheless does not neglect the impact of culture and ideas on social existence (Maduro 1982:152). Admitting to the ideological role that religion has played in various historical eras, Maduro seeks a solution not in the desertion of religion, but in the revisions and mutations arising from religious innovation (1982:141). Such a position allows religion to play a relatively independent role which is not totally subordinate to the ideology of a dominant class.

The root of the thesis arguing for a positive and active role for religion in social and economic life is grounded in Max Weber's original and influential study *The Protestant Ethic and the Spirit of Capitalism* (1958). As opposed to Marx, who firmly believed that religious values and interpretations were exclusively a byproduct determined and conditioned by economic factors, Weber stressed that religion also played an important determining role. In his words:

not ideas, but material and ideal interests ... directly govern men's conduct. Yet very frequently the "world images" that have been created by "ideas" have, like switchmen, determined the tracks along which action has been pushed by the dynamic of interest. "From what" and "for what" one wished to be redeemed and, let us not forget "could be redeemed", depended upon one's image of the world. (Gerth and Mills 1958:280)

He supported his argument further by examining the role that the Calvinist ethical system had played in the rise of capitalism in Europe and concluded that there was a positive and direct correlation between the two.[2] This conclusion, however, should not be taken to suggest that Weber believed in a determinate relationship between the Protestant Reformation and the rise of capitalism. On the contrary, as he himself pointed out, his goal was only "to ascertain whether and to what extent religious forces have taken part in the qualitative formation and the quantitative expansion of that spirit over the world" (Weber 1958:91).[3]

The model illustrated below reflects a mutual and interactive relationship between the material modes of production and the ideas or culture in which the former are situated; neither is totally independent of or the cause of the other. The modes of production refer to a socially structured set of relations shaped and constructed partially by human will, but mostly by the content of organizable resources. As opposed to the purely economic Marxist conception of human relations, this understanding sees the modes of production as constituting a *regime* which indirectly influences other non-economic aspects of social life (Maduro 1982:45).[4] It will determine what kind of activities will be impossible, undesirable, tolerated, secondary, urgent or primary. As far as religious culture is concerned, the modes of production will both limit and orientate its activities and scope, highlighting particular aspects of the faith at one time while dimming the same aspects at another. In this respect the religious culture is conditioned by its social setting (Maduro 1982:45–6). Simultaneously, the religious culture plays a role of its own, stimulated by its own dynamics, and which is relatively autonomous of the social context. "Autonomous," means that religion is not totally shaped by social structures, conflicts or transformations. Instead it plays an active role in the construction

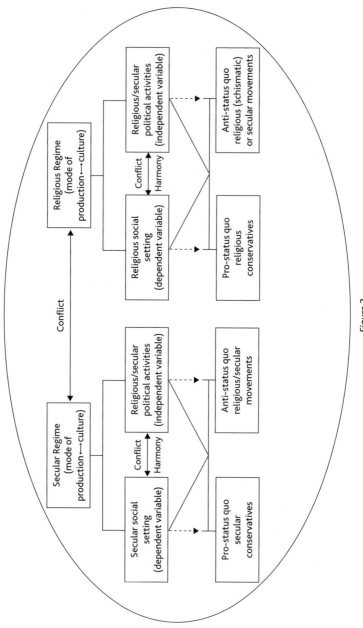

Figure 2

of a subjective, objective, and institutional worldview which shapes the social experience of the collectivity both generally—in terms of heritage, culture, norms, beliefs, traditions—and particularly through furnishing the fertile ground for the emergence of a founding charismatic leader (Maduro 1982:83, 87–8, 154 fn. 90).

The modes of production and the ideas and culture of the society thus constitute the components of the regime which shapes and forms the social setting (secular or religious) while limiting and orientating the various different religio-political activities and interpretations. Both the social context and the religio-political elements are in a constant state of interaction which may be harmonious, if the two are compatible and congruent, or conflictive.[5] In a secular social setting conflict will arise as a result of the autonomous orientation of politically active religions. Under such circumstances harmony can be restored only if religion renounces its political activism or if the secular regime is able to neutralize religious opposition either through repression, or by presenting a feasible and successful alternative, or by a combination of both. In the case of a religiously based social setting conflict is likely to arise between opposing secular forces or between different religious interpretations; in the latter case the outcome is possibly, though not necessarily, schismatic. Harmony in this case can be achieved either through the establishment of a pluralistic tradition that accepts different interpretations, through successful repression or through the emergence of a charismatic figure capable of embodying or transcending the different conflicting currents. Whichever the case, there will be an overlapping of methods adopted. Figure 2 may help to illustrate the point.

The model's point of departure is a secular regime in power facing opposition from religiously orientated political groups which are trying to reconstruct the order in congruence with their own image of society. In so doing religious activists are in fact attempting to shape and influence the prevailing social arrangements in a fundamental way which is both exclusive and uncompromising. This inevitably endows the religio-political movement with an innate revolutionary dynamic which, if victorious in the face of pro-status quo conservative opposition, feeds back into the regime and in turn is influenced by it. This process continues as long as the revolution continues and has not reached its equilibrium state or *Thermidor* (Brinton 1959).[6] Once in power, the new regime will recast the structures of society in a new mould while limiting and orientating the concomitant religio-political interpretations, which are most likely to be those of a charismatic leader or group.

The second round of developments in the model will then envisage a reversal in the roles played by the relevant variables. Once the religious regime is securely situated in power, and especially after the inevitable demise of charismatic leadership, it will eventually attempt to institutionalize and preserve the status quo. The revolutionary regime will adopt a conservative attitude and will not be inclined to change.[7]

The subsequent nature of interaction between the social and religio-political forces will depend on the ability of the new regime to achieve a consensual social acquiescence which perceives congruence, or at worst minimal divergence, between theory (religiously based convictions and aspirations) and practice (social arrangements and structures). The greater the discrepancy between the two the more likely it is that a conflictive situation will arise in which social action will be the independent determining variable. The nature of opposition—whether religious or secular—will depend on the types of existing structures capable of mobilizing resources and on the social configurations of power. Whichever the case, social conflict will be an inherent idiosyncrasy of those forces opposed to the status quo. A secular challenge which attempts to restructure society along non-religious lines will render the religious setting a dependent phenomenon. If, however, the challenge is emanating from a different religious interpretation, then there will emerge a series of overlapping variables in which religion is both a determining and determined element. Religious dynamics may therefore become a source either of unity or of divisiveness. The problem then becomes one of identifying the factors which contribute to either orientation.

A corollary to this problem is the question of power and control. Are the rules of the power game the same irrespective of who is at the apex of the regime hierarchy or do they vary with the change of ideology and ruling elites? Another question arises for those who subscribe to the belief in natural historical processes: is the history of mankind one of inevitable progression toward secularism, or one of inevitable cycles of religious and secular swings? If it is the latter, what then are the factors which cause the shift from one regime to another? I will now address some of these issues and problems associated with religion and politics, using Maduro's model, in an attempt to explain the relationship between religion and social change.

RELIGIONS AND SOCIETY: AN EPISTEMOLOGY OF THEORY AND PRAXIS[8]

In his second thesis on Feuerbach Marx made a definitive statement regarding the interplay between theory and praxis insofar as they contribute toward the attainment of "truth" or "real knowledge":

the question whether objective truth can be attributed to human thinking is not a question of theory but is a *practical* question. Man must prove the truth, i.e. the reality and power, the this-sidedness of his thinking, in practice. The dispute over the reality or non-reality of thinking that is isolated from practice is a purely scholastic question. (Marx and Engels 1981:121)[9]

On this interpretation, social reality is not only the outcome of subjective mediation but also an active participant in its own creation. Far from being just a dependent component of "truth," praxis is in effect also an independent agent of certitude. Just as much as praxis, truth remains dependent on human activity. "The truth of doctrinal statements," as Moltmann has emphasized, "is found in the fact that they can be shown to agree with the existing reality which we can all experience" (Moltmann 1967:18). This reality of course has, in one way or another, to reflect a certitude so as not to allow adaptive praxis to turn into *pragmatism* which "in all its forms," as René Guénon put it, "amounts to a complete indifference to truth" (Guénon 1962:85).

Elegant and persuasive as Marx's thesis may be, his reduction of religious consciousness to a mere super-structural reflection is less than convincing. His emphasis on the social relations of production as the infrastructural determinant of human praxis overlooks the impact of revelation as a subjectively autonomous and causal domain of action. The neo-Marxist Otto Maduro, arguing for a more complex understanding of religion and social change, criticizes Marx's reductionist approach to faith (Maduro 1977). Highlighting his fundamental break with classical Marxism, Maduro makes the following observations regarding the role of religion in society:

1: Religion is not a mere passive effect of the social relations of production; it is an active element of social dynamics, both conditioning and conditioned by social processes. 2: Religion is not always a subordinate element within social processes; it may often play an important part in the birth and consolidation of a particular social structure. 3: Religion is not necessarily a functional, reproductive or conservative factor in society; it often is one of the main (and sometimes the only) available channel to bring about a social revolution. (Maduro 1977:366)

Such observations offer significant help in understanding the dynamics of religious thought. The conventional Marxist premise that religion is a static force which can express itself only in the form of reactionary and anti-progressive impulses gives way before the undeniable reality of contemporary religious social and political activism. Marx's contention that religion is the opium of the masses, far from being the dogma it used to be, has become the object of intense re-interpretative efforts at best, and of intellectual embarrassment at worst. One defense of Marx's statement claims that it is a "sociological affirmation" bound by time and place rather than an ahistorical "metaphysical assertion" about the essential nature of religion (Maduro 1982:xx).

The function of religion is to establish a sacred universe within which existential human experiences can be assessed with respect to a consecrated cosmic order. By its very nature it initiates a dialectical process in which religion as an external principle contributes to the creation of communal worldviews. At the same time it is conditioned and orientated by human social interactive interests and configurations. Insofar as religion continues to function as a conflictive element it will acquire the ability to produce, reproduce, and transform social relations, and hence to play a social role (Maduro 1982:116, 118). Despite modern reductionism this role can never be negated in any practical sense. The position of the "holy" or the "sacred" in mundane human affairs remains intrinsic and fundamental. It constitutes, as Weber indicates, the source of ultimate answers to the problem of meaning, and when these are internalized and institutionalized they play a causal role in determining human action. Religion, in other words, maintains a functional relation to the system of action at all times (Parsons 1954:208–9).

Writing in the 1940s Kingsley Davis rejected the notion that secularization would continue to the point where religion would become totally nonexistent. In a far-sighted perception about religious regimes he poignantly stated that:

Secularization will likely be terminated by religious revivals of one sort or another. The precise nature of the revivals is impossible to predict. The details may resemble nothing we know now, but it is safe to assume that they will perform the same functions and have the same basic principles that have heretofore characterized all religion in all societies. (1961:544–5).

These functions would involve the maintenance of equilibrium as the "normal condition" of society where a change in any particular social variable produces change in other variables so as to maintain a uniform state.[10] Religious activities which in the process do not contribute to social harmony are perceived in this context as "dysfunctional," "anomalous and sociopathic" (Maduro 1982:118). The functionalist school of thought, therefore, ignores the dynamic and potentially revolutionary role that religion can play in social processes.

The problem with such an approach is that it does not recognize that the symbolic components which converge at a particular historical conjuncture can have their own unique dynamics. In different societies at different times religious and structural processes combine or fuse in a variety of independent formations. The basic implication of this is that there is no unique or universal set of rules or functions that religion might *a priori* be predetermined to fulfill. Its social role or manifestation will instead largely depend on the historical and structural vicissitudes within the interplaying domains of social and religious impulses. That is to say, the social functions of religion can be determined only after the relevant socio-religious dynamic variables have been examined experimentally. After all, "we are treating the particular social functions of a particular religious society, situated in space and time." This is something that can be established only "*a posteriori*—after an empirical investigation of the phenomena we want to analyze" (Maduro 1982:119–20). In other words a scientific study of religion requires a multifaceted empirical method that cannot be substituted or anticipated by theoretical constructs (Maduro 1982:366). The point to be made here is that religion *per se* does not perform a predetermined well-defined social role which lacks functional variability. Religious influences and roles instead can, and do, mutate, and their historical and structural metamorphosis is conditioned by the limits of time, space, and social affiliations. In other words the social functions of any religion will largely depend on the objective social conditions of any particular society together with the position and internal circumstances of the religious sphere itself (Maduro 1982:129).

An understanding of the interplay of these various factors is of basic importance for any theoretical framework of analytical or predictive power. Reaching such an understanding will certainly involve a close scrutiny of different socio-religious variables such as the qualities of religious beliefs and practices, the cognitive framework of the culture, the social location of religion, and the internal structure of religious organizations and movements (McGuire 1981:197–203). Within such a dynamic framework, the religious field, as a terrain of mediation, can be examined as an agent of either social hegemony or oppositional autonomy, entangled in a conflictive social context. The realization of oppositional autonomy will be a direct function of *oppressed group consciousness, oppressed group organization* and *oppressed group mobilization*. A progressive polarization of these distinct yet complementary levels of action, however, is unlikely to occur in the absence of the main dynamic instruments of religio-theoretical autonomy: innovation and mutation. Their impact will be all the more profound if they are capable of supplying a consumable product to an alienated, religiously mediated subordinate social group.

It becomes necessary therefore that those instruments, while attempting an anti-hegemonic breach with religious tradition, maintain a respectable measure of continuity with the past. This configurative fusion of continuity and change in the religious field constitutes the principal challenge to the realization of an autonomous, religiously inspired revolutionary transformation. Tactical or strategic fusion errors may ultimately render innovation simply an adaptive change which may end up in sheer pragmatism, or, if the breach goes too far, in producing an incomprehensible and marginalized sectarian offshoot (Maduro 1982:137–42). A delicate balance therefore has to be struck between innovative change and authentic continuity so as to render possible—given a conducive social context—a dynamic and guided outburst of human emotions. Whatever the case may be, the practical manifestation of such a process will be in the form of a distinct orientation within the monopolistic religious field, or if that is not possible, a potentially schismatic movement of conflictive and divisive dimensions.

What made the clerical role so important in the Iranian revolutionary experience was the fact that they had come to constitute *organic intellectuals* who were spontaneously sought out by the subordinate classes to gather, systematize, express, and respond to their aspirations. If enough space exists in the religious field to allow for the articulation of popular clamor against hegemony, or if the field itself is autonomous in creating theological innovation, a situation prone to the consummation of clerical revolutionary potential is produced. This situation remains particularly relevant in social regimes where all other avenues of protest against economic, political, and cultural tyranny have been blocked by the state (Maduro 1982:142–3). Subjective religious autonomy hence emerges as the most viable, if not the only, channel of opposition capable of leading to an objective manifestation of doctrinal and popular defiance.

To assert that religion at times plays an autonomous and independent role in the formation and structuring of social life is not, however, to attribute to it an absolute idiosyncrasy. Religion at any time and in any place is a socially situated phenomenon which, notwithstanding its metaphysical qualities, has to be relevant to the contextual and environmental realities of its field of action. Such relativeness remains an imperative if religion is to protect itself against the impotence of absolutism. What this means, in effect, is that the faithful who adhere to and practice a particular religion actually do so within the confines of a finite set of objective choices which militate against attaining absolute religious standards. Such choices are determined to a large extent by the social context and international pressures which allow for different degrees of religious impact and alternative policy implications and outcomes (Maduro 1982:43). The most fertile grounds for religious formations, therefore, are collectivities which are prone to express their concerns and beliefs in a transcendental and "metasocial" form. Such collectivities or social groups tend to develop a "religious interest" which purports to translate their religious worldview into a communicable representation of their milieu in a way that will permit them comfortably to act and socially situate themselves. Religious interest is defined as

that need present in some societies and some social groups, to situate and orientate themselves—and to act—in their natural environment and social milieu through the mediation of a view of this milieu that is referred—centrally or laterally, totally or partially—to metasocial and supernatural forces upon which the group feels dependent and before which it considers itself obliged to a certain conduct. (Maduro 1982:43)

This religious interest gives rise to an autonomous persuasion which drives its subjects to exert an effort to reconcile their natural and social environment with a transcendentally and subjectively perceived idea.

Both religious interest and the concomitant effort to bring an "ideal" down to reality converge at a particular historical conjuncture to provide the necessary conditions conducive to setting in motion a process of religious production. This process reflects "the effort motivated by religious interest to develop a world view that would permit the subjects of a particular religion to situate themselves, and act in the most satisfying manner possible in their natural and social environment" (Maduro 1982:82). The process is usually initiated through the experience of a charismatic figure or group of figures who are capable of incarnating in themselves the hopes and aspirations of the religiously interested social group. All three factors (religious interest, social effort, and charismatic leadership) constitute the necessary and sufficient conditions for the initiation of a relatively autonomous religiously inspired social process. They do not however determine whether the outcome of the process is to be successful or unsuccessful.

THE IRANIAN REVOLUTION:
AN ISLAMIC EPISTEMOLOGY OF GOOD AND EVIL

The challenging message of the Iranian revolution as a perceived anti-Western phenomenon is that it provides new religious standards for moral references which are seemingly opposed to secular traditions of popular ethical judgments and conceptions of popular sovereignty. It thus represents a basic rejection of the Western modern project in theory and praxis. The novelty of the situation was explicitly expressed in the astonished remark of a White House aid: "The notion of a popular revolution leading to the establishment of a theocratic state seemed so unlikely as to be absurd. ... What was truly 'unthinkable' ... was not the Shah's demise but the emergence of a clerical-dominated Islamic republic" (Arjomand 1988:3). This new republic attempted to reconstitute the organic relationship between morality and its objective environment through a process of religious reinterpretation and reconstruction of society. The ultimate project was to create a new religious field of action in which the faithful could express their religious interest in a manner consistent with the corresponding social and political reality. The Islamic militants had recognized that the essential field of hermeneutical investigation was not the relationship between doctrine and history but the nature of the bond between theory and social praxis, and that in order to be relevant the revolution had to be well grounded in its own socio-cultural milieu, notwithstanding its "fidelity to original and traditional elements in religion" (Fierro 1977:121). The religious militants, in fact, "fortified an already vigorous religion with the ideological armor necessary for battle in the arena of mass politics" (Arjomand 1988:210).

The final outcome of the dialectical process in the religious sphere in Iran remains to be seen. The immediate goal of the fundamental transformations under way is to supply an adequate religious commodity relevant to an unsatisfied demand which is rendered acute by the crushing onslaught of modernity, and to mobilize increasingly alienated social forces in order to embark on the transformation of the "anomalous" structural components of the religious field. This has necessitated a basic change in the epistemological foundations of religion incorporating a far-reaching dialectical process of historical demythologization.[11]

The aim of this process is not to eliminate myths or even to challenge them, but rather to interpret them in existentialist, anthropocentric contexts rather than simply in cosmological terms. The process has involved going beyond old myths and toward the creation of new ones relevant to contemporary circumstances within the context of a well-discerned and delineated "epistemology of good and evil" (Pellicani 1981:41). This epistemology, produced by the discourse of the Islamic revolution, has provoked a hostile attitude from secular and Westernized scholars who have failed to see, beyond the revolutionary violence, the overall dynamics of a profound and historically unique process of social transformation (Farhang 1985/86:260–2). With the outbreak of the Iranian revolution, conflict between secular and religious regimes became inevitable. The dimensions of this conflict were visible to John Stempel who observed that

Historically, the most important consequence of the revolution may prove to be the rise of religion as a significant political factor. Blending theocratic ideology with power on a sustained basis offers an alternative revolutionary model to supplement Marxist and other paradigms. It is a way to replace the authority and legitimacy of a monarch or other secular leader with another kind of power based on a different justification. Tactically it accomplishes its aim without resorting to massive sustained violence. In this case the fundamentalists proved that even a powerful armed force can be destroyed from within. The most disturbing element about Ayatollah Khomeini's Islamic movement is not its doctrine but its effective mobilization of a diverse society into a political organization supporting a religious government. Clerical supremacy as asserted by Ayatollah Khomeini is an implied standing challenge to secular governments everywhere. If it continues to exist and prosper, a centuries-old Western trend of separation between church and state would be reversed. (Stempel 1981:311)

Free thinkers: discourse as epistemology

Any attempt to analyze and understand the objective factors which ultimately created a revolutionary consciousness among the Iranians and succeeded in mobilizing them must take account of the subjective idiosyncrasies of this society. In many respects, the Iranian revolution exhibited many of those structural features identified by scholars of social change as causal and determinate (Davis 1979:148–67; Deutsch 1971; Eckstein 1970:171–95; Gurr 1971; Johnson 1968; Moore Jr, 1967; Olson 1971). It is, however, the confluence of the subjective historical and cultural traits of the population and its clerical leadership which have shaped the revolution's religious impulse, and the praxis of the revolution has reflected it, precipitating what the Italian scholar G. Scarcia has described as "a confluence between Shi'ism and the popular spirit, taking on the form of national consciousness" (Algar 1969:25). Behind the structural causalities of the Iranian revolution lies an intellectual movement which has fused religion and politics in the crucible of revolutionary praxis. This movement combines Iranian Shi'ite idiosyncrasies with the Islamic heritage in a reinterpreted context of futuristic immanency. While Grand Ayatollah Khomeini provided the revolution with its praxis leadership, Ali Shari'ati provided it with its discourse. On the basis of his Western training in social sciences, Shari'ati paved the way for the emergence of a radical manifestation of Islamic revolutionary expression. His theory and Ayatollah Khomeini's praxis therefore proceeded on parallel lines, to converge at a particular historical conjuncture when the former mobilized the intellectuals and the latter the masses. In this sense the theory and praxis of the Islamic revolution reflected what Hugo Assman has termed "the epistemological privilege of the poor" (Brown 1978:61), or *mustadafin* (the oppressed), to use Islamic terminology. This privilege attributes a more realistic view of the world to those who perceive it from below (the oppressed), as opposed to those who perceive it from above (the oppressors).

Both figures based their exhortations on a qualitatively and symbolically altered appeal to the cognitive standards of reference of their respective audience. Both were able to strike a sensitive chord in the subjective and objective make-up of the Iranian Islamic identity, which merged in an authentic cultural revival and doctrinal praxis. Their innovative contributions provided for the crystallization of mass consciousness, organization and mobilization into a well-defined program of religious and political action. Underlying the philosophy and ideology of Shar'iati and Ayatollah Khomeini was a clear understanding of the major cultural principles governing social and human interaction in Iran in the realms of the sacred and the profane. These cultural principles, deeply rooted in the Iranian identity structure, involve a dialectical relationship between the spiritual internal and the materialistic external, reflected in a state of "dynamic tension" within a cosmic equilibrium. Within this equilibrium, however, a balanced discrepancy between reality and the perceived ideal is maintained and tolerated (Beeman 1983a:74–5). While a distinction between the internal and the external exists in many societies (Geertz 1973), in the Iranian case it remains of particular significance. Iranian Shi'ism, according to Beeman, "has been built up over the centuries on a base of native pre-Islamic (Zoroastrian) belief and flavored with particularly Iranian aesthetic and philosophic doctrines" (1983a:74). This complex belief system envisages a constant struggle between two diametrically opposed and polarized forces of good and evil. The internal represents the prized core of human spiritual perfection which strives to overcome the unsavory external periphery. The constant tension between core and periphery, internal and external, esoteric (*batiri*) and exoteric (*zahir*)[12] thus constitutes the teleological domain of human strife.

A mere discrepancy in this dialectical relationship *per se* need not necessarily be a source of disturbance or anxiety. After all, apart from the case of the chosen few (the prophets and the imams), perfection can only be sought, not attained. A condition of crisis can emerge, however, and this occurs not when perfection fails to be actualized but when the very process of striving for the ideal comes to a halt or goes into reverse. The internal/external distinction thus exists not only in the Shi'ite religious consciousness but

in the political and historical consciousness of Iranians as well. The struggle between the pure core of Iranian civilization and the external forces that threaten to destroy it is one of the principal popular idealizations of Iranian history. ... In extreme situations of personal suffering or national need, the resources of this symbolic core can be marshaled for political action. (Beeman 1983a:76)

Within this context it was possible for Shari'ati and Ayatollah Khomeini to present to the Iranian nation a religious framework which brought Islam to the forefront of subjective consciousness and objective political activism. Contrasts between good and evil as embodied in confrontation between Moses and Pharaoh (Fischer 1986),[13] Hussain and Yazid,[14] Abel and Cain (to use Shari'ati's dichotomous parlance), Ayatollah Khomeini and the Shah, the oppressed and the oppressors, the righteous few and the Great Satan (Beeman 1983b:191–217),[15] provided new meanings and definitions of identity and added a new focus of liberation to the symbolic cognitive core of the masses. Revolutionary mobilization was therefore not only a product of the fervent exhortations of revolutionary leaders but also the result of the conjunctural cathartic function of the passion plays which reenacted and kept alive the memory of the martyrdom of Imam Hussain at Karbala'. "The climax in such plays," Akhavi tells us, "is the Imam's martyrdom, but the triggering mechanism of martyrdom is the repeated question of participants: 'May I be your Ransom?' In the Christian tradition, the sacrifice of one leads to the salvation of all. The Shi'ite tradition requires that the sacrifice be borne equally" (Akhavi 1983:195–221).

The Karbala' metaphor was thus manipulated in order to unify disparate social groups into one mass movement; its popular meaning also altered. The Karbala' passion changed from a passive act of mourning for Hussain and anticipation of the return of the Twelfth Imam into an active demonstration of opposition to and defiance of tyranny. The Islamic revolution thus constituted a "social drama" or a "successful passion play" with distinctive Iranian and Shi'ite characteristics (Fischer 1986:74–83): injustice inflicted in the past was at the present moment uniquely rectifiable in the context of the revolutionary discourse articulated by Shari'ati and consummated by Ayatollah Khomeini. Shari'ati's thinking was based on an analytical distinction between two alternative types of Islam: a static Islam characteristic of the oppressors and a dynamic, liberating Islam committed to the oppressed. It is the duty of what he calls the "free thinker," who is conscious of his own human condition and the condition of his society and of the period in which he lives (Shari'ati 1980a:8),[16] to reveal, on the basis of his own strong convictions rather than any imported ideologies, the sometimes subtle difference between the two. In fact, as Shari'ati indicated, if Muslims seem to be oppressed everywhere despite their commitment to Islam, this should not be a cause to doubt the faith, but only the understanding of this faith. "If we are Muslims, if we are Shi'ites," he stated,

and believe in the Islamic and Shi'i precepts, and yet those precepts have had no positive results upon our lives, it is obvious that we have to doubt our understanding of them. For we all believe that it is not possible for a nation to be Muslim, to believe in Ali and his way, and yet to gain no benefit from such a belief. (Bayat-Phillip 1980:156)

The foundation of a true understanding of the faith is to be able to distinguish between the Islam of Abu Zarr, the ascetic companion of Prophet Muhammad (570–632 CE), and that of the *Umayyad* kings. Both are brands of Islam, yet their implications are inherently antithetical (Hussain 1985:79–80). It is only in the former type of Islam that Islamic concepts such as Umma, *imam*, *adl* (justice), *shahadat* (martyrdom), *hijra* (migration), *intizar* (awaiting), and *tawhid* (unity of God) can bear dynamic underpinnings. It is when these concepts acquire a transformatory meaning that Islam can become a praxis-orientated religion.

How then was this to be achieved? Shari'ati suggested a method which he believed that the Prophet had adopted in conveying his revolutionary social and spiritual message to the pagans of Arabia. Conservatives cling to the past, revolutionaries break with it, and reformists seek gradual change over time. The Prophet's method, by contrast, was to preserve the form of a custom while transforming its meaning. The Prophet, states Shari'ati,

preserves the form, the container of a custom which has deep roots in society, one which people have gotten used to from generation to generation, one which is practiced in a natural manner, but he changes the contained, the contents, spirit, direction and practical application of this custom in a revolutionary, decisive and immediate manner. (Shari'ati 1980b:65)

For an example of this method Shari'ati referred to the *hajj* or pilgrimage. Through revelation the Prophet was ordered to maintain the ritualistic form of the *hajj* as it had been practiced by the idol-worshippers, and yet fundamentally to change its focus of reverence toward "the unity of God [and] the oneness of mankind" (Shari'ati 1980b:66). In so doing the Prophet in effect initiated a qualitative, revolutionary leap which transformed the *hajj* into a ritual that is "completely contrary to and opposite of its original use" without challenging the cognitive framework of his audience. What was involved here was a "shift in consciousness" which facilitated the internalization of the new message without inflicting upon its subjects the "anguish of having to dispense with historically rooted and emotionally valued traditions and rituals" (Irfani 1983:122). It was in fact a shift in consciousness which impressed upon the Arabs the "revival and ... cleansing of their eternal customs" (Shari'ati 1980b:66).

Shari'ati believed that by adopting this method "one can reach revolutionary goals without forcibly bearing all the [consequences] of a revolution and without opposing the basis of faith and ancient social values" (Shari'ati 1980b:67). He pointed out, for example, a new symbolic understanding of the ritual of *hajj* which went beyond its significance as a mere religious observance and imbued it with social and political content. The stoning of the three idols which is part of the *hajj* rituals symbolized for Shari'ati a condemnation of the three tyrannies of oppression, ignorance, and hypocrisy which stood against the attainment of true faith, or *tawhid*. The stoning in effect constituted a "revolutionary act" which revealed to mankind "the clear horizon and free way to migration to eternity toward the all mighty Allah" (Shari'ati 1978:1). To migrate toward Allah one has to rebel against tyranny as Abraham did—even at the expense of being thrown into fire. Those who follow Abraham's footsteps and willingly accept being thrown into "fire" shall by no means be burned to ashes, but instead "Allah will make [for them] a rose garden from the fire of Nimrods" (Shari'ati 1978:36). There is no place here for a withdrawal into a monkish life in isolation from human concerns. Self-centeredness is the only outcome of such a withdrawal, which by its nature is antithetical to real faith. Only through exercising generosity, kindness and devotion to the community (Umma) can one attain self-realization. The ultimate manifestation of devotion is the willingness to sacrifice one's life on the path of God; this is, by becoming a "*shahid*" (martyr). *Shahadat* (martyrdom) is being present, alive, palpable, and visible. A shahid is an everlasting witness and visitor; he exemplifies an eternal being (Shari'ati 1978:28–9). Self-realization also involves the knowledge that "guidance," "self-consciousness," "deliverance," and "salvation" can be attained only through the praxis of "jihad" (Shari'ati 1978:62). This is the knowledge that

... the way of righteousness, the road toward Allah may never be approached without practicing devotion, self-denial, transpersonal generosity, captivity, torture, exile, pain, endless danger, even the firing squad. This is how one may walk with the people and step in the direction to approach Allah. (Irfani 1983:123)

The archetypal shahid was of course Imam Hussain, who was not merely a historical figure but represents humanity's eternal struggle for liberation, salvation, and perfection. He is the symbol of the fight against tyranny and corruption everywhere and at any time. He set the standards of revolutionary praxis where "only blood could distinguish the boundary between truth and falsehood," irrespective of the end result. As a matter of fact

... whenever and wherever a liberated person has refused to submit to despotism and its attempts for distorting supreme values, and has preferred death to a dehumanized purposeless existence under a monstrous regime and inhuman social system, it is a response to Hussein's call. Wherever there is struggle for liberation, Hussein is present on the battlefield. (Irfani 1983:131–2)

Shahadat thus becomes a matter of choice rather than an imposed necessity, for Hussain could have avoided it had he wanted to. It becomes in fact the harbinger of revolutionary liberation and the cornerstone of a sublimated forthcoming order. Through it "Islam ... would spearhead the revolution for creating a new transformation in history to fulfill the Qur'anic promise that the *mostad'afin* would inherent the earth" (Irfani 1983:132).

Human strife therefore constitutes a perpetual dynamic and dialectical flux between the divinely spiritual and the profanely material in man. This flux is reflected in the constant altercation between his base component (clay) and his sublimated spirituality (soul) which strives for perfection and transcendence. His objective history is that of the conflict between Abel and Cain from which all historical contradictions inherent in the opposing forces of *tawhid* and *shirk* (idolatry) emerge (Shari'ati 1979:97–8). Shirk represents the evil forces of Cain (injustice, tyranny, oppression) which seek to destroy the liberating message of Abel. In the modern context this conflict takes the form of a constant struggle between Islam on the one hand and the tyrannical regimes and their imperialist supporters on the other. It expresses a conscious and cognizant commitment to a liberative praxis which pits faith against capitalist exploitation and Marxist atheistic materialism

(Shari'ati 1980c). A constant evolution toward liberative perfection renders *intizar*, or the quietistic awaiting of the Imam, a dynamic concept. Man's "obligatory" pursuit of truth can after all never be a substitute for the role of the Imam as the realization of this ideal. Intizar thus becomes a religion of protest and absolute denial of the status quo.

Intizar not only does not negate man's responsibility, but indeed it makes his responsibility for his own course, the course of truth, the course of mankind, heavy, immediate, logical, and vital. The religion of *intizar*, which is a "positive philosophy of history," a historical determinism ... is ultimately a philosophy of protest against the status quo. (Akhavi 1980:155)

In other words, man is responsible for his secular salvation inasmuch as he is responsible for his transcendental deliverance. Both are distinct yet harmonious components of the divine will of *tawhid*. A Muslim's progressive evolution toward higher moral perfection is after all contingent on his social consciousness and praxis within the Islamic plan of salvation (Motahhari, *Kayhan International*, May 20, 1989).

Revolutionary praxis within the Karbala' and shahadat metaphors is neither utilitarian nor goal-oriented. It is an intrinsic value in and of itself: "anyone believing in the liberating spirit of truth had to put up a fight against falsehood, even if that meant sure death for oneself" (Irfani 1983:131). Legitimate revolutionary violence is thus a struggle for power, not as a goal in itself but as a means of establishing an Islamic moral order. Power in this case is not the *outcome* of a triumphant strife but the *actual* praxis of strife itself. In May 1984, for example, Ayatollah Khomeini exhorted non-Iranian *ulama* to "speak out." "Do not wait until you attain power so that you can speak," he declared. "Speak and then you will have attained power" (*Kayhan International*, June 10, 1989:6). The same sentiments were expressed by Shari'ati in a speech on Imam Hussain:

The great teacher of martyrdom has risen to teach a lesson to those who believe that struggle against dictatorship should be waged only when victory is possible, and to those who have despaired or have compromised with the Establishment, or have become indifferent to their environment. Hosein teaches that *shahadat* is a *choice* through which a *mujahid*, by sacrificing himself on the altar of the temple of freedom and love, is irrevocably victorious. Hosein has come to teach the Children of Adam how to die. He declares that people who submit themselves to all forms of humiliations, injustice and oppression just to live a little longer are destined to die a "black death". Those who lack the courage to choose martyrdom, death will choose them. (Irfani 1983:133)

For Shari'ati the blood of the shahid is the most important element in historical dynamics. Shahadat is the act of supreme sacrifice which maintains evolutionary purification and sublimates revolutionary consciousness. It is the engine of social protest which crushes all obstacles, and the pulsating heart that throbs with life.

Just as the heart injects life in the body by pumping blood through its dry veins, so the *shaheed* is the heart that transmits his blood and gives life to the dried-up and dying body of the society—a society where people have submitted to false values, coercion, and oppression so as to survive a little longer and are content with sheer physical survival.

Shahadat is thus "an invitation to all generations and for all times that if you can, then kill the oppressor, and if you can't then die" (Irfani 1983:133).

Principles such as *jihad* and *martyrdom* introduced new dimensions in politics and conflict in much the same fashion that the "nationalism" of the French Revolution, for example, had previously brought about in Europe. Clausewitz, observing the Revolution and its total and absolute wars, perceptively indicated:

It is true that war itself has undergone significant changes in character and methods, changes that have brought it closer to its absolute form. But these changes did not come about because the French government freed itself, so to speak, from the harness of policy; they were caused by the new political conditions which the French Revolution created both in France and in Europe as a whole, conditions that set in motion new means and new forces, and have thus made possible a degree of energy in war that otherwise would have been inconceivable. (Clausewitz 1976:610)

The influence of these ideas on the praxis of the Iranian revolution can hardly be exaggerated. The willingness of the masses to die can hardly be matched in any other similar upheaval in contemporary history. The "cult of martyrdom" in effect became the symbol of the wrath of the revolution and the crucible of an emotional outburst which had been suppressed for close to fourteen hundred years. Martyrdom in the Iranian context was not just an interpretation of jihad but a step beyond it. It was not the mere acceptance of death but the actual choice of it. It constituted an act of supreme negation of utilitarianism and materialism and the paramount affirmation of spiritual purification. It was the vindication for the "guilt complex" among those who fell short of the standards of Karbala'. Here was a chance offered to them to salvage their spiritual defeat in the most sublime and transcendental way. Here was the battle of Hussain and Yazid reenacted between Ayatollah Khomeini and the Shah. Here was the chance to relive Karbala', and better yet to win.

Shari'ati's contribution to the revolutionizing of Islam was of pivotal importance in raising the consciousness of the masses—especially the students—toward expressing their protest in Islamic terms. His acceptance of historical dialectics, however, meant that, directly or indirectly, Islam became an instrument of these dialectics, and therefore a component subservient to them. Shari'ati presented to his audience a *revolutionary Islam*, yet the clergy, led by Ayatollah Khomeini, wanted an *Islamic revolution*. What the latter sought was a revolution that served the purposes and values of Islam, and not a religion that served the purposes of revolution. While recognizing that Islam certainly envisaged struggle as a legitimate instrumental praxis of faith, they did not see internal conflict—an intrinsic component of dialectics—as an inevitable or desirable end. On the contrary, while recognizing dialectical contradictions in and with other non-Islamic societies, they offered Islam as the alternative solution to this dilemma (Motahhari 1985:201–19).

The Islamic revolution was a phenomenon of religious consumption that took place as a result of the convergence of an unsatisfied religious demand with a satisfactory supply of religious production. This religious production involved a fundamental shift in paradigm from the conventional "national modernization" model to a model basically concerned with the "moral purification of a corrupt society" (Najmabadi 1987:203). The shift was fundamental: religion was not concerned simply with criticizing the mode of modernization or its shortcomings and failures, but instead perceived the whole undertaking as undesirable from the start. Ayatollah Khomeini articulated the position of his Islamic Government thus:

Let them [the West] go all the way to Mars or beyond the Milky Way; they will still be deprived of true happiness, moral virtue, and spiritual advancement and be unable to solve their own social problems. For the solution of social problems and the relief of human misery require foundations in faith and morals; merely acquiring material power and wealth, conquering nature and space, have no effect in this regard. This conviction, this morality, these laws that are needed, we already possess. (Khomeini 1985:36)

Ayatollah Khomeini's success as a revolutionary leader was therefore largely due to his ability to secure a considerable degree of solidarity among the clergy and to rally the traditional loyalties of the masses by highlighting the revolutionary elements of Twelver Shi'ism in a subtle manner that did not openly contradict classical or traditional thought. Above all, he was able to fuse the elements of divine law, Islamic government, and just order into one image of an "ideal Utopian apocalyptic world" that transcended the corrupt and unrighteous mundane order (Calder 1982:17–18). In this context, power, means, and ends were not to be measured or judged by the general critical standards of secular relativism, but by the absolute standards of revelation, which brings into existence the structures that are required to reflect the harmonious relationship between man and God and their unity of purpose. Islam holds that man is primordially good, but through his erring may choose to be corrupted. Unjust social structures are thus simply the outcome of man's erring choice and not of necessity or divine ordination. From a theological perspective, religious absolutism exercises vigilance over secular relativism and it is the former, therefore, that sets the epistemological criteria of judgment. What determines an Islamic society, then, is not its position on the left–right political spectrum but its own standards of social, economic, and political justice, and the types of structures which lead to and/or reflect such standards.

The introduction of this metaphysical component into politics transformed Iranian political practice, as distinct from that of other nations, supplementing a two-dimensional plane of worldly secular concern with a third dimension of metaphysical continuity. Within this religio-political domain, Islamic politics represented "a new kind of preoccupation with the self, a search for an original identity that only in a completely untainted form is deemed capable of unlocking the true source of social well-being" (Najmabadi 1987:204). In this search, as Afsaneh Najmabadi points out, "lies the otherwordliness of Iranian politics today and its virtual incomprehensibility to all those not caught up in the new paradigm" (Najmabadi 1987:204). This new paradigm expresses its innermost specificity in its perception of the dialectical relationship between the Islamic East and the materialist West.

CONCLUSION

In this chapter I have tried to reach a more profound understanding of the relationship between religion and social change by identifying perspectives for observing the dynamic interaction between two processes inherent in man's social existence. I have also tried to delineate the discursive/structural and religious factors which, inseparably from each other, have contributed to polarization within society and to a new dynamism in internal religious logic. Interplay between *ideas* and *structures* and resultant *action* have provided the basis for a paradigmatic shift in modern conceptions of the role of religion: from the idea that religion is obsolescent to an understanding that religious dynamics play a principal and formative role in the structuring of social reality.

The implications of this shift for the discipline of social science in general and for the field of political science in particular are dramatic. The introduction of a religious dimension in modern politics has transformed our understanding of human means and ends in a way that has called into question the basic modern premises of rationality and cause–effect relationships. The basic assumptions of unilinear secular progression and development to which modern political literature is so attached have been strikingly challenged. Jerrold Green has come to the following conclusion:

Characterizations of the Iranian Revolution in the West are incorrect and lack understanding, failing to recognize the fundamental role of religion as the source of strength and sustenance for adherents of innumerable faiths over countless centuries in all corners of the world. Such commitments are especially salient aspects of the modernization process, with religion serving as a particularly effective refuge from the more dehumanizing and anomic aspects of dramatic and rapid social change. Moreover, in light of the absence of conventional participatory mechanisms, formalized religious organizations can, and in the view of some religious leaders, should serve as vehicles for improving the quality of life for their adherents. Those disturbed by such religio-political movements must ask themselves: Are religions any more troubled than the societies that house them? In religiously homogeneous societies, religious-based political activity can serve as an accurate reflection of wider social needs while at the same time leading to dramatic political consequences. (Green 1982:150)

For the above reasons among others, an increasing number of Western scholars have come to recognize their failure—so far—to explore new horizons or examine other options (Wiarda 1985b:xi). In all probability an alternative method will have to overcome the shortcomings of reductionism and relativism in favor of a holistic approach toward the various dimensions of human existence. It has, after all, proven next to impossible to understand human nature without taking its spiritual constituent into account, or by reducing its dimensionality to the merely quantitative indices of economic and material progression. Perhaps a vital key to a deeper understanding of human nature lies in revelation as well as in the artificially constructed yet fallible assumptions of human reasoning. The following chapter explores further some of the possible epistemological implications of such a supposition.

2
Islam and the
Appropriation of Modernity

THE PROBLEM

Much of the burgeoning politics of Islamic resurgence relate to challenges posed by global and "civilizational" forces. These forces served to reawaken previously dormant and presumed settled issues of authenticity and identity structures. Correlated social and political anxieties, as well as acute concerns about perceived existential threats to Arab and Islamic values, imposed on many in the Muslim world— including both secular and religious groups, and by virtue of the same condition—a renewed though *contradictory* insight into their past, present, and future. This led to a stressful and pathological state, as the past, the present, and the future appeared to lose much of their sense, diffusing meaning and dissipating energies. This had serious consequences. A nation in a seemingly perpetual condition of anxiety and trepidation, may very well fall into a state of historical nihilism and perplexed visions. For to a society that "is full of confusion about the present, and has lost faith in the future, the history of the past will seem a meaningless jumble of unrelated events" (Carr 1986:xxxv). This may very well bring about a loss of vision or the adoption of false ones. And, "[w]here there is no vision," as Irving Babbit has put it, "people perish. Where there is sham vision, they perish sooner" (Nixon 1994:174).

Reinstating the dynamics of Islamic history, however, largely hinges upon the dialectics of the past, present, and future creating a new consensus or a confirmation of *who* Muslims are, *what* they want to be, and *how* they want to be. These queries constitute structural and existential concerns over identity which must be addressed if Muslims are to confront their perceived disenchanted condition. A renewed understanding of the past therefore calls for an enhanced "insight" into the future as the past ceases to be an object of defense or attack, while the future becomes the focus of planning and preparation. The present, in turn, becomes the locus in which a newly envisioned past and a projected future collectively merge (Carr 1986:xxxix).

The trials such complexities have given rise to were poignantly articulated by Mohamed Arkoun:

[t]he Muslim intellectual must today fight on two fronts: one against social science as practiced by Orientalism in a disengaged, narrative, descriptive style; the other against the offensive/defensive apologia of Muslims who compensate for repeated attacks on the "authenticity" and the "identity" of the Islamic personality with dogmatic affirmatives and self confirming discourse. And beyond these two obstacles always present but at least identifiable, the Muslim intellectual must contribute through the Islamic example to an even more fundamental diagnosis, especially regarding questions of ethics and politics: what are the blind spots, the failings, the non sequiturs, the alienating constraints, the recurrent weaknesses of modernity? (Arkoun 1994:9)

Nevertheless, a gradual yet identifiable concern appears to be slowly emerging among many Muslims regarding the distinct options of both intra- and inter-civilizational interaction. Its basis is the stance that Muslims, as a community, as countries, and as individuals, should adopt in their relations with the West. As this concern builds up, it is likely to constitute the broad framework within which Islamic–Western civilizational relations will be conducted and pursued. The ensuing question may thus be formulated in terms of how to construct this complex framework.

The absence of a relevant methodological framework capable of setting the boundaries and rules of verification for any interactive process involving the incorporation of the achievements of non-Islamic civilizations exposes much of the vulnerabilities of the receiving party. It further manifests a condition of dependency on the donor civilization's epochal formations and definitions of reality. Emulation becomes the illusionary source of progress and the very dynamic by which a culture undermines its own vitality. In response to such exigencies, a detailed study was undertaken by the Iranian Journal *Kayhan Al-Arabi*, in an attempt to explore the opinions of a large number of Muslim intellectuals regarding the best means of implementing an activist Islamic strategy in response to the Western media's hostile representation of Islam. Reflecting a good measure of maturity in thought, and perhaps realism, a middle course attitude permeated as the strategic alternative to an unredeeming hostility toward or unbridled embrace of Western values. In its conclusion, the study contended that "total rejection of the heritages of other civilizations like total acceptance, is not an Islamic path. Nor does it behoove an Umma whose commandment to read and learn preceded that of praying and of fasting" (Darwish, 1994:2).

While the broad strategy is crystallizing in shape and form, much of its details remain contentious. Its viability, methods, and instruments, together with the inherent risks and potential paradoxes involved in it, continue to irk the polarized consciousness of secular modernists and Islamic traditionalists. Mutual suspicion, lack of communication, and conceptual limitations further exacerbate bifurcations detrimental to a focused and dedicated collective effort. Resolving those problems at the tactical level remains as important as consensus on the strategic plane. Social polarizations, increasingly making themselves felt in Muslim societies, may then be partially diffused by situating both antagonists within a commonly reconstructed methodological and referential framework. This framework should be capable of reconciling and subsequently transcending polar entrenchments, while maintaining a healthy and dynamic tension between the two. A brief critical look at works of three Muslim intellectuals: Burhan Ghulyun, Arkoun, and Hassan Hanafi may serve as a constructive launching pad in this direction.

INTELLECTUAL CURRENTS: COMMON CONCERNS AND DIFFERENCES

Islamic normativity and the problem of cognitive reductionism: where justice is never served

According to Ghulyun, Muslims' willingness to accept the setting of historical modernity (Western-*ism*) as the unchallenged criteria of creativity has led in effect to the loss of their own standards, and, epistemologically, to the mere explanation of the object by itself, i.e. subjectifying that which initially was intended to be observed. This condition inevitably reduced them to a state of being mere consumers to what the "*other*" produced; creativity having been defined in the "other's" very own terms. Not only has this undermined the very foundations of civilizational creativity, which constitutes a group's very identity and subjectivity, it has further contributed to the destruction of this very same process. Failure to recognize and sense the imperatives of such dynamics could only lead to the dismantling, deconstruction, and final dissolution of the Islamic religio-cultural matrix. Consequently, elites in Islamic countries have become mere reflections of the Western civilization's productive and intellectual capacity (Ghulyun 1990:282). This, according to Ghulyun, had less to do with the incessant flow of new meanings, symbols, and significations from the West than with the methods by which Muslim societies have attempted to deal and cope with them. Nothing after all, as he put it, can stand in the way of such cultural inflows as long as their source is a predominant and all-encompassing civilization (Ghulyun 1990:279).

Having critically and analytically identified the problem, Ghulyun's subsequent tackling of the "modern" dilemma suggests a process of "consciousness elevation" with regard to Muslims' conceptual norms and edifices, together with the constant revision of their methodological imperatives. Through praxis and experience, collective Muslim consciousness would then grow, develop, and progress. This, as he put it, would advance its credibility and consolidate its independent understanding of reality. Reason and cognitive strategies in this context, would have an exceptional role to play (Ghulyun 1990:252, 312–13).

Ghulyun's cognitive analysis, while sophisticated and perceptive, logically and inevitably leads to a commensurate reductive solution. Dealing with Islamic issues solely at a reduced cognitive level sets in effect "determining presuppositions" embedded in an alien discourse. This is why, despite his impressive critique of both salafi and modernist movements in the Arab world, Ghulyun ultimately reaches a dead end. He fails to suggest any strategic alternatives. Acknowledging the criticisms addressed at this shortcoming in the final section of his book, Ghulyun vacillates (Ghulyun 1990:353). He rejects any of the salafi, modernist or synthetic "ideological" constructions, or for that matter the possible existence of any monolithic ideology capable of bringing together the diverse thought currents of Marxism, nationalism, and Islam (Ghulyun 1990:254–5). He further resigns himself to the fact that there is no ready-made solution for the crisis of identity and the bifurcation of consciousness from within the (Islamic) culture itself (Ghulyun 1990:356). What could be done at best is to alter the nature of the relationship between the diverse existing ideological currents from one of antagonism and hostility to a relationship of dialogue, interaction, and coexistence, i.e. pluralism. In what overarching framework would such pluralism take place? Ghulyun responds in the only way his reductive cognitive method could lead him to—democracy. His eschewing of the concept of *Shura* (counsel) implicitly recognizes that democracy requires a secular structural context. Shura would require an Islamic normative fixture that would counter his reductive espousal of ideological diversity. His appeal for tolerance of the latter betrays in effect a predetermined ideological stance. Toleration of ideological diversity can, after all, only take place subsequent to a definable epistemic continuity. This is why Michel Foucault could argue that, despite all the apparent challenges that Marx's ideas presented to the power and domination of ruling classes and their commensurate ideologies, "[a]t the deepest level of Western knowledge, Marxism introduced no real discontinuity." And while the erupting conflict and opposition to Marx's ideas "may have stirred up a few waves and caused a few surface ripples ... they [were] no more than storms in a children's paddling pool" (Foucault 1970:261–2). Marxism's epistemic continuity allowed it, despite its exploits, to be tolerated in the ranks of its liberal opponents.

The "revival" that Ghulyun talks about, through which creativity as a product of differences, contradictions, and free dialogue becomes possible, must by necessity recognize the above considerations. It may be true that those elements are necessary for a dynamic take-off, as Ghulyun stresses. Yet, this provides no reason for the circumvention of the imperatives of indigenous methodological and self-referential frameworks in favor of a Foucauldian "experience of order"—a given epoch's conception of knowledge ultimately grounded in the fundamental way in which things are seen to be connected to one another. Such connections ultimately determine the modalities of existing thought and influence its development. What this conjures up is a power relationship guiding a normatively open Islamic system continuously required to adapt to secular environmental inputs. Islam becomes vulnerable to an alien episteme, or "the system of concepts that specifies the notion and structure of knowledge" for a modern secular era. And while this episteme may reflect "rectifications of earlier [concepts] and contain them as special cases of a broader and more adequate explanation of the world" (Gutting 1989:139; Foucault 1970:xxiii–xxiv; 218–19), the relevance of this system to the development of an Islamic conceptual framework is moot. As a matter of fact, the substance of thought which shapes the fabric of an Islamic society becomes marginalized in favor of the epoch's experiences of order and configurations. An authentic Islamic episteme undaunted by external impositions can only be launched through the re-founding of its own discursive group of relations "between authorities of emergence, delimitation, and specification" (Foucault 1972:4). And while "different discursive formations may have many of [even, in theory, all] the same rules ... different discursive relations among their rules will differentiate them" (Gutting 1989:139). How one orders relations between possibly identical rules should thus constitute the principal guiding effort in order to guard against confusing rules for identical discursive relations. This is a common pitfall which many intellectuals from the Islamic world fall into, and which Arkoun, following Ghulyun's footsteps, also confronts.

In his work *Rethinking Islam*, Arkoun calls for implementing a "modern cognitive strategy," which aims at "moving beyond practices bequeathed by the past, whether within Islam, Christianity, or the secular West," while "violating dogmas and subverting theories and standard definitions" (Arkoun 1994:123). Along a post-modern line of thought, he proposes a process in which "[r]eason questions its own status in the psychological configuration of the mind, and certainly, in the unfolding of all cognitive activity." This presumably would allow scholars to "revise their images of so-called archaic, traditional, and modern cultures, their attitudes toward cultural interchange and their practices within the logosphere defining each language" (Arkoun 1994:127). Subsequent reconstruction may then aim at "creating space for the emergence and construction of notions, concepts, and categories to be found in all types of culture and in all domains of semantic and semiotic activity" (Arkoun 1994:125).

Presenting himself as a "wronged plaintiff" stating his case against an historical injustice imposed upon Muslims by the West, Arkoun proclaims that despite undergoing "a generalized crisis" heavily influenced by the "end of Marxist eschatology," the "West" has continued to maintain its pressure on the rest of the world and to refuse to entertain external "forms of thought." The Western discourse, Arkoun proceeds, has incessantly imposed upon "critical voices expressing solidarity with the history of Muslim peoples [a demand] to be more 'objective,' more 'neutral,' less 'polemical' or 'engaged' in recurrent forms of protest against the West." At the core of this power discourse, an essential call for conversion to the values of the West is promulgated. As a result, "the history of the hegemonic world rolls on, perpetuating a sovereignty over human beings that was once attributed to God, while secondary actors exhaust themselves in imitating, adapting, reproducing, and confirming the productivity and insuperability of that World." Ironically, in Arkoun's words, while Western intellectuals may be willing to admit the weakness of Enlightenment reasoning, the crisis of political thought, the disappearance of all ethical discourse, the weakening of the philosophical quest for meaning, the deterioration of the providential welfare state, the increasing fragmentation and abstraction of literary and artistic production, they are not willing to tolerate nor accept alternative assessments. This attitude, he stresses, is governed among other reasons by the "introspective" critical currents of Western thought. Thus, when Islamic thought, for instance, "points out the dangers of uncritical allegiance to these same forces of disintegration and alienation, [Westerners] tend to reaffirm the untouchability and universality of their model" (Arkoun 1994:4).

One would have expected after such fervent indictments that Arkoun would embark on the methodological exercise of exposing and dismantling this violent hierarchy of power. Instead, he turns against his own Islamic heritage, deconstructing its cognitive systems and ethico-juridical codes, and historicizing its beliefs. His cognitive approach to Islam within a Foucauldian power framework renders him susceptible to much of the paradoxical trappings of the latter, in addition to inconsistencies of his own. Not only does Arkoun propose to undertake this exercise in the absence of a presumably reconstructed Islamic methodological order as a legitimating precondition, but in applying a cognitive approach to Islam, he inadvertently consolidates the very victimizing power hierarchy that he claims to have condemned. In typical apologetic language, he explicitly declares his aim to be to "modernize archaic attitudes as well as to rehabilitate a sense of the living cultural traditions of Muslim societies in the intellectual and cultural practices of the West" (Arkoun 1994:121). This was to take place within the confines of some ambiguous, unidentified, to-be-constructed cultural matrix that would require a seemingly fair and benign universal desertion of any claim to absolute truths. Since "signs" and "symbols" have always been used by different ethno-cultural groups to legitimate power drives, so Arkoun's logic goes,

[a]ll "believers," whether they adhere to revealed religions or contemporary secular regions [sic], would thus be equally constrained to envisage the question of meaning not from the angle of unchanging transcendence—that is of an ontology sheltered from all historicity—but in light of historical forces that transmute the most sacred values. (Arkoun 1994:9)

This "open-minded secular" approach, "applied with a critical perspective to any aspect of knowledge and understood as a search for the most neutral, least ideological form of expression out of respect for the free will of the other person, constitutes significant progress of the mind" (Arkoun 1994:20). Such neutrality, only possible, according to Arkoun, through *secular* thought, would ultimately produce a "liberal, critical 'Islam' open to change ... far situated from fundamentalist ideological closures and the ... recurrent force of orthodoxy as an instrument of control" (Arkoun 1994:3, 124).

Arkoun's suggested approach unequivocally situates Islam as the unprivileged and controlled term in relation to a cognitive, secular, and supposedly "neutral" hierarchy of power. Alleged claims to neutrality under those conditions can only reflect a contradiction in terms. Like Ghulyun before him, Arkoun sets this referential matrix in a discursive relationship with respect to an Islam required continuously to adapt and conform to external guiding principles. Instead of attempting to reestablish the independence of Islamic self-referentiality, he offers a theoretically and methodologically alienating exercise in which Islam is ultimately reduced to the confines of Western cognitive matrices. After all, how could a revelation emanating from the Divine and essentially concerned with setting the standards of truth and error be reduced to a cognitive and neutral realm, historicized and de-ontologized? What would be left of its essence? Nor is it credible that the dismantling or epi-phenom-enalization of Islam's normative matrix, such as is strongly implied in Arkoun's work, would constitute a prerequisite for a liberal critical Islam. The collapse or marginalization of this matrix as a matter of fact would ultimately eliminate a necessary and essential condition of his liberal inclinations—freedom. It is the consolidation of the Islamic matrix, as Ghulyun has put it, which ultimately justifies socio-religious and political *ends*, and their commensurate *means*. In its absence as a guiding standard, it becomes almost impossible for Muslims in general, and as individuals, to exercise free choice based on their own initiative. Many of their options would ultimately hinge upon mere circumstances shaped and formed by an overpowering adversarial reality. Muslims would un-circumspectly surrender their fortitude, to be marginalized as instruments and blind machines designed and run by the embodiments of a stronger and more powerful will (Ghulyun 1990:254).

Arkoun's attempt to introduce a "counter power" ultimately collapses into the premise of cognitive reductionism and consequently the trappings of this same framework's power horizons. In order to escape this Foucauldian paradoxical "universe" of power, and in a proposal reminiscent of the famous Egyptian liberalist Taha Hussain, he suggests a philosophy of history that projects a ubiquitous interest and consciousness in a recomposed humanistic "Mediterranean culture." This was not to take place within an Islamic self-referential framework, but rather through a process of a radical rethinking in which the "relationship between thought and sign and between thought and symbol," is envisaged from within the perspective of a "comparative history and a philosophical critique of all the cultural and cognitive systems present" (Arkoun 1994:121–2); the seeming underlying goal being to "operate a decentring that leaves no privilege to any centre" (Foucault 1972:205). In so doing, Arkoun dismantles an ontologically centered (centripetal) Islamic value system from within the very power horizons of an epistemologically decentered (centrifugal) Western system of knowledge. In the framework of all possible contingencies, the latter system, judged in its own terms, would thrive and prosper while Islam, judged in the Western system's own terms, could only be exhausted and impoverished. Any semblance of equality is shattered and, in the very jargon of post-modern language, a *differend* erupts. *Differend* refers to a conflictive situation between two (or more) heterogeneous discourses which cannot be equitably resolved due to the lack of determining presuppositions applicable to all parties involved. This condition arises "when the 'regulation' of the conflict that opposes them is done in the idiom of one of the parties while the wrong suffered by the other is not signified in that language." Any judgment made in this context can only "wrong" one side because "the rules of the genre of discourse by which one judges are not those of the judged genre or genres of discourse" (Lyotard 1988:9, xi). Equal procedural application to binary opposite value systems can only lead to inherently profound and substantive inequalities. After all, if "all knowledge," as the post-modern approach seems to suggest, "rests upon injustice," and if "there is no right, not even in the act of knowing, to truth or a foundation for truth" (Foucault 1977:163), where does this leave the Qur'an, the Prophetic tradition, and Islamic revelation as sources of knowledge? Where does this leave Islam? That which makes claims to truth, and defines its source from outside of history, cannot relinquish its rights to both justice and universality without forsaking its own essence.

Rethinking Islam cannot allow, by any measure, such discrepancies to stand. Yet, Arkoun simply assumes them away by delving into cognitive matters and ignoring cosmology and normativity. As a result he fails to validate either the inherent superiority of his approach or genuine claims to "universal tendencies" (Arkoun 1994:123). In his implicit subservient concurrence to the logic that "only that which can be validated under the regime of cognitives is real" (Teubner

1989: 743), Arkoun—the plaintiff—is compelled to prove any damage he alleges cognitively, while ignoring Islamic self-referential rules. However, if

the regime of phrases to which the plaintiff belongs is different from that of cognitive phrases, and thus necessarily different from that of the only tribunals he can appeal to, then he is certain to lose his suit. This is the case, for example, with a philosophy whose regime of phrases ... cannot by hypothesis be limited to the cognitive regime. (Benjamin 1989:353)

Ghulyun and Arkoun's cognitive propositions, despite denials of ignoring normative considerations, inevitably constrain and predetermine the reductive outcomes of their approaches. Much of their critical effort, aimed equally at both the Islamic East and the secular West, backslides into the very web they so tenaciously try to escape. Neither one of them breaks loose from the cognitive imperatives to which they have chained themselves. In the final analysis, they fail to reverse and liberate the violent Western/Islamic hierarchy or to dismantle the rhetorical and metaphysical structures at work through such an order of oppositions. By deferring to cognitive logic, both authors surrender to its reflections of reality. Both Ghulyun and Arkoun, despite their different though complementary approaches, lose their case—their shared claim to "equality," in effect, "hides differands" (Benjamin 1989:356). Justice, wherever it is sought, cannot be served.

Occidentalism: the case of Hassan Hanafi

In contrast to Ghulyun and Arkoun, Hanafi attempts to go beyond critical exercises toward suggesting counter-discursive strategies of engagement. He identified the basic challenge confronting the Muslim Umma today to be the dilemma of identity preservation in the process of engaging other cultures and civilizations. Aware of the oppositional problems involved in a cognitive hierarchy, he proposed a methodological alternative in the form of a radically constructed *Occidentalism*. Its immediate purpose was to halt and reverse the seemingly unimpeded Westernization process overwhelming the Islamic world by attempting to reconstruct the self-defining Islamic identity and overcoming its alienation; an alienation most conspicuously experienced by upper strata in Muslim societies who can no longer identify themselves with a tradition perceived to be stagnating and ossified. Rather than bearing their responsibility toward their own heritage by altering its configurations, readjusting its axes, and selecting from among its categories, they have opted instead for the easier and uninhibited immersion into an alien system of intelligence. Occidentalism, according to Hanafi, purports to bring those estranged social groups back where they belong. It constitutes a necessary first step toward bounding the Western civilization and alleviating its overwhelming weight which overshadows alternative creativities.

The complexity of this situation reflects the polar fluidity associated with self-centeredness and rejectionism on one hand, and collapsing into the confines of emulative dependency on the other. According to Hanafi, the resolution of this seeming paradox constitutes contemporary Muslims' civilizational task. Within this task, both Islamic and Western heritages must be critically and objectively evaluated from a vantage point that eschews either apologetic or condemning pretensions. This remains a process applicable to both heritages and, as opposed to emulation, which Hanafi correctly stresses "is not a source of knowledge" (Hanafi 1991:26–7, 83), is conducive to inciting methodological innovation without which internal civilizational dynamics lose their vitality. As a creative act capable of meeting such requirements, this reconstructive effort not only allows for self-assured civilizational interaction, but also simultaneously for the feasible transference and adaptation of elements of one experience to the needs and requirements of the other. The predominant Western civilization may then be comprehended within the context of its own unique historical development. In tandem, a methodological segregating approach may be developed in the framework of which the seemingly intractable link between modernity and Western-ism could and must be resolved.

Despite his approach's philosophical undercurrents and its recognition of the *non-linear* self-referential dimensions of *Islamic history*, Hanafi does not delve far enough into that history's full implications, or into the circular laws of sufficiency.[1] As far as these laws are concerned, he deals with them either superficially or borders on fusing them with the necessary conditions for an Islamic revival. At best he stops short of explicitly identifying them. In so doing, he limits the full potential of his "Occidental" approach. Conditions of sufficiency are particularly important in order not to lose sight of the fact that the current disenchanting position of Muslims has not been wrought upon them merely by the intellectual superiority of Orientalists. Rather, it was largely inflicted as a result of the objective material power at their disposal without which many of their bearings may have been rendered innocuous. Confronting the West at the "Occidental" level in the absence of many of the capabilities that rendered Orientalism effective may well reduce its challenge to nothing more than a mere intellectual curiosity. At the level of necessity, Hanafi's Occidentalism certainly contributes to stopping the condition of objective defeat from becoming an internalized subjective conquest. However, in this sense, it is merely defensive and reactive. Reaction remains an adaptive process, largely determined by the actions of an independent and imposing power, and subject to its linear environmental imperatives. Consequently, what Arab and Muslim intellectuals may or may not do remains a function of the other's determinations and a reflection of their own objectification.

A revival as such does not hinge solely on matters of rationality, heritage, and culture, but more so on the resultant confluence of a myriad of socio-economic and historical and planning coincidences, which expand or limit the horizons facing nations aspiring for rejuvenation. There is, in other words, no blueprint, scheme, or quantitatively calculated linear projection for a "revival." Linear progressions at best may be able to identify *results* (cause–effect relationships) but not *consequences*. The latter being outcomes of non-linear events that "cannot be deterministically predicted" (Lazlo 1991:x). And while events may be partially dependent on objective material conditions, they are by no means constrained by them. As an ideological orientation, historical linearity necessarily fails to deliver on promises of progress or say much about future historical occurrences. By its very assumptions, something like the Iranian Islamic revolution could never have been contemplated nor for that matter have been feasible. After all, in light of the Iranian Islamic phenomenon, if the predominance of the West is perceived as an event rather than as a linearly determined progression, this would contextualize its civilizational order as an historical contingency rather than as a universal necessity. The Western civilization would no longer be able to claim control over history and would become subject instead to the vagaries of consequential events. As such, it ceases to set the laws of history, or be capable of making triumphalist proclamations about the end of history. The failure of the Iranian revolutionary experience, therefore, more than merely being a matter of objective Western interest, constitutes an indispensable subjective necessity.

Hanafi's work, nevertheless, although broadly philosophical and wanting in terms of methodological concreteness, remains a serious attempt at articulating and formulating these dimensions of opposition. The more so, as it contributes to reversing the subject–object order which hitherto governed much of Western–Islamic mutual perceptions. Its major significance lies in the horizons it opens for the introduction of a normative dimension, which by reducing the cognitive aspect to its natural boundaries, allows for de-fusing the predominance of Western civilization from concomitant notions of universality. In the absence of normative closure, a cognitive approach that internalizes the standards of the external system of intelligence that produced it would render synonymous *preponderance* and *universalism*. The historicity of the former is consequently con-fused with the ahistoricity of the latter. In the process, the productions, regressions, consistencies, and contradictions of a relative historical experience project themselves as the dynamics of absolute and linear determinism. In this regard, Occidentalism responds to a growing need for a foundational discourse from within which critique and counter-discursive engagements may be launched. Through its structural reversal of Orientalist logic, Occidentalism purports to dramatically alter the terms of interaction (Hanafi 1991:9ff).

Expanding beyond its limitations remains necessary however, in order both to avoid falling into the "reactive trap" which Occidentalism may lead us into, and to (re)establish the historical non-linear independence of Islamic history. Evading this trap requires a methodological and practical regime of action, unencumbered by intra-Islamic pathologies, burdens of historical baggage, or the bearings of this epoch's insecurities. This must be qualified of course by a necessary and total commitment to the imperatives and untouchable foundations of Islamic principles and identity structures. Thus, despite the poorly articulated idiom of Islamist groups, the slogan "Islam is the solution" constitutes more than just a rhetorical proclamation or miraculous invocation to be cynically dismissed. Rather it underscores the expectations of Muslims' civilizational resurgence and the infusion of meaning in history. By obeying God and devotedly following his will as expressed in the Law (Shari'ah), events become subject to a universal power that wills them to converge, beyond mere objective causality and "results," toward the necessary and sufficient "consequential" conditions of revival. Other than being a mere act of piety, Shari'ah becomes the praxis through which human and divine will are harmonized, the confluence of which instates the requisite presuppositions of revival and resurgence. Meaning and action consequently converge, in the course of which Islamic history becomes reinstated as the dynamic unfolding of a divinely heralded universal and ahistorical scheme of events. Based on the interplay of the constituent elements of *variation*, *selection*, and *retention* (read ijtihad), and their corresponding time dimensions—the future, the present, and the past—Islamic history may then proceed to evolve. Ijtihad ceases to reflect discrete cases of innovation, and becomes instead a continuous process of expansion. This non-linear pattern of growth must be circular, so as to allow the future to be largely a reflection of the past.[2] "According to this innovatively repeating cycle there is some novelty in recurrence; each cycle moves society along a given axis, vague as the fate of future cycles may be" (Lazlo 1991:50). In those terms, linear "reactionary" and "progressive" conceptions of historical dynamics lose much of their relevancy and meaning. Where the past and the future link, and continuity is reinstated, "traditional–modern" dichotomies make little sense. Islamic action and capabilities must thus be reinstated and mobilized at the level of sufficiency through an initial non-linear (circular) transformation that would allow for the subsequent dynamics of autonomous action and meaning. From this, it follows that while the laws of necessity may be cognitive those of sufficiency must be normative with determining presuppositions applicable to both. A "linear" break between the two would constitute a *differend*.

TOWARD REINSTATING ISLAMIC HISTORY

"Rethinking" Islam is a most serious proposition that may be enunciated only in full cognizance of its commensurate responsibility. Responsibility calls upon Muslim intellectuals to maintain and sustain the continuity of their history, and to project the Islamic vision into the future in such a way that would give a more profound and lasting insight into the past. Otherwise, attempts at renewal may very easily slip into their opposite as a reaction against the foundations and imperatives which must always remain rooted, secure, and untouched. Absence of guiding parameters and explicit conceptual frameworks of reference capable of determining and constraining the purposes and ends of civilizational interaction and dialogue would ultimately reduce "interaction" to a colonizing *lebenswelt* and turn dialogue into a discourse. Commensurate attempts at self-criticism would further reflect nothing more than a futile exercise in self-deprecation.

Looking at Islamic history through the prism of their contemporary times, and projecting the problems of the past as a key to understanding those of the present, Ghulyun, Arkoun, and Hanafi have, to varying degrees, fallen into a "purely pragmatic view of the facts." According to this "cognitive" insight, the "criteria of a right interpretation is its suitability to some present purpose" (Carr 1986:54). Yet, an authentic Islamic episteme would require of intellectuals the daunting "capacity to rise above the limited visions of [their] own situation in society and history" (Carr 1986:xxii, 21), and to lead a kind of "exilic" and "marginal" existence in which social and economic "deprivation" as the cost of integrity and courage becomes "a unique pleasure" (Said 1994:62 and front flap).

Cognitive and pragmatic indifference to truth, under the banner of intellectual reform and renewal, allow Arkoun's historical confusion to effectively dismantle the Islamic identity structure, Ghulyun's "critical disenchantment" to lead us nowhere, and Hanafi's more serious Occidentalism to confine us to a reactive attitude. Such pitfalls may appear natural in light of the current Islamic historical predicament. However, if Islamist and secular intellectuals are to rise above the limited visions of their own situation in society and history, they will need to construct indigenous methodological maps, and develop the ability to transcend historical conflicts and problems. This may require they be less concerned with theorizing and more with regaining methodological initiative. After all, much of the dependency of intellectuals from the Arab and Islamic world on Western social theory may be attributable—among other reasons—to a perceived rigidity and ossification in Islamic methodological development. Loss of such requisite dynamism accentuated the process of entropy in Islamic thought and was perceived to have confined reason to a marginalized and reclusive domain. This has contributed to a concomitant tense if not hostile relationship between traditional scholars and intellectuals versed in Western rationality. Methodological innovation thus remains a requirement at the core of which the dynamics of Islamic growth and ijtihad may be reinstated.

Shafi'i's Risala and self-referentiality: continuity beyond *taqlid* (emulation)

In his introduction to Imam Muhammad bin Idris al-Shafi'i's (767–820 CE) *Risala* (The Treaties), Majid Khadduri indicated that the Shari'ah was the embodiment of the Islamic ideal life and the framework of Islam itself. In its particular usage, the concept of Shari'ah has come to designate an Islamic legal worldview, reflecting the essential qualities of the Islamic community. In broader terms, it disclosed a self-contained, self-referential socio-economic and political system. As such, it acquired the character of a religious obligation and constituted a political sanction of religion (Al-Shafi'i 1987:3).[3]

It was due to Al-Shafi'i's genius that the foundations of Jurisprudence (*usul al-Fiqh*) were given precision and parametrically articulated. In an early historical encounter with the problem of authenticity, Al-Shafi'i continuously confronted other jurists of his time in disputations "against the use of sources which might infuse into the law elements of human legislation" (Al-Shafi'i 1987:44). His outstanding contribution lay in his awareness that the Shari'ah as a normative system could maintain its unity and identity only by being entirely self-referential in its operations and processes. As the highest standard of authenticity, it was perpetually required to produce "its elements, structures, and processes, its boundaries and its unity in a circular way." Circularity suggested a self-validating closure, which does not in any sense negate the environment in which the system operates, yet imposes that the Shari'ah in all its operations reproduces itself only for the purposes of internal evolution. This helps in focusing practical and theoretical attention on the procedures that dictate the premises, content, and consequences of the Shari'ah's constructions of social reality (Teubner 1989:752).[4] The current problem of the nature of the Shari'ah's interplay with the socio-economic and political environment may hence be reformulated as a matter of "how circular causal processes are subject to external influences." Circularity becomes "eminently suited to generating hypothesis for causal relationships," imputing complexity to the causal models which influence the Shari'ah externally. This allows us to move from the simple input–output, cause–effect logic toward a rationale of "perturbation"[5] (Teubner 1993:35, 48). By sustaining its own dynamics and structure, the Shari'ah becomes and remains a "subject reproducing its own conceptions of itself and of society" and a "sovereign" with respect to the constitution of identities and differences (Teubner 1988:2, 6, 7). It cannot consequently import identities and differences from the outer world, but will have to decide upon them itself. In so doing, it establishes a "recursively closed system which does not derive its operations from its environment" (Luhmann 1988:18). In contradistinction to open and adaptive input–output systems, the Shari'ah constitutes a unified counterpart which while "open to energy" is "closed to information and control" (Ashby 1956:4). As such, only a self-reproducing closed Shari'ah system is capable of ijtihad and/or evolution.

The methodological problem that the Sunni process of ijtihad has historically faced, was that in attempting to limit legal reasoning solely within the confines of Islamic sources, Al-Shafi'i "paid less attention to the problems of developing new principles of law [cognitive evolution] than to the problems of how to demonstrate that all the principles and rules that existed in his time were derived from recognized Islamic sources (normative ijtihad)." He was keener on establishing the methodological foundations of self-referential religio-normativity than on engaging with the evolutionary dynamics of cognitive openness. This "closure," reflected in the confinement of legal reasoning within the framework of Islamic sources, "inevitably narrowed the free use of legal reasoning, and the tendency toward taqlid [= cognitive closure] ... may be said to have begun at that time. In the following century, taqlid became the dominating rule." The space required for evolution and continuous growth in complexity was consequently increasingly and considerably reduced. Subsequent developments contributed further to the structuring of the Shari'ah in a way which "tended to become gradually divorced from the practical needs of the individual and oriented toward the common interests of Islam" (Al-Shafi'i 1987:43–4). This separation, one might add, remains substantively different from the same process of "de-centering the subject" underway in the West, which multiplies the "centers of cognition." Social discourses in the latter become "new epistemic subjects that compete with the consciousness of the individual ... moving the subject away from its privileged position as the sole and ultimate center of cognition." Islamic social discourse of de-centering, on the other hand, has always moved centripetally—i.e. outside of the individual subject yet toward a center. Islamic–Western civilizational interactions, therefore, have to be distinctly cognizant of the consequences arising from the interplay of a centripetal worldview, and an opposing centrifugal and increasingly "centerless" and "epistemically fragmented" Western counterpart (Teubner 1989:741, 738).

Al-Shafi'i's intellectual and scholarly legacy has thus contributed to two major historical processes: one positive and one negative. In the former terms, Al-Shafi'i has brilliantly established, for his time and beyond, that only with reference to itself must the Shari'ah continue to organize and reproduce as a system, differentiated from the environment, and autonomous from its current besieged situation in society and history. In the latter terms, and probably as a consequence of his methodological prowess, *taqlid* became increasingly entrenched, leading to gradual stagnation, loss of energy, and eventually to scholarly entropy. Al-Shafi'i's *Risala* nevertheless remains a crucial springboard toward rejuvenating the dynamics of Islamic history in general and stagnating Sunnism in particular. The significance of his work, after all, "lies not so much in the detailed matters it discusses ... as in the comprehensive view of the whole subject of *usul* [foundational closure] and the logical and systematic method Shafi'i provided for legal reasoning." In both their negative and positive aspects, the "impress" of his legacy which has never been superseded in Islam has remained, in Khadduri's words, "permanent" (Al-Shafi'i 1987:41, 4).

Ijtihad and the evolutionary continuity of Islamic history: the normative/stem–cognitive/branch link[6]

Moving beyond Al-Shafi'i's normative/methodological closure should not be perceived, therefore, as an attempt to break with historical precedents, but rather as their complex consolidation (retention) in response to environmental perturbations, through both ijtihad (= normative continuity) and evolution (= cognitive change). The most important feature of both categories is the maintenance of the Shari'ah's internal circular structure, not its ability to adapt to the environment (Teubner 1993:55–6). As long as the Shari'ah's "circular organization is not interrupted" it may undergo any requisite change. However, whereas "normative closure requires symmetrical relations between the components of the system where one element supports the other and vice versa, [c]ognitive openness ... requires asymmetrical relations between the system and the environment" (Luhmann 1990:230). Evolution is thus introduced not as an unequivocally goal-oriented dynamic, but rather as a "teleonomic" process which continues to build upon the established system of Shari'ah. This allows the Islamic religious field to be re-constructed according to "immanent rules of regulation." Though at times irreversible, this process does not necessarily lead to a state that is "better" or "worse" than its predecessors. Nor does it guarantee greater viability or security, more "good fortune" or "consciousness." In this sense evolution is not "evolutionist," i.e. it does not support the eschatological political doctrine of evolutionism, according to which mankind, following a "logic of development," progresses from stage to stage until the "goal" or merely the "end of history" is reached (Teubner 1993:56, 48). This was evident in Al-Shafi'i's self-referential and procedural methodology. He explicitly indicated that the Shari'ah can only be changed by itself, and that the "abrogation or the deferment of any [Qur'anic] communication cannot be made valid save by another [Qur'anic] communication." The same applies as well to the Prophetic Tradition (The Sunna). While Qur'anic communications may supersede the Sunna, this may take place only after the latter has been first abrogated by another Sunna, i.e. abrogated itself. In this latter process, the Qur'an circularly and symmetrically, though indirectly, refers to itself through the Sunna (Al-Shafi'i 1987:125).[7] Since there is no law outside of the Shari'ah, there by definition could be no input or output of law in relation to its social environment. Consequently, there is no instruction by the outside world and only construction of the outside world by the Shari'ah (Teubner 1989:740).

While the historical corpus of Islamic jurisprudence has dealt extensively with matters of ijtihad (*stem*), it has significantly marginalized in the process the cognitive identity of its evolutionary *branch*. In typical traditional fashion, the necessary latter was collapsed into the presumably sufficient former. Contemporary complexities however, may no longer allow this to be either feasible or justified. As such, the Islamic cognitive problem will need to be re-formulated in terms of how to bring forth the identity of the evolutionary branch. Subsequent to that, the problem will be how to link it to the stem (ijtihad) in a dynamic and vibrant systemic unity in which closure and openness reflect "reciprocal conditions" rather than "contradictions." In this unity, "the openness of the system bases itself upon self-referential closure [i.e. evolution], and closed [self-referential] reproduction refers to the environment [i.e. ijtihad]." Systemic unity, in other words, requires corresponding structurally congruent normative-cognitive mechanisms. In order to reinstate the methodological and symbiotic stem–branch, ijtihad–evolution and centripetal–centrifugal dynamics of appropriation, such dynamics must combine "symmetrical and asymmetrical, general and specific commitments" (Luhmann 1990:229). The dynamics of the respective former elements (i.e. stem: ijtihad, centripetal, symmetrical) incorporate the circular "filter" mechanisms of "variation, selection, and retention" (Teubner 1993:49, 56), while the respective latter elements (i.e. branch: evolution, centrifugal, asymmetrical) are based on the corresponding cognitive mechanisms of hierarchical and discursive Western/Islamic *reversal*, Islamic/Western *capture* and Islamic/Islamic *closure*.

Reversal, capture and closure constitute the cognitive appropriative dynamics which have to take place and be completed before linkage to the stem is possible or viable. *Reversal* initiates a deconstructive process pertaining to the concept or system of concepts to be appropriated. It constitutes the first step toward an Islamic cognitive strategy through which, by using social theory's own "stratagems" against itself, a force of dislocation is produced "that spreads itself throughout the entire system, fissuring it in every direction thoroughly delimiting it" (Derrida 1978:20). Reversal, in other words, permits the disorganizing of the Western/Islamic binary order and the dissonant invasion of the former by the latter. This initial cognitive step is particularly crucial because all knowledge "depends on its concepts," or names of ideas which "determine the questions one asks and the answers one gets ..." (Thompson 1961:4). They are a "condensation of experience" (Viaud 1960:76), and a "kind of unit in terms of which one thinks" (Gould and Kolb 1964:20).

While exposing conceptual tensions and binary oppositions remains necessary, deconstructive reversal is insufficient to resolve their challenges. To be purposeful, it must undergo additional steps in order to transform its centrifugal push into centripetal anchorage. An intermediate *capturing* mechanism proceeds to re-construct a new Islamic/Western conceptual hierarchy. This visionary phase involves the construction of imagery for a contemporary Islamic existence, to be compared, contrasted, and ultimately extended from a corresponding ideal historical imagery. Both may then be linked— if needed—through a reduced and deconstructed social theory in order to capitalize on the elements of *precision* it may provide. Social theory as an "instrument" of linkage remains hemmed in between two or more Islamic conceptual frameworks or ideal types. Parameters thus exist which guide where one is coming from and where one is heading to.

Once the exercise has been deemed successful through the irruptive emergence of a new and independent Islamic concept, a *closure* may be effected which disposes of previous links with alien tools of investigation. As the final stage of the cognitive appropriative process, an Islamic/Islamic circular (as opposed to the preceding two hierarchical sub-strategies or stages) closure establishes self-referential autonomy. A qualitative transformation takes place at this cognitive juncture which appropriates social theory as a rich and innocuous source of energy, contributing to the authentic reconstruction of the Shari'ah in the same fashion that a branch contributes to the reproduction of its own stem. In this sense, appropriation is circularity and "circularity is validity" (Luhmann 1990:231). Once the organization of self-referential circularity and structural identity is achieved, it becomes possible to transpose the cognitive evolutionary functions to the Shari'ah system itself.

This process of internalization shifts the dynamics of evolution from the environment into the [Shari'ah] system itself and subordinates it [to the latter's circular dynamics]. What we are witnessing here is a shifting of the balance from "external" social mechanisms of evolution toward "internal" [ijtihad] mechanisms. External evolutionary mechanisms can now have only a "modulating" effect in [Shari'ah] developments, as internal structural determinants begin to play a key role in the evolutionary process. (Teubner 1993:56)

The internalized evolutionary branch may then be linked to the stem along three options: a—if the appropriation of the concept or system of concepts has been deemed fully realized, it/they may be incorporated according to the normative mechanisms of ijtihad as a source of energy; b—if the process of appropriation has been judged faulty or unsuccessful, the concept or system of concepts may be rescinded until further re-appropriation would render them accessible; and finally, c—if the appropriation of the concept or system of concepts is deemed insufficiently meritorious to be fully incorporated, yet useful enough to preclude rejection, it/they may be instated as a cognitive branch to a normative stem. This condition becomes a source of dynamic tension within the overall Islamic stem–branch or *Tree* methodological framework. In this organic unity, normative "retention" and cognitive "closure" form the valid point of internalization or convergence between both domains.

Beyond the theoretical level, this dual strategy may offer useful practical insights. By introducing elements of complexity, a vibrant and dynamic Shari'ah system may help in resolving some current real-life problems and issues within the Islam world. For instance, a problem of particular concern to the Islamic regime in Iran is the nature of the relationship between the *fuqaha'* (jurisprudents; sgl. faqih) and the intellectuals, expressed institutionally in terms of the relationship between religious seminaries (Hawzas) and secular universities.[8] Difficulties have arisen as a result of the secular philosophical foundations of universities in their present form.

Maintaining a hierarchical order between the two is unlikely to contribute to a mutually cooperative relationship, and more seriously would compromise the necessary symbiosis between the respective normative and cognitive institutions. Thus far into the third decade of the revolution, this matter does not seem to have been adequately resolved, as perhaps exemplified by some student protest movements. Appropriation may serve as a relevant mechanism of problem solving and systemic unity. Through its mechanisms, the "centrifugal analytical" dynamics of secular universities may be transformed to their "centripetal appropriative" counterparts. Rather than solely being secular-cognitive institutions open merely to input–output environmental adaptations, mechanisms of reversal, capture, and closure would serve to maintain the universities' cognitive properties while appropriating and internalizing secular philosophical perturbations through the very elements of the normative system. Universities could then shed their secular identity while maintaining their cognitive essence. Due to the structural identity (circularity) of the appropriative process, they may now serve not only as a valid source of energy to the Hawzas, but also as a neutralizing front base against cultural and informational imperialism.[9]

By effecting this philosophical and conceptual change, a gradual shift in consciousness would take place over time from secular toward Islamic cognition. In the process, the latter could capitalize on the accomplishments of the former. The dynamic unity between stem and branch, normativity and cognition, Hawzas and universities may thus be reinstated both intellectually and institutionally. A common language and discourse would eventually develop in which the two dimensions of systemic unity may communicate, agree or disagree. Intellectual *differends* and social bifurcations may then be resolved.

WESTERN HISTORY AND ISLAMIC MODERNITY: TOWARD A HYPER-APPROPRIATIVE STRATEGY

Given that the current epoch is one in which the predominant civilization is Western, Muslims are inevitably confronted with a contradictory and paradoxical situation. The non-linear, symbiotic, and centripetal dynamics of Islam contrast sharply with the linear and centrifugal dialectics of the Renaissance, Reformation and Enlightenment. And since structural identity is necessary within the Islamic religious field for normative-cognitive continuity, it follows that this must also be the same dynamic of the historical epoch in which this process takes place. An Islamic modernity in other words, will have to exhibit the same circular structural identity in consonance with, and as a reflection of its own unique historical configuration. When this dynamic interplay breaks down the configurative element of Islamic civilization collapses. Reinstating it presages the necessary requisite order for an Islamic modernity or episteme.

The fact that many intellectuals—both Islamist and secular—have fallen into the trap of seeing modernity and the West as synonymous largely constrained their options and defined their attitudes. Both translated an empirical historical experience into an epistemological conclusion only to find out, to their surprise, that the West itself is questioning its own historical experience. On both sides of the polar scale, they were reduced to mere reactive dependants, with the whole of the modern problem confusingly formulated in a fashion that reflected this condition. In the process, infighting between the proponents of either choice (e.g. secularists vs. Islamists), obscured the subject matter or the paradox(es) that needs to be resolved. The very premises from which both parties launched their respective discourses remained almost identical. If a premise is wrong then the conclusion derived from it is unlikely to be true either. The polar conclusions they arrived at, therefore, more or less reflected two sides of the same coin. Furthermore, if how one formulates a problem determines to a large extent the type of answers one shall ultimately get, the vicious circle that both Islamists and secularists fall into does not bode well for either side.

That the West can neither be rejected nor embraced projects it as a most formidable challenge and the essence of Muslims' historical dilemma. The logic of Western predominance—especially in a technological age—makes the options of an Islamic "rejectionist" position prohibitively limited and in most cases untenable. The logic of Islam, by the same token, does not allow for adoption of what would basically cast threatening shadows of doubt on religio-cultural identities and certainties. In addition, the immense gravitational pull of each polar stance rules out largely tenuous adaptations. This seemingly un-resolvable paradox may have inspired the works of numerous Arab and Muslim intellectuals—including those discussed above—yet none appears to have adequately tackled it. Depending on their vantage point, it was traditionally dealt with in either/or fashion; either one embraces the West or one rejects it. Where a compromise would be suggested, method remained wanting.

Transcending and reformulating problems in appropriative terms is one way of dealing with paradox(es). Since no Islamic civilization, or for that matter Islamic authenticity and identity, can evolve within the reduced confines of a linear-centrifugal historical stream, the whole question of the compatibility with and adaptability of Islam to secular cognition as a Western manifestation must be reformulated. Engaging the West summons the means and methods of appropriation through which the linear-centrifugal dynamics of historical modernity (Western-ism) may be transformed into their non-linear-centripetal Islamic counterparts. Modernity ceases to be imported into the Shari'ah system as an input or independent reality, and instead is constructed within it by operations of the Shari'ah system itself. This process does not render the distinction between the latter and the broader Western environment irrelevant, but reinterprets and connects this distinction to the difference between normative and cognitive operations (Nerhot 1988:9). In much the same fashion as normative closure has been sustained as the very condition of cognitive openness, appropriation becomes the term under which incorporation translates into the very act of preemption.

The paradox of historical dynamics: centrifugalism vs. centripetalism

According to Isaiah Berlin,

there exists a great chasm between those, on the one side, who relate everything to a single central vision, one system less or more coherent or articulate, in terms of which they understand, think and feel—a single, universal, organizing principle in terms of which all that they are and say has significance—and, on the other side, those who pursue many ends, often unrelated and even contradictory, connected, if at all, only in some de facto way, for some psychological or physiological cause, related by no moral or aesthetic principle; these last lead lives, perform acts, and entertain ideas that are centrifugal rather than centripetal, their thought is scattered or diffused, moving on many levels, seizing upon the essence of a vast variety of experiences and objects, for what they are in themselves, without consciously or unconsciously seeking to fit them into or exclude them from any one unchanging ... at times fanatical, unitary inner vision. (Tehranian 1995:360)

Conventional wisdom has it that the Enlightenment brought about the age of reason, heralding its triumph over religious and metaphysical relics. This reflected the linear dialectics and centrifugal dynamics of the Western civilization. Reason allegedly ushered in the autonomy of man and his rational and critical independence.

Through its faculties, man was to seek his own happiness and self-fulfillment, always falling back upon himself to correct himself. Skepticism became the self-referential mechanism by which humanity was to continuously perfect itself, and reason consequently was appropriated as the standard of social and moral judgment.[10] In so doing, it was declared, man asserted his will in history.

For various historical reasons, Muslims took such unique dialectics for granted, accepting them as referential judgments and, in the maze of their own historical disappointments, externalized themselves. A quick glimpse at the Qur'an would have enlightened them to the fact that reason, whenever mentioned, has always been linked with faith and certainty and not skepticism, and that the autonomous skeptical mind has been referred to in the same source as "*hawa*" or passion (i.e. as a binary opposite). Within the Qur'anic definition, passion does not mean the lack of reason but its claim to autonomy.[11] Both constitute substantively distinct even if procedurally similar rational manifestations of human existence.[12] In those terms, the dialectics of the Enlightenment have come to produce the centrifugal dynamics of passion and skepticism, and a Westernism whose inertia and very logic merely created, in Max Weber's words "[s]pecialists without spirit [and] sensualists without heart." A "nullity," he judged, which "imagines that it has attained a level of civilization never before achieved" (Weber 1958:182).[13]

The Western appropriation of reason, or what in essence is passion, disguised the true substance of the Enlightenment project, and such would also be the case with any attempt at emulation. If modernity was supposed to be the age of reason, Enlightenment ushered in the verdict of its failure. That it has admittedly led to loss of meaning, an empty self, "discontinuity" and an "irrational rationality" (Brzezinski 1993:x, 29), instead of self-realization, in its very abode of origin, is a testimony to historical modernity's reneging on its promises. In its obsession with "fragments," "fractures," and denials of universal truths, its advanced stage of passion—euphemistically termed post-modernity—has attempted to conceal this failure by condescendingly denying universality to itself *and* others. That it should only be speaking for itself reflects the same dominative universal tendencies which it denies. In its discursive and Orwellian double-talk, post-modernity simply represents the latest attempt at universalizing Western values in the guise of modest self-denial or "unmaking" (Hassan, quoted in Wellmer 1985:338). Its claims to benign rejection of the "tyranny of wholes" which could lead to "totalitarian" experiences conceals both totalitarianism and nihilism as end results of centrifugal historical processes. These polar manifestations provide for neither an improvement nor a blueprint for a substantively different historical unfolding.

The mixed feelings with which the end of the Western "universal" experience has been met was implicit in Zbigniew Brzezinski's ambivalent reference to the French historian Jean-Marie Domenach's remark that, "in applauding the failure of Marxism, Westerners have not fully grasped the fact that they may be saluting the last Western attempt to rationalize and universalize history" (Brzezinski 1993:48). Marxism, which had plausibly been presented as a "form of religion" (Gellner 1994:xiii), has provided for the visible repressive and dominative elements of secularism which, while concomitantly serving the rational interests of its Liberal counterpart, allowed the latter to plead innocence. With Marxism's collapse, liberalism has been faced with the task of having to do the job itself. And since it is not equipped by its very logic to manifestly claim universal truths, post-modernity reflects the latest tool in the liberal-democratic secular arsenal to universalize itself while still pleading innocence. If secularism has failed to prove its universality (a contention which the Iranian revolution has perhaps irreversibly challenged) then let there be no universality at all—so the logic goes. Ultimately this constitutes a new bottle containing the same old liberal wine, where everything boils down to a "universally" fractured and fragmented opinion. Since Western consciousness is mainly an historical product, it can rest reasonably comfortable within the confines of such spatial and temporal limitations. These limitations however, cannot constrain Islamic cosmo-normativity. Calls for Islamic adaptations to what it vehemently condemns, even if expediently appropriated as reason, could only reflect a tragic absurdity and a contradiction in terms. Yet it was this tragic contradiction which guided much of the intellectual efforts of secular and Islamist thinkers. Confusing Western *passion* for modern *reason*, the branch for the stem, they narrowed their options down to the confines of the respective formers. Desperate to reconcile Islam with the (post-) modern spirit of the age, they ended up channeling their talents toward chasing mirages and skeptical illusions.

Post-modernity, in effect, constitutes nothing more than the appropriated euphemism for (pseudo) nihilism in the same fashion that reason constituted the appropriated euphemism for Western passion.[14] Much of the contemporary achievements of Western civilization, after all, were claimed to be built on foundations that never really existed. It was basically built on misnomers. This tenuous exercise in (post-) modern futility can only sap away energy which otherwise might have been channeled toward significantly more productive and authentic foci. Any claims regarding Western universalism, or for that matter the lack of it, must consequently come to an end. Within the limits of those binary opposites, Western intelligence is unlikely to find a way out. By the same token, intellectuals from the Islamic World may well heed not trying to get in.

Reason as the cognitive aspect of revelation must by its very nature remain anchored and maintain a centripetal dynamic with respect to the latter. Perpetually, it must embark on the eternal journey toward such certainty. For those who incessantly try to reconcile Islam with a secular (post-) modernity, it is imperative at the outset that they explain how they propose to merge a centripetal worldview and an opposing centrifugal historical dynamic, or for that matter, if they choose one or the other, how will they maintain the other system's identity. Thus for instance, Muhammad Abed al-Jabri's critique of what he termed the Islamic "explicative mode of knowledge"[15] (al-bayan), while possibly warranted in light of its apparent limitations, fails to address this basic paradox, i.e. the nature and method of possible linkage between the opposed dynamics of the centripetal (al-bayan) and the centrifugal (al-burhan; the demonstrative/reason). While he does recognize that al-bayan always returned the branch (far') to a foundational stem (asl), i.e. proceeded from conclusions to premises, and that al-burhan moved in the opposite direction, proceeding from premises to conclusions (Al-Jabri 1996:113), he does not propose a new solution other than the conventional critiquing, analyzing, and unfettering of the Arab mind from the domination of the past (Al-Jabri 1996:565ff). As a matter of fact, in trying to answer the question as to how to renew and modernize from within "our own" Islamic tradition, Al-Jabri retorts by saying that "renewal and modernization are both a practice and an historical process and thus the question asked is not an epistemological question ... [but] a practical one; a question which finds its gradual, evolving and renewed answer from within experience and not before, above or outside of it" (Al-Jabri 1996:568). Implied in such an answer is the very epistemological aspect which he denies; the very centrifugal dynamic of the Western civilization where experience and praxis determine the historical course of action.

Subordinating the present to the past may be fettering and at times quite frustrating. Yet, critiquing the "Arab mind" as a means of breaking loose from this hierarchical relationship and in the absence of an ontological-epistemological framework could very likely unleash destructive centrifugal forces of such magnitude as to effect a break with the past. Paying lip service respect to tradition in the absence of a proposed resolution to this basic paradox lacks all credibility. Islamic history would inevitably and teleologically follow the very linear dynamics of the Western civilization, permanently moving away from its origin. A modern Islamic coping with matters of continuity and change requires the transformation of the hierarchical relationship between revelation and reason, into which tradition has collapsed, toward original symbiotic stem–branch circularity. In such circularity the branch's complementary identity (reason) is to be reinstated, undaunted by tradition's negating encroachments. The question should then be re-formulated not so much in terms of how to break free from the authority of the past, but in terms of how to reinstate Islam's historical continuity into the modern age; a continuity which has been disrupted by Western centrifugalism and Tradition's complacency. The Islamic stem (past)–branch (present) methodology remains crucial to addressing this question and in reinstating the centripetal and symbiotic relationship between continuity and change. Normative continuity requires the appropriation of the present into the past (stem; e.g. Al-Shafi'i and Ayatollah Khomeini's thought). Corresponding cognitive change requires appropriation of the past into the present (branch; e.g. Ali Shari'ati's thought and potentially Hassan Hanafi's). By establishing circular identity between the past and the present as a prerequisite to historical linkage, the centripetal dynamics of Islamic history may hitherto be unleashed (the Iranian Islamic revolution).

Centripetalization: a paradox resolution mechanism?

In order for Muslims to gauge what they want of modernity and how they envisage their position and action in it, they must be able from the outset to know what this "worldview" means for them in the first place. This is of profound importance because:

The very notion of an action requires the idea of the actor's end or purpose. That is, for an action to be perceived, purpose and meaning must be perceived. Thus a change in the perceived meaning or purpose entails a change in the action that is perceived. (Wilson 1970:67)

Emulation is increasingly becoming less of an option among Muslims who want to preserve their own unique identity against collapsing into "schizophrenic" alternatives. It is not feasible for Muslims, after all, to live or accept modernity defined in terms of the withering away of "substantive" values in favor of "secularism, scientism and hedonism" (Kolb 1986: xii). Such definitions merge both modernity and Western-ism, confusing what occurred as the result of the latter with the former. And while this has been rendered possible by historical default, centripetal appropriation may help prohibit this experience from becoming commensurately a universal epistemological imperative. Centripetalization takes place by linking an independent branch to its corresponding stem. In contra-distinction to its traditional historical antecedent, this methodology does not limit itself to the confines of Islamic juridical normativity. Instead, it reflects the normative-cognitive strategy pertaining in most cases to the non-linear linking of a Western conceptual branch (the cognitive) to an Islamic normative stem. This would establish a centripetal dynamic which substantively transforms the original concept not only into its Islamic counterpart but also into its very own anti-thesis and/or binary opposite: Rationality/Passion attached to an Islamic stem is transformed into Revelation/Rationality/Reason. While the latter respective concepts remain procedural counterparts, stemic linkage opposes them substantively. The same structural process can apply to other secular concepts that may need to be appropriated. Rationality/Westernism may be attached to a stem transforming the former conceptual branch into Revelation/Rationality/Modernity. Westernism becomes substantively transformed into its antithetical Islamic opposite and ceases to exhibit identity with modernity. Connecting the respective transformed concepts of reason and modernity allows us at this stage to separate what is being thought by the West from what ought to be thought, and thus to reinstate the Muslim *subject* mind. As opposed to the traditional past, in which revelation dominated reason in a hierarchical fettering relationship, modernity reinstates the circular and symbiotic (stem–revelation/branch–reason) relationship between the two. Henceforth it becomes possible to define Islamic modernity as the epoch in which revelation and reason converge at their narrowest point;[16] the epoch in which Islam's pristine past and the present merge to reestablish the universality of revelation and reason—the future.

The echoes of Samuel Huntington's observation that "there is a failure to distinguish between what is modern and what is

Western," and that "[t]he one thing which modernization theory has not produced is a model of Western society ... which could be compared with, or even contrasted with, the model of modern society" (Huntington 1988:365), may perhaps find resonance in this methodological alternative. Centripetalization both appropriates and qualitatively transforms what it incorporates. Appropriation in turn helps separate the hitherto merged conceptions of modernity and Westernism, allowing for the development of a non-Western model of modernity to which the West may be both compared and contrasted. Knowledge produced by the West comes to constitute matter to grapple with, appropriate, and ultimately to authenticate. The horizons that this process of (de)appropriation opens for Arab and Muslim intellectuals could therefore be limitless.

Binary opposition could also be applied to a myriad of other concepts. Rationality/hedonism attached to the Islamic stem would change into Revelation/Rationality/Salvation. Hedonism as autonomy or "salvation" from the Law (a centrifugal concept) becomes transformed into Salvation as freedom under the Law (a centripetal concept). By extension, the linking of the Rational/Democracy branch to a stem would produce Revelation/Rationality/Shura. The interplay of the substantive concepts of salvation and Shura could have extremely important implications regarding the nature of any proposed Islamic political system. It re-formulates the problem away from the discursive/euphemistic diatribes of how to bring freedom to the Muslim World by democratizing it, into one where the main focus becomes how to evolve the ideal Islamic political system of salvation. This would allow Muslims to set their own agenda as opposed to having it set for them. The qualitatively transformed concepts, in turn, must be structurally consistent with the stem–branch link which made the initial process feasible in the first place. They must be progressively breakable into stem and branch respectively; thus, reason is breakable into primordiality (*fitrah*/sublimated human instinct) and passion; Modernity into revelation and reason; salvation into virtue and freedom; Shura into allegiance (*bay'ah*) and choice (*ikhtiar*), and so on. In all cases and under all circumstances, the structural elements (i.e. stem and branch) must both link and protect their unique identity roles. Otherwise, collapsing the branch into the stem would inevitably dismantle the dynamics feasible only under such conditions. Primordiality (stem) with collapsed passion (branch) leads to stolidity; revelation with collapsed reason leads to *traditionalism* and sheer emulation (*taqlid*); virtue with collapsed freedom leads to hypocrisy; and allegiance with collapsed choice leads to tyranny; hence the deviation and consequent stagnation in Islamic history. Rectification of these conditions requires a (re)constructed stem–branch regime of inclusion (asymmetric relations), as opposed to a collapsed stemic regime of exclusion (symmetric relations). This would ultimately touch on all aspects of a Muslim society from gender relations in the family and minority relations, up the social ladder to institutional structures and political systems. What becomes required for thought reform, revival, or ijtihad, consequently, is not a process of critique of Islamic history (a centrifugal dynamic), as many intellectuals seem to concede, but of appropriative reinstatement (a centripetal dynamic). Rationality/critique centripetalized becomes Revelation/rationality/appropriation. The latter may then be further broken down into (re)instative normative closure and evolutionary (possibly revisionist) cognitive openness.

The three pronged circular mechanisms of hyper-appropriation may thus be identified as: 1—ijtihad/normative closure (variation, selection, retention); 2—evolution/cognitive openness (reversal, capture, closure); and 3—centripetalization (normative stem/ rationality/cognitive branch), or correspondingly the full dimensions of individual existence (spirit/mind/matter). Though circular and appropriative each in their own right, together they constitute the unity of the Islamic hyper-appropriative strategy. And while the operations of the first two mechanisms must always remain distinct until such a time when the circular structural identity phase may allow them to be linked, the third may operate the normative–cognitive link simultaneously, reflecting a continuous and dynamic *process*. Centripetalization, that is, constitutes the reciprocal self-referential link between normative closure and cognitive openness.

ON CONCEPTUAL HIERARCHIES

Scholarly studies of Islam, modernity, and Islamist movements need to avoid confining analyses of these phenomena to superfluous and largely obsolete "reactionary-progressive" and/or Orientalist conceptions of historical dynamics. Labels of moderation, extremism, and adaptability attributed to such issues and their political currents in the Islamic world simply reflect ideological impositions and discursive manipulations. Worse yet, they contribute to the consolidation of a serious epistemological crisis that can only serve to widen the *differend* between Islamists and secularists. Such a shift in scholarly focus is of great significance because while the Shari'ah

cannot take over full epistemic authority and responsibility for the reality constructions involved ... at the same time it does not totally delegate epistemic authority to other social discourses. Rather, as a precondition for the incorporation of social knowledge, the [Shari'ah] system defines certain fundamental requirements relating to procedure and methods of cognition. (Teubner 1989:751, 750)

Incorporation of social theory in Islamic methodology serves the purpose of providing a healthy tension and "variety pool" for evolution (cognitive openness), continuously subject to Islamic ijtihad and its methodological limitations (Teubner 1989:751, 750). This is necessary in order to avoid cognitive hierarchies, temporal limitations, and/or intellectual–mass alienation.

While an Islamic religious worldview sets revelation as the foundational stem and reason as its branch, secularism reverses this relationship. A secular worldview involves the subversive re-ordering of the elements of its religious counterpart. Islam and secularism, in other words, constitute binary opposites which inevitably extend their opposition to their irruptive concepts. Whether Islamic and secular worldviews are compatible must therefore constitute the initial problem setting. In order to avoid this distinctly clear and straight-forward exposition, the posing of which would invite a more or less straightforward response, the concept of democracy for example, is invoked by secularists as a discursive substitute that basically conceals a shifting and steering ideological formulation—a shot, so to speak, fired from the arsenal of secularism. The recurrent question as to whether Islam is compatible with democracy defers in effect a religious worldview, with its own epistemic constitution of elements and concepts, to the latter—a concept. This concept does not stand on its own as an independent construct or mechanism of choice, but as a product of a secular *Weltanschauung*. To put it forward as the vision for a "comprehensive view of an Arab social project," as Ghulyun for instance has promulgated (1990:359), is inevitably to argue for subservience to the discursive and epistemological foundations of the Western *Weltanschauung* which underlies this structural concept. This could very well lead, quoting Theodor Adorno, to a "[w]rong life [that] cannot be lived rightly" (Adorno 1951:39).

To those who still prefer to pose the question in its ideological form, democracy's compatibility with Islam can logically only become a matter of how the former would strengthen Islam's centripetal dynamics at the level of process, and its circular organization at the level of structure. Incorporating democracy—a conceptual product of secularism—into the Islamic worldview qualitatively transforms it into its corresponding *shura*, a case where internal relations metamorphose seemingly identical rules. From thereon, one may test whether both concepts and/or systems are compatible, taking into consideration that *shura* constitutes a subset of Islam in much the same way as democracy is a subset of secularism. A different formulation of the matter would discursively require the dissolution of the Islamic worldview (i.e. universal set) into a concept (subset) or more realistically into a binary opposite universal set (secularism). The implications are not difficult to gauge. Oppositional worldviews predetermine respective oppositional concepts. The non-linear circular dynamics of Islamic history require corresponding non-linear and circular concepts; a privilege that the concept of democracy, among other linear concepts, does not enjoy. And while a worldview is all encompassing (= universal set/stem), a concept is a partiality (= subset/branch). Since a universal set can never be incorporated into its own subset, let alone an alien one, the former can never be incorporated into the latter.

Secularism's challenge to Islam and, for that matter, religion in general, goes far beyond the ideological to the higher plane of doctrine and essence. The conflict underway to varying degrees of intensity in the Islamic world between Islamists and secularists cannot be understood or perceived solely, therefore, at the cognitive (ideological) level since it persists more importantly at the cosmological as well as the normative-structural (deontological and doctrinal). The diversity that an Islamic civilizational order can, and as a matter of fact has to, tolerate, is that of *mazaheb*—the branches erupting from a common Islamic stem. Irrespective of their internal epistemological breaks, *mazaheb* are an ontological necessity that prohibits the subversion or discontinuity of the original or primary order of thought. Other subverting currents of knowledge which proceed from the skeptical foundation that there exists no truth cannot consequently be tolerated. The limits of tolerance therefore must be critically ascertained. Accordingly, Islamic militants are not to be understood merely from within the confines of a superimposed ideologically motivated "(fundamental)ist" or "terrorist" label, but from those of a political *mazhab* whose parameters identify the varying yet legitimate alternatives of circular interplay between the religious, the social, and the political.[17] The dynamics of Islamic events and movements should be examined, within the context of a common language, as manifestations of the practical application of the Shari'ah itself as defined by the Shari'ah itself, that is, circularly. Action, in turn, is to be assessed and evaluated in terms of the Shari'ah's own determinations and presuppositions, that is, in terms of the extent to which it contributes to maintaining the latter's internal cyclical structure and dynamics, as opposed to that of pretenders to other legitimacies. As opposed to secular linear depictions of ideology, and by maintaining epistemic continuity, a *mazhabi* approach is breakable into a categorical–stem (*Muhkam*) and allegorical–branch (*Mutashabeh*) (Qur'an 47:20; 3:7) system of elements necessary for the structural order of understanding. By linking identity structures and action, it serves to narrow social bifurcations. In lieu of the nature and order of this linkage, a *mazhabi* approach may be defined as a normative-cognitive, *ijtihadi*-evolutionary framework in which the "rational assessment of action is dependent on the belief system" (Larijani 1995:43). The socio-institutional implications of these structural and methodological principles could be quite significant insofar as they set effective limits to the political instrumentalization of Islam. Otherwise, the Shari'ah's "development would ... be contingent rather than the necessary consequence of its recursively organized operations" (Teubner 1993:15–16).

Armed with the proposed Islamic hyper-appropriative strategy, the requisite scholarly shift may become feasible.[18] In contributing to the evolution of a universal Islamic counter-discourse capable of setting its own necessary and sufficient rules of interaction, it may be possible as well to engage "Western history," while simultaneously incorporating and substantively internalizing that experience. By re-formulating discursive mechanisms and power formations in terms of an internalized self-referential Islamic episteme, it would help preempt the self-proclaimed "moral" pretensions of external political pressures. Its strategic parameters would allow the discursive question of compatibility between Islamic worldview and secular concepts/systems to be exposed not only as ideologically false but also as blatantly illogical. To the dilemma of how one can be genuinely modern and authentically Islamic, it offers a foundation for a methodological solution by re-formulating the question of how Muslims are to fit into a predominantly Western episteme toward one of how to appropriate the modern epoch—i.e. create one's own episteme. The ensuing configurative mix of concepts such as reason, modernity, salvation, and *shura* would ultimately produce a unique and internalized civilizational order fundamentally different from that produced by the configurative and binary opposite episteme of passion, Western-ism, hedonism, and democracy. This epistemic map may eventually help persuade secular intellectuals in the Arab and Islamic world, through a shift in consciousness, to re-orient their attitudes and approaches toward a more authentic and independent civilizational order. Storming into the fray as a constitutive agent of existence, Islam would then be able to create its own reality from the very womb of current predicaments, reinstating in the process the "Muslim" as a subject of history. In laying down its own epistemic foundations, this "post-Western" Islamic order may hence be equipped to embark on re-producing its own knowledge, sciences, philosophy, and values. Toward this end, this approach remains a preliminary initiative in a long and arduous task that, needless to say, requires the collective labor of all interested and concerned. In this direction, the next chapter attempts to elaborate on these theoretical and epistemological expositions, by looking at the concept of leadership in Islam, and at the particular relevance of the theory of *Wilayat al-Faqih* as manifested in the case of the Iranian Islamic revolutionary experience.

3
Wilayat al-Faqih:
An Islamic Theory of Elite Hegemony or,
Assabiyyat al-Khawass[1]

Leadership, wrote James Mcgregor Burns, "is one of the most observed and least understood phenomena on earth" (Burns 1978:2). Methodological, theoretical, and ideological considerations persuaded many secular (Western) analytical systems to emphasize less the personal attributes of leadership than structural imperatives associated with the behavioral and pluralistic underpinnings of Western social sciences (Tamadonfar 1989:2). Religiously (Islamic) mediated socio-political systems in the modern world, on the other hand, have lapsed into confusion and uncertainty at the crossroads between traditional and non-traditional values of leadership. Whichever the case, "all paths to the study of leadership," as Aaron Wildavsky has observed, "end up by swallowing their subject matter" (Wildavsky 1980:12).

Political approaches to leadership emphasized the power content of the concept viewing it in light of preconceived notions of power's violent hierarchy. Those who seek to examine and analyze "leadership" roles, quite often fall into the trappings of power approaches, which frequently deviate from original intent. "At the cost of a steep intellectual and political price, viewing politics as power has blinded us to the crucial role of power in politics and hence to the pivotal role of leadership" (Burns 1978:11). Consequently, leadership continues to elude us as one of the most wanting principles of social and political organization.

Religious and particularly Islamic concerns with the same concept have remained largely stalemated by the unwillingness of Orthodoxy to give ground for differentiated interpretations of leadership, and its inability to gain ground beyond the Caliphial representation of authority, or to provide solid claims in its favor. Muslims' failure to move backward or forward was reflected in the form of stagnated if not ossified discourses on leadership.[2] The debilitating impact of such a condition unleashed social and political centrifugal forces which have severely taxed the moral and religious fabric of Muslim societies. The leadership and legitimacy crises in most Islamic countries are largely a result of the absence of religio-political dialectics. A rigid orthodoxy, that is, bifurcated from the dynamic requisites of ortho praxis.

The main issue this chapter attempts to address therefore pertains to the criteria and parameters of an authentic Islamic leadership–state–society relationship, given the modern condition. How, that is, can an Islamic existence be structurally effected which is modern yet not Western? What organizational form should leadership, state, and society—the foundational constituents of an authentic Islamic order—take in order to produce insular and preemptive mechanisms against religious instrumentalization or a relapse into unmitigated politics? This chapter suggests that any attempts at analyzing Islamic issues and/or events cannot take place in the absence of a relevant methodological frame. It further proposes that a preliminary synthesis of the salient aspects of works of three historical figures—Abd al-Rahman Ibn Khaldun (1332–1406), Antonio Gramsci (1891–1937), and Grand Ayatollah Rouhullah Khomeini (1902–1989)—may partially contribute to the development of such a frame.[3]

METHOD AND THE PROBLEM OF SYNTHESIS

Synthetic attempts incorporating Western theoretical models and tools of investigation and Islamic social and political concerns frequently give rise to expressions of doubt and cynicism. Axiological divergences impose limitations on value syntheses between perceived incompatible systems. Western social sciences have largely appropriated and claimed for themselves a monopoly over rational and objective knowledge, proclaiming discursive hegemony as their legitimate prerogative. On the other hand, "social theory" as Robert Wuthnow has observed,

prevents us from understanding what it means to be an "infidel" civilization. To understand requires abandoning social science as a privileged framework and shifting toward a view of multiple discourses, each illuminating the meaning of events in different ways. ... Taking religion seriously [therefore] means granting it parity as an interpretive framework. (Wuthnow 1991:14)

Violent collision of first principles consequently imposes demands for a hierarchy of significance reflective of the ranking of values and meanings from which (ontologically) and toward which (teleologically) the struggle for explanation and theorization originates and ends.

Islamic approaches to leadership still lack much of the analytical precision characterizing their Western counterparts. To a large extent they do not go beyond broad philosophical conceptualizations regarding the source and nature of legitimate authority, the requisite personal and moral characteristics of the Caliph or Imam, and the functions that he performs in terms of upholding and implementing the Shari'ah (Islamic Law). Apart from Grand Ayatollah Khomeini's theory of Wilayat al-Faqih—a theory embedded in the Shi'ite Imamite tradition—no major genuine methodological innovation has been made since Ibn Khaldun's Muqaddimah (*Introduction to History*) in the Islamic social and political domains. Ijtihad has been deemed increasingly desirable in light of modern contingencies. It is further justified by the predicament of Islamic social and political analysis which, to date, has failed to develop its own tools, rendering initial vulnerability to external borrowings a contentious yet perhaps inevitable condition. Such vulnerability though, is neither permanent nor preordained. It is rather contingent upon Muslims' willingness and ability to eventually broaden their empirical and analytical horizons beyond their initial needs. Preliminary vulnerability and dependency thus may be perceived as a dutiful chastisement for the lack of intellectual creativity and the general preference for readily served methodologies. A harsh yet perhaps justified critical departure.

Securing an Islamic outcome from the synthetic process therefore requires the adoption of two opposite yet symbiotically nurturing strategies of deconstruction and reconstruction. In so doing, synthesis becomes "the strategy of using the only available language while not subscribing to its premises, or 'operat[ing] according to the vocabulary of the very thing that one delimits'." It becomes the strategy "of a discourse which borrows from a heritage the resources necessary for the deconstruction of that heritage itself" (Spivak in Derrida 1976: xviii). This would necessarily involve the exposition of the Western/ Islamic violent hierarchy of binary opposites in which the former controls the latter both axiologically and logically (lxxvii). "The task is ... to dismantle the metaphysical and rhetorical structures which are at work in the (privileged terms), not in order to reject or discard them, but to reinscribe them in another way" (lxxv). The desired outcome should then reflect the "irruptive emergence of a new 'concept' ... which no longer allows itself to be understood in terms of the previous regime (system of oppositions)" (lxxvii). In time, this process may permit the disorganizing of the Western/Islamic binary order and the dissonant invasion of the whole sphere of the former by the latter. Such a reversal may be feasible insofar as Western analytical tools of investigation remain in a captured state within a newly reconstructed Islamic/Western violent hierarchy. Ultimately, a form of closure, i.e. Islamic/Islamic hierarchy, may be affected beyond which a viable and independent Islamic field of analytical knowledge could be established. This field may then be equipped with the necessary inventory of tools which allow it to embark on sustaining, reproducing, and finally, reconstituting itself.

ELITE HEGEMONY:
A CONCEPTION OF LEADERSHIP, STATE, AND SOCIETY

A framework of analysis

In broad terms, Robert C. Tucker has defined leadership as a "relation between leaders and followers in interaction" (Tucker 1981:13). Burns perceived this relation to be exercised "when persons with certain motives and purposes mobilize, in competition or conflict with others, institutional, political, psychological and other resources so as to arouse, engage, and satisfy the motives of followers" (Burns 1978:19). In structural terms, this exercise of leadership requires an examination of concomitant social and political organization both founded and transformed by the leader, together with an analysis of the political and psychological legitimations which help establish leadership and authority on a base of followers (Rustow 1968:689).

Notwithstanding the crucial importance of the leadership–follower relationship, the responsibilities of an Islamic state or government, especially in light of modern exigencies, will need to expand beyond such a mere link. It suffices no more to reiterate the general consensus of Muslim scholars—despite different Sunni and Shi'ite opinions— about the role of the Imam or Caliph as a protector of the faith, administrator, and upholder of the Shari'ah. Nor is it enough to proclaim that legitimacy and authority are solely derived from those functions. A clear methodological link between religion and politics will have to be established in order to delineate the legitimate and verifiable boundaries of their dialectical synthesis. Legitimacy, in addition to being derived from the Shari'ah will have to be derived also from concrete religio-political projects. The success or failure of Islamic regimes to bring about the highly prized and necessary political unification of various political entities or states for example, should reflect as well on their legitimacy. To be defined as Islamic and legitimate, the state and/or leadership will have to extend beyond mere structural or ritualistic appearances toward linking with process, while bridging at the same time the gap between the domestic Islamic order and the general orientation and thrust of its external outlook. This would inevitably require the establishment of an Islamic regime defined not simply in terms of structures, but further as "sets of implicit or explicit principles, norms, rules, and decision-making procedures around which the [Umma's] expectations converge" (Krasner 1982:186). Irrespective of any number of structural forms that it may take, Islamic governance becomes the reflection of a continuum of internal and external behaviors infused with religio-political norms and imperatives which distinguish it from other exclusively politically guided regimes. The pertinent questions then become how to establish such a regime and who is to bring it about?

Addressing those questions is necessary if an Islamic discourse on leadership, state, and society is to be developed or reconstructed. The frame in which this venture will be pursued here integrates the theory of Wilayat al-Faqih (dependent variable), as formulated by Ayatollah Khomeini (1985), and Gramsci's theory of Elite Hegemony (intervening variable). To constrain it by the space and limitations of Islamic axiological imperatives, this synthesis will take place within the Islamic framework provided by Ibn Khaldun's theory of *assabiyya* (independent variable). By so doing, Gramsci's hegemony becomes embedded in a broader Islamic grid which both verifies and delineates the concept's legitimate boundaries and parameters while avoiding the trappings of analytical alienation. In tandem, Ibn Khaldun's concept of assabiyya can then be expanded beyond its narrower historical connotations, while further detailing Ayatollah Khomeini's political theory of al-Wilayat beyond its specific Shi'ite location toward its broader Islamic horizons. The purpose is to link the traditional (Ibn Khaldun) with the innovative (ijtihad; Khomeini) through a modern medium (Gramsci).

Regimes and patterns of leadership

Ibn Khaldun, a Muslim historian and sociologist, identified three broad types of regimes in his Muqaddimah, which reflected different forms of leaderships: 1—governance/leadership based solely on natural social solidarity (assabiyya as unmitigated power); 2—governance /leadership based on reason and natural law in conjunction with assabiyya; and 3—governance/leadership based on Divine Law

(Shari'ah), again in conjunction with assabiyya (Mahdi 1964: 263). Within those three regime typologies, assabiyya figures prominently in all, while the rational and religious dimensions are introduced in the second and third classifications respectively. Should the purpose of assabiyya or core leadership mitigated by reason be solely concerned with the worldly or mundane good of both the rulers and their subjects, then this polity would fall under what Ibn Khaldun termed as a rational regime. Should however the religious dimension be introduced such that the leadership is concerned as well with the good of the subjects in the hereafter (*akhira*), then a Regime of Law unfolds as the superior order of existence (Ibn Khaldun 1958:383–5). The latter regime's inherent superiority lies in its intrinsic goal of maintaining a balance between both life dimensions, providing for moderation against excessive mundanity and/or hedonism. Above all, it becomes a community (Umma) upon which God's favor and pleasure is bestowed.

Against this Khaldunian backdrop Gramsci's theory of hegemony will be utilized as the intervening tool of investigation, situating the civil society in the superstructure and linking the former's assabiyya with Ayatollah Khomeini's theory of Wilayat al-Faqih. Taking religion as a superstructural phenomenon, hegemony in the Gramscian sense becomes particularly useful as a "modern" conceptual correspondence to Ibn Khaldun's religious/Islamic designation of assabiyya. Each concept refers to a common socio-theoretical position embodied directly or indirectly in a broadly based philosophical/religious *Weltanschauung* focused largely on the nature and goals of leadership. Hegemony and assabiyya are differentiated as two entirely different worldviews and moments of history with their own autonomous and independent discursive engagements. In as much as the concept of hegemony is essential in bridging the gap between the social sciences and moral/political philosophy, as Robert Bocock argues (1986:58), so is the concept of assabiyya crucial in linking the social sciences to Islam. Such linkages help incorporate a "social theory about the part played by conceptions of the world and their associated values in social change" (Bocock 1986:83). The essential difference between the two concepts lies in their alternating hierarchies of absolutes and relatives, i.e. in the nature of the hierarchical order of the two first principles of revelation and rationality. Hegemony or assabiyya therefore, not only comprise analytical devices, but are in fact constitutive elements of a philosophical/religious discourse that influences and structures both conceptions and actions. Within this frame, the three regime typologies above provide for three corresponding patterns of power and governing relationships: 1—domination (tyranny–autocracy); 2—hegemony (rational regimes–democracy); and 3—assabiyya (Regime of Law—Shari'ah). While each pattern does incorporate the element of power, they remain, in an ascending order of superiority, exclusive in terms of their justifications and legitimations. Rationality and Shari'ah, as opposed to tyranny, infuse the power element with differentiated bases of authority.

Domination reflects a pattern of power relationship that is largely based on coercion, arbitrary force, and ultimately in political terms on tyrannical or autocratic rule. It evinces mankind in his most pristine nature as a power seeking *homo politicus* (Laswell 1976:39). Domination consequently comes to constitute the weakest form of leadership in as far as it seeks narrow and parochial interests. In those terms one is inclined to agree with Burns in his exclusion of tyrants or autocrats from leadership status, although for different reasons (Burns 1978:27). While the condition for active consent may not figure prominently in a tyrannical rule, a *de facto* leadership–follower relationship may nevertheless be established with its own internal logic and justifications. If domination, as a coercive pattern of power, is to be excluded from the definition of leadership, it does not suffice then to focus simply on relational aspects. It becomes crucial to identify the qualitative *legitimating* principles which further underlie those bearings.

This qualitative concern serves to introduce us to the other two patterns of authority in the frame of which one may reflect on "what it is that leaders do, or try to do, in their capacities as leaders, [and] what functions they perform in the process of exerting influence upon their followers" (Tucker 1981:13). Such reflections are important if we are to avoid the frequent confusion of non-democratic, non-liberal but Lawful (*shar'i*) patterns of assabiyya with the arbitrary methods of tyranny or authoritarianism. The boundaries between the two after all may be subtle enough not to allow for ready distinctions. Yet, the division between the two is sufficiently pronounced so as to merit a clear vision of differences.

Assabiyya as a regime and a pattern of authority in the Islamic state is more than a mere ideology or a mode of socialization. Essentially it is a reflection of a religio-political mandate geared toward producing a "form of strategic leadership" capable, in the context of a modern order, of reformulating the scenario of Islamic transformation (Buci-Glucksman 1982:117–18). This leadership comes to comprise a ruling elite/*khawass* who, by virtue of their consensually and popularly recognized intellectual and religio-moral superiority are entitled to a place of honor and authority in the religio-political hierarchy—an entitlement that is, to rule. This prerogative however, should reflect a social group's ability to rule and govern not only after it has gained power, but more importantly before having access to it (Gramsci 1980:57–8). As a matter of fact, the latter becomes a prerequisite to the former. Moral abstractions are no substitute to concrete organizational projections embedded in the very nature of assabiyya. Leadership, as Ibn Khaldun has rightly observed, is not possible without popular consent as well as a popular willingness to translate this consent into assabiyya (Issawi 1958:108–9); an active consent, that is, legitimated, and therefore reinforced and strengthened, by religious ordinances and the collective Islamic social consciousness of the Umma. Assabiyya as a regime should thus be responsible for, and capable of, fusing the compulsions of "dominion" and "intellectual and moral" authority in the body of the leadership (Issawi 1958:108–9; Gramsci 1980:57). While initially the coercive aspects of dominion may be more observable—given that most processes of regime change are violent by nature—it is imperative that this remains a transitional condition hinging upon the ability of the new leadership to universalize its existence by expanding its values—making them at the same time the values of other social or subordinate groups. While the Islamic practical translation may largely be the expression of this leadership's understanding and historical experience, its values should ultimately become detached as images or projections of its political outlook (Adamson 1980:177). Assabiyya, that is, must stand on its own, not through a social group's position in the socio-economic hierarchy, but rather through the Islamic values which it carries. This condition should delineate the cutting edge between the founding of a regime and self-serving interests. Pure socio-economic and political analyses consequently cease to occupy the position of independent explanatory variability and instead are reduced to the level of intervening variability.

Assabiyya as Islamic leadership is thus not "imposed" in as much as it is legitimately "conquered" through a combination of intellectual and moral superiority on the one hand, and a tight web of guiding relationships which "must open a collective perspective to the whole of society," on the other (Buci-Glucksman 1982:120). It has less to do with domination and coercion and more with the active and direct elements of consent which reflect the genuine reciprocations and circularity of this pattern of authority (Buci-Glucksman 1982:118). As opposed to passive or indirect consent, reciprocation takes place "from the base upwards," erupting from the civil/traditional society and expanding via the consensual vehicle of Shura through "all the capillaries of society" (Gramsci 1978:212). And while the politico-institutional reflection of a secular hegemonic order incorporates democracy in its varied forms, assabiyya discloses the Islamic counterpart. The former absolutizes popular will; the latter reduces it to an input. Circumscriptions imposed on popular will are compensated for by the infusion of assabiyya throughout society, allowing for the expansiveness of active consent, while opening the way for followers to join the ranks of leadership through their own religio-moral and intellectual excellence. Consequently, a universal Islamic active consciousness or *Weltanschauung* emerges, based on both a solid popular foundation and a commonly shared Islamic value system "that unites, albeit in their contrasting interests, the different parts of society and guarantees the ideological cohesion of the social body and its very existence as an [Islamic] community" (Pellicani 1981:33).

Determinants of Islamic analysis

In light of the above, the work of the Moroccan writer Muhammad Abed al-Jabri on "The Arab Political Mind" (Al-Jabri 1990) becomes of relevance. His historical analysis of Islamic social and political development has identified three key organic determinants which he believed to have constituted the basic components of a pre-modern Islamic historical superstructural order: The tribe (collectivity); the spoils (economics); and the faith (Islam) (Al-Jabri 1990:48–50). Over different historical periods, these determinants expressed themselves in different dynamic configurations, with each determinant playing an equal or more prominent role than the other two, although under no circumstances separate from them (Al-Jabri 1990:60–1). Together, they came to shape and form not only the collective consciousness of the Muslims both in the past and in the present but also the institutionalized social and political patterns of relationships as represented by the ruler (Sultan), the elites (*al-khassa*) and the masses (*al-'amma*) (Al-Jabri 1990:342, 356ff). Al-Jabri attempts to explain Muslims' tensions with modernity, and the roots of the dominative patterns of relationships so prevalent to varying degrees in their societies, as inherent in the very history of Islam. He condemns Muslims not only in the present, but also in the past, for not being or not even having the potential of being modern, liberal, and democratic. As he puts it within the context of his Islamic historical reference, "consciousness of the necessity of democracy has to pass through a consciousness of the roots of tyranny and its foundations" (Al-Jabri 1990:365).

By implicitly recognizing that a superstructured order is pre-capitalistic, and therefore by extension, necessarily pre or non-modern (Al-Jabri 1990:7–53), Al-Jabri, dissipated the full potential of his analysis and methodology. By the constraints of his own reasoning, he could no longer broaden the horizons of assabiyya into a modern superstructural principle (Al-Jabri 1990:48). The latter, after all, is presumed redundant. Instead, he had no choice but to confine it to its original form of tribal and clannish relationships, rendering it a residual concept. Preserving "complete historical independence" (Al-Jabri 1990:44), as he has stressed, should prohibit the pre-positioning of a superstructured historical order with respect to a totally different historical experience. Despite his cautious attitude, Al-Jabri stumbles into this contentious ground by fore-structuring Islamic history instead of reinstating it and flowing with its own dynamics through a critical merger with experience (1990:372–4). Consequently, his conclusions fail to follow from his premised organic approach toward reading Islamic history, and veer instead toward a Western epistemological finale. By implying that it should teleologically follow the same path of Western historical development, Al-Jabri inadvertently aborts any potential independent Islamic approach to modernity.

The inevitable outcome of what one is inclined to perceive as a methodological error is the bifurcatory problem. In the practical social, political, and institutional realms, bifurcation frequently leads to expressions of dominative relationships. The internal consistencies of assabiyya, as a superstructural concept, collapse once a conclusion embedded in one system of intelligence/values, with its own premises, is alleged to be following from the premises of a totally different system of intelligence/values. Contradictions in "intelligence" and "foresight," as Ibn Khaldun has observed, may be "defects" which could spell ruin for society insofar as they represent externalities or unconstrained "excess of thought." In the process people may be driven "beyond the requirements of their nature," giving rise to the objective intellectual, social, and political conditions of oppression and domination.[4] The very conditions, that is, which "intelligence" seeks to alleviate. Furthermore, Al-Jabri's pre-inclination toward submitting the understanding of Islamic history and its social and political organization to the discursive formation of liberal democracy lead him to equate it with *shura* (Al-Jabri 1990:365–6). In the process, he ignores the respective religious and secular foundational distinctions between the two principles. The bifurcatory inconsistencies, which emerge as a result of such impositions, are a problem that Al-Jabri concedes (Al-Jabri 1990:340) yet which he does not avert. He appears to fall into the trap of translating empirical historical observations—pertaining largely to Western history—into normative and epistemological conclusions—pertaining largely to the Islamic mode of existence. He then concludes that "in contemporary times there is no other than the methods of modern democracy, which is a heritage for the whole of mankind" (Al-Jabri 1990:372). If such is democracy, then what is Islam? Where does Al-Jabri stand and how, as a prerequisite to his project, does he define himself? Ultimately, he defines his own Islamic existence in light of the "other"—the West. Suffice it here to quote G. Lowell Field and John Higley who observed that "the way in which socio-economic (and political) development occurred in the West was sufficiently fraught with historical accident as to make its occurrence again in other parts of the world highly unlikely" (1980:116). They conclude:

It is only in the developed, affluent Western countries ... that any large number of persons are individually carriers of Western values in their specific and subtle details. And it is largely only in those countries that one finds the elite structure and the institutionalized stability without which large numbers of people cannot have either the security for social benevolence or the opportunity for meaningful participation in social and political decision-making that are the essence of Western values and ideals. In any reasonable view of historical contingencies, therefore, Western civilization, once lost, would probably never be seen again, or anything like it. (Field and Higley 1980:116)

Al-Jabri's analysis of Islamic history does, nevertheless, provide us with some analytical insights which, contrary to his own conclusions, allow for the projection of this history in the present and into the future. Those insights aid in undergoing the complex and sophisticated classificatory process necessary for identifying and ascertaining what is purely modern as opposed to what is modern-cum-Western. They further help contribute toward identifying the strategic and analytical distinctions between the two.[5] Breaking loose from the limitations of Al-Jabri's logic, however, remains necessary if we are to move beyond the narrow Khaldunian definition of assabiyya, toward creating a modern operative concept in the fold of which "men gain consciousness of their [Islamic socio-political] position and tasks" (Femia 1981:74). Assabiyya as a modern Islamic pattern of authority and process preserves the essential organic nature of the above three key determinants vital for the modern authentic functioning of an Islamic leadership, state, and society. A crucial Islamic concept thus becomes liberated from the violent hierarchy of Western methodology, and is pulled out of the confines of its narrow historical context, establishing its own dynamics as an independent tool of investigation.

CONCEPTUAL CHANGE, CIVIL SOCIETY, AND TRANSITION TO AN ISLAMIC SOCIETY

The meaning embodied in conceptual formulations is frequently of significant religious and political consequences. As a matter of fact, conceptual change becomes intrinsically charged with the momentum of religious, political, and social transformations (Ball, Farr, and Hanson 1989:2). Alasdair MacIntyre for instance observed that, "since to possess a concept involves behaving in certain ways in certain circumstances, to alter concepts, whether by modifying existing concepts or by making new concepts available or by destroying old ones, is to alter behavior" (MacIntyre 1966:2–3). Adequate and authentic conceptual tools therefore, are a necessary condition for the consistency and reconciliation of (political) means and (religious) ends. They constitute the armory of any independent methodology or approach, which sets the criteria of action, judgment, and appraisal.

Situating civil society in the religious superstructure introduces the dynamics of conceptual change which, in itself, is a "species of ... innovation" (Ball et al. 1989:2). The superstructure becomes re-phenomenalized as the embracing fold of the different matrices of socio-religious relationships. No longer would the state be an autonomous territorial structure in which laws are enacted or made by the government or society at large, but more a heteronomous collectivity in which the Shari'ah is administered. In this collectivity assabiyya together with its institutional translations become a reflection of an authority-bound regime. As opposed to authoritarian-ism in which the civil society is dominated by the state, and is largely therefore a pattern of power relationship between the two (Linz 1970:251–83), an authority-bound regime is a condition in which the character of the equilibrating relationship among the leadership, state, and society is ordained according to a common Islamic frame of reference. The nature of the problem of relating those designations becomes consequently transformed into a problem of classifying the relationship internal to the superstructure. Society then becomes the substratum upon which the assabiyya of the leadership may be viably expanded. Concomitantly, the state is perceived not simply as a "political society" but rather as the "equilibrium between political society and civil society" (Adamson 1980:216–17). The authenticity and success of any Islamic movement may be judged henceforth as a function of its ability to make this strategic transition, and its ability to effectively induce a conceptual change in the image of the state.

This methodological approach should help in galvanizing the principles of Islamic analysis by organically fusing the dynamics of leadership, state, and society, in the context of which modernization, as opposed to Westernization, becomes feasible. It further prohibits the fragmentation and isolation of "key determinants" for analytical purposes, allowing for the concomitant possession of substantially similar modern aims (i.e. being "developed") but clearly differenti- ated identifications and strategies for attaining them. The strategy of choice becomes then a principal condition of Islamic analysis capable of incorporating the religious meaning dimension which mere cultural approaches have difficulty bringing out. Thus, even if the Iranian state is perceived to have been strengthened or consolidated as a result of the Islamic revolution, it was no longer as an absolute existence—at least conceptually speaking. And while conceptual change may frequently precede objective conditions, eventually it may pose a practical constitutive agent of an altered reality. Islam as a religion—as opposed to an ideology—structurally brings forth the doctrinal justification for the dissolution of the modern/Western state organization should circumstances allow. It reintroduces the dialectical contradictions of the state—resolved elsewhere through the mass politics of totalitarianism and/or democracy—by challenging the principles of state autonomy and popular sovereignty, while incorporating and transcending the territoriality associated with both. It is in those terms that Islam may be expected to project itself as a *revisionist* discourse, not only in its capacity as the religion of Muslims but perhaps more extensively as the ideology of those disenchanted with the national and world order.

Islam by its very structure and by its reductionist approach to the state calls commensurately for the establishment of a web of traditional networks and relationships as stable foci of loyalties, independent of the state. While civil society is placed in the religious superstructure, allowing for the totalizing embrace of assabiyya and the unification of the fragmented Muslim societies, traditional built-in mechanisms remain in existence which guard against merger with the state or totalitarian tendencies. The state can no longer legitimately demand individual or mass loyalty beyond what traditional structures and the faith would allow. Locating civil society in the religious superstructure, in other words, transforms society without necessarily infringing upon its autonomy. Society consequently gradually sheds its civil nature in favor of a transition toward tradition, while maintaining at the same time an independent existence from the state. Civil society eventually becomes the Islamic content of the state and the expanse of its assabiyya—the Islamic Society. By being authentically Islamic yet genuinely modern, this society should then be well equipped to confront the "disabling" and "built in distortions" of the modernization process (Sharaby 1989:22–3).[6] That this society may incorporate older forms of socio-political organization and action should not persuade one, however, to perceive those forms as "direct reenactments of their forebears" (Richards and Waterbury 1990:331). Nor should its overlapping modernizing tendencies be confused with the basic elements of Western values. Rather, it is the Islamic society's ability to sift through and appropriate the basic elements of modernity from within its own parameters that will determine its essential capabilities and the feasibility of its differentiated strategies. The personified expression of the leadership or Islamic bloc most capable of consummating and sustaining this appropriative process and of wrestling with its dialectics come to constitute *al-khawass*. As a distinct concept, *al-khawass* ceases to carry elitist connotations of pure interests and instead is treated as a "value-free" (Mosca 1965:53; Pareto 1968:8) term applicable to individuals and groups in society who—within the assabiyya circular pattern of authority—score highest on the scales measuring religio-political values.

The introduction of the concept of *khawass* constitutes a deliberate attempt at highlighting an important distinction from the commonly abused term—*Ulama*. As a group, the Ulama have largely come to be understood as those individuals who specialize in religious knowledge so as eventually to be qualified to make sound and independent religious rulings (fatwas) based on their own ijtihad. In practice, they have come to be a source of religious rigidity with their "ijtihad" simply being a government or state instrument. *Al-khawass*, instead, attempt to introduce connotations which incorporate the principle of *ilm* (knowledge) but also take it upon themselves to bear the practical social, political, and economic consequences of religious rulings. *Al-khawass*, that is, uphold the values and standards of the society, but also bear the strategic implications associated with such a responsibility. They are competent not only in religious affairs, but also in the religio-political dialectics which allow them, while maintaining the hierarchy of sound religious rulings, to reconcile sound strategic decisions. In addition to their erudition, they are those who command formal and informal popular respect through their independence, courage, virtue, righteousness, and administrative capabilities. They are the ones required, in other words, to competently and by example reinstate ethics and morality into the pure political process, which has largely torn through the fabric of Muslim societies. In an Islamic state, ruled by *al-khawass*, politics is no longer defined in terms of unmitigated power or conflict, but restrained to the extent possible by the moral imperatives of the faith. At the superstructural level it thus becomes possible to transform leadership into an Islamic bloc capable of bringing about the intellectual and moral unity of the various social groups which articulate society. Since the ultimate loyalty of this bloc is to the sovereignty of the Law (Shari'ah) rather than to popular sovereignty, potential contradictions between the latter and incumbent politics are largely circumvented if not resolved outright. The issue becomes no longer whether or not there should be elites, but instead which elites, which bloc?

This condition one may hasten to add is by no means an attempt at envisaging a perfect or utopian existence. Essentially, it is a situation in which the state through its qualified leadership is responsible for creating and maintaining a regime of objective public conditions which would allow Muslims as a community to practice their faith on a daily basis in the absence of a threatening environment. It is not responsible however to elicit perfection out of every individual or to presume the possibility of wiping out private human frailties. Ultimately this becomes a personal choice and an individual responsibility toward God. That Islam incorporates the Shari'ah after all is evidence of its non-utopian nature, the presumption of which implies the potential obsolescence of the Law.

Wilayat al-Faqih: the assabiyya of Islam?

"Every [assabiyya] relation, is necessarily pedagogical" (Pellicani 1981:43) insofar as it is able to inject and socialize the people in a society—Muslims and non-Muslims alike—into the Islamic religious and cultural *Weltanschauung*. At the same time, it involves the procurement of moral and intellectual autonomy in order to be able to expand the terrain of its leadership and to have access to a viable space of action capable of mobilizing broad and active popular consent. After all, "no religious movement can succeed" as Ibn Khaldun has observed, "unless based on an (assabiyya)," by virtue of which the masses ('amma) would be willing to "be moved to action" (Issawi 1958:133).

In light of the deep crisis facing the secular regimes in the Islamic world, both at the moral and legitimation levels, and which has reduced their initial hegemony to the level of a dominative relationship, those with the traits of a counter-hegemony or assabiyya will disclose themselves as the alternative. While control over the instruments of coercion may help sustain a dominative regime for a period of time, short or long, ultimately this regime is doomed. Perhaps it is this condition that has driven a prominent Egyptian intellectual and critic of Islamist groups such as Hussein Amin to express in a mood of resignation his conviction that an Islamic state in Egypt is inevitable (Weaver 1993:83). Should this be the case, the transition from a dominative or hegemonic pattern of power to that of assabiyya, will no longer be determined by the institutional location of the conflict but rather by its qualitative transformation.

At the heart of this conflict is a condition which Ibn Khaldun most perceptively articulated over five hundred years ago. It may be appropriate, therefore, to quote him here at length. As he put it:

The vanquished always seek to imitate their victors in their dress, insignia, belief, and other customs and usages. This is because men are always inclined to attribute perfection to those that have defeated and subjugated them. Men do this either because the reverence they feel for their conquerors makes them see perfection in them or because they refuse to admit that their defeat could have been brought about by ordinary causes, and hence they suppose that it is due to the perfection of the conquerors. Should this belief persist long, it will change into a profound conviction and will lead to the adoption of all the tenets of the victors and the imitation of all their characteristics. This imitation may come about either unconsciously or because of a mistaken belief that the victory of the conquerors was due not to their superior solidarity (hegemony) and strength but to the (inferiority of) the customs and beliefs of the conquered. Hence, the further belief arises that such an imitation will remove the causes of defeat. (Issawi 1958:53)

Secular hegemony imbued with the values of the Western "conquerors"—to use Ibn Khaldun's language—attempted to expand its terrain of leadership through the development of a secular discourse consolidated by a pattern of alliances which included local traditional elites, secular neo-elites, and representatives of the colonial powers. This pattern of power created a bifurcatory condition which, while co-opting some into its domain, excluded the broad mass base, offering it no choice but to fall back upon the traditional values of its own society. Assabiyya consequently came to reflect both a reactive and proactive Islamic counter-hegemonic process, aiming at alleviating the above conditions while rejuvenating the spirit of self-identification and resistance to internal dominative and external hegemonic patterns of power. Its theoretical and practical implications found the most conspicuous expression in the principle of Wilayat al-Faqih and the Iranian Islamic revolution. This revolution reflected the moment of hegemonic struggle in which the Fuqaha' (Jurisprudents; sgl. *Faqih*)—despite their lack of instruments of coercion—were able to actually rule society and to launch a frontal assault on the state which, despite its control over the coercive apparatus, had lost the loyalty and active consent of the masses. This loss of legitimacy inherent in the "vanquished" syndrome, involves necessarily a structural–superstructural dislocating process profoundly detrimental to the religious, cultural, and identity definitions of the Muslim self. Since secular leadership in most Islamic countries is located in the former (structure) while the *Weltanschauung* of the masses is embedded in the latter (superstructure), the internal consistency of hegemony and its authority patterns inevitably collapses. This then becomes the essence of the bifurcation problem which gradually yet eventually dismantles the systemic postulates of the leadership–followers relationship.[7] While there is not necessarily an inevitable outcome that such conditions may lead one to expect, in broad terms any outcome will likely range along a continuum from apathy to revolution, or shades of both thereof. Whichever proves to be the case, society loses its essential characteristics, cohesiveness, and balance, exhibiting a condition largely reflective of social pathology. Under those circumstances any arguments for blind imitation, as opposed to authenticity, lose their force and appeal, and ultimately deprive any leadership of the dimension of meaning so vital for its bond with its followers.

Thus, in broad terms, a leadership imbued with the requisite hegemonic patterns of authority becomes the historical bloc most capable of, and therefore responsible for, articulating a "grand strategy." This strategy, in the words of the late Egyptian writer Adel

Hussein, is to rule both the thinking and actions of leaders and followers, government and opposition (Dwyer 1991:73). In specific Islamic terms, this bloc is the one most capable of reflecting the hierarchical Islamic articulation of the diverse political, economic, and cultural expressions of the Umma. Those expressions constitute "partial totalities of potentially equal significance which are knit together or drift apart in accordance with the political actions that people carry out in concrete historical circumstances" (Adamson 1980:179). Thus, when Ayatollah Khomeini described the fuqaha' as the "fortresses," "guardians," and "citadels" of Islam (Khomeini 1985:73, 132), and built the case for their right and obligation to rule and govern (Khomeini 1985:55ff), he was in fact designating them as an Islamic bloc and the repositories of assabiyya. He was placing the burden of hegemonic struggle on their shoulders as the focus of leadership, bringing forth their ruling capacities as active and innovative *khawass*/elites from within the religious field. Once this universalization process has been underway a junctural hegemonic conflict erupts as the "most ... political phase," marking "the decisive passage from the structure to the sphere of the complex superstructure" (Gramsci 1980:181). Since religion is a superstructural phenomenon and the fuqaha' are situated in the religious field, it follows that their leadership or Wilayat al-Faqih is also lodged in the superstructure; a necessary first step toward resolving the bifurcatory problem. Assabiyya then becomes the most complex religio-political phase, which allows for the decisive passage of the civil society into the sphere of the religious superstructure. Its aspect of dominion gradually recedes into the background as "people forget their original condition," and the representatives of assabiyya eventually become "invested with the aura of leadership." This allows their followers to obey them voluntarily (Issawi 1958:110). The process of universalization, however, is not merely a function of time or "successive generations," as Ibn Khaldun would lead us to believe (Issawi 1958:110). More so, it is the outcome of a complex social and political process in which time constraints impose normative limits on the transitional process. A transitional period should not exceed that of one to two generations, after which promises will have to be delivered upon. Beyond that, the active voluntary character of obedience may be compromised as the memory of the pre-transitional period fades away.

During the pre-revolutionary triumph period, Wilayat al-Faqih produced a discourse which was capable of universalizing its assabiyya among both traditional and secularized Iranians. It allowed Ayatollah Khomeini to conclude for instance that "all segments of society are ready to struggle for the sake of freedom, independence, and the happiness of the nation," and that their struggle, embedded in the religious superstructure, would then be transformed into a *jihad*, with all the implications and connotations that this term implies (Khomeini 1985:132). Jihad (focusing on the tragedy of Karbala' and the martyrdom of Imam Hussain in the seventh century) then constituted the universalizing discourse which brought about the diverse and necessary alliance of social forces against the ancient regime. Its inclusive and incorporative nature, at least during the period when revolutionary violence was underway, allowed for a unity and commitment to action, while the Islamic character of the revolution and the assabiyya of the Islamic bloc sustained it at the superstructural level. Perhaps this is why purely structural or sociological analyses of the Iranian revolution can never grasp the full dimensions of the transformation, or at any rate provide an Islamic understanding of an Islamic phenomenon. Assabiyya, as an Islamic concept and principle, attempts to transcend those limitations.[8]

A major challenge to Wilayat al-Faqih in the post-revolutionary period and into its third decade, however, is how to sustain its inclusive discourse by maintaining its universalizing capacity while addressing its diverse target constituencies. It will have to be able to secure the process of situating the civil society in the religious super-structure long enough so as to sustain this condition indefinitely. It will further have to be able to continuously produce and project assabiyya leadership from within its ranks while co-opting the "plurality of creative minorities" and increasing the "material and spiritual patrimony of the collectivity" (Pellicani 1981:32). The measure of success and authenticity will largely rest on this Islamic bloc's ability to establish an assabiyya that could then, with its own logic, dynamics, and rules of engagement, be thrust into modern times and in effect produce its own modern Islamic vision of social and political organization and legitimations. To accomplish this demanding task the Islamic bloc will need to display a composite of rational and religious discourses directed equally at their secular and traditional constituencies. The most effective discursive mechanism at the disposal of the Islamic regime has been the formalization of Friday sermons, through the readily available mosque structures, into a religio-political event (Azodanloo 1992:12–24).

As the theoretical and practical projection of assabiyyat *al-khawass*, Wilayat al-Faqih enjoys the unique potential in the Islamic religious field of meeting the above challenges and of engaging the secularists and co-opting them into the broader horizons of Islamic rationalism. Not only would conversing with the secularists on comprehensible grounds expand the terrain of assabiyya, but more importantly this would ease and mitigate the passage from a secular to an Islamic *Weltanschauung* while minimizing any violence that may erupt as a consequence of hegemonic conflicts. By preserving the form while altering the content of rationality, assabiyya as a pattern of authority and leadership becomes capable of effecting a shift in consciousness without inflicting upon its subjects the pain of having to totally forsake previous emotional attachments and historically cherished patterns of hegemony (Shari'ati 1980b:65). Minimal effectiveness should eventually be capable of eliciting, for example, a passive consent reaction similar to that of an Iranian exile who had recently returned to Iran. After spending nine years in France where he had acquired a *pied-à-terre*, this returned exile acknowledged: "we've ended up coming round to the idea of an Islamist regime." Such former exiles, as the *Manchester Guardian* has observed, "do not seem to have strong feelings about the Iranian regime, and are certainly not afraid of it" (February 21, 1993:21). The regime, however, should never cease to attempt to gradually transform this passive consent into its active counterpart. This constitutes an important ingredient of any consolidation process. Sustained long enough, assabiyya should eventually be able to bring about the formidable alliance between the nationalist and Islamic forces. This alliance, which should necessarily avoid any confrontational postures or colliding paths, is essential if the dynamics of social and political change are to come into play in the Islamic world. By infusing nationalism with religio-moral content and transcending its chauvinistic elements, while maintaining its nuclear core essential for action, assabiyya becomes the mobilizing principle of the Islamic regime.

As an ijtihad based on revelation and reason Wilayat al-Faqih thus signals fundamental challenges to what has been pejoratively referred to as *al-fiqh al-sultani*, or the theological apologetics justifying the absolute powers of the rulers, so prevalent in Sunnism and to a lesser extent in the Shi'ite principles of quietism (*taqiyya*) and awaiting (*intizar*). By conceptually changing the role of the "Faqih" and situating politics in the religious superstructure, al-Wilayat innovated a politically active role for an Islamic bloc which established its

pattern of authority on the twin Islamic requirements of assabiyya—
al-khawass and *al*-Umma.

Rationality within this new medium ceases to be merely the capacity
for abstract thinking, or a scientific and philosophical method whose
ideological imperatives transform reason into an absolute standard
for intellectual polemics. Instead it becomes the means by which the
totality of basic and interrelated convictions become prioritized and
through which every society and culture attempts to incorporate and
represent its objective reality. To the extent that rationality becomes
an active organizational principle capable of challenging historical
conditions and transforming them into an identifiable reality, to
that extent it gains anchorage, consistency, and credibility (Ghulyun
1990:158). Rationality situated in an Islamic superstructure comes to
reflect the Umma's reconstruction of its own reality and its problem-
solving capacities from within the horizons of the existing historical
conditions (Ghulyun 1990:159). It no longer becomes the allegedly
neutral and absolute application of reason as appropriated by Western
systems of hegemony and their social and political frames, and
instead becomes coextensive with the specific historical location of
the Islamic Umma and the principal values which it upholds.

The rational discourse of Wilayat al-Faqih therefore, cannot
be complete without being commensurately critical. Its critical
dimension will need to develop the discourse most capable of
restoring the internal consistency of the Islamic religious field, by
distinguishing and exposing the "conflicting logics of sense and
implication" (Norris and Benjamin 1988:7) inherent in counter-
discourses. Consistency and rational objectivity requires that the
designative nature of the Islamic discourse be identified with its
original intent and not with any other discourse. This is most crucial
because "what a speaker expresses is not a document on the structure
of what has been spoken." In many instances the purported intent
is in opposition to the perceived objective (Ghulyun 1990:251). As
a necessary condition, any Islamic assabiyya will have to confront
this discursive challenge since it is at this level that the problem of
minorities—religious, ideological, or ethnic, will have to be addressed,
and it is among those groups that assabiyya will have to be rationally
universalized.[9] Needless to say, corresponding institutional structures
will have to be created to bring about and sustain this condition. The
ability to infuse assabiyya into the Umma, comprising of all those
who live in the abode of Islam, expands concomitantly a common
Islamic moral language which counters the bifurcatory problem. "As

this common moral language extends, so does society; as it breaks up so does society" (Jouvenal 1957:304), and of course, so does any bloc's legitimate claim to leadership.

On the nature of the Islamic state: assabiyya or theocracy?

While the above analysis addresses several Islamic issues, it begs nevertheless one more important question: Whether or not a religio-political system based on Islam in general and Wilayat al-Faqih in particular is by necessity a theocratic regime? Significant ambiguity exists as to the conceptual distinctions between theocracy and an Islamic state. The subtle differences between the two frequently render them synonymous.[10] Theoretical and practical overlapping and variations in definitions and understandings further compound the problem. Where similar definitions are expounded, abstractions and generalizations render vulnerability to confusion highly likely.[11]

Notwithstanding these words of caution, Wilayat al-Faqih—given the centrality of the populist elements in it—need not be presumed *a priori* as an attempt at establishing a theocracy, as H.E. Chehabi for example would lead us to believe (1991:70). Given the Islamic principle and doctrine of "Seal of Prophets" (Qur'an 33:4), the very structure of the Islamic faith does not allow for any person to make a "credible" claim to represent or speak for God, nor for any human mediating location between man and God. And while in Islam many believe there is no separation between Mosque and state, fusion or subordination of political power to religious ordinances remains an interpretive effort based on legitimate ijtihad, which by definition can make no claim to infallibility. As a matter of fact, the very principle of ijtihad, which structurally necessitates diverse opinions and schools of thought (*Mazaheb*), does not allow for religious centralization and consequently any form of a theocratic/hierarchical pattern of authority. A fatwa or religious ruling based on the ijtihad of a qualified faqih is religiously obligatory (*fard*) only if there is unanimous consensus among other fuqaha'—a rare occurrence—and religio-politically binding (*wajib*) if issued by a legitimate ruler—an Imam. Only in the former case, that is, is it a primary obligation directly derived from the Shari'ah. In the latter, it becomes a secondary ordinance, binding yet not necessarily obligatory, based on the legitimating credentials of the leadership and the circular covenant of *allegiance*. In this vein it has more to do with the practical necessity of governance than with doctrinal Islamic imperatives. The intimidation of some of the Grand Ayatollahs during the early years of the revolution, who did not agree with Ayatollah's Khomeini's ijtihad, had more to do with the secondary rather than primary ordinances of Islam and the situational imperatives of the time. Several of the *Mujtahids* who did not agree with Wilayat al-Faqih succumbed to its authority on political rather than religious grounds. Their rejection of this ijtihad in many respects carries the same religiously authoritative weight as that of Ayatollah Khomeini. It was religious politics, however, that made the difference. The issue of blasphemy, associated with direct denial of primary obligations, therefore does not arise.

Al-Wilayat did not, then, alter the basic structural relationships in the religious field. Clergymen "continue to disburse funds, aggregate followers on specific issues, articulate needs, wield the symbols of culture, administer shrines, manage and own lands" (Akhavi 1980:179). The religious field in Iran, despite the fusion of political and religious powers, remains independent, polycentric, and dynamic. Organizationally, this helps mitigate the erection of an institutionalized centralized hierarchy pivotal to the establishment of a theocracy. The fusion of religious and political powers does not necessarily alter this condition. This simply implies a choice of a political course of action from among varied legitimate religious opinions rather than the negation of ijtihad's plurality. Policy in this case becomes the religiously legitimated decision-making process.

Moreover, the circular leadership–follower–leadership relationship through which individuals have the freedom to choose their own *mujtahids* to follow and whom they could change at will, challenges the very essence of hierarchical concatenation central to a theocratic order. By stressing informal popular recognition of the Faqih's benevolence and wisdom, significant constraints on the risk of relapsing into a dominative pattern of power emanating from the fusion of religion and politics do exist. The Council of Experts which chooses him for that role, taking popular recognition of the Faqih's preeminence in hindsight, further structures and formalizes this process. Nor did the late Ayatollah Khomeini, despite his charisma and authority and despite his control over the state's coercive apparatus, seriously attempt to bring the full force of the latter against the religious field's polycentric and circular structure. Neither has his successor Ayatollah Ali Khamene'i, tried to do anything of the kind. As a matter of fact, even in his capacity as the *Waliy* (guardian), religio-political, Faqih of Iran, Ayatollah Ali Khamene'i has permitted the followers of the late Grand Ayatollah Abul-Qassem al-Kho'i to continue to follow his rulings and emulate him despite his death and despite the fact that he did not accept Wilayat al-Faqih (*Kayhan Al-Arabi*, August 29, 1992:1).[12] The expanded terrain of assabiyya, instead, has brought forth the historically ignored popular dimension into the Islamic religio-political domain. Thus, unlike the broad vertical perceptions of authority associated with theocracy, an Islamic bloc's pattern of leadership is circular, based on the mutual obligations of the leaders and followers to each other. There remains, in other words, an inherent conflict between the authority patterns of theocratic hierarchy and assabiyya circularity; the latter does not allow for the former.

Practical considerations furthermore come into play. As a long-term strategy of survival, the establishment of a theocracy, in the sense of centralizing the religious field, may be counter-productive and self-defeating. The polycentric character of the clerical organizational structure provides an opportunity for potential opposition to channel its energies and find expression through and from within the religious field itself rather than from outside of it. Diverse popular demands, consequently, can find a differentiated religious/clerical response, which allows for the transmission of those demands to the interior of the religious field. This is particularly important should the principle of al-Wilayat, for whatever reasons, falter or lose its vitality over time. Theoretically and practically therefore, Ayatollah Khomeini's political theory, contrary to some prevalent views, is not a theocratic principle sanctified by the totality of a divinely commissioned sacerdotal order. Like any ijtihad it remains contingent and thus not necessary to Islamic doctrinal belief. Institutionally, Wilayat al-Faqih reflects a circular pattern of religio-political power within the frame of a religious field that is structurally non-hierarchical, and which therefore does not justify a theocratic pattern of authority. At the same time, while it does confirm the leadership of the fuqaha' as an Islamic bloc or *khawass*, this remains subject to the fuqaha's ability to maintain their authority and legitimacy through their assabiyya and bloc capacities. Were this bloc to compromise or fail to perform its universalizing responsibilities, as is largely the case among the Sunnis, then the whole principle of al-Wilayat would collapse. For this reason and others it may be less relevant to raise questions as to how theocratic the Islamic Republic of Iran is, whether Wilayat al-Faqih is a theocratic principle or not, and whether Ayatollah Khomeini actually wanted to establish a theocratic state or not, and instead focus on the dynamic emergence of the fuqaha' as an Islamic bloc, on what are the objective conditions for the emergence of such blocs, on how and to what extent have they been able to expand the assabiyya of Islam, and on what other equivalent or alternative Islamic blocs do or may exist among the Sunnis? This would eventually allow for the expansion of the analysis to the Sunni domain where, should the assabiyya of Islam rest in an Islamic bloc other than the fuqaha', claims to leadership as a result would rest elsewhere. This is important given the different political traditions of the two branches of Islam.

On the dynamics of al-Wilayat: a principle in flux

Developments in the dynamic understanding of Wilayat al-Faqih help in providing signals as to the expected political course of action of the Islamic regime within Iran. Taking the Islamic principle of "enjoining that which is good and prohibiting that which is evil" (Qur'an 3:104, 110; 9:112) as his point of departure, Sayyed Muhammad Hussain Fadlallah addressed the issue of political opposition and factionalism in the Islamic state and within the parameters of al-Wilayat (*Kayhan Al-Arabi*, December 14, 1992:9). The basic thrust of his reasoning postulates that governance based on the Shari'ah and a scrupulous implementation of Islamic principles does not in and of itself guarantee freedom from error or immunity to deviation. While the justice of the ruler, for example, may prohibit him from deliberate error, it will not vouch against him falling into it otherwise through mistaken ijtihad, oversight, forgetfulness, or as a result of internal weaknesses or external pressures. The fatwas of the Faqih after all do not represent an "absolute objective condition," but rather an ijtihad in response to an existing reality. Thus, there is no obligation toward obedience should error be determined to have been committed. Nor is the leader's right of obedience an autonomous condition intrinsic to the person of the Faqih, but a public one linked to the Umma's interests and causes (*Kayhan Al-Arabi*, December 14, 1992:9). One important implication of this logic initiates the gradual de-personalization of the office of "Faqih" and the move toward institutionalizing it. A natural development, given the demise of Ayatollah Khomeini's charismatic presence, and the tendency of all revolutionary regimes to eventually normalize once the new institutions have been well set in place. Contrary to Said Arjomand's claim, therefore, that Wilayat al-Faqih "demands unconditional obedience" (Arjomand 1988:183), Sayyed Fadlallah argues both critically and differently. In fact, he argues against the very blind obedience that Arjomand has attributed to the ijtihad.

According to Fadlallah, criticisms hurled by opposition or factions on the basis of alternative ijtihads and from within the lawful parameters of the Shari'ah become a means of cooperating with the regime toward upholding the values and principles which it represents. Based on the social and political criteria of mediation, consensus, and benevolence, opposition ceases to be a way of scoring points and instead becomes a lawful right (*Haq Shar'i*) based on the Shari'ah and on the Umma's entitlement to oversee the process of convergence between theory and practice. Factional differentiation from within the religious field, therefore, should by no means be taken as an exemplary of intra-clerical relations or as a basis for conclusive inferences. At the heart of the matter there remains the strategic concern with preserving and maintaining monopoly of the legitimate exercise of religious power, the extension of public audiences, and the protection of the religious field and religious interest from the jeopardy of conflicts and crises. Superficial inquiry into factional tactical and strategic differences would practically shed no light on these issues (Akhavi 1980:179). Nor should the existence of distinctive tendencies induce us to perceive factions as the evolutionary harbingers of a multi-party system. Factionalism, as long as it takes place within the context and constraints of a stable superstructure, simply reflects the interplay between the two dimensions of religious absolutism and popular relativism. The fluidity of this dynamic relationship accords with the functional parameters of the Islamic state paradigm, which is capable of guarding against tyranny despite religious constraints on popular sovereignty. At the same time, it allows for the exercise of the Umma's will, as the embodiment of an expanded assabiyya, within the parameters of the faith. This determines the nature of the Islamic state away from the implications of theocratic governance as understood in the West. Factional formalization, on the other hand, incorporates substantive as well as procedural alterations which characteristically transform the superstructural nature of the Islamic mediating-consensual political and decision-making process, and introduce elements of partisanship and interest as determining variables. The fluidity required by the former becomes stymied by the structured boundaries and borders set by the latter. As a matter of fact, it is at this juncture that Islamic and secular hegemonies diverge most and conflict becomes most intense. Ayatollah Khomeini's decision in 1987 to abolish the Islamic Republican Party (IRP) reflected his keen awareness of the commensurate implications.

Fadlallah's discourse, which engages such concerns, appears to suggest a practical method by which assabiyya could be universalized. If, according to him, "the Umma lives the idea of criticism as a means of confirming the regime on a solid ground of righteousness and veracity, it will in due time actively cooperate with the regime and the opposition to help focus positions on a firm foundation" (*Kayhan Al-Arabi*, December 14, 1992:9). Implicit in Fadlallah's emphasis on cooperation in "due time" appears to be a cautioning word against excluding or totally alienating the secular elements, many of whom acquire skills needed by the Islamic Republic. There also looms a fair optimism regarding the possibility of expanding the assabiyya of al-Wilayat among them. This should be possible once the supremacy of the religious superstructure as the determining moment of history has been confirmed, and once the political struggle between secular hegemony and Islamic assabiyya has been resolved in favor of the latter. At the same time nevertheless, Fadlallah warns against giving unlimited freedoms to parties or groups which do not believe in the founding philosophy of the state and who present themselves as counter to this very same philosophy. Islam, that is, and as Eric Voeglin would concur, "is not a suicide pact." Nor is a genuine Islamic regime, same as any other, democratic or otherwise, "supposed to become an accomplice in its [own] overthrow" (Voeglin 1974:144). Fadlallah makes the important distinction between opposition to government and opposition to regime. In the political frame of al-Wilayat, the twin pillars of an Islamic order remain the Islamic bloc (Imam/Faqih/Fuqaha') and the Umma.[13] Together, they constitute the foundation of the assabiyya of Islam.

CONCLUSION

The purpose of this chapter has been to introduce new concepts and expand upon already existing ones in order eventually to develop a viable and independent field of Islamic social science and methodology. The political and institutional conceptualizations of such independence would then reflect on the authentic nature and qualitative characteristics of government and leadership in an Islamic state and/or society.

Recognizing that conceptualizations detached from practical applications lose much of their impact, if not credibility, I have attempted to link them as much as possible with the Iranian Islamic revolutionary experience as the closest thing to an ideal type that one could come up with. At the same time, being aware of the risks inherent in the usage of alien tools of analyses on the Islamic *Weltanschauung*, I have attempted to mitigate those risks by reducing the former from independent to intervening variable. This has been made possible by employing the classical theory of Ibn Khaldun as the overarching independent frame within which the link between Western and Islamic variables could be made. It is my belief that such reductionism remains a methodological necessity if one is interested in understanding Islam and its burgeoning politics in the Middle East outside and beyond ethnocentric and Orientalist approaches. It is also necessary if the hierarchical "reversal" of binary opposites is to become feasible, and if the "captured" use of helpful and insightful Western tools and concepts in the Islamic field is to be legitimized.

Henceforth, it becomes possible to bring about a "closure" and to reconstruct and reconstitute an Islamic *Weltanschauung*, while reintroducing it as a feasible modern project. The structural consolidation or monolithism of Islam, which some scholars have tended to dispute on cultural and interpretive grounds (Said 1981:x), may then be reconfirmed on those very same grounds. Cultural, social, and political vicissitudes become less a reflection of diversity than of unity—level of analysis issues than independent frames of comprehension. The widespread tension and violence taking place currently in many parts of the Muslim world between secular hegemony and Islamic assabiyya, remains largely a product of the former's attempt to epiphenomenalize Islam as a consequence of characteristics and idiosyncrasies inherent in the very nature and requisites of secularism. A superstructural approach, based on the three-pronged strategies of *reversal*, *capture*, and *closure*, becomes thereby a viable option for "remonolithizing" and "re-phenomenolizing" Islam as a prerequisite for any hegemonic struggle. This struggle is by no means confined to the domestic and internal concerns of the Muslim state. It extends beyond its borders to the expanses of the international and global environment as internal and external hegemonies mutually reinforce each other. This necessitates that one extend this approach and analysis from the state structure to the world beyond its own boundaries. To this we turn in the following chapter.

4
The Islamic Paradigm of Nations: Toward a Neoclassical Approach

As late as 1966 Martin Wight could still pose the question "why is there no international relations theory?" By this he meant the absence of a tradition of speculation about relations *between* states, families of nations, or the international community, comparable to that of political theory as speculation *about* the state. To the extent that it did exist, it was marked by "intellectual and moral poverty" caused both by the prejudice imposed by the sovereign state and the belief in progress (Wight 1966:15–16, 19). Unlike political theory, which has been progressive in its concern with pursuing interests of state as the "theory of the good life," international politics as the "theory of survival" constituted the "realm of recurrence and repetition" (Wight 1966:25, 32). Essentially, therefore, it had nothing new to offer. This challenging viewpoint spawned a dynamic range of intellectual activities, which by the 1990s had enriched the discipline of international relations in ways earlier unforeseen. The assumptions of repetitiveness and recurrences, which had hindered the field's potential for expansion and risked limiting its horizons, were contested. No longer was the field constrained by a preoccupation with state survival or a lack of appropriate concepts with which to theorize about global politics. The discipline drew on advancements in the cognate fields of social and political theory, which opened new horizons of theoretical unfolding. It became sufficiently enriched and diversified to be able to challenge claims to a "consensually recognized or determined" nature of world politics and to overcome conceptual paucity and rigidity (Burchill and Linklater 1996:7–8).

Much of what Wight indicated in the 1960s may not be as pertinent to the current state of Western international theory, given the gamut of intellectual developments that have taken place since. In surpassing the simplicity of earlier approaches, the field, in fact, became a victim of its own success. Well into the 1990s it continued to suffer from a lack of an authoritative paradigm on the one hand, and a confusing array of proliferating paradigms on the other (Holsti 1985:1–7). Nevertheless, the dynamism exhibited in addressing these contentions reflected a positive attitude toward problem solving, the highlighting of which could perhaps inspire similar outlooks among constituents of diverse cultures.

However, there appears to be a continued relevance to this caveat as far as a potential Islamic theoretical counterpart is concerned. Since classical times, from around the eighth century CE, the Islamic paradigm of law of nations has basically divided the world into two opposing domains. One constitutes the abode of Islam (*dar al-Islam* or *Pax Islamica*), comprising the "sovereign" Islamic state ruling over both Muslims and protected non-Muslim communities (see Figure 3). The other, falling beyond the pale of *Pax Islamica*, represents the abode of War (*dar al-harb*) (Khadduri 1966:11).

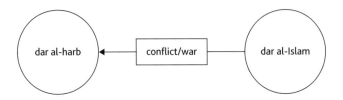

Figure 3   Representation of the simple classical Islamic theory dividing the world into the two broad categories of abode of Islam and abode of War.

This law of nations is not considered to be separate from the broader aspects of Islamic jurisprudence, but rather as an extension of the Shari'ah or sacred law, and as it developed and found its full expression under the Abbasid Dynasty (750–1258 CE) it came to acquire a kind of "sacrosanct soundness" as part of the Shari'ah itself (Al-Ghunaimi 1969:133). Hence it made no clear distinction between the sources and sanctions of domestic or municipal law, and the analogous categories pertaining to external relations (Khadduri 1966:6).[1] The Islamic external outlook thus came to be persistently based on perceptions of foreign relations as guided and heavily influenced by a religiously based "domestic analogy" (Suganami 1989:9). This was natural given the universality of Islam, and the fact that *dar al-harb* was not recognized on an equal footing as legitimate or sovereign. It was the territory yet to be brought from the "state of nature" into the fold of the Divine (Khadduri 1966:13).

This static view had much to do with the Islamic paradigm's religio-legalistic foundation. Since absolute moral values rarely change, theory acquired metaphysical dimensions. Elevated to the religio-moral level, theory lost its essential cognitive characteristics.

Despite obvious and unrelenting transformations in the nature and structure of the global system, the classical paradigm endures as the realm of recurrence and repetition. Yet it continues to shape and influence Muslim consciousness, even as it increasingly comes under heavy strain. To what limits, though, it might sustain such influence, in the face of a starkly inhospitable global reality, and without reinstating the cognitive aspects, has become a question of importance. Its "analogous" structure raises further questions as to the extent to which it is possible to develop an Islamic theory of international relations without having first re-delineated this relationship. According to one view expressed by F.L. Oppenheim, "international" law assimilated by a domestic legal system beyond a certain demarcation is likely to contradict its own essential qualities. Once crossing a threshold, it would cease being "international" law, as the medium through which relations are conducted between sovereign nations (Suganami 1989:67). The dilemma this poses for Islamic jurisprudence is obvious. In conducting relations with *de facto*, though not necessarily *de jure*, non-Muslim "sovereignties," whose law is to govern and set the conditions of interaction? To disrupt the inside/outside continuum is to subordinate sacred imperatives to positivist or non-Islamic values. This remains the case even where values may overlap, as the sanctioning source must continue, in principle, to occupy a super-ordinate position. Thus the basic structure of the paradigm does not allow for conducting foreign relations, and if any sustained relations are to be conducted, the paradigm is rendered inapplicable. Nevertheless, only limited and unsystematized speculation about expanding the theory's horizons has been pursued, allowing it to be judged by some Muslim scholars, perhaps hastily, as practically anachronistic and irrelevant (Abu-Sulayman 1993:61, 97).

The purpose of this chapter is to introduce new elements of dynamism into the theory's static structure and hence contribute to reconstructing and reexamining its possible relevance as a neoclassical conceptual device. This highly needed "therapy" for theoretical irrelevance aims at restoring "intelligibility" and "awareness" to the theory, and at founding a new, cleaned-up basis for conceptual and methodological construction and formation (Sartori 1984:50). Ability to conceptualize is a prerequisite for any possible shift from being simply an object of world politics toward being a subject and a participant. Only subsequently would it be possible to reestablish the significance of the Islamic theory of law of nations as a religious, ideological, and political regime in the service of policies and strategies that touch upon world events.

CONCEPTUAL AND THEORETICAL ISSUES

Discussing matters of strategy and war, B.H. Liddell Hart emphasized the crucial importance of conception as a guiding principle in peace and/or conflict. He underscored the fact that distracting the mind and expectations of opponents deprives them of their freedom of action as a sequel to their loss of freedom of conception (Liddell Hart 1967:341–2). The effectiveness of a strategic vision depends more "on the ability to paralyze an enemy's action rather than the theoretical object of crushing his forces" (Liddell Hart 1967:341–6). Such is the significance of this that in many instances of strategic or grand-strategic contestation it takes only conceptual maneuvering to determine a winning or losing outcome. Fighting becomes secondary or redundant as opponents lose their sense of self-representation and consequently change their purpose, consciously or otherwise. Conception and strategy in the logic of this argument compose two mutually consolidating and fortifying constituents of reality. The absence of one almost invariably undermines the other.

The same underlying principles apply to matters cultural and religious. Whereas Liddell Hart stresses the organic relationship between conception and strategy in the military realm, Edward Said highlights the corresponding categories of culture and imperialism in the intellectual–ideological domain. The connection between the two categories rests on the power to narrate, or to block other narratives from forming and emerging. Cultural narratives reflect conceptual constructions which, from opposite vantages, justify or condemn imperial domination. Predators and prey become narrations in and of themselves, each in their own way (Said 1993:xiii). The very grand narratives of emancipation and enlightenment produced by the colonial predators served to mobilize colonized people against their former dominators, and therein were unveiled their inherent contradictions. In adopting the very idioms of their colonial masters, the colonized people, or preys, actually end up perpetuating and reproducing the very power relations of those narratives, thereby revealing the dynamic consistencies of imperial discourse.

Out of these combined and seemingly paradoxical manifestations, loss of conception leads to strategic disarray, cultural/religious dissipation, and hegemonic resurgence. Commensurately, imperial repression invites the return of the repressed (Sayyid 1997:3). Counter-eruptions categorized under the rubric of "religious nationalism" (read assabiyya) are the most conspicuous result (Juergensmeyer 1993). In their inflamed expression, these take the form of both random and/or organized violence. In their more sober manifestation they induce a renaissance-like intellectual effort that aims both at reinstating and reexamining a people's own identity, thought, history, and experience. At the heart of this effort is a concern, under constraints and conditions of globalization and uncertainty, with the nature of the interaction between and among diverse cultures, religions, and consciousnesses.

While there is a commonality of concerns and issues among humanity at large, the diversity of priorities, agendas, interests, and above all consciousnesses and worldviews find their expression in different narratives or conceptual schemes. These refer to the manifold "languages" used in expressing, representing, and reflecting collectivities' distinct ways of perceiving or thinking about the world and of "ordering" the "data" of experience. People with different conceptual schemes are frequently concerned with the same properties of objects or with corresponding data. The "given" though, is "somehow 'organized,' 'ordered,' 'interpreted,' differently" (Walton 1973:1, 3). The "givens" of international and global issues are no exception. Both classical Islamic and Western traditions regarding relations among nations have been largely cognizant of analogous matters. This can be observed from the early treatise (*siyar*) of the eighth-century Muslim jurist Muhammad bin al-Hasan al-Shaybani (750–804 CE)[2] through Hugo Grotius, down to contemporary thinkers such as Hans Morgenthau and Kenneth Waltz (1979). Broadly speaking, common themes that animate juristic and intellectual interests in the subject revolve around three overlapping considerations: 1—the causes and justifications of war and the conditions of peace, security, and order; 2—power and position as an/the essential actor (unit of analysis) in the community of nations; 3—conceptions and images of the international system and of the role of the "state" in that system (Holsti 1985:8). These considerations of power and politics came to be largely articulated in the modern Western theory of (neo)realism. However, embedded in an Islamic theoretical counterpart, an alternative conceptual categorization is rendered essential in order to depict the ensuing substantive differences.

Ibn Khaldun's typologies of assabiyya (i.e. power, rational and legal) remain relevant here and may be extended from the internal domain to the external environment (Mahdi 1964:263), incorporating realism and neorealism into the category of rational regimes, and not too infrequently into that of pure domination. Classical Islamic theory would fall under the regime of Law. Like the rational category, the Islamic law of nations constitutes a way of thinking about the world, a conception of "order," and a research program with its own set of assumptions and premises from which Islamic derivations and arguments can be developed and analyzed (Mastanduno 1999:19). In contradistinction to regimes of the rational category, however, it designates an entirely different conceptual worldview and moment of history with its own autonomous and independent discursive engagements. Assabiyya, as a corresponding conceptual device grounded in the regime of Law, constitutes in the Islamic theory of nations what the concepts of power and capability are to realism and structural neorealism. Just as "power" serves the purpose of bridging the gap between international structures and processes, so is the concept of assabiyya crucial in linking international-global understanding to Islam. Such linkages help incorporate a religio-political theory about the part that can be "played by conceptions of the world and their associated values" in bringing about a desired change (Bocock 1986:83). (Neo)realism and Islamic theory, together with their concomitant concepts of power/capability and assabiyya respectively, not only comprise analytical devices, but are in fact constituted and constitutive elements of distinct philosophical and religious discourses which influence and structure both conceptions and actions. Rationality/realism and Shari'ah/assabiyya, in other words, infuse power with differentiated substantive bases of action and hence reflect two categories of political behavior. The former constitutes "relational power," which seeks to maximize values, influence behavior, and control outcomes from within a given institutional structure or regime. The latter reflects a "meta-power" concept and refers to efforts and behavior that seek to change existing institutional structures and alter the rules of the game (Krasner 1985:14).

Assabiyya is rooted in three types or categories of belief structures: 1—worldviews; 2—principled beliefs; and 3—causal beliefs. These embody cosmological, ontological, and ethical notions respectively, rendering them broader than mere normative outlooks (Goldstein and Keohane 1993:8–10). Worldviews merge with peoples' conceptions of their identity, beliefs, and focus of loyalties. Islamic law or Shari'ah falls in this class, and when it is compared with secularism, for instance, it is clear that they comprise two different and largely opposed worldviews. The second category, of principled beliefs, embraces normative conceptions about values. Frequently, though not always, these take the form of binary opposites such as justice versus injustice, right versus wrong, falling within the pale, versus falling without, or abode of Peace versus abode of War. Principled beliefs interpose themselves between worldviews and policy outcomes by translating key doctrines into guidance for present human conduct. This is equivalent to Islamic jurisprudence or *fiqh*, as the "media of making the *Shari'ah* accessible to common believers" (Al-Ghunaimi 1969:133).[3] The Islamic law of nations constitutes one manifestation of such an exercise. Thus it falls short of a totalizing worldview and its full sanctity, but is more than a mere theoretical construct or policy guideline, to be subjected nonchalantly to allegations of irrelevance or variability.

Causal beliefs pertain to "cause-effect" relationships based on the opinions or consensus of members of "recognized elites," through whom authoritative rulings or decisions are made. They come closest to being the detailed paradigmatic judgments or *ara'/fatawa* (singular *ra'y/fatwa*) of an Islamic epistemic community or *ulama*, the consensus among whom constitutes *ijma*.[4] Causal beliefs fall at the interface between the normative and the cognitive. They entail strategies of attaining goals "themselves valued because of shared principled beliefs, and understandable only within the context of broader worldview outlooks" (Goldstein and Keohane 1993:10). Thus changes in the conceptualization of this latter category tend to be more flexible and frequent than in the former two, which reflect constants and continuities. All three categories, however, constitute a closure based on symmetric relationships among Shari'ah, *fiqh* and *fatawa*, for which assabiyya becomes the operationalized or cognitive *praxis*. What is meant by closure is the domain within which the micro maintains its symmetrical relation to the macro, and where asymmetrical political and strategic insights fit into a larger Islamic whole (Luhmann 1990:230). Normativity maintains its symmetry by being non-adaptive, that is, "closed to information and control." By linking with a cognitively open framework it can nevertheless remain "open to energy" and non-entropy (Ashby 1956:4). Normative closure and cognitive openness constitute the systemic self-referential unity of the reconstructed Islamic theory of nations.

THE MODERN STATE AS A SYSTEM OF DURABLE INEQUALITY

Beliefs and ideas play an important role, tangible though sometimes less visible, in the differing ordering, organization, and interpretation of "data," beyond the mere justifications of pure interest. By providing conceptual order to the world, they contribute to shaping agendas and programs. Particular ideas and beliefs chosen rather than others act as "blinders" or "invisible switchmen" influencing policies and possibly effecting their transformation. They serve to reduce the number of conceivable alternatives, and to channel action onto certain tracks while obscuring other outlooks (Goldstein and Keohane 1993:12). They can further assist in unsettling discredited institutional frameworks in favor of alternative formations (Jackson 1993:119).

Modern state structures and currently emerging blocs are congruent with particular international and global designs and their constitutive and/or constituted interests. They incorporate certain symmetrical ideas, beliefs, and concerns while excluding others. The crucial question from the Islamic theoretical perspective is who and what has been excluded by international and global structures, and what role the modern state plays in such exclusion. Ian Clark, for instance, observed that "a theory of the global is itself an integral dimension of a more plausible theory of state." Theorizing about the latter structure thus carries us over the "great divide" between the inside and outside, to how we think about relations between states. According to this vision, the state is "the common but contested ground that brings the national and international together, rather than ... the barrier which marks the line of separation between them" (Clark 1999:17–18). This is in stark contrast to the assumptions of the realists and neorealists about power and anarchy; particularly where neorealists have yielded to the international system a distinctive and virtually autonomous existence.

Neoliberals in their turn have come to perceive the state as the instrument through which external demands of capital flows are imposed on domestic target groups. This constitutes both a reversal in its earlier role of projecting national economic demands into the international system, and an alternative form of structuralism to that of neorealism. Instead of the latter's "anarchic/power configuration," organization shifts to the "competition/neoliberalism" of the global economy (Clark 1999:94). State formation in its modern structural sense is further attributed by Charles Tilly to war. Demands imposed by violent conflict promote the dynamics of state-making processes, which range from territorial consolidation and centralization to administrative differentiation and monopoly over the means of coercion. "War made the state," as he put it, "and the state made war" (Tilly 1975:42). In contrast, Ibn Khaldun perceived the rise of the state as an outcome of human cooperation rather than anarchy. People cooperate because they stand to benefit more, and out of such cooperation, which represents the "human condition," emerges the state. This human condition is based on reason, social reproduction, and social cohesion, or assabiyya. Unlike Thomas Hobbes, Ibn Khaldun rejects the "state of nature," which pits all against all, rendering man willing to accept tyranny rather than live under conditions of sheer self-help (Pasha 1997:60).

The purpose here is by no means to present a theory of the state or its origins. Rather, it is to stress that the concept of the state is both contingent and variable, simply reflecting the varying empirical realities with which theory and practice concern themselves (Nettl 1994:11). "Competing theories of the state," in fact, "invariably come perilously near to being competing ideologies" (Ferguson and Mansback 1989:4). To challenge the territoriality of the state thus does not contest the concept's abstract necessity. Rather it simply affirms its contingent structural underpinnings and vested inside/outside interests, and by the same token denies any inherently "natural" existence of the form that the modern state has taken. The "universalization" of the "sovereign" equality of states, for instance, was a contingent development based on pressures from newly independent and weak states hoping to protect their new freedoms, on analogies made to domestic politics of juridical equality, and on great power calculations of interest (Krasner 1985:74). This suggests that inferences derived in each historical setting about political conduct are unique (Ferguson and Mansback 1989:3).

Religio-political reconceptualization of the modern state as contingent rather than necessary is a prerequisite for the effective representation of an updated Islamic theory of nations, yet one which retains the essential qualities of its classical antecedent. As a first step this entails the deconstruction of the modern state concept and its normative connotations, which served to reflect this relatively novel structure as a competing consciousness and discourse. The contingency of the state allows us to deconstruct it as a structure of domination and to perceive the underlying sources of tension between Islam on the one hand and the modern state and the ensuing international-global system on the other. This helps expose the violent controlling hierarchy of axiological and logical opposites (territorial/nonterritorial, progressive/regressive, equality/inequality, for example) (Derrida 1976:lxxvii).

Landscapes, of which the modern nation-states are constitutive structures, have come to be seen as "texts" and discourses combining narratives as well as conceptual, ideological and signifying representations (Barnes and Duncan 1992:8). In this light the "state" constitutes an inter-textual artifact actualized to reflect a particular self-image constructed and reconstructed through historical and political processes. The contemporary meaning it has come to bear has been produced from "text to text" rather than between "text and the real world." The consequence is that

writing is constitutive, not simply reflective; new worlds are made out of old texts, and old worlds are the basis of new texts. In this world of one text careening off another, we cannot appeal to any epistemological bedrocks in privileging one text over another. For what is true is made inside texts, not outside them. (Barnes and Duncan 1992:3)

Both Western theory and the "nation-state" are examples of spatio-temporal inter-textuality, which has rendered the state "like virtually all concepts in the field of international relations ... drenched with normative connotations" (Ferguson and Mansbach 1989:3). Being more or less the product of a common Western civilizational matrix, one can refer to an inter-textuality that is intra-textual. R.B.J. Walker was to the point when he indicated that theories of international relations are aspects of contemporary world politics, which need to be explained rather than being an explanation. They are to be comprehended as a typical discourse of the modern state and a "design" for constitutive practice which seeks to limit and delineate the horizons beyond which political action by "others" would be risky or prohibited (Walker 1993:6). Imperial and hegemonic constitutive designs require the support of structures of power, which sustain their greatest impression by availing themselves of clearly articulated ideas. The outcome has been a conception of "order," which inherently benefits some at the expense of others (Paul and Hall 1999:3). The modern state is the vital instrument of that order. Initial hopes that the principle of state sovereignty would protect the weak through the universalization of legal "equality" have proven false as many states crumble and collapse under the weight of the global system. This is the logical consequence of a "Euro-centric" international order, which reflects not only leading states' power and material interests, but also the constitutive aspects of their identities (Ruggie 1998:14). In this sense Frantz Fanon sees notions of "respect of the sovereignty of states" as a colonial "strategy of encirclement" (Fanon 1963:71). Whereas before nineteenth-century European nationalism Muslims defined their "*self*" first and foremost in religious terms, as Islam would normally have demanded of them, the subsequently superimposed nation-state structure introduced competing secular Eurocentric instruments of identity formation. Islamic autonomy, conception, and self-referentiality were challenged at the normative level, and behaviorally at the state and systemic levels. With the current wave of hegemonic neoliberalism this threatens to reach down to social structures (the family, for example) and individual attitudes. Very few of the failed Muslim pseudo-state structures are likely to be able to meet this challenge, nor does the global system afford them a substantive change of policy in response. The "state" in the "abode of Islam" remains a constituted object not a constitutive subject, existing as a contingent byproduct of outside formations and not as a necessary sign of internal principles. It has receded into a self-reinforcing condition of dependency, penetrated by external actors, and a reflection of extra-textuality. As such, it continues to strike at the very identity of this abode, the most conspicuous manifestation of which has been the recognition by a significant number of those states of the region's antithetical identity: Israel.

What applies to the Western world in a changing global system is thus different from what applies to Muslim nations in the same system. In contrast to the former, for the latter there is no mutual global and state reconstitution that would allow for intra-textuality or even for a measure of inter-textuality. In many ways, the relationship between globalization and the international system resembles that between post-modernity and modernity. As far as the Muslim world is concerned, globalization seeks to deconstruct their "state" structures, along non-territorial, pre-colonial, "preorganizational" lines, if possible, so as to re-inscribe them. In this sense, globalization seeks neither to destroy nor to consolidate the state, but basically to reconstruct it in a particular image. The question hence is not whether the "modern state" as a sovereign entity is going to be undermined as such, but rather which states will be dismantled, deconstructed, consolidated, nominalised, reinscribed, and how. Like post-modernity, globalization may be post-international, coming after, yet representing a return to and questioning of, earlier constructs (backward-looking) in order to reconstruct (forward-looking). It is an act of restoration and a forward-looking dynamic simultaneously, still within the normal progression of Western history. Despite all the uncertainties associated with globalization, it remains simply the autonomous linear sequel of that history, reflected in the form of continuation of an American hegemonic order (Ikenberry 1996:89–91; 1999:125).

The world this gives rise to will likely be based on intra-textuality versus extra-textuality, or what some observers have termed "a tale of two worlds" (Goldgeier and McFaul 1992; Singer and Wildavsky 1993:3). One world consists of a core or "great power society" of non-unitary actors, focusing primarily on maximizing wealth, sharing common liberal norms, and a horizontal relation of cooperative interdependence. The other world, into which Muslim societies fall, consists of periphery states, largely dependent on the core, and conducting their policies among themselves according to the tenets of anarchy and structural realism (Goldgeier and McFaul 1992:468–70). Essentially, then, there will be two separate worlds with horizontal cooperative and anarchic relations respectively, and which stand in a vertical hierarchical relationship *vis-à-vis* each other. A relationship, that is, of inequality.

"The state," as Michael Walzer once observed, "is invisible; it must be personified before it can be seen, symbolized before it can be loved, imagined before it can be conceived" (Walzer 1967:194). Deconstructing the modern state structure in the abode of Islam requires developing a discourse and an ideological thrust which, while undermining its force as it stands, constructs a conceptual alternative. This calls for the reconstitution of the state by changing its dimensions, signification, and content, and from thereon its meaning (Zartman 1995:267); an "essentially ... normative" as well as a "scientific question" (Holsti 1985:7). While it is not uncommon in Eurocentric discourses to come across arguments supporting such transformations, the significance and implications for the two worlds remain worlds apart. To the great power society such transformations will mean more integration and unity in the style of the European Union (EU) or the North American Free Trade Agreement (NAFTA) between Canada, Mexico, and the US, or the consolidation of the power and hegemonic influence of the Jewish state of Israel over its neighbors. Israel, according to this discourse, would become the Trojan horse for a regional, imperial neoliberal power structure. For the Muslim world, in contradistinction, the same discourse regarding the state translates into "humanitarian intervention," "minority rights," and "right to secession" or self-determination, among other supposedly lofty yet practically fragmentary principles. For, as Barry Buzan has indicated, "the idea of the state, its institutions, and even its territory can all be threatened as much by the manipulation of ideas as by the wielding of military power" (Buzan 1991:97). Whereas for the society of great powers the above values are mutually constitutive and therefore inter- and intra-textually sovereign, for the Muslim Umma they represent an authority over their Islamic values and their social and political structures. The practical outcome of this extra-textual discourse is to reconstitute notions of "sovereignty," "recognized borders," and entitlement to "independence," allowing for a new and massive wave of colonial expansion to proceed unhindered by formal legalistic encumbrances. The purpose is to serve global neoliberal interests as the supreme loci of power. This not only further delegitimizes Arab/Muslim pseudo-state structures but also deconstructs them for the purposes of new inscriptions. Sovereignty of Islamic values is further undermined as a stepping-stone toward their total marginalization, depriving them in the process of any possible competing domestic or external functioning space. The consequence, as the Islamic landscape readily manifests, is social and political fragmentation, identity crisis, splintering, diminution, conflict, and, in the final analysis, colonization.

As a prerequisite to expanding the horizons of an altered meaning of sovereignty under global conditions, what is required is a transformation in the "epistemic dimension" of social life, or the system of meaning and signification embedded in collective mentalities. In order to allow for relational changes between the inside and the outside, the extra-textual apparatus, which ruling regimes in Muslim countries have come to draw upon in imagining and symbolizing forms of political community, will have to undergo a fundamental reorientation (Ruggie 1998:184). So will their very conception of problem solving. No longer is the state simply a means to power and wealth from the inside shielded by sovereignty from the outside—which some may call corruption—but a structure of "durable inequality" of which the former predicament is but one source (Tilly 1999).

Self-referential standards of "civilization" set by a European model of statehood and state organization, serving what were basically European interests and reflecting their own moment of history, are all congenial to the structuring and perpetuating of a world system of inequality (Kingsbury 1999:74). Binary oppositions associated with the state correspond to "invisible" discursive categorical differences locking groups in permanent structural relationships of contrasts. Categories of inequality—even when evidently employing cultural labels, justifying for a particular group its own inferior position, relative or absolute, thus rendering it natural—always depend on far reaching socio-political organization, belief, and enforcement. In the field of international relations these translate into the structural–global, the ideological–neoliberal, and the power–imperial respectively. Durable inequality among categories develops because great powers that control access to "value-producing resources" solve defined systemic problems by means of categorical distinctions based on constructed systems of closure, exclusion, and control (Tilly 1999:7–8). Policies that sought to maintain colonial rule over "non-sovereign" territories came to depend increasingly on the structuring of categorical and binary distinctions among ethnic and racial groups (civilized/uncivilized, for example). Many of those excluded and controlled, on the less privileged sides of the categorical divide, eventually developed and acquired stakes in the formulated solutions, despite their dominating hierarchies. Afro-American civil rights activist Malcolm X had this point in mind when he used the example of the slave in the field versus the slave in the master's house. When they met in their free time, the latter would tell the former about the joys of serving at "home." In his speech he would use the first person plural: in "our" house, "our" mansion or "our" palace, whatever the case may be, "we" do so and so. Unlike the slave in the field who recognizes the reality of his status and resents it, the slave in the house is doubly enslaved: once by the fact of being a slave and twice by acquiring a stake in being a slave.

Categorical institutionalization of this kind serves to sustain relations of durable inequality, as the master divides and conquers. Should the slave in the field rebel, his counterpart at "home" can have only the limited option of being his antagonist. This condition is the inevitable outcome when debilitated Muslim states feel obliged to sign a human rights convention, a peace treaty or clauses of specific gender "empowerment," all supposedly bearing connotations of universal equality. Not only do they submit to the bidding of a great power like the USA in such instances, but also in so doing they tie down their future options as they face greater prospects of exacting compliance. Lacking significant influence on the principles of international commitments to which they put their signature, they become exposed to both external impositions and internal structural fragility. "Globalization" in other words, "affects not just their bargaining power at the time of negotiation, but more widely, their relative power to make choices in the future" (Hurrell and Woods 1995:456). It is thus inextricably intertwined with the propagation of inequality. Globalization, that is, negates in practice what universalization of values demands in theory, and thus any "relationship between globalization and human rights," for instance, becomes "far from straightforward" (Clark 1999:131). Or perhaps it is that the latter is nothing more than an instrument of the former. As "particular" identities are being developed with reference to the vision of the "universal," and as globalization is being universalized as a system of durable inequality, it becomes clear that human rights is nothing more than the ideological underpinning of such a global order. It is basically an old/new colonial project aimed at re-inscribing Muslim "state" and society, by justifying intervention and enforcement. After all, as Andre Beteille has insightfully observed, "Western societies were acquiring a new and comprehensive commitment to equality at precisely that juncture in their history when they were also developing in their fullest form the theory and practice of imperialism" (Beteille 1983:4). W. Michael Reisman has recently provided a consistent sample of this pattern. Attempting to build a legal case for foreign intervention he argued that national sovereignty in its classical sense has become "anachronistic" and that it is legitimate to intervene in countries deemed "undemocratic." Human rights constitute the basis for such intervention. State sovereignty is no longer to be a protective shield if popular sovereignty is suppressed. Much in the same fashion that the "wealth of a country can be spoliated as thoroughly by a native as by a foreigner," so can popular sovereignty be "liberated as much by an indigenous as by an outside force." He adds, however, that such suppression constitutes only "a justifying factor" for intervention, "not a justification *per se* but *conduit sine qua non*" (Reisman 1990:871–2). American global interests no doubt would be the determining factor.

Like any political system, globalization requires mechanisms of control, which in a global hierarchy function as sources of durable inequality. These include exploitation, opportunity hoarding, emulation, and adaptation. The first two come at the systemic level of analysis, and are largely responsible for the installation of the categorical boundaries of inequality. The latter two, at the state and also the individual-leadership levels, reinforce, consolidate, and generalize the former arrangements (Tilly 1999:10).[5] *Exploitation* occurs when powerful actors in the global system (insiders) command the resources and values from which they draw increased returns. This takes place by coordinating the efforts of weaker actors (outsiders) who are excluded from the full value added by that effort. *Opportunity hoarding* provides stakes to the latter categories. It offers monopolized rewards or valued interests selectively to the segregated structures of the "sovereign" state in order to undermine the force of revisionist or unificationist tendencies, while keeping the "unequal" states divided. *Emulation* generalizes the state system not only by copying or imposing it as an established organizational model, but also by attempting to transplant its concomitant yet alien social and political relations from one cultural and historical milieu to another. It further serves to lower the costs of maintaining the status quo below the costs of any of the modern states' potential or theoretical alternatives. *Adaptation* articulates and elaborates regimes of systemic interaction among states on the basis of a presumably recognized categorical inequality. The purpose is to render the costs of moving to theoretically available alternatives prohibitively high. Adaptation thus locks in categorical inequality by taking it for granted. Emulation serves in proliferating categorical inequality by producing "homologies" of form and function. Together, these mechanisms create the illusion of the "ubiquity" and therefore the "inevitability" of the modern state, rather than its variability (Tilly 1999:10, 190–1).

Each of the above four mechanisms constitutes a "self-reproducing element" and together all lock neatly into a "self-reproducing complex" (Tilly 1999:191). Their impact can be clearly followed in the historical process of emulation and adaptation which took place in the Muslim Ottoman Empire during the nineteenth century (it was abolished in 1924) and subsequently in the fragmented Arab states during the twentieth century. The aim of achieving parity and equality with the West in fact achieved the very antithesis of those goals. Yet this process is still under way as a "state" project increasingly opposed by societal forces. In contrast to the European "nation-state," the outcome has been a "state" against the "nation," to use Burhan Ghulyun's apt depiction (1994:27–8). In the European historical experience the state affirmed the nation; in the Muslim adaptive and emulative counterpart, the state negated the nation. Infusing this same state structure with new ideas, sound or mistaken, while possibly mitigating or exacerbating the effects of the four mechanisms described above, will neither stymie nor necessarily initiate them. Democratic principles, applied within the modern state—the structure that has come to embody those elements—will not contribute to rectifying this systemic configuration of inequality. Allowed to function seriously, democracy is likely to bring Islamist forces to power, which both religiously and ideologically cannot accept such a global order or state structure. This helps explain the absence of any real systemic interest in having a functional democracy in the Muslim world, and the intense American hostility to Islamic values. Nor, by the same token, would the mere implementation of the Shar'iah provide a ready solution as the "state" would inevitably come to confront a hostile environment. Being constitutive of Islamic identity, the Shari'ah means neither emulation nor adaptation. By extension it challenges the control and distribution of resources and values undertaken by exploitation and opportunity hoarding. Yet the holistic dimensions of the Shari'ah cannot be fully expressed as the force of those mechanisms come into play. A change in organizational forms—the installation of different categories, or the transformation of relations between categories and rewards—therefore becomes necessary (Tilly 1999:15).

Defining those alternative organizational structures is part and parcel of any possible autonomous and self-referential conceptual change. The crisis that the Muslim world faces thus extends beyond the issue of the legitimacy of regimes to that of the legitimacy of the *state* structure itself. The Muslim states will have to relent reciprocally on what is by now a fictional sovereignty—a seemingly paradoxical dynamic of surrendering intra-sovereignty to gain in inter-sovereignty. Despite inevitable systemic resistance this will have to proceed in such a fashion as to make it necessary that "the 'domestic' is as much a part of the fabric of the international system as any abstracted 'structure' of the relations between states" (Clark 1999:5). If a theory of state is largely a theory of its external environment, and if the international-global order as it stands is not what Islamic values and Arab and Muslim people would readily accept, then it follows that to alter or significantly influence that system they will have to transform their extant state structures as well. Much in the same fashion that a domestic change in the attributes of the family, as the basic unit in society, would lead to transforming society and social relations, and vice versa (agent-structure), so would a change in the attributes of the state, as the basic unit of the international-global system, alter the system and its relations, and vice versa. With form and content in the Muslim world no longer coinciding, either the state structure must be altered to fit the Umma's principled beliefs, or the Islamic worldview must be diluted to suit the requirements of this structure. Between an Islamic choice opting for the former, and global forces opting for the latter, the modern Muslim state and its contradictions have reached an historical impasse.

TOWARD A NEOCLASSICAL ISLAMIC FRAMEWORK

Much like globalization, Islamic theory merely induces a particular conceptualization of the meaning of the state. It does not necessarily negate statehood as such, even as it challenges its territoriality, but rather contests the association of identity formation with bounded territory. The state in this new/old conception is a means toward securing an Islamic or "good" life and not an end in itself. Islam, as Ayatollah Muhammad Hussain Fadlallah has put it, was not revealed in order to establish a state as an end, but to spread a message based on which a state would come into existence only as a subsequent means toward achieving this goal (Fadlallah 1996:28). Whereas globalization is increasingly setting the state in service of the transnational flow of capital, goods, and information, Islam sets it in the service of moral and religious values. The equality of Islamic universalism is about to confront the inequality of American globalism. A new binary dichotomy is taking shape, not just between historically fixed categories, but more so among dynamic flows of forces and values. The trajectory of the previously marginalized Islamic law of nations seems to be catching up with the flow of current history.

Within the abode of Islam, the nature of external relationships between states will have to be transformed. This means that Muslim states cannot continue to maintain the structure of their relationships on the basis of supposedly unitary actors engaged in an anarchic self-help power setting. They must move to an *abodic*/macro, that is "civilizational," level based on meta-power or assabiyya, as an endogenous/cooperative–exogenous/conflictive concept. Unlike mere Third Worldism, which sought to guard security and independence by jealously defending the pseudo nation-state structure, notwithstand-ing calls for transnational unity of one kind or the other, assabiyya seeks to promote those very objectives, among others, by challenging the very imagery and conception of the modern state. Substantive issues of this kind pose both theoretical and practical revisionist challenges to the status quo, particularly so as issues of identity come to the forefront. The crucial and most central issue is thus to determine where the assabiyya of Islam lies and to coalesce around it, transcending territorial and vested or modern state interests. It is the rational and reasoned tackling of primarily political and strategic questions of this kind that will determine answers in the light of which categorical provisions of the Shari'ah and determination of Islamic interests could be made.

Theorizing about the state, under such conditions, must itself begin by subverting the framework of the great divide, whether between the inside and the outside or between the abode of Islam and the abode of War. This does not mean eliminating categorical distinctions, but rather recognizing that the stability of fixed categories under conditions of fluidity and transformation is likely to experience powerful pressures (Clark 1999:16, 31). Fixed categories are inherently disposed toward maintaining closures. Closure generally leads to entropy as loss of energy and openness to entropy as loss of identity. The seeming opposition between both forces frequently contributes to distress and uncertainty, particularly so as elements of conservatism creep in, opting in response for the security of static norms in preference to the insecurity of dynamic interaction. This is problematic because systems of thought, as well as geopolitical structures, which seek to seal themselves off from outside forces will tend to exhaust their ideas as well as their human and natural resources respectively, and hence undergo high levels of entropy (Demko and Wood 1994:28). A branchless tree may continue to grow for some time until it reaches certain limits, beyond which it cannot go. Only the branches, however, allow it to "procreate" and in a sense reproduce itself. Manifesting closure, recurrence, and repetition, the Islamic law of nations collapsed theory into law, the branch into the stem, and the part into the whole. Its potential evolutionary and contributive energy is thus exhausted.

Shifts in the systemic order and capabilities are strongly intertwined with qualitative and quantitative factors ranging from conceptual change and political, economic or social structural organization to an increase in space, resources or more favorable external conditions. Non-territoriality, as one such organizing principle, is linked to relative and absolute power changes in the international-global system, not simply as a matter of extension or expanse, but also in terms of the concomitant changes necessary for the effective management of space. To talk about non-territoriality is thus to incorporate qualitative as well as quantitative transformations both at the state and *abodic*/macro/civilizational levels. If successfully constitutive of a new geopolitical and strategic reality, the impact could eventually translate into a broader measure of global influence or better internal control over the external environment, and hence a relative reduction in conditions of inequality.

Two "postulates" may help in justifying the principle of non-territoriality, and perhaps in developing the argument further in harmony with rational Islamic theoretical underpinnings and religious principles. First that, "*a state's relative capability in a system will increase when its rate of absolute growth is greater than the absolute growth rate for that system as a whole (the systemic norm).*" Second, that "*a state's relative capability for growth will accelerate for a time and then (at a point of inflection) begin a process of deceleration*" (Doran 1991:4). Both assumptions transcend the divide between the inside and outside in that intra-Muslim state borders and sovereignty lose much of their significance while at the same time new reorganizing principles of state are introduced. Reforms which may cause a positive increase in a state's capabilities are likely to be constrained and limited by territoriality and thus will reach their limits long before being able to attain an essential actor role. Conversely, in the hypothetical situation where two or more Muslim states happen to unite without internally reorganizing, the same sources of failure will simply be transposed from what was previously a smaller structural failure to a larger one. Should both reform and unification occur simultaneously, a situation might emerge in which the absolute growth of the "Islamic state" could be greater than that of the system. This is one important reason why the US is hostile to Islamic geopolitical conceptions and values, which seek to change the connotations of the state. These considerations have less to do with Islamic "radicalism" or "moderation" as such, and more with systemic idiosyncrasies. This is illustrated by American policy toward the experiences of two countries, Iraq and Egypt. When the US mobilized to reverse the Iraqi invasion of Kuwait in 1991 it was, among other reasons, to protect the ultimate structure of "sovereign" states, and the mechanisms serving that purpose—the arbitrarily bordered Arab "state." Breaking the borders "taboo," irrespective of intentions, would have allowed for a change in conception regarding the ubiquity and inevitability of the state structure, and an increase in the relative autonomy and power of an emerging regional power. This was not only in the case of Iraq. When Egypt attacked Libya in 1977, with the prospect of taking over the oil fields of that country, the US made its disapproval amply clear. Despite American hostility to Muammar Qadhaffi's regime and friendly relations with the Egyptian counterpart, a warning was conveyed to Egyptian President Anwar Sadat indicating opposition to such a takeover. The US would not countenance an increase in Egypt's capabilities at an accelerated rate once it had laid its hands on Libya's oil (Heikal 1996:228, 247). This might have been explained by reason of international law had the US not previously supported Iraq's invasion of Iran, and had not American international behavior in other cases been similarly aggressive. In addition, it remains highly unlikely that the US would at any point look favorably on, say, a possible union between Egypt, Libya, and Sudan, even if it were to be consummated peacefully. The reasons have much to do with the idea of global order and the bordered state system "switching off" a unified Arab and/or Muslim nation as with considerations of absolute and relative power.

Robert Gilpin has observed that "a more wealthy and more powerful state (up to the point of diminishing utility) [can] select a larger bundle of security and welfare goals than a less wealthy and powerful state" (Gilpin 1981:22–3). Whereas the consolidation and mobilization of a collective Islamic–Arab identity in response to globalization would have been required, systemic interests have sought instead to impose the state secular identity as the highest value. As a result primary and/or secondary identities are imposed not chosen. Supporting a tribal emir in Kuwait—in a state of perpetual fear of an "inside" neighbor and in need of permanent "outside" protection—to stay in power constitutes a self-reproducing mechanism of regional control and durable inequality. Even by the standards of primacy of state values, the Muslim state has been a failure. Yet Muslim states continue to pursue contradictory and conflicting state policies ultimately leading to a progressive dynamic of fragmentation, bringing them under total systemic colonization and domination. The tragedy of the Muslim community/Umma, if one may paraphrase Rousseau, is that it is in all Muslims' religious and value interests to unite under a commonly agreed-upon sovereign/imam in order to have a better chance of attaining a larger security bundle. Yet it is in the interest of each single regime or state to obviate that authority when it is to its own expediency (Williams, Wright, and Evans 1993:100). Calls for Muslim states to develop policies of cooperation and mutual assistance in different forums and at different levels (Abu-Sulayman 1993:xiv), while continuing to maintain their structures of durable inequality, are unrealistic and naive to say the least. First, global imperatives may render such cooperation untenable, and may compel its norms in such a fashion that Muslim regimes may find it more rewarding and in their interest not to cooperate—most such regimes being highly penetrated and dependent, if not outrightly colonized. Second, as Geoffrey Garret and Barry Weingast have put it, "to assert that institutions help assure adherence to the rules of the game is to overlook a prior and critical issue. If the members of a community cannot agree to one set of rules, the fact that institutions might facilitate adherence to them would be irrelevant" (Goldstein and Keohane 1993:18).

Mere cooperation, therefore, is no substitute for unity, both functional and political. As a matter of fact, in a world of realism the former is highly unlikely without the latter. Only the ability of a centralized (federal or otherwise) authority to extract the collective resources of the Umma would allow the state to exert more control over its external environment. The resources at the disposal of the Muslim world cannot be mobilized or extracted through goodwill, moral exhortations or sympathy. Notwithstanding the necessity of the former *bona fide* factors, they must be translated into centralized and structured imperatives. Fareed Zakaria made an insightful point when he distinguished, in his politico-historical study of the USA, between state and national power. Only when the "state" was able to establish centralized control over the extraordinary resources of the American "nation" by 1890, was it possible for the US to pursue a coherent foreign policy, which would serve that country's purpose of exerting control over its external environment well into the twentieth century and beyond. Until such a hold could be established, despite its tremendous resources, the US remained a "weak divided and decentralized" state, providing policymakers with "little usable power" (Zakaria 1998:55). The same could be said about the EU. Despite the abundance of resources at the EU's disposal, which matches if not exceeds that of the US, the EU remains limited in the amount of control it can exert on the external environment, whether in terms of foreign or military policy. No effective sovereign and/or centralized extractive institutions so far exist which could translate wealth into power. Both the US and EU federative experiences thus provide comparative empirical evidence in the light of which Islamic unifying religio-political concepts such as the imamate and the caliphate could be reformulated and operationalized geopolitically. The modified restoration of the caliphate/imamite as an institution, contrary to claims projecting this as an unrealistic return to the past, constitutes the perhaps as yet unarticulated Islamic equivalent to the secular EU project and even to that of the US "federation." Yet it is dubbed regressive even as it transcends the modern state, and is hence visionary and futuristic.

Other relevant historical cases must also be examined and analyzed, such as those of the Austro-Hungarian Empire, the Soviet Empire, and most significantly, the Ottoman Empire. Their rise and decline, in the framework of assabiyya, among other potential concepts, could provide for a fresh historical and Islamic outlook—assabiyya in this context referring to the right and eligibility of a particular group to rule or otherwise, and thus strongly intertwined with legitimacy. A *comparative* analysis between rational regimes and regimes of law (Shari'ah) as related to those empires could lead to insightful conclusions. So would examining the possible links between assabiyya as theory of state and corresponding increased control over the external environment as a systemic reflection—these being two aspects of a single dynamic breaking the inside/outside divide.

Breaking this divide requires the cognitive opening of the closed categories of the Islamic classical theory. This means being able to discriminate between closed normative aspects (law–stem) and the theoretical and practical underpinnings (theory and praxis–branch). Khadduri made an important point in this respect when he distinguished between *jihad* as a doctrine of permanent state of war and the condition of actual and continuous fighting (Khadduri 1955:64). A distinction of this kind is useful in elaborating and transcending the boundaries of fixed categories. The fact that both were considered stemic normative wholes or universals led to the diffused incorporation of the partial (branch) and contingent condition of actual fighting into the normative abode of War category. This implied that no distinction was made between the abode of War as a closed and necessary category on the one hand, and the open and contingent issues of peace and war on the other. One was basically inherently implied in the other. Thus under circumstances in which fighting, as a contingent category, was neither feasible nor perhaps required, doubts were as a consequence cast on the normative category: a case in which the theoretical "system" turned against itself rather than opting to evolve while maintaining its own integrity.

A neoclassical Islamic framework is needed, therefore, to provide for new conceptions of relationships between norms and values on the one hand and interests and interaction on the other. A relational distinction must be introduced between the macro-abstract worldviews and principled beliefs, and the micro causalities. This is in contrast to the classical framework, which allowed the macro and the micro to diffuse into each other. In an Islamic frame of reference, normative principles as well as cognitive interests bear an originative influence in determining action. The starting point of a neoclassical framework is thus to reformulate the cognitive problem in terms of how to bring forth the distinctiveness of the evolutionary branch in a dynamic unity such that closure and openness reflect "reciprocal conditions" rather than "contradictions," thus recharging energy and consolidating identity. In this unity, openness of the Islamic value system bases itself upon self-referential closure, and closed reproduction refers to the environment (Luhmann 1990:230). This is a different way of referring to subversion of categorical inside/outside distinctions in favor of mutual adaptation of a specific kind. Synthesizing Ibn Khaldun's cyclical theory of state (assabiyya) and historical dynamics with the Islamic law of nations caters to a promising ontological–epistemological Islamic framework, combining theory of state with international theory, forming what may be called a "power cycle theory," one which "encompasses both the state and the system in a single dynamic" and which reflects structural change at the two levels concurrently. It unites the structural and behavioral aspects of state international political development in a single dynamic and can be analyzed on each level by means of a variety of approaches. These may include religious interpretations, history, understanding of international and global political behavior, or empirical testing (Doran 1991:19–20).

However, the fact that the concept of "statehood" is also being concomitantly transformed elevates such a power cycle theory to the meta-level. In this context, introducing the leadership principle of Wilayat al-Faqih as a potential model and an empirical expression of assabiyya could help in building a commensurate theory of state. The dynamism of this contingent causal belief grounded in Islam, and its institutionalized practical and empirical manifestations, justify it as an operational Islamic conceptual construct. At this point, then, we could perhaps imagine three concentric circles including Wilayat al-Faqih (innermost), assabiyya (middle), and abode of Islam (outermost) (see Figure 4). The first indicates *who* is to rule (causal beliefs/*fatawa*), the second explains *why* (principled beliefs/*fiqh*), and the third delineates the non-territorial domain or "state"—*where* (worldview/*Shari'ah*). A neoclassical Islamic theory that introduces these elements of complexity into its structure could help explain potential influence on global and international relations caused by the cyclical dynamic of state ascendancy and/or decline.

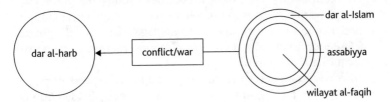

Figure 4   Diagram introducing an element of complexity and depicting the suggested neoclassical "state" approach.

At the same time, the closed normative categories of abode of Islam versus abode of War would carry the different yet symmetrical connotations of identity (constructed) and self (inherent) rather than of permanent conflict and hostility. Branching out of them are the cognitive asymmetrical aspects of (a) peace (*dar al-ahd*), (b) tension (*dar al-sulh*), or (c) actual war or aggression (*dar al-baghy*) (see Figure 5).[6]

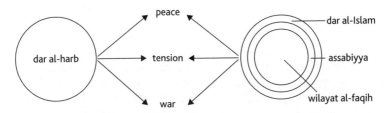

Figure 5   Diagram representing the "branching-out" or the cognitive opening of the normatively closed categories reflecting the different states of peace, tension or war. Peace = *dar al-ahd*, tension = *dar al-sulh*, war = *dar al-baghy*.

The proposed system allows for a measure of flexibility, fluidity, and inference, and hence dynamism, as opposed to the static framework of fixed and immutable categories. The "West" is still to be perceived in terms of the classical category "abode of War," but the definition of *War* is no longer simply that of *conflict* but refers more to the "other" or *separate identity*, with mutual relations varying on the basis of political contingencies. The latter definition reflects the security of social relationship, a sense of being safely in cognitive control of the interaction context. It is relational at the most basic level of interaction: that of the mutual knowledge which is a condition of action, and which derives from a sense of shared community. Essentially it becomes a source of "ontological security", which "relates to the self, its social competence, [and] its confidence in the actors capacity to manage relations with others" (McSweeney 1999:157), a condition of closure, that is, being the prerequisite for openness.

In correspondence with the above cognitive aspects of peace, tension or conflict/fighting, the "West" may be subdivided into (a) non-imperial powers, (b) semi-imperial powers, and (c) imperial powers respectively (see Figure 6).

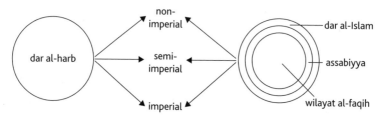

Figure 6 Depiction of a policy framework that, while normatively closed, is cognitively open. It is based on policies rather than generalized closed categories but also protects identity structure. The non-imperial, semi-imperial, and imperial identifications correspond to the respective conditions of peace, tension, and war in Figure 5.

Conflict would hence shift from a fixed "Western" category toward a fluid imperial counterpart, as actors' roles might change or alter over time. Reformulated accordingly, the "abode of War," against which *jihad* or *just war* may in principle be conducted, becomes imperialism and not the West as such, policies not categories. In this sense *jihad* re-appropriates its just and defensive connotations. Fluidity by the same token requires the expansion of cognitive skills (*fatawa*) into fields of strategic planning, prioritization, and political analysis as categories change, mix or transform. It demands further the sharpening of dynamic theoretical inferences, while remaining at the same time cognizant of normative closures and red lines related to religious values and interests. It is perhaps this framework that has allowed the Iranian Islamic experience to evolve successfully, despite great systemic opposition, from revolution to a revolutionary state and then to an institutionalized state, while remaining loyal to Islamic principles both domestically and externally. Its normative closure was the very condition of its evolution and cognitive opening.

This is in contradistinction to the Arab "state," which is normatively open and cognitively closed. No wonder the former is dynamic and evolving, the latter static, fragmenting, and decaying.

CONCLUSION

The preceding discussion helps justify the continued relevance of a duly modified classical Islamic approach to relations among nations. Modification requires moving beyond the simplicity of normative closures toward a dynamic relationship with the complexities of cognitive openness. As such, a neoclassical framework heralds the end of simplicity in much the same fashion that the end of the Cold War ushered in the end of simplicity associated with a bipolar structured world.

The respect with which the classical paradigm of nations has been held by many Muslims through the centuries is, therefore, not necessarily misplaced. Where such respect is perhaps out of place, however, is when it becomes a form of veneration which does not allow for intellectual expansion, elaboration, and complexity, combined with a state of paralysis and immobility emanating from a feeling of insecurity about being unable to preserve religious identity in a perceived hostile global environment. Islamic beliefs and ideas, for a myriad of historical reasons, have been largely detached from national and global structures and processes. As such they have been unable to play an active role in shaping national and government policies or to reach out beyond to influence systemic configurations. To the extent that beliefs determine and sway policy, and thus are potentially constitutive of the domestic and possibly the external environment, such insecurities could be mitigated.

The fears and concerns of many Muslims are, nevertheless, not simply a product of a vivid imagination, but are seriously rooted in perceived attacks on their identity structures and faith, fueling anxieties about their continuously being an adaptive object rather than a constitutive subject. These attacks are signified by the distinctive reshaping constructs of *democracy*, *liberalism*, and *human rights*. Essentially, these three mutually re-enforcing values and interest configurations are perceived by many Muslims as comprising the main discursive weapons of the "abode of War," supported and imposed by consolidating economic, political, and military powers. They constitute therefore the main subject matter and critical focus of the following three chapters respectively.

5

Islam, Iran, and Western Discourse: Behind the Democratic Veil

Reflecting on the 1991 Gulf War during which the Iraqi invasion of Kuwait was reversed and the Iraqi regional power curtailed, S.R. Gill observed:

It is the most recent chapter in the historical struggle between the Arab World and the West, in contemporary times over the control of oil. More fundamentally, however, it partly reflects not simply the struggle between states ... but also the struggles over the organizing principles of society—struggles which began at least as early as the Middle Ages and the era of the Crusades—between Western capitalist secular materialism and the metaphysics and social doctrine of Islam as well as more secular pan-Arabist forces in the shape of the Iraqi regime. In this sense, the Gulf war is rooted in the social struggles and transformations which have occurred in the world over many centuries. (1991:275)

In the same vein, commenting on the rising tide of Islamic activism, Bernard Lewis concurred that:

We are facing a mood and a movement far transcending the level of issues and policies and the governments that pursue them. This is no less than a clash of civilizations—the perhaps irrational but surely historic reaction of an ancient rival against our Judeo-Christian heritage, our secular present, and the worldwide expansion of both. (1990:60)

Gill, Lewis, and Samuel Huntington, all appear to converge on the same understanding and contemplate conflict between civilizations as the "latest phase in the evolution of conflict in the modern world" (Huntington 1993:22). In a more practical policy reflection of the above, former assistant Secretary of State for Near Eastern and South Asian Affairs under the George Bush Sr. administration, Edward Djerjian, proclaimed the tidings of the "fundamental values" which undergirded the American foreign policy in the Arab and Muslim World: "Reviewing the main thrust of our policy in the Middle East," he stated, remind us that, even in the 1990s, our national interests in the region continue to exert a powerful claim on our attention. But there is more to our policy agenda than protection of vital resources and conflict resolution. Another pillar of US policy is our support for human rights, pluralism, women's and minority rights and popular participation in government, and our rejection of extremism, oppression and terrorism. These worldwide issues constitute an essential part of the foundation for America's engagement with the countries of the Middle East—from the Maghreb to Iran and Beyond. (Haddad 1993:88)

In short, the lines are being sharply drawn between the West and its old nemesis, the World of Islam. Such demarcations reflect two distinct *abodic*/civilizational orders with their own specific and dynamic understandings of the nature of congruency between cosmo-normative standards and social existence. Implicit in such a process are the fundamental considerations of epistemology and ontology, and the very foundations upon which civilizations and *abodes* are built and consciousness shaped.

What follows however, is not an excursion into the origins of ideas or their comparative standing. Nor is it a broad exposition of a particular case or experience. Rather, it is part of the general endeavor at formulating a methodological approach toward the development of an Islamic social and political counter-discourse, and an attempt to provide indicators that would contribute to a deeper analysis and examination of Muslim contemporary reality. As Fazlur Rahman has poignantly pointed out, "the survival of the Islamic world as Islamic is conditioned not only on activist ferment, but on patient and complex intellectual labor which must produce the necessary Islamic vision" (1981:25). Only then could Muslims engage in the "politics of civilizations," not solely as the "objects of history as targets of Western colonialism," but "as movers and shapers of history" (Huntington 1993:23).

This chapter, as well as the following two, will attempt to examine the role of discourses, particularly those of the democratic and liberal variety, as they seek to contest Islam and hence, intentionally or otherwise, to de-legitimize it. It will focus on some salient aspects of the presumed civilizational or "*abodic*" clash. The basic contention here is that the multi-dimensional conflict between the Muslim world and the secular West should be resolved first and foremost at the foundational levels of epistemology and consciousness. I proceed by expounding some essential sources of conflict, and by deconstructing liberal democracy as the political and ideological manifestation of the Western hegemonic system. I further suggest some criteria for assessing the Iranian revolutionary experience as a budding nucleus of an Islamic transformation, within which this phenomenon can be analyzed, assessed, and understood.

MUSLIM CONSCIOUSNESS AND THE CHAOTIC REALITY: A STATE OF EPISTEMOLOGICAL DUALISM

"World politics," wrote Huntington, is "entering a new phase" in which "the fault lines between civilizations are replacing the political and ideological boundaries of the Cold War as the flash points for crisis and bloodshed" (Huntington 1993:22, 29). As opposed to the earlier polarization, the new demarcations are "basic," "fundamental," "consciousness" based and "less mutable" (1993:25–7); in short, essential. Both the West and the Muslim World, understood in their broadest cultural and religious identity respectively, are poised to engage in this old–new form of conflict. Even loyal Muslim regimes, which have devotedly served Western interests, have come to be exposed to these new demarcations. In an article in the influential American journal *Foreign Affairs*, for instance, Daniel Pipes and Patrick Clawson suggested that "Washington needs to view Saudi Arabia as a *temporary* ally with whom numerous and profound differences remain, and to keep open other *options*" (1993:132; my emphasis). As for Turkey, they strongly advised against the mistake of perceiving it as "just another European state," and suggested moving it administratively in the State Department from the bureau that handles European countries, into that of the Middle East. This was to constitute "a small but significant step to begin the process of seeing the country in its *proper* context" (1993:137; my emphasis). Under these circumstances, intellectual curiosities about cultural and/or sub-civilizational diversities become less relevant or rather superfluous. In practice, both civilizations/consciousnesses increasingly come to see and to act towards each other monolithically.

Consciousness of the internalized normative standards according to which identity and basic reality are perceived to be, or as they ought to be, is a direct product of a legitimized system of knowledge/values and its epistemological constructs. The foundational structures of society or civilization erected by any group of people are a direct product of an epistemological and/or ontological prerequisite concerned basically with the limits and constraints of verifiability. Epistemological considerations, that is, are crucial to the construction and appraisal of social and political interpretations at both the secular and religious levels (Connolly 1967:69–70). The Western consciousness internalizes rationalism, secularism, democracy, liberalism, capitalism, and human values as its essence and basic civilizational identity. Notwithstanding the critique and controversy which surrounded Francis Fukuyama's thesis about those values ushering in perfection and the end of history (Fukuyama 1992a & 1992b; Huntington 1992), his views were not necessarily in dissonance with their overall milieu. At the other end is the Islamic world community or Umma, which defines itself essentially as based on revelation and therefore divinely ordained,[1] One/Unique,[2] and the most Elevated of all human communities[3] with whom earlier receivers of divine revelations will always attempt to maintain a power relationship.[4] In those competing claims it is not hard to discern the very basic roots of conflict. Without excluding intra-civilizational confrontations, a line of demarcation is entrenched which is easily observable once certain essential values are challenged by a foreign "consciousness," and beyond which intra-diversity subsumes a secondary position of importance. Conflict erupts at the level of consciousness all the way up to the multi-dimensions of human existence. At stake are the dynamics of "objective ... and subjective self-identification of people" (Huntington 1993:24).

In the political domain, this spills over into addressing the nature of authority, its ultimate source, its legitimation, and how the Muslim Umma perceives and determines the parameters and constraints within which it is to deal with other communities. Only the resolution of such essential and self-identifying questions would determine whether the "Islamic" praxis of any regime which lays claim to such credentials is organic to its social and political thrust or is simply instrumental. In many instances a thin line separates the two norms of practices. Yet despite all the subtleties, differences between the two remain discernible in their distinct attempts at separating or merging religio-political morality in a regime's behavior. Merger involves the very process of creating and embedding the criteria of meaning in an independent Islamic consciousness. The ultimate expression of this process is the Shari'ah.

Islamic ontological-epistemological foundations—as opposed to the reduced epistemological basis of Western consciousness— presuppose Islam's transcendence as a revelation that is external and independent of social reality. This remains true even if interpretations of it are often influenced by historical conditions. Adopting Western criteria of religious culturalism as the *valid* knowledge thus represents not only an epistemological contradiction, but above all the very process of superimposition of one consciousness upon the other. At one level, there is an Islamic consciousness that is required to shape reality according to a preconceived principle. At the other, there is a conflicting Western empirical reality which attempts to shape consciousness. At the heart of this process the Western project of cultural domination is consummated, and the dilemma of Muslims' existence and adaptation in modern times lies.

The relevance and importance of cultural approaches is undeniable. However perceiving Islam merely as a cultural phenomenon of symbols and meanings in isolation of its revelatory nature is not only reductionist, but erroneous. To perceive Islam reductively is to perpetuate a condition of epistemological reversal which subsumes the absolute under the rubric of the relative, reducing the seriousness with which religion is taken while increasing feelings of indifference toward it. Revelation thus becomes constrained by the dictates of reason as a "religion of culture." This religion of culture, as Habermas has stated, failed to develop "any synthetic forces that could renew the unifying power of traditional religion" (Habermas 1987:86).

Muslims' contacts with the modern West have historically taken place within the context of this discursive formation which sustained a relative power relationship. That power being Western necessitated that this discourse be both hegemonic and repressive of the Islamic East. It was not a dialogue between equals nor a conversation, but a will to power which attempted to reconstitute Islam and Muslims both at the level of consciousness and at the empirical level. Under those circumstances, historical discourse became an "asset—finite, limited, desirable, useful—that has its own rules of appearance, but also its conditions of appropriation and operation," and which "from the moment of its existence (and not only in its 'practical application'), pose[d] the question of power" (Sheridan 1980:101–2).

The impact of this historical experience is not difficult to discern. Its structural expressions in the Islamic environment be it in the educational or political sphere, continue to reproduce themselves in a fashion that perpetuates this constitutive power relationship. In their distribution, those structures comprise the means of power by which Westernized elites maintain or modify the appropriation of discourses through qualifying speaking subjects and constituting doctrinal groups (Sheridan 1980:127). They continue to formulate and disseminate language and knowledge in a discursive formation reflective of the character and personality of the predominant civilization (Al-Attas 1985:127). That elites in most Islamic countries are largely a product of this violent experience is a testimony to their detrimental existence as native products of superimposed constitutive educational and political structures. In this lies the essence of the polarization and bifurcation between elites and masses in the Muslim world.[5]

Muslim and Arab intellectuals, imbued with the Western discourse of rationality, have entered political life as natural allies of the local traditional elites and the colonial West. The broad mass base on the other hand, had no choice but to fall back upon the traditional values of their own society to protect themselves from the excesses of the new class; a class which sought to pattern its life and values along Western lines. Commitment to traditional (Islamic) values thus reflected a defensive posture which aimed at rejuvenating the spirit of internal cohesion and self-identification against the disintegrative effects brought in by patterns of modern life. It further reflected an indigenous consolidation against the danger of destruction of the national balance, perpetrated by external pressures (Ghulyun 1990:242).

Outside impositions of structural formations thus determined the extent and horizons of elite–mass bifurcation. In as much as these formations constituted the nature of elite power and the justification of its appropriative claims to alien systems of validation, to that extent social cohesion and breaking through the cycles of underdevelopment remains an unattainable goal. Their disintegrative consequences, underscored by dislocated elites and insecure masses, and exacerbated by external discursive practices, have turned the national entity in the Islamic world into a condition of social and structural *centrifugality*. Consequently, it becomes almost impossible for the state to deal legitimately with strains upon it, penetrate society, regulate its social relationships and extract its resources. In the presence of such bifurcations and in the absence of an overarching consciousness that unites and merges its subjects at all levels of the social scale in a commonly circumscribed meaning and common criteria of validity, there can be neither strong societies nor strong states. This is a point which Joel Migdal seems to overlook in his study of *Strong Societies and Weak States* (Migdal 1988:4).

Conflicts of civilization/consciousness, however, deprive the parties concerned of the luxury of doubts about their own essential and basic values. It goes without saying that objective material factors contribute to the shaping of human consciousness. A perpetual state of material subjugation of one consciousness to another is likely to elicit tendencies toward subjective submission. At this confrontational juncture, the role of the elites becomes supposedly crucial in countering such tendencies sweeping much of the Islamic world to one degree or the other. In light of the changing nature of polarization on the world scene, secularists/doubters and secular institutions in the Islamic world appear to be least equipped for this daunting task or for handling its civilizational/abodic demands. Isolated from their own societies and, with the end of the Cold War, potentially dispensable to their Western mentors, those elites have found themselves in a twilight zone. Turning more violently against their own people through the power of coercion, the subtleties of democracy and its human rights variant, and peace/alliance with Israel, they have sought to buy their last ticket to redemption. Having nothing to draw upon other than the spiritual and material reinforcement provided by the very adversary they are supposed to challenge, they constitute a submissive condition which extends beyond military overpowerment to the displacement of their vanquished inner consciousness with that of the victor's. In the separate *abodic* configurations of Islam and the West, maintaining and preserving uniqueness and differentiated identities and expressions of consciousness become a prerequisite for survival. This requirement stands in sharp contrast with the words of the Saudi ambassador to Washington Bandar bin Sultan, after the signing of the Gaza-Jericho agreement between Yasser Arafat and Israel, that "everything is possible" (*Kayhan*, September 18, 1993:12). In fact, less than a decade later in 2002, the then Saudi Crown Prince Abdullah presented an initiative which offered Israel full recognition in return for Arab lands occupied in 1967. The following year in March 2003 Iraq was invaded by the US. The Saudi initiative, apparently still-born, was exhumed and resuscitated at the Riyadh 19th Arab summit, held on March 28–29, 2007, at a time when the US appeared to be seeking to build a so-called "moderate" Arab–Israeli anti-Iranian front, targeting its nuclear power project and possibly assisting in any American military attack against Iran. For such a front to materialize without major opposition, the entire region's "*abodic*" identity structure is in fact being altered in order to allow for the antithetical Israeli counterpart to be totally normalized. Islamic Iran, an organic component of the regional identity matrix, and in the same vein as Iraq before it, can then be declared an enemy. Everything, after all, is possible.

Thus, when Bassam Tibi, for example, proposes the secularization of Islam (Tibi 1990a:69), and calls approvingly for a substantive "renewed understanding of Islam" along lines similar to the Christian reformation (Tibi 1990a:9), he fails to distinguish the historical development of Christianity and its nature *vis-à-vis* Islam, or to indicate where the reformation has left Christianity today. He seems to be calling for a wholesale adoption of the Western value system as the infrastructural foundation of modern societies. In those societies, pluralism appears to be a socio-structural correlate of the secularization of consciousness (Berger 1967:126). In return for epiphenomenalizing Islam, Tibi finally throws in the magic word and calls upon the West to generously *democratize* "international social relations," by allowing the integration of the technological-scientific culture in less developed countries (Tibi 1990a:194). The bargain, it may very well appear, is to exchange the Islamic soul and identity for Western technology. That such a bargain can only lead to "torn" societies—of which Huntington cited Turkey as an example (Huntington 1993:42–3), though a country like Egypt would also fit very well—does not appear to bother Tibi. As an example of Said's "native informant" (Said 1979:324), it is difficult to distinguish here between what Tibi says and the Orientalist Sir William Muir's claim that "the sword of Muhammad and the Kor'an are the most stubborn enemies of Civilization, Liberty, and the Truth which the world has yet known" (Hourani 1967:222).

In the final analysis, Tibi deals with Islam within the confines of Western paradigms which simply reduce religion to sociological and cultural epiphenomena, ignoring its distinct claims to validity and its internal communicative meanings. Islam in those terms is comprehended not in light of its own independent standing, but in light of an alien constitutive formation and image. In the process, secularized Arab and "Muslim" elites/intellectuals have come to comprise nothing more than the indigenous instruments of Orientalist discursive hegemony. They evolved into a "class of educated people whose intellectual formation is directed to satisfying market needs," shaped and reinforced by Western "socio-political and economic exchange" (Said 1979:325). Such chronic dependency by elites on Western paradigmatic approaches to understanding themselves and their own religio-cultural expressions lends particular credence to Ali Shari'ati's distinction between elites/intellectuals and "free thinkers" (Shari'ati 1980a:8). Participating in their own "orientalization," the former have entrenched what the Algerian thinker Malek bin

Nabi referred to as the essential and psychological "susceptibility to colonialism" (Nabi 1961:36–7). By orientalizing themselves and objectifying their own consciousness, they have ultimately subscribed to transforming their own societies into colonizable ventures.

Not only that. By virtue of setting pseudo-scientific categories as criteria of validation over the Islamic consciousness, Westernized elites/intellectuals have actually constrained themselves to scientific consumption rather than scientific production. This becomes the natural development once those elites/intellectuals have determined their position *vis-à-vis* their Islamic reality and decided upon abandoning and forsaking it. They embarked on a pre-determined "disengaged/objective" approach which would eventually omit this reality from consciousness, and ultimately from existence (Ghulyun 1990:211).

Tibi's claims, therefore, that assertions regarding religion being embedded in social reality are universally valid and "recognized sociological findings" (Tibi 1990a:187–8), fail to see that sociological and pseudo-scientific validations need not be religiously relevant. Ignoring such considerations allow Tibi to issue a liberal call for the "reduction," "de-sacralization," "secularization," and "doctrinal renunciation of the Islamic claim to superiority" (Tibi 1990a:194), without accounting for the inconsistencies and contradictions inherent in such claims. Nor does he explain why, if such processes were to take place, underdevelopment would be surmounted—a theme which he stresses (Tibi 1990a:69)—overlooking the historical development of the West, the structural constraints imposed by international polarities, balances of power, and strife over limited resources. Valid empirical observations of Western historical experiences need not, after all, be translatable into epistemological conclusions (Mannheim 1970:111). Even if cultural reductionism were to help in surmounting underdevelopment according to Tibi's logic, this would necessarily require surrender at the level of consciousness. Tibi does not address the implications of such surrender nor does it seem to concern him. His Arab and "Islamic" background notwithstanding, he falls into the web of Orientalist discourse, which Said rightly perceived as the "sign of European-Atlantic power over the Orient" (Said 1979:6). It is ironic that, while Said observes the hegemonic propensity of the European culture—"The idea of European identity as a superior one in comparison with all the non-European peoples and cultures," and which seeks always to maintain "the relative upper hand" (Said 1979:7)—Tibi states

A doctrinal renunciation of the Islamic claim to superiority would appear inevitable from the perspective of cultural pluralism. This is in any case a doctrine that today has no material underpinning. As a source of an ideology of intolerance it stands in the way of establishing a true cultural pluralism. (Tibi 1990a:194).

It follows, therefore, that Muslims' existence cannot allow for the perpetuation of such a conflict between two opposed levels of consciousness vying for their common loyalty. One is Islamic, constitutive of their subjective identity, and the other secular-discursive, constitutive of their objective material susceptibilities. This setting calls uncompromisingly for the consummation of a process of divorce between these two anti-thetical levels. While not sufficient, it remains a necessary condition for resolving this "confused" state of affairs, and for creating a clear Islamic consciousness that is dialectically receptive to other systems of knowledge. "Divorce," in other words, while necessary for terminating the Western discourse in its present formation, is at the same time a first step toward furnishing the grounds for a future and inevitable dialogue. The nature of this dialogue and its outcome is to be determined primarily by the parameters of an independent Islamic consciousness.

This breaking-off process therefore, is not to be understood as a call for isolation or for nostalgic reminiscence. Rather, it is a retrenching experience necessary for the independent re-initiation of the dialectics of ijtihad on its own ground rules and as the foundation for an Islamic theory of change. For this reason, Rahman's valid point that early Muslims practiced ijtihad by acting "first upon their experience of the totality of the Qur'anic teaching and introduced the citation of particular verses only at a secondary stage" (Rahman 1982:24) remains wanting. What legitimized such a decision-making process in the first place was the fact that it was made in a world still governed by religious certainty, and undertaken in an environment shaped and governed by Islamic principles. How relevant or possible such a process might be in the absence of a constitutive and politicized Islamic vision, and in an environment shaped and governed primarily by secular, "antitraditional traditions" (Shils 1981:321), remains an open question.

Ijtihad, it is important to note, is preconditioned and cannot be initiated based on an *ad hoc* individual or collective decision. Nor is any genuine and authentic ijtihad possible in the absence of a cleansed Islamic consciousness. Insofar as it becomes possible, the concept of authenticity gains a meaning that extends beyond the nostalgic attachment to the past which can never be again except as a continuous project. As Habermas has pointed out, a "teleological thought that contrasts origin and goal with each other loses its power completely" (Habermas 1987:87). Ijtihad, as authenticity, becomes not only, in Leonard Binder's terms, "the reassertion of the historical truth of the earliest period *of* Islam as the true being of Islam" (Binder 1988:294), but also in a present practical sense the conscious consummation of this process of divorce "as the medium in which modernity makes contact with the archaic" (Habermas 1987:87). Subjugated adaptations to a secularized reality would largely reduce Islam's certainty to the skepticism of a competitive arena of varied "reality-defining ideologies" (Berger 1967:126). Without the requisite milieu, anything similar to what Rahman has called for can only lead to "little more than forcing from the divine texts that particular interpretation which agrees with preconceived standards subjectively determined"; in short, to "juristic opportunism" (Coullson 1964:75, 152) undertaken by *pseudo-ulama*.

LIBERALISM, DEMOCRACY, AND ISLAM:
THE DECONSTRUCTION OF A DISCURSIVE FORMATION

If the Islamic–Western discourse has taken place within the framework of a particular power formation, the liberal-democratic variant represented its most potent constitutive practice. The nature of this power relationship is likely to assume new dimensions of potency given the apparent annulment of the balancing constraints within Western intra-discursive legitimations. Islam is about to engage a liberal democracy invigorated by a fresh victory over its communist archrival, and consolidated by totalizing claims of superiority. That this discourse will have to be maintained and if possible elevated to new heights, necessitates that it be continued with more vigor and perhaps to an extent never known before. In the absence of communism as a challenger in the politico-moral arena, new challengers will have to be created and vanquished, old ghosts will have to be rehashed and exorcised. Islam poses a most likely candidate, and Muslims' commitment to their faith will be tested to the limit.

Democratic discourse basically refers to what in language theory is called an *illocutionary* speech act, where the utterance itself is the act. By saying "democracy" a (self) proclaimed representative moves the particular case into a specific area, claiming a special right or justification by virtue of the "word-act" (Buzan 1991:17). Labeling an individual or group as being democratic or undemocratic in many ways becomes the secular equivalent to the religious affirmation of faith or of excommunication. The "non-democrat" becomes essentially the "non-believer" whose life and property is fair game. This was the discursive tactic used by the US when all other reasons and justifications for the invasion of Iraq in April 2003 had failed or had been exposed. Through such a word-act, means and ends are merged and seemingly inherent contradictions are presumably resolved, away from any accusations of double standards or hypocrisy. For in the name of democracy everything and anything, as well as their opposites, become legitimate or justified. Hence, on the one hand, religion is denied as a legitimizing principle yet makes a sudden and welcome comeback to justify the existence of Israel on religious grounds. On the other hand, when Arabs complain that Israel's means and ends of coming into existence, and colonial actions and policies, are undemocratic, it is not uncommon to hear the retort, which seeks at the same time to steer clear of any details of the matter, that Israel is the only democracy in the Middle East. Essentially it turns out to be a matter of what you win with (*the word*), you play with (*the act*).

If Muslims are to *engage* liberal democracy, it is therefore most vital for them to recognize not only what the latter says, but more importantly what it does not say. They will have to distinguish the "conflicting logics of sense and implication," with the object of exposing the fact that liberal democracy as a text need not say what it means nor mean what it says (Norris and Benjamin 1988:7). In Jacques Derrida's terms: they will have to deconstruct liberal democracy through a rhetorical close-reading which is capable of identifying its language not solely as a reflection of reality, but as a constitutive agent of existence that both influences and structures conceptions (Derrida 1976:lxxv).

An Islamic discursive engagement with liberal democracy necessarily entails the *deconstruction* of the truth/veil, freedom/domination binary oppositions so as to discern their practical meanings to Muslims in contradistinction to their Western manifestations. The privileged first two terms will have to be exposed as "accomplices" of the "violent hierarchy," which controls the latter two terms. Through this method, binary oppositions could be unraveled by showing how a single term carries a meaning and its antithesis in its own structure and helps expose that behind liberal democracy's appropriation of the concept of freedom lies a structure of domination inherent in its very meaning. Eventually, this would provide the opportunity to engage in the political practice of dismantling the logic by which this particular system and its concomitant political and social structures maintain their force (Eagleton 1983:148). This force came to be held in place not by any conclusive logic, but by the dominant impositions of metaphor and rhetoric. As Richard Rorty put it:

> We are heirs of three hundred years of rhetoric about the importance of distinguishing sharply between science and religion, science and politics, science and art, science and philosophy and so on. This rhetoric has formed the culture of Europe. But to proclaim our loyalty to these distinctions is not to say that there are "objective" and "rational" arguments for adopting them. Galileo, so to speak, won the argument and we all stand on the common ground of the grid of relevance and irrelevance which modern philosophy developed as a consequence of this victory. (Rorty 1979:330–1)

In its broadest terms, liberal democracy refers to the limitations and locus of state power (Holden 1988:12). John Hallowell however, indicated that the relationship between liberalism and democracy has historically been so intimate that they were often spoken of as synonymous terms (Hallowell 1973:68). Bertrand de Jouvenal, furthermore, pointed out that "discussions about democracy ... are intellectually worthless because we do not know what we are talking about" (Jouvenal 1948:338). He was faintly echoed by Robert Dahl who observed that "there is no democratic theory—there are only democratic theories" (Dahl 1956:1). Democracy, that is, has become the "loosest label of its kind" (Sartori 1968:vol. 4, 112).

It is not the purpose here to choose from among the many definitions of democracy, but instead to project an *Islamic hierarchy of understanding* on it. As used in this context, liberal democracy will simply refer to the discursive manifestations of the Western world; a discourse that is based on the essential relations and structures of Western liberal democracy which, given all its transformations, remains deterministically unalterable in its interaction with the Islamic system of knowledge. Liberal democracy in these terms reflects *a secular legitimizing principle, representative of the Western cultural and political systems. Through a medium of tolerance, it transfers ultimate authority from the religious domain to the popular realm, and separates public morality, as socially and contingently determined, from private morality, thereby relaxing religious consciousness and its structural cohesiveness without directly confronting it.*

Thus, when John Stuart Mill, for example, argues for protection against what he terms "the tyranny of the prevailing opinion and feeling," and "against the tendency of society to impose ... its own ideas and practices as rules of conduct on those who dissent from them" (Mill 1985:7), a conflict between two inherently conflictive principles is most likely to arise. One Islamic, which defines opinion as an exertion (ijtihad) within the framework of a universal and normative standard of truth, and one secular, where opinion—as a function of a separate private–public conscience—is expressed in the free market.

Contrary to the Western conventional understanding of religion as a social formation, the Muslim Umma defines itself as a religious phenomenon and a conscious Islamic existence. Its essence is defined in terms of the Divine purpose of creation: "I have only created Jinns and men that they may serve Me" (Qur'an 51:56). In light of this purpose, Islamic social and political organization is to be translated and structured. Institutional formations constitute mutual supportive organs of an inseparable private and public religio-morality which encompasses all fields of cultural, literal, artistic, and philosophical knowledge. The Umma, as a will, provides the structural constraining parameters for the creation and preservation of an Islamic consciousness, formed and shaped by, and in harmony with, the precepts of revelation. Consequently, "if the right to be irreligious is won," as Owen Chadwick put it,

the institutions, privileges, customs, of a state and society must be dismantled ... to prevent the state or society exercising pressure upon the individual to be religious if he wishes not to be religious. The liberal state carried on logically, must be the secular state. (Chadwick 1975:27)

In this state, "no social or educational pressure is exerted in favor of one religion rather than another religion or no religion," and thus, there is a total detachment from religious [or irreligious] teaching or practice (Chadwick 1975:27). The secular state, in other words, reduces religion to the level of opinion, leading gradually and inevitably to the secularization of human consciousness.

Much of the potency of the liberal democratic discourse lies in this ability to relax religious consciousness leading to its eventual omission from public life. This it does without making claims to elimination, and without confronting religious consciousness at any stage. In an Islamic context, such a relaxing process or creation of *indifference* can mean nothing but a condition of de-Islamization, and therefore by definition irreligiosity. In its essential characteristics, secularism is irreligious, and therefore anti-Islamic. By extension, so is liberal democracy.

Liberal democracy, thus, does not stand on its own as an independent construct, but as a product of a secular *Weltanschauung* and the constitutive agent of the very violent hierarchy that needs to be reversed. To argue for a liberal democratic political system, as many Westernized intellectuals in the Muslim world do, is to argue for subservience to the discursive and epistemological foundations of the Western *Weltanschauung* which underlies this structural concept. *Liberal democracy, in its practical meaning, becomes a systemic underpinning of secular knowledge, instrumentalized to create open societies susceptible to Western infiltration and domination at both the cultural-intellectual and empirical levels. Ultimately, it becomes the conscious and unconscious instrument of a chronic perpetuation of an inferior and subservient relationship vis-à-vis the West.* These problems constitute structural flaws in the very basis of democracy and not simply, as Fukuyama's triumphalism would have us believe, an "incomplete implementation of the twin principles of liberty and equality upon which modern democracy is founded" (Fukuyama 1992a: xxi). Insofar as it denies any principle superior to individuality, and insofar as it reduces knowledge to individual and collective rational, free market choices, liberal democracy espouses pragmatic and inductive principles consistent with its essential logic. Rationality and motivation according to this logic are determined by the individual pursuance of self-interest defined in material terms. Rationality in this sense becomes a foundational order of knowledge pertaining to the understanding of human nature.

From an Islamic point of view, the claim that a rational human being is one who pursues his own self-interest does not necessarily constitute a metaphysical truth.[6] Rather, it is a manifestation of a *reasoned* self-fulfilling dialectical process, reflective of selective institutional and structural formations. A human being from an Islamic perspective is intrinsically equipped with the necessary qualifications to see beyond his self-interest, and is therefore responsible, guided by revelation, for creating structures reflective of this understanding. This understanding opposes the reductionist approach toward a human rationality incognizant of the non-rational dimension of human essence.

The credibility and legitimacy of an Islamic state order, therefore, is largely based on deductive reasoning, that of liberal democracy largely on induction. Thus, Islamic Shura (counsel) and liberal democracy should not be confused as similar or synonymous. In fact there is a fundamental difference which is methodological and foundational, and therefore essential. Shura and liberal democracy represent two entirely different systems of knowledge—two different epistemologies. A state structure which is by nature bound to constrain individual rational and non-rational choices according to the precepts of the Islamic system of knowledge cannot therefore, in the words of Binder, be a liberal polity (Binder 1988:31). Said therefore was wholly to the point when he defined the purpose of his seminal study on Orientalism

as a step toward an understanding not so much of Western politics and of the non-Western world in those politics as of the strength of Western cultural discourse, a strength too often mistaken as decorative and "superstructural." My hope is to illustrate the formidable structure of cultural domination and, specifically for formerly colonized peoples, the dangers and temptations of employing this structure upon themselves and upon others. (Said 1979:25)

Those dangers and temptations threaten the very foundation of consciousness-formation in the Islamic world through an epistemo- logical displacement which, as Said stressed, is neither decorative nor superstructural. The liberal democratic discourse, as the political manifestation of the predatory Western epistemology behind the veil of freedom, is in effect a consciousness imposition and therefore, by definition, a dominative project. Through its bifurcatory impact, it creates dependent and attached indigenous elites as instruments of this discourse. More than an idea or an organizational principle, liberal democracy emerges as a practical interest which binds the commitments of those elites to the West. For a process of conscious divorce or reversal to be consummated, this whole conceptual edifice will have to be dismantled as an idea, a structure, and an interest— a monumental task, no doubt.

In confronting the Western discourse, Islam can only shape reality rather than adapt to it. If it is to do so, Islam will definitely have to be re-politicized and restored to its true essence as a political religion capable of overcoming historical conditions. Only by reversing the violent hierarchy, which governs much of the understanding of Islam in Western discourses, that is, reverse the Western/Islamic hierarchy (domination/subservience) → Islamic/Western (cognitive openness) à Islamic/Islamic (ijtihad, closure), could Islam become a positive constituent of existence, and only then could it regain its essential characteristics as a *Weltanschauung* in its own right. The alternative can only be a Western discourse of power formation and a perpetually subjugated and demoralized Islamic community.

THE ISLAMIC REVOLUTION OF IRAN: THE END OF A DISCOURSE?

Liberal democracy constitutes in its essence much more than a mere claim to freedom or equality. While freedom is an essential component of it, the concept is not reducible to that component or synonymous with it. In fact it is not reducible to all its declared components since many of its practical and theoretical implications remain veiled and undisclosed. That which is known, in terms of its claims to freedom, justice, equality, popular sovereignty, and so on, is of a certain reductive nature which renders those components distinct from their absolute Islamic equivalents. Claims of compatibility, based on mutually recognized values are, therefore, inherently fallacious and prohibit the process of reversing binary opposites and reverting to essentials.

Binder's claim that "we look in vain for unique ideological elements that will explain the radicalism of those presumably influenced by Sayyed Qutb," whose calls for social justice, equality, freedom, order, and economic justice conform well enough to Western liberal notions, is a typical example of this fallacy (Binder 1988:185). In his expectation that Islam should conform to Western liberalism as the standard of reference, Binder betrays a lack of insight into the dimensional distinctions between religious and secular language. Those ideas, be they expressed by Qutb or any other Muslim activist, are subject to a totally distinct governing principle. Expressed linguistically—in small and capital letters—it is the distinction between social justice and Social Justice, equality and Equality, freedom and Freedom, and so on. Binder's search need not be in vain. In fact, his obsession with stamping Islam with the seal of the liberal bourgeois state betrays a patronizing and condescending discourse which he claims to have set out to avoid. So does his call for the appropriation of religion by the bourgeois ideology so as to preempt its appropriation by some rival, "undesirable" force (Binder 1988:17). In effect, he becomes part and parcel of the power relationship which justifies the ending of what he termed "dialogue."

At the same time, Binder fails to detach himself from the Western linear-causal paradigm of modern development in his understanding of a complex phenomenon such as the Iranian revolution. In a tone of inevitability, he states that the Iranian masses "have not yet emerged from their material, cultural, and moral wretchedness sufficiently to recognize the contradictions between their own interests and the structure of the regime of the clergy" (Binder 1988:214). By implication, no sound, morally healthy, and economically prosperous society could ever be or allow a religiously based government since— reducing issues of consciousness to a matter of interest—the nature of the organic relationship between the clergy and the masses in Iran does not matter. And of course neither does the bifurcation in the Islamic societies between the Westernized elites and the masses, itself caused by the very ideology of the bourgeoisie. What matters is the Western-oriented liberal bourgeois state.

Binder's tone of inevitability echoes a similar expectation voiced earlier by Theda Skocpol. Referring to the Iranian clergy, Skocpol concludes with certainty that:

Those Islamic Jacobins may well endure quite a bit longer than their eighteenth century French predecessors. Nevertheless, they cannot last indefinitely. For when the oil runs out, or if international demand goes severely slack for a prolonged period, then the material basis for an unproductive revolutionary utopia will be gone. (Skocpol 1982:280)

While ignoring the issues of legitimacy and authority in Islamic societies, which the Iranian revolution addresses head on, Skocpol does not make it clear why she arrives at such conclusions. Why, in other words, should the Iranian revolution be anticipated as unproductive? Why would the clergy not be aware of the dangers posed by being a rentier state? And, why would they not be willing to do something about it? Too many presuppositions seem to be involved here which shed doubt on the clergy's ability to handle what perhaps is seen as an appropriated secular domain of competence. Instead of reexamining their preconceptions and the assumptions of their Western paradigms in light of the Iranian revolution as a religious phenomenon and an authentic Islamic paradigm, Binder and Skocpol choose to deny the facts in favor of their presuppositions. The Iranian revolution, that is, could not *be* because the Western system of knowledge has sanctified it that, in a modern world, religiously founded social relations and actions cannot *be*. Thus, Binder lumps the Iranian revolution led by Imam Khomeini with the instrumentalization of Islam by figures such as Sadat, Fahd, and Zia al-Haq (Binder 1988:212), in an attempt to deprive it of its genuineness and authenticity. After all, as he put it, "as mere ideology,

Islam may ... serve any political design" (Binder 1988:212). As if no criteria or system of validation exists or could be developed to determine the parameters of Islamic action. In the final analysis, it is all a matter of convenience, expediency, and interpretations.

Typical of Western methodology and Orientalist approaches to Islam, uncertainties, variations, alleged contradictions with "modern reality," and cultural reductionism are emphasized. This is done in contradistinction to the attempted universalization and generalization of Western liberal democratic values and norms. Such a process appears to be ideologically motivated to weaken the structure of the former while strengthening that of the latter. Binder's work does not strike one as an exception. Neither do the ideological, ethnocentric, and predatory nuances of his discursive work. Instead of coercively denying the authenticity of the Iranian experience, Binder freely projects it into the free market and the murky quagmire of opinions. Since everything is a matter of opinion, cynicism and skepticism become the Islamic criteria of self cognition. Islamic certitude becomes shaken by the founding principles of secular consciousness. "A whole series of 'interests' which, by such means as scholarly discovery, philological reconstruction, psychological analysis, landscape and sociological description," is created and maintained. This takes place through a discourse which is "produced and exists in an uneven exchange with various kinds of power, shaped to a degree with power political ... power intellectual ... power cultural ... [and] power moral" (Said 1979:12). Under the rubric of objectivity, falsely presented as a detached insight into experiences, those interests are presented as necessary knowledge. Objectivity in reality becomes *the reasoned articulation of a discursive bias*. As a claim to detachment after all, it makes no sense other than as being a reflection of a false consciousness—an ideology.

Merely exposing this ideology of *objectivism* however, is not enough. In the absence of alternative concrete and practical criteria, critique offers limited help. Ziauddin Sardar has suggested that only a "steady state" based on the principles of "homeostatic growth, domesticity, social justice and cultural (Islamic) authenticity," could ensure the perpetual move of the Muslim community toward its ideal being (Sardar 1987:248). The Iranian revolutionary experience may be understood and analyzed dialectically, in light of its provision of this steady state. Rather than attempting to fit the Islamic revolution into Western paradigmatic criteria, its structures and processes are to be judged and assessed independently in terms of the above principles.

A prominent consideration is to determine how far the revolution has been able to achieve a steady state as opposed to the chaotic condition pervading most Islamic societies. As a regime, how far has it been capable, through a process of selective growth, to respond to change while maintaining its fundamental, internal balance? The policies of Iran in the post-Khomeini era, for example, can be assessed in terms of their maintenance of the relevant critical variables within identified limits acceptable to the regime's value and organizational structure (Sardar 1987:245).

At the level of domesticity and as part of the Muslim Umma, Iran's policy performance can further be measured in terms of its strategy of "selective interdependence" with other Muslim communities to achieve maximum self-sufficiency and self-reliance (Sardar 1987:246). This would include the process of institutional creation which, on the domestic level, should be capable of establishing social justice, and on the international level of pursuing a foreign policy in light of Islamic principles and interests. Within the context of such formulations, Islamic authenticity should be reflected as the essential criteria of purposeful change. As Sardar put it, this is "the principle that ensures that traditional and cultural values of Islam are not undermined by pursuing goals and policies that on the surface are innocent enough but, in essence, incorporate Occidental values and norms" (Sardar 1987:248). Grand Ayatollah Khomeini's theory of Wilayat al-Faqih could be tested as an innovative reflection of such authenticity and as a criterion for future innovations.

It may be fair to argue that the Iranian revolution has to a large extent achieved a steady state in as far as it has consummated— though not necessarily finalized—the process of divorce from Western discourse and systems of knowledge. While much still needs to be done before the full horizons of Islamic existence are unfolded, the revolution—given its situational constraints—has substantively laid the necessary foundations for a genuine conversation between the Islamic political process and its socially translated existence. In modern Islamic history the Iranian revolution represents the single credible experience that is both theoretically and empirically testifiable. It remains the first genuine and authentic religious phenomenon which has endeavored and expressed the will to comprehensively operationalize Islamic principles. Above all, it addressed the complex issue of the relationship between religious *Legitimacy* and popular will. In short, it provides Muslims with something concrete to work with.

The real significance of the Islamic revolution and its structures of authority as an empirical model have been frequently overlooked by Sunnis. As a result of ignoring that experience as well as Shi'ite jurisprudence, a wealth of knowledge of immense potential benefit to the debilitated state of Sunni *fiqh* and political theoretical development is simply excluded. The fact that Shi'ites have historically been a minority has had its effects on Shi'ite jurisprudence, which provides for *fiqh al-aqalliyya* (the minority). Having been persecuted and weak, it provides for *fiqh al-istidhaf* (the weak/downtrodden). Having never closed the gate of ijtihad, it provides for the dynamism of *fiqh al-ijtihad*—a talent which Sunnis have apparently lost in favor of *taqlid* (emulation), whether of their predecessors or of the West. Having represented opposition to the Sunni ruling establishment, it provides for *fiqh al-thawra/alkhuruj* (revolution), particularly in light of the Iranian Islamic revolutionary experience. Having been able not only to establish an Islamic state but also to institutionalize it under the aegis of the Wilayat al-Faqih principle, it provides for *fiqh al-dawla* (the state). Finally, having been able to deal dynamically with, and to exert increased influence on, the external environment while credibly holding fast to Islamic principles, it provides for *fiqh al'ilaqat al-kharijiyya* (external relations). These six aspects of jurisprudence provide for a comprehensive theoretical, empirical, rational as well as religious corpus of Islamic knowledge. In a reconstructive effort of this kind, Sunni–Shi'ite relations must be seen through a strategic rather than a historical prism.

Within the context of such a foundational structuring, the Iranian revolution has the unique potential to offer two additional and overlapping services to the articulation of an Islamic paradigm. In the context of this experience the issue of *freedom* as perceived by Islam can be de-appropriated and made distinct from its virtual monopolization by liberal democracy. This monopoly allowed the latter system to address the issue of freedom within its own exclusive parameters. While the Islamic regime in Iran has been responsive to political expressions of popular will through voting, elections, and the circular nature of the Faqih–followers relationship, the concept of freedom should not be confused. Islamic Freedom remains subliminal, liberal freedom remains hedonistic. Both understandings of freedom, that is, are different in form, substance, and essence.

Nor should the expressions of popular will be confused with democracy. While the authority of the Iranian government rests on the consent of the people, its *Legitimacy* is based on its commitment to Islam. The Umma, as Binder rightly observed, "is not the constituent power in the sense of originating the constitution. The constitution of a Government of Muslims is the Qur'an and the Sunna" (Binder 1988:130). The Legitimacy of the Islamic government, in other words, is based on a higher principle than the authority rendered to it. Contrary to liberal democracy where legitimacy and authority are derived from the same source of popular obligation, and therefore are two sides of the same coin, the two concepts in an Islamic system are derivatively distinct. *Legitimacy* is derived from upholding the Shari'ah as an approximation of Divine will, and therefore absolute. *Authority* on the other hand, is derived from the control of the instruments of political power, based on the Umma's recognition, and is therefore relative. Thus, while popular will is the determinant of authority as government, both are constrained by an independent criterion of Legitimacy. It is the pattern of interplay between those two components which helps determine the nature and authenticity of an Islamic regime.

One perceived implication of such distinction is that people are deprived of any legitimate claim to abandoning or altering the nature of the Islamic state. While this may be seen as an expropriation of freedom of choice in the democratic understanding, it is important to observe here that as an Islamic criterion, the Umma can provide the government, whatever its nature, with authority, but only its Islamic character will provide it with Legitimacy. Only then could the Umma's consciousness and its socio-political structures be reconciled and harmonized. For this reason, no measure of democracy in the Islamic world will resolve its political crisis of legitimacy. Far from being a solution to the problem of freedom, democracy in fact constitutes the essence of its contradictions. In the absence of the necessary settlement of the issue of Legitimacy, or in Sardar's terms the attainment of a "steady state," liberal and democratic superimpositions will simply exacerbate two destructive tendencies overwhelming Islamic societies to various degrees; conflict among those conscious of their challenged worldview, apathy among those who are not. In either case no society can lead a healthy existence or achieve a steady state.

The second major service that might be rendered by the Iranian revolution follows from the first. As a populist phenomenon, the

Islamic experience of Iran has imaginatively patterned the interplay between religious absolutism and popular relativism in a fashion that narrowed the perceived discrepancies between the two dimensions. Late ayatollah Murtaza Mutahhari once observed:

> It is true that relying on the people generates power for the Ulama but it takes away their freedom. ... A religious leadership which relies on the people is able to struggle against injustices and aggression of governments but is weak and unable to fight the ignorance of the people, whereas religious leaders who rely on governments are powerful in fighting the habits and customs of the ignorant [masses] but weak in fighting the injustices of governments. (Rajaee 1990:69)

Owing to the revolution, the Ulama no longer need to rely on one or the other. The circular nature of the Faqih–followers relationship, in which the former both leads and follows the masses, and the polycentric nature of the religious field, represent the functional parameters of the Islamic state paradigm. Those parameters should be able to restrain the system from turning into a tyranny despite religious constraints on popular sovereignty. At the same time, it allows for the exercise of the Umma's will, as the embodiment of Islamic consciousness, within the parameters of faith.

In those terms, the Iranian revolution offers what the late Egyptian writer Adel Hussein termed a "Grand Strategy." This strategy is capable of ruling the thinking of both government and opposition, thereby controlling contradictions and bifurcations in society. Only then, according to Hussein, could the foundations of any "truly independent nation" be laid, and only through such a strategy could the Iranian revolution's attempts to strengthen the "civil society" within an Islamic polycentric structure succeed (Dwyer 1991:73).

CONCLUSION

An Islamic state, as an existence, is a dialectical condition between socio-political structures and the Umma's consciousness. Both support each other, neither is effective without the other. A Muslim consciousness neutralized by an alien superimposition, and a political regime governed by external principles, constitute therefore the two pronged dominative foundations of the Western discourse. The potency of this discursive formation does not derive solely from its confrontational practice, but more so from its subtle nature and euphemistic language. Its intricacies make it extremely difficult to expose its theoretical and practical meanings and implications without an elaborate deconstructive approach. With the exception of Iran, this discourse has been largely successful in neutralizing the dialectical process of *politics* and *consciousness* in most Muslim countries.

As long as those two poles are kept apart, liberal democracy as a dominative project will continue to slice irresistibly through the Umma's consciousness irrespective of the nature of its ruling regimes. In the process, it will displace political Islam as a promise of salvation rooted in a Western discourse. Unless this veil of salvation is torn down, the Muslim Umma will remain in a perpetual state of spiritual and material defeat. For all practical purposes, liberal democracy may have freedom to offer to the West; for the East, however, it has only domination to impose. The East and the West, after all, are much more than mere geographical poles.

As a religious phenomenon, the Iranian revolution represents a major breakthrough in relation to the discursive formations of the West, at both the theoretical and empirical levels. As a broad typological scheme and a nucleus for an Islamic paradigm and grand strategy, it has contributed immensely to the development of Islamic political theory and to the practice of Islamic authenticity. In light of its typology, organic elite, structural and processes theories could be developed, which eschew the bifurcatory impact of Western paradigms. More concretely, and despite its distinctive characteristics, the revolution provides Muslims with a genuine experience to adopt, to adapt to, or to go beyond. As Ayatollah Muhammad Hussain Fadlallah has observed:

The Islamic Republic of Iran does not claim infallibility in its political guidelines, nor does it claim for itself the representation of the absolute truth of Islam. Instead, it acts, through its responsible leadership, on the basis of what it understands from the actions of the totality of Islamic principles on the detailed conditions of the Islamic movement. (*Kayhan Al-Arabi*, July 1, 1991:9)

6
Liberalism and the Contestation of Islamic Sovereignty[1]

The outcome of diverse but cumulative and consistent Western intellectual traditions has been to penetrate only the shadows of Islamic subject matter rather than its reality. As a result, the intellectual horizon toward which social theory continues to strive in order to comprehend and understand Islam remains seemingly as remote as ever. In the haziness of the shadows, Islam is perceived not as one but many, as a culture not as a religion, as a constructed artifact not a transcendental revelation. Nevertheless, mixed feelings of hope and frustration continued to hover over the scholarly community that social theory may still hold to its promise of providing answers and explanations. However, events, ranging from the Arab–Israeli conflict, the attacks against the United States on September 11, 2001, to the ensuing war in Afghanistan (2001) and its expansion against other Arab and Muslim nations including the occupation of Iraq (2003), have all added to a strong sense of ominous doubt. Two worlds, with divergent and competing value claims, stand face to face on the edge of what may prove to be a fateful collision course. Social theory and its affiliated discourses are unlikely to take a neutral stand, nor observe benign silence. As part and parcel of a consciousness-shaping arsenal, both contribute to conflicting claims and paradoxes. They make liberative claims which are associated with dominating constitutive influences over individuals' innermost mental perceptions.

Contrary to the reading of many, this may not necessarily be the product of intentional scheming or sinister devising minds, but more the effect of inherent ontological and epistemological limitations. Normally, such a problematic might simply have continued to be debated within the relatively safe confines of academia, had it not been for the divisive political and mental structuring affecting popular perceptions on both sides of the *abodic*/civilizational divide. The terms according to which this theoretical and practical "system of knowledge" has been implemented continuously failed to translate positively onto the Islamic landscape. Their secular underpinnings reflected serious tensions with a religion that relegates standards of judgment only to itself, rather than to alternative value systems. It was no coincidence, therefore, that Ernest Gellner reached the interesting inference, made on "rational" grounds, that Islam is a "secularization-resistant" religion (Gellner 1992:6). In this, Gellner may have simply made an empirical observation or arrived at an epistemological conclusion. In either case, what he stated is justified whether one agrees with or contests his conclusion. For by rendering religion a contingent rather than a necessary value, religion is partly or wholly "falsified" (Hodgson 1977:vol. 1, 57). And if self-referentiality constitutes Islam's methodological imperative, then to secularize Islam is effectively to undermine and to overpower this imperative.

This chapter carries on the discursive give and take of the preceding one, expanding and delving into the broader "Liberal" discourse and ideology, and its contending presumptions *vis-à-vis* Islam. This is of considerable importance because ensuing hardening images, real or constructed, will determine how both sides—Islamic and Eurocentric/Western—will continue to see each other as well as themselves, and will significantly shape future actions and influence subsequent outcomes.

CONCEPTUAL MEANS AND METHODS OF CONTESTABILITY

A confluence of varied intellectual constructions and strands have come together over time to exacerbate a sense of contestability among the Muslim community. This was commensurate with a perceived condition of pathological social and political fragmentation. Three broad factors, roughly speaking, may be identified as possible contributing reasons. The first has to do with the theoretical confusion between "a religious view of history and a historical view of religion" (Rahman 2001:198). History understood religiously is marked off from religion comprehended or interpreted historically. This is not necessarily meant in any dichotomous sense, but in terms of the distinct yet symbiotic relationship between the two. Revelation informs history, and history enlightens revelation defined and understood self-referentially on its own terms. They relate as *asl* (stem/foundation) and *far'* (branch/experience), to apply Islamic jurisprudential language, where only in their *unity* do they provide legitimate grounds for interpretation, understanding, and ijtihad. The lack of such conceptualization prodded Charles Adams to observe that the conventional wisdom ... has been that historians of religions have failed to advance our knowledge and understanding of Islam as religion, and that Islamists have failed to explain adequately Islamic religious phenomena. The third factor—increasing Muslim sensitivity to Islamic studies in the West—far from resolving the issue of how to approach the study of Islam as religion to the satisfaction of either religionists or Islamists has created still more strident divisions. (2001:vii)

This has led to "the apparent lack of meaningful relationship between the systematic scientific study of religion on the one hand and the work done by Islamists on the other" (Adams 2001:viii). Striking an optimistic note however, Adams pinned his hopes on the "systematic and phenomenological concerns" absorbed by a new generation of younger scholars at the feet of their religionist mentors (2001:ix).

In practical terms, some Muslim scholars reacting to an acute sense of malaise emanating from the stress of a general crisis, and under the rubric of an undefined "liberal" Islam, have come to project contemporary historical (read Western) experience on revelation, while overlooking the latter's plans for history. Such pitfalls may sound natural in light of the current historical Muslim predicament. However, an Islamic meaning in the *meta-narrative* sense imparts both an anchoring reference point and a framework for conceptualization, two necessary conditions providing for focus and crisis-handling competence. Within this unifying framework of revelation and history, neither the presence of liberalism or democracy nor their absence may have any necessary direct bearings on changing the course of events.

Secondly, social theory has reduced Islam from a meta-narrative to middle ranged categorizations based largely, though not exclusively, on what different Muslim adherents are perceived to say or do. Despite bringing with it a good measure of empathy, methodological momentum privileged what *is* over what *ought* to be, frequently paying little attention to autonomous Islamic standards of judgment. While recognizing the normative ideals of Islam, social theory brought to bear the maxim that religious reality had "its locus in the experience of the devotee" (Adams 2001:ix). This translated into reducing ontology to epistemology, with profound strategic political and intellectual implications. A Muslim counter-dominating response to imperialism, for instance, becomes simply one Muslim experience among others, one that *is* (for example, terrorism), rather than an Islamic response that *ought* to be (for example, jihad/just war). Thus, imperial and colonial experiences become normalized as a relationship of domination with Muslim societies, yet one that presumably does not present a challenge to Islam itself. The organic-epistemological link between Islam and Muslims can hence be severed. Any one Muslim experience becomes as legitimate as the other and, better yet, externally categorized, between "our" Muslims and "other" Muslims. Essentials become blurred by the murky grounds of expediency and discourse; a stark instance of conflicting logics of sense and implication. In those terms, contestability does not mean the mere challenging of an Islamic worldview *per se*, but more seriously the strategy of contesting its essentials, or de-essentializing the faith—hence *essential contestability* and *mystification*. Social theory in its different variants, ill equipped to deal with the revelatory aspects of Islam, ultimately reduces it to a culture, or a functional structure superseded by the imperatives and progressive march of modernity or post-modernity. An Islam subjected to such stratagems becomes less of a religion and more an *opinion* reflecting "many" Islams. This remains an inter-discursive effect despite incidences of Western or Eurocentric intra-discursive debates or disputes.

In such contestation both categorization and secularization, understood as compartmentalization of knowledge and the privileging of epistemology, played crucial roles. One serious outcome has been to contest the foundations of Islamic representation. The sub-field which came to be known as "Islamic studies" categorized Muslim scholarship and societies into two broadly distinct, contradictory and exclusive binary opposites—"Westernized modernists," and "traditional fundamentalists" (Ahmed 2002:200). These were further divided into sub-categories depending on how some observers perceived modernists as reflecting an Islamic experience, and fundamentalists as exhibiting modernist tendencies. In their different divisions and sub-divisions it is not difficult to sense inherent binary verdicts as to who the "good guys" and the "bad guys" might be. The former are "liberal," well versed in Western knowledge, the latter are "extremist," content with their otherworldliness and possessed of an ancient historical dogma. Despite the fact that such categorizations may be best suited for Western political analysis rather than for comprehending Islamic reality, they provided a discursive path followed somewhat uncritically by a good number of (self)proclaimed "liberal" Muslim thinkers. Hence rather than revealing the complexity of Islam, they served to confound it (Ahmed 2002:200), while at the same time building structures of *durable inequality* among categories

(Tilly 1999). Policies which seek to maintain a dominating rule over competing sovereign value structures come to depend increasingly on the erection of inter- and intra-group categorical distinctions as means of de-legitimation. Binary simplifications of this kind comprise value-laden interests and constructions.

The same goes for compartmentalization—the methodological separation and privileging of epistemology over ontology, history over revelation, experience over foundation, and autonomy over heteronomy. Muhammad Abdul Rauf made an insightful point when he noted that the educational system as it historically evolved within the limits of an advancing Islamic civilization has always "expressed the basic Islamic impulse of personal salvation." Never losing sight of the role of education as the medium through which Islamic values are transmitted and perpetuated, "representatives" of Islamic knowledge laid the *usul* (foundations) which safeguarded against any possible divorce between learning and belief in God and the tenets of Islam. This did not mean that all knowledge was solely religious knowledge, but that the notion of an Islamic versus a non-Islamic subject of study, that is, compartmentalization, was neither a legitimate nor an irreconcilable form of categorization. All knowledge was regarded as Islamic, and in its service (Rauf 2001:181).[2] The collapse of this order of things, made susceptible by Muslim scholarly complacency and political tyranny, on the one hand, and then largely brought about by a colonial experience and legacy on the other, exiled Muslims from the natural course of their divine history. "The age of the complete Islamic man, the scholar and traveler," lamented Akbar Ahmed, was long over in the Muslim world, giving way to the age of mediocrity. The *alim* would be reduced to the mere level of a myopic clerk, the pious to that of introverted escapists, the scholar to a self-righteous bigot, and the ruler to a petty tyrant and pathetic figure. "Henceforth, a scholar, saint or ruler would tend to work within his own defined arena reflecting the caste and class system of European imperialism. They would condemn each other with shrill voices employing sterile labels taken from Western scholarship" (Ahmed 2002:200). The end result being to reduce and categorize themselves in Western constructed opposites, largely formulated by whatever the rules of discursive engagement may require. In the process, Islamic texts were being "over interpreted" by forcing upon them inconsistent fictitious counterparts and opening them to an endless array of meanings which cannot or should not, in good conscience, be conveyed (El Fadl 2001:55–6; Eco 1990:23–42). Thus, Islam stands contested on its own ground, undermining its assertion to being a separate and independent guiding principle.[3] It has to be qualified and improved upon or made to fit preconceived preferences.

Thirdly, and following from the above, enter post-modernism with its "incredulity toward metanarratives" (Lyotard 1984:xxiv) and integration of high and low culture (Turner 2002:29). Juxtaposing discourses in an "exuberant eclecticism" and mixing diverse images into unconnected wholes, post-modernism was the latest in the arsenal subverting universal religious conceptions (Ahmed 1992:25). While its skepticism of grand narratives may be justified when applied to the very system of knowledge of which it too is a product, or when applied to pure human thought and institutional constructs, it is by no means a legitimate exercise when applied outside this framework, and certainly not when it comes to religion. In effect, it perpetrates an act of *violence* against Islam, both in its revelatory *and* jurisprudential/thought components. While the discursive sleight of hand has been to claim that one was distinct from the other, this appears to be "a word of truth where error is sought," to quote Imam Ali bin Abi-Talib.[4] The objective in many cases being to establish this dubious assumption as a truism which would then allow the necessary space to invade, subvert, deconstruct, and then reconstruct new meanings in the image of a non- or un-Islamic reality. The purpose is to use an Islamic value system's "stratagems" against itself while not subscribing to its premises, in order to produce in the process a force of dislocation. This force, to quote Derrida again, "spreads itself throughout the entire system, fissuring it in every direction thoroughly delimiting it" (Derrida 1978:20)—essentially that is, deconstructing Islam.

In making claims to the separation of Islamic thought as branch from revelation as foundation, mechanisms of *control* and *durable inequality* (exploitation, opportunity hoarding, emulation, and adaptation) are subsequently set in place. The connection between them rests on the power to narrate, or to block other narratives from forming and emerging (Said 1993:xiii). Here, many Arab and Muslim "intellectuals" are frequently vulnerable to serious qualms. Unlike the lamented *alim*, who both in his successes and failures was at least committed to an Islamic value system, or the intellectuals of nineteenth and early twentieth century Europe who represented the role of "cultural legislators" (Turner 2002:29), both Arab and post-modern intellectuals have come to symbolize something much more unassuming.

Modern Arab intellectuals emerged as faint images of their European colonizers, largely as inter-cultural consumers and interpreters, rather than productive intra-cultural legislators. As such, they never really experienced the relatively sovereign status that their European counterparts at one time enjoyed. Consequently, elites in Muslim countries became mere intellectual reflections of the "other" or the "abode of war," rather than free thinkers, capable perhaps of performing mental exercises, yet uncommitted to the value imperatives of their own societies (Shari'ati 1980a:8), harboring "cool loyalties" to those standards (Turner 2002:27). Their spiritual lifeline and loyalties extended across the boundaries of their own societies. Post-modernity even made things relatively easier. Intellectuals now can argue for a discursively justified detachment from their own societies in the name of cosmopolitanism, irony, and skepticism, covering in many instances for outright indifference and self-centered interests. Intellectuals of this kind "operate within an academic marketplace that is global and largely borderless ... and may be accused of intellectual prostitution, in a context where the marketization of knowledge means a transfer of loyalty and identity to a more ironically indifferent pattern of the global village" (Turner 2002:30–1). The issue of Islamic representation is thus largely circumvented, allowing for the mechanisms of *emulation* and *adaptation* to be introduced smoothly. The former serves to universalize a dominating discourse the latter to entrench a *status quo* based on categorical inequality (Tilly 1999:190–1).

Mechanisms of durable inequality open the door wide for the *essential contestability* of Islam. They serve to reduce Islamic religion to a mere dependent function of a constellation of "other" concepts, largely secular, drawn in to shape comprehension of Islam; an Islam congenial and laudatory perhaps, yet devoid of essentials. The *usul*, or the symmetric, self-referential foundations, which historically maintained and preserved the integrity of Islam both as religion and knowledge, is thus challenged from quarters which have no loyalty to such integrity. Yet it is only interpretive communities with such allegiance, and harboring knowledge, competence, honesty, and commitment, that can make legitimate claims to the representation of Islam. If alternatives to the classical foundations are sought, they must be justified on the basis of being able to perform better at providing for such integral requirements. Before contesting different interpretations, Islam must be recognized for what it is, a revelation, rather than in terms of what it could be made into; the latter contingency being defined in light of the former imperative. Otherwise faith would be controlled by mechanisms outside its pale. Most modern approaches, however, whether hostile or sympathetic, tend inadvertently or otherwise to employ such mechanisms of control or variants thereof.

One reason for this state of affairs is a self-inflicted vulnerability which opened the doors wide to contestability and de-legitimation. The religious and historical development of Islamic epistemology, never separated from ontology, charged the faith with the dynamism necessary for the ongoing process of overcoming and overpowering contestations. In this open process contestation became the very practice of affirmation. Its eventual collapse into a mere set of closed positive commandments/ontological structures (*ahkam*), detached from the process and methodology of jurisprudence (epistemology cum ontology—*fiqh*), led to closed deterministic affirmations associated with a collection of arbitrary and conflicting religious rulings (fatwas) (El Fadl 2001:171). Breakdown in the ontological/ stem–epistemological/branch balance created stagnation rather than an ability to illuminate, comprehend or conceptualize. As a result, calls for Islamic (re)interpretations under the guise of exercising "ijtihad" become nothing more than the mere process of emulation and adaptation to largely un-Islamic settings or qualifying categorizations. Essentially, ijtihad becomes a self-negating objectifying process, where comprehensiveness is substituted for by selectivity, honesty and integrity by fraudulence and duplicity, principled stands by opportunism, competence by incompetence and, autonomy by dependency. Hence, when Islam is contested, this state of affairs cannot rise to the challenge, and at best can only do so defensively, apologetically, or at times simply by lashing out. Islam, through the collapse of its epistemology, no longer overpowers contestation, and is invasively undermined and fissured, losing its autonomous capacities in the process, and thus in need of constant external categorical qualifications. Such a condition inevitably leads to being culturally dominated, and ultimately, in Burhan Ghulyun's terms, to the "assassination of the [Muslim] mind" (1990).

Social theory's irredeemable shortcoming is that it can only deal with Islam as "information," rather than as a revelatory essence and therefore as a source of true knowledge. This is why a non-Muslim who happens to "acquire information" about Islam inside out, can never be legitimately qualified to issue a fatwa. Had information sufficed it may have been possible. Knowledge of Islam, that is, can never be separated from belief—a necessary even if not sufficient condition.[5] This inseparability (re)introduces the foundational principle of incontestability. For as Jacob Neusner has indicated:

> Even though, through philology, we understand every word of a text, and through history, we know just what happened in the event or time to which the text testifies, we still do not understand that text. A religious text serves not merely the purposes of philology or history. It demands its proper place as a statement of religion. Read as anything but a statement of religion, it is misunderstood. (Martin 2001:17)

Intellectually this means that any starting point for observing variations in Muslim life must begin from the defining revelatory premise, followed by symmetrical conceptual extrapolations. Only secondarily, and once the terms of Islamic discourse have been set, can one interact asymmetrically with "external" conceptual frameworks. Cultural variations in Muslim societies may thus be understood in terms of Islam's standing with respect to 'araf (sgl. urf; customs, traditions), and not for instance in terms of "many Islams" whose essence is mystifyingly arcane, trapped beyond empirical reality. A non-essentialist epistemological approach applied to the Islamic concept of Umma, for instance, rather than unifying it by questioning how Islam may help to bring diverse groups together despite cleavages based on ethnicity or unequal economic relations (Ahmed 2002:184), would fragment it by notions of ethnic and gender identities, rendering it one among other concepts, largely meaningless. This as opposed to a Europe which seems for all intents and purposes to be moving toward forming a community of its own based on some perceived notion of European identity that, as of yet, does not appear to exist—a perhaps insightful example as to how the same epistemology and methods applied in different contexts would lead to diametrically opposed results; and also a reflection of what happens when, through this very epistemology, mechanisms and parameters of control are applied.

Consequently, if and when someone uses terms such as liberal Islam or Islamic democracy, it is legitimate to ask where linguistically one might find those terms, "liberalism" and/or "democracy," in Islamic primary and/or secondary sources, in order to satisfy the condition of symmetry. If someone were to argue that by Islamic democracy is meant "*shura*," then one is entitled to ask, why not use the Islamic term with all its connotations and denotations instead? If an argument is made justifying such usage in terms of practical reasons of comprehensibility, then one is still entitled to question the complacency of those who wish not to exert an effort to clarify and recharge Islamic concepts, who are not sufficiently aware of distinctive theoretical, conceptual, and empirical applications, and who ultimately feel it necessary to depend on an external system of knowledge to clarify one's own. For those who fail to see the point, perhaps they need to speculate on what kind of reaction may be elicited were Islamic-laden concepts to be imposed in order to clarify and judge their social theory counterparts. Very likely it will be characteristic of the reaction to a de-legitimizing threat.

Adding to the above queries are claims to conceptual *compatibility* between social theory and Islam. Frequently the question as to whether Islam is compatible with democracy is formulated in such a fashion so as to elicit a polarizing and fragmenting response. Much in the same way that *Amr bin al-As* advised *Mu'awya* (both opponents of Imam Ali) to create a situation in which, if Imam Ali were to accept, disagreement would ensue, and if he were to reject, his ranks would still break down—in contemporary strategic parlance, to lock an opponent on the "horn of a dilemma." The ploy was to raise the Qur'an on top of the spears and call for its invocation as an arbiter between their warring faction and that of Imam Ali. In modern and "changing" times, democracy, invoked instead as the sacred text, is raised on the barrels of the guns. If the Muslim response to the dilemma of Islamic–democratic compatibility is in the affirmative, then ultimately Islam falls under the epistemological spell of social theory, and is consequently contested and mystified. If the answer is negative then they could easily become defensive targets to discursive accusations, of the type of "clash of civilizations" or worse. Alternatively, if the response is equivocal, with some adherents saying yes, others saying no, then a polarized situation is created in their societies, allowing convenient space for social theory's epistemological "management of crisis"—supporting "our Muslims" against "other Muslims." Muslims are thus situated in a seemingly lose–lose situation. This visibly reflects on their performance in all domains—whether they wage war, make peace, conduct negotiations, engage in dialogue, set a plan, conceptualize, attempt organization, or whatever the case may be. Consequently it becomes much easier and more credible to put the blame for failure at the door of the "irrational" Islamic belief system, to contest its universality and henceforth its relevance and legitimacy; the necessary prerequisites and very processes inherent in goals of cultural domination and identity reconstruction.

Three further challenging implications appear to me to be associated with the way the issue of the compatibility of Islam and democracy is formulated. First Islam, a worldview, is reduced to the level of a democratic concept. Second, it is then linked in this reduced and particularized re-conception, in a de-privileged *contingent* relationship to the alternatively universalized and *necessary* democratic tenet. If democracy, broadly and substantively speaking, is understood here as a secular legitimizing conceptual principle, then we have an interesting process where Islam is reduced to a concept, then linked to another concept belonging to an alternative secular worldview, as a means of subsuming the Islamic worldview under secular principles. Third, it mystifies first by obscuring that worldviews and concepts ought to be compared and contrasted with their respective counterparts, not with each other; Islam *vis-à-vis* secularism, and *shura*, for instance, *vis-à-vis* democracy. And second, by concealing the real question that ought to be asked: is Islam as a worldview compatible with secularism as an opposing counterpart and organizing principle? By willingly and enthusiastically engaging in the deceptively benign formulation of compatibility, as "liberals" tend to do, Muslims end up relinquishing their right to being subjects of history in favor of being its objects. Essentially and rather incontestably, they undermine their standing by applying the very mechanisms of durable inequality upon themselves. In the process they block their right to an alternative narrative.

CULTURAL DOMINATION AS A DISCOURSE OF DE-LEGITIMATION[6]

Cultural domination recalls the Khaldunian observation about the proneness of the "vanquished" to emulate the victors, in the hope that imitation would alter their condition of defeat (Issawi 1958:53). The irony is that usually it does not, particularly when the emulator objectifies himself, and instead becomes the very source perpetuating the condition of subjugation as it keeps reproducing the mechanisms of control and their blocking narratives. While the general Arab and Muslim colonial experience over the past two hundred years or so attests to this, there remained one major obstacle that incessantly prohibited the total subjective transformation which Ibn Khaldun had alluded to—Islam. It proved impractical for social theory to commit a direct act of "violence" against the Qur'an, the formidable repository of Islamic certitude (whether intentionally or otherwise is totally irrelevant), which had proven immune to secularization or to the kind of textual critique applied to biblical scriptures. The onslaught took the different approach of undermining Islamic tradition and institutions. By making claims that Islamic thought was all a matter of interpretations and, therefore, mere human knowledge (Soroush 2000), the ground is set for alternative "modern" interpretations. Yet, in the absence of a functioning Islamic epistemology, these "interpretations" in most cases, constitute nothing more than a mere process of adaptation and emulation, that is, mis-interpretation. Both mechanisms contribute to softening the subjective setup of the "object" while commensurately facilitating exploitation and opportunity hoarding. The first step, it would appear, is to deprive Islam of its cognitive structures or thought; as a precursor to contesting the Qur'an and *Sunna*, given that cosmo-normative structures isolated from a cognitive shield are presumed to be highly vulnerable (Luhmann 1990:230). Khalid Abou El Fadl rightly asserted that both the Qur'an and *Sunna*, as the primary sources of Islam, were irrevocably interwoven and intertwined with the juristic tradition such that to negate one is inexorably to deconstruct the other (El Fadl 2001:175).

Legitimate Islamic (re)interpretation must always remain rooted in the three concentric circles/closures of belief structures—a sacred worldview, principled beliefs, and causal beliefs (Goldstein and Keohane 1993:8–10). Commensurate with these closures, respective determinations must be made among signs and references to Islam, the Islamic, and the "Islamicate" (Hodgson 1977:vol. 1, 57). When one talks about Islam, one is referring to the universe and cosmology of revelation as uniquely represented by primary texts and scriptures. Hence there is only one Islam, and not many Islams. To make such a claim reflects a contradiction in terms, for there is only one revelation not many, and besides, if there are many Islams, what is "common" or "essential" among all of them so as to justify referring to supposedly different manifestations of a "phenomenon" with the same term? In the second closure or level of normative principled beliefs, one may talk about that which is *Islamic*, referring to the symmetrical and self-referential elements of jurisprudence. The "Islamic" of course may refer to more than one, however, in its diversity, it remains finite and delimited. Finally, at the causal beliefs level of closure, one may engage in the broad pseudo-infinite Islamicate manifestations of *'araf* (sgl. *urf*; cultural customs), or the asymmetrical interaction between Muslims and their environment, which Islam or that which is Islamic approves of, enjoins, condemns, or is silent about (Hodgson 1977:vol. 1, 58).

Within this framework of closure and openness—which conceptualizes the systemic *self-referential* unity and dynamic give-and-take between the universal, the macro/abodic, and the micro/local—it may become more possible to discourse with control mechanisms of durable inequality on more leveled grounds. By contrast, the analytical framework of social theory—which de-links the innermost circle(s) from its whole, adaptively reconstructs it by infusing it synthetically with alien conceptual structures, refitting it as "many Islams" rather than an Islamicate construct, while ignoring or rendering irrelevant the universal closure—constitutes a most subtle fissuring, contesting, mystifying, and therefore de-legitimating exercise. While short term and partial perceptual intellectual satisfaction may ensue, this is likely to be at the expense of the integrity of the whole.

THE MUSLIM CRISIS: AN ISLAMIC VIEW OF HISTORY

Few would contest the fact that Muslim societies are facing a deep existential crisis, living in a contemporary world governed by challenging control mechanisms and subverting values. *Crisis*, as understood in medical usage, "refers to the phase of an illness in which it is decided whether or not the organism's self-healing powers are sufficient for recovery." Inherent in a crisis condition is "the idea of an objective force that deprives a subject of some part [large or small] of his normal sovereignty. [Hence] to conceive of a process as a crisis is tacitly to give it a normative meaning—the resolution of the crisis effects a liberation of the subject caught up in it" (Habermas 1976:1).

Both subverting values and their control mechanisms allow fewer and much more limited possibilities for the Islamic value system to solve problems than are necessary for its continued existence. Both perpetuate a persistent dynamic of disturbances to system integration, rendering its very survival at stake. Crisis assumes intolerable proportions as it precipitates the disintegration of value-producing institutions and impairs the consensual foundations of normative structures so as to render society anomic (Habermas 1976:2–3). A serious reflection of such anomie is the undermining of social consensus toward religious representation. This constitutes a condition and strategy of contestation and de-legitimation, since it is only when the meaningful perspectives of different groups are brought into agreement that institutional socio-religious action becomes possible (Luhmann 1989:x).

The contemporary world, as observed by Abdolkarim Soroush, having become the "ethical inverse of the old world," has brought about the dreaded apocalyptic prophecies of Islamic revelation, where passion overpowers reason, the internal is dominated by the external, and where traditional vices have become modern virtues. This inverting dynamic has become the life blood and fuel of present life, as a new "morality" displaced the official books on ethics. A transformation of values, freed from internal constraints of traditional piety, maintained the new order, social, legal, and political, through the invocation of an autonomous system of checks and balances (Soroush 2000:43). This system espoused a certain mode of command, but not the virtues of "justice" and "piety" in the broadest moral understanding of both.

If such readings are true, few should then wonder as to why Islam and secularism will remain in conflict, why a sense of deep crisis permeates the Muslim psyche, and why a liberal and/or democratic order of checks and balances is viewed with suspicion. The formidable challenge that a so-called "Islamic liberal-ism" will have to confront is how to make credible its ability to create a "liberal" order which at the same time preserves and consolidates Islamic principles of religiosity. So far, this has not gone beyond paying lip service to Islamic values while propounding mostly secular liberal tenets. Essentially, Islamic raw material is manipulated to build up a Western discourse, with some Muslim intellectuals opportunity hoarding by twisting this material to emulate and adapt Islam to its ethical "exploitative" opposite. The thrust of this effort has fallen into sheer pragmatism, or the historical understanding of religion. Most polemics and counter-polemics between liberal Muslims and their opponents tend to be conceptualized within this framework. Liberals explaining Muslims' crisis in terms of failure to adopt Western values, wholesale or adaptively; hence their sloganeering "democracy is the solution." Religionists claiming that Muslims have abandoned God, who in turn has abandoned them;[7] hence their sloganeering, "Islam is the solution." Both opposed explanations however, seemingly remain wanting as one party discourses at the *secondary* "free will" level of causality, the other at the *primary* "predestined" counterpart—a dialogue of the deaf of sorts.

In what follows therefore, I shall briefly attempt to suggest elements by which a religious/Islamic conceptualization of history may be construed, touching upon principles of free will and predestination, but certainly not attempting to resolve their complexities. The purpose is to attempt to provide some sense of the extant crisis in terms of Islamic "imagery." This is done rather heuristically, with no intention of arriving at any final conclusions. At the outset, it is important to point out that to justify modern progress and development solely in terms of Western liberal values is to make claim to a one-to-one correspondence between those values and the end sought; the same causes and/or inputs would produce the same effects and/or outputs. This has been rendered a potent argument given *default* perceptions juxtaposing both as historically and organically linked. Yet in many ways, this constitutes a denial of the relevancy and imperatives of historical contingencies and accidents which could very well lead to same causes and inputs producing totally contradictory results. In the language of the religionists such "unknowns" are understood as divine intervention or will acting upon history as it unfolds according to God's own predestined plan; not always in ways understood by people, but where revelation provides meaning. While Christopher Columbus, for example, may be said to have exercised his free will by embarking on a voyage to find an alternative route to India, only to discover the Americas in 1492, nothing of his own necessitated that he make such a discovery. It was a contingency in secular language, predestination in religious idiom. With all the wealth, opportunities, and newly opened horizons that the discovery of a new world brought about, it was time for the "sovereignty" of the *Rum'*—the West. Every Umma, be it Islamic or non-Islamic, as the Qur'an states, has its own divinely appointed time, both a beginning and an end.[8] This time frame, from an Islamic perspective, constitutes the context of predestination and free will (social theory may refer to this same framework, reduced to secular history, as *dialectics*).[9] Opportunity hoarding, emulating and adapting to secondary causes, which less fortunate nations resort to in order to enjoy the fruits of the "sovereign" nation, or to accelerate its downfall and, by implication, their own rise, are all likely to fail, in reality *or perceptively*, in this religious view of things. For it may not be meant for them to adopt values largely inconsistent with those of revelation,[10] nor may it be meant for them to be sovereign if their time is not yet due, nor could inheriting the sovereign nation be expedited as divine will cannot be rushed, and is totally autonomous of what man wills, desires, or covets.[11] This is a matter of predestination, where human free will has no direct power to determine the unfolding of events. Claims to the contrary constitute the arrogance of power.[12]

From this line of argument, it would appear at first glance that one is inevitably led to arrive at a logical conclusion which denies much room for human agency. However, the Divine law of circulation (*tadawul*) and succession (*istikhlaf*) of nations affirms human will rather than denies it, even if within the very limits of divine purpose.[13] While what a community of people, faithful and unfaithful alike, may do or not do would neither extend nor expedite the appointed time of the sovereign nation, their freely willed actions determine whether they shall be entitled to or excluded from the right to succession.[14] Furthermore the possible confluence of their efforts, even if at one time seemingly incoherent, insignificant, or ineffective may ultimately coalesce at a specified future time to offer coherence, significance, and effectiveness.[15] One is tempted to speculate whether if Imam Hussain had not been martyred in Karbala' in the seventh century CE, in a seemingly futile effort to oppose corruption, an Iranian Islamic revolution would have occurred in the twentieth century.

The very process of emulating and adapting to the values of "sovereignty" will not, therefore, be the source of salvation since, as sovereignty runs its course, so will its values. Control mechanisms tie the fate of the seemingly "less fortunate" to that of the supreme nation and its appointed time. As the real representatives of those values reach their assigned course, the same fate may very well await their fake imitators.[16] The latter therefore are on the receiving end of the worst of all worlds, neither sovereign nor inheriting, never really knowing how to walk properly, yet having forgotten how to fly.[17] An outcome that liberal Muslims should perhaps ponder, as they embark on their discourse of liberal-democratic salvation.

By the same token there appears to be no inherent reason for Islamic religionists to arrive at the pessimistic conclusion that the disenchanting condition of Muslims is a sign of divine punishment and displeasure, and therefore abandonment by God. The Prophet and his companions were chased out of their homes and properties, they were soundly defeated at the battle of *Uhud* (625 CE/3 Hijri), and almost extracted at the battle of the *Ditch* (627 CE/5 Hijri). This was not necessarily a sign of divine displeasure. At the same time, the Post-Guided Caliphate (632–661 CE) Islamic empire continued to expand and grow in wealth and power under a largely corrupt Umayyad dynasty, whose most notorious accomplishments were to massacre the family of the Prophet (*Al al-Bayt*). This was not necessarily a sign of divine pleasure. If there is no essential one-to-one correspondence between Western values and mundane success, however this may be defined,[18] neither is there inevitably a one-to-one correspondence between Islamic piety and devotion on the one hand, and material wealth and power on the other. Piety and devotion would have been too easy and, in fact, too "enjoyable." The divine law of succession must apply to Muslims and non-Muslims alike, otherwise a *sunna* or law of God would be countered. The historical loss of Muslim sovereignty may of course be legitimately explained in terms of divine punishment for Muslim frailties. But it may also be just as legitimately explained in terms of a divine testing of their faith and fortitude in preparation for future divine purposes; a trial and "weeding out" process.[19] The former pessimistic fallback need not carry more weight than the latter optimistic outlook.[20] However, which view Muslims uphold will have serious implications for their self-image and morale. Pessimism would render them mentally and psychologically fettered by counter de-legitimating epistemologies and discourses; simply blaming their failures on the West, while also hoping for salvation from the West—the West gives the West takes.[21] Such a situation could very easily erupt into pseudo-nihilistic chaos emanating from utter despair, or, as the West becomes Muslims' "fate," turn into servile susceptibility to overpowering discourses of domination bearing the false signs of a natural order.[22] Alternatively in order to make informed decisions and choices in a difficult situation a sense of liberated conceptualization and meaning becomes necessary; meaning being a "determinate strategy amongst alternative possibilities" (Luhmann 1989:x). Optimism would re-energize Muslims' missionary zeal, re-inspire confidence in their heritage and what they already have, and knowledge-wise perhaps assist in unfettering their minds as free, capable, and worthy subjects of history and of God.

"Islamic liberalism" and its discontents

People, as James Baldwin observed, "are trapped in history and history is trapped in them" (Hall 2002:1). This is particularly true when it is a revealed history. Islam and history constitute the inseparable components of an unfolding sacred plan; hence Islam as a "secularization-resistant" religion. Yet apparently this is the type of resistance that modern Muslim liberalists are seeking to overcome. Their professed claim, in the name of freedom, is to liberate Muslims from the limiting confines of their own history and by extension from the sacred.

In the typical fashion of identifying a "dissenter"—celebrating him as exemplary of a cause, stage-managed to undermine an "undesirable" order, political or religious—Robin Wright, "and many after her," have acknowledged Iranian intellectual Soroush as the "Luther of Islam" (Soroush 2000:xi).This is pointed out by the Iranian translators of Soroush's work so as to endow the claim with Western authorial weight. They go on to state that "if as the Christian West has shown, the establishment of, and disenchantment with, a visible 'City of God' leads the way toward the 'Secular City,' then Islamic civilization is on the verge of a decisive and familiar breakthrough" (Soroush 2000:xi). Islam that is, must have its "Luther," its "Reformation," and its "secular" historical dynamic, otherwise, it has no history or for that matter, no future. One is disposed to conclude they do not recognize any autonomous space for Islam's own dynamics. An autonomy which allowed two non-Muslim intellectuals to observe that, within Islamic tradition, critical Muslim intellectual practice takes a "tajdid/renewalist" rather than a "romantic" or "scientistic" form (Esposito and Voll 2001:11). An observation consistent with the Prophetic tradition to the effect that God will send at the head of every century (read interval of time) someone to renew the religion of the Umma. The former reflects an empirical observation, the latter establishes an epistemological principle. Nothing in Islamic history therefore suggests the experience of a city of God collapsing into a secular city as a legitimate or stable condition along Western lines. By extension, if democracy is the most inspiring legitimating principle of the secular city, and if Islamic history may not be secularized, then a democratic interjection is unlikely to solve the crisis of legitimacy in Muslim societies. Democracy, more than a mere voting mechanism or procedure, is a value-laden principle incorporated in a secular epistemological whole. Applied in other than its historical context, it could very well become a discursive instrument of domination, mystification, and contestability.

By all means such discourse may carry a liberal element with it to Muslim societies, but not necessarily freedom nor salvation. The subtle yet substantive distinction between liberal manifestations and freedom must not therefore, be lost. On the one hand, captured in a history not of their making, Muslim consciousness and will become "locked" into and captivated by a specific categorized authoritarian and uncontested historical determinism, presented as inevitable, final, natural, and conclusive (El Fadl 2001:93). Giving up on their sovereignty Muslims as a result forsake their freedom. On the other hand, breaking the sacred *covenant* (Islam) linking their history to the divine, they renounce their justification to *vicegerency* (*khilafa*) and hence their worthy claims to salvation.[23] In the Islamic universe, vicegerency entitles mankind to *representation*, and is the underlying cause behind man being created, as an act of divinity, in the image of God. The legal implications of this principle allow members of the covenant, if not to speak *for* God—the prerogative of Prophets—then to speak *in* his name. Mankind's role and purpose on earth is derivative from this permanent *covenant* as conditioned by divine revelation. When a people rupture the necessary connection between Shari'ah and the purpose of their existence (some may call this 'secularism'), in a fashion perhaps similar to a renunciation of citizenship, the covenant is broken and their right to representation/vicegerency is no more. This is why in Islam apostasy is considered, in principle, to be a capital crime, not simply because it constitutes a betrayal of the Muslim community or state, as some scholars have suggested (Moussalli 2001:6), but because it is the ultimate rebellious forfeiture of purpose, right, and honor of vicegerency/representation. Delving into the relationship between Islam and liberalism or democracy, the uniqueness of such cosmological and conceptual intricacies and complexities must not be underestimated or overlooked.

This is not to obscure the fact that some Muslims are more expressive of faith than others and are therefore liable to bear higher authoritative and representative responsibilities than others.[24] By way of analogy, all citizens of country X may be argued to commonly represent country X's values in one way or the other. This is the case despite the fact that individually they may hold diverse opinions about almost everything and have different capacities and competence. However, some overarching commonality of *citizenship* binds them together. Thus, their attitudes, behavior, culture, civility, and so on, reflect on their country's image. By the same token, some citizens represent country X more than others. An ambassadorial emissary represents his country more than an ordinary citizen, given his training, competence, position, and consequently the authority vested in him, to directly speak in the name of his own country, or indirectly and by delegation, for his country. This does not deny the right of ordinary citizens to still speak in the name of country X as members of its citizenry, but what we are talking about here are *different levels of representation*. A *legitimate* head of state constitutes an even higher order of representation where it may be claimed that not only does he speak *in* the name of country X, but actually *for* country X, having possibly decided on a particular policy course among other options, perhaps even contrary to options preferred by significant parts of his citizenry.

Thus, to claim that divine will is indeterminate and that *fiqh/*jurisprudence (literally *fiqh* means understanding or comprehending with progressively higher levels of insight) is a mere reflection of human interpretations is only partially true. For if one can never determine divine will, then revelation becomes largely superfluous. If religious interpretative constructs are mere opinions, then this is to deny the hierarchy of representation and levels of meaning. Islamic *mazaheb* constitute one conspicuous manifestation of such an exercise.

At the causal-Islamicate level each and every Muslim is entitled to his own ijtihad or representative views that bind him personally, given his diligent and *bona fide* grasp of his faith. On the collective plane of principled Islamic beliefs however, this can only be done by a group or class of people qualified and competent to make such representative decisions, both in religion and in politics—politics being the institutional realm in which contested interpretations and conceptions are played out, re-infusing faith with epistemological vigor. Hence the inseparability of religion and politics, and hence the Qur'anic injunction to obey those charged with authority (4:59), that is, those of a standard most competent and qualified to speak in the name of God. Perhaps therefrom comes the Prophetic tradition that "every *mujtahid* is correct" (El Fadl 2001:33). And it is in this sense and by right of principled ijtihad that Grand Ayatollah Khomeini's theory of Wilayat al-Faqih has come to constitute a crisis-solving principle which sought to reclaim Islamic representation and sovereignty, translated into action.

Many "liberal" Muslims, and other scholars, in their presumptions about Western values, tend to overlook the crucial importance of such matters for the reinstatement and reconstruction of the consensual basis of representation in Muslim societies. This is a precondition for challenging mystifications associated with issues of legitimacy, governance, and methodologies of social sciences and essential con-testability. Charles Kurzman (1998), in his edited collection of essays by Muslim liberals, provides a case in point. He includes, among others, figures such as Mohamed Arkoun, Muhammad Said Al-Ashmawi, Benazir Bhutto, and Fatima Mernissi. In the absence of a standard of levels of discrimination, the representative adequacy of their opinions becomes both unclear and questionable to say the least. Certainly as Muslim individuals they are entitled to the common and general right of representation. One should never lose sight, however, of the fact that Islam is a system of values, beliefs, and commitment, not simply of information. And while an individual's faith is an exclusive relationship between that individual and God, there always exist markers (*dalalat*) by which it is possible to observe and distinguish interested knowledge from disinterested intellectual information (or for that matter, from mere manipulation), instrumentalization or diverging claims from intended purposes and implications. These markers pertain to the level of *credibility*, based in some cases on narrower and formally articulated standards, in many other instances on broader informal Muslim recognition, and still in other situations on the interplay between both standards and recognition. Of course this cognitive structure must be set in the broader cosmological and principled closures of Islam and the Islamic.

Much of the liberal effort is geared toward expanding the non-religious space while limiting that of the religious. Kurzman identified "three principal modes" of liberal Islam in this regard (1998:13–18). The first mode claims liberal positions to be sanctioned by Islamic law. Essentially, that is, the Shari'ah is liberal, a claim for which support is selectively sought from Islamic sources. The problem of course is that counter non-liberal justifications can also be put forth. A belief system which incorporates both liberal and non-liberal manifestations within its value structure, or cuts across both, cannot therefore be determined to be one or the other, but will rather be independent of both.

The second mode seeks to take advantage of areas perceived to be outside the pale of the Shari'ah or about which the Shari'ah is presumed to be silent. In such instances liberals emphasize human independence and ingenuity, in addition to the legitimacy of borrowing from other people's knowledge experiences. This includes the insights and methods of social theory and its liberal values. However incorporation of social theory, liberal or otherwise, in Islamic methodology for "evolutionary" purposes (cognitive openness) must be continuously subject to Islamic normativity and its methodological limitations (see Teubner 1989:750–1; 1993:60, 48).[25]

The third and most common mode of liberal discourse stresses the distinction between revelation and interpretation, the latter set in the realm of pure human knowledge. However, while ijtihad by all means allows for varied yet informed religious opinions, this is very different from being a free market of all opinions.[26] Otherwise, we are faced with a situation in which the Shari'ah is practically reduced to mere human interpretations bearing no more weight than any other opinions of the learned or free market type, religious or irreligious (Chadwick 1975:27).

Thus, when Mahmoud Mohammad Taha (d. 1985) in his "Second Message of Islam" engages in a rather acrimonious interpretive exercise to argue that first-generation Muslims did not receive the actual and intended message of Islam because they were not ready for it, one is certainly struck into paying close attention. According to him, while revelation incorporated both messages, the companions were introduced to dogma or the first message of Islam pertaining merely to external and apparent submission (al-zahir; the exoteric) (Taha 1998:271–2). The second message of Islam previously abrogated and yet to unfold constitutes true Islam in its essence (al-batin; the esoteric). Beyond dogma it will represent real knowledge and the real essence (Taha 1998:272). So far so good, but what is the nature of this true message of Islam? Sure enough, it is socialism by reason of economic equality, democracy by reason of political equality, and both socialism and democracy by reason of social equality. Socialism and democracy reflected the original and intended divine revelation, but which the society of the companions of the Prophet, being below required capacities and standards, could not grasp (Taha 1998:280–3). In one masterstroke both secular ideologies are provided with theological foundations—they become revelation in its highest manifestation.

The introduction of the notions of a first and second message of Islam is apparently an attempt to circumvent the uncontestable Islamic doctrine of finality of revelation. The idea seems to come to Taha from the first and second coming of Jesus Christ, which is recognized by Muslims, despite the "seal of Prophethood" doctrine. How such eclectic ideas may contribute to the cause and credibility of "liberal Islam" remains a question of interest. For implied in Taha's argument is that the first message is irreconcilable with modern ideological constructs, since this can only be the case with the second and real message. Now if it may be argued that the first message is also the final message, then we have a situation here whereby Taha's very logic supports his opponents' very objections against such ideologies. The polemics that are likely to emerge out of such contestations and mystifications are predictable, and in the case of Taha have in fact been tragic.[27]

Mohamed Arkoun also seeks to "rethink" Islam, justifying it by the need to think about what was made "unthinkable" by the triumph of orthodoxy, and the need to open new horizons of knowledge through a systematic cross-cultural approach to problems of human existence (Arkoun 1998:213–14). Orthodoxy is then set within the framework of discourse of power, and judged accordingly (Arkoun 1998:209). Nothing is inherently illegitimate about this approach, although some of its methodological limitations need to be noted. The first pertains to the ambiguity of the concept of power which beyond its immediate coercive manifestations may turn out to be both all inclusive and *unfalsifiable*. On the one hand, anyone who does not happen to believe in the Prophethood of Muhammad or the revelation that he received may have no compunction about attributing all or at least most of his actions and motives to a search for power. For a believer, on the other hand, the whole issue of power is a non-issue and a non-starter. By the same token, Imam Ali, a paragon of piety and knowledge, believed himself to be entitled more than anybody else to the succession of the Prophet. Was he simply an ideologically motivated power-hungry person and would a framework of power allow us to understand his motives and intentions? Do not the substantive elements of piety and knowledge account for something? If they do, then one can conclude that Ali was right and Mu'awiya was the transgressor. If not, then basically Ali and Mu'awiya are simply two men of the same caliber. If such are the contrasts, should not these concerns be dealt with self-referentially rather than cross-culturally, even where the matter of "power" does arise?

Arkoun further claims that the idealization of the Prophet, and other companions, by Sunnis and Shi'ites alike, were simply legitimizing constructions of a developing community; the product of Qur'anic discourses and myths (Arkoun 1998:219). Yet, the Prophet cannot be said to be idealized to the extent that idealization reflects human constructions. For if the Qur'an clearly states that the Prophet is of "unimpeachable character" and a "universal mercy" this sets him as a standard by a source autonomous of mankind.[28] By definition this constitutes true knowledge, not constructions, perceptions, or myths; unless of course the Qur'an is dealt with simply as a source of myths and discourses. Perhaps Arkoun's purpose is to shock and challenge "orthodoxy." Yet if this is the case why not do so while attempting to preserve the integrity of the religious field. For instance by thinking about the "unthinkable," and reconstructing the Islamic history through a common Sunni–Shi'ite framework of comprehension—the comprehensive view emerging from taking both power and opposition into account. Not by any means to score points or to prove who is right and who is wrong, but to overcome scholastic and theological boundaries which render any view of such history largely partial. A unified comprehensive framework may then open the door of opportunity wide for epistemological and juridical renewal—perhaps through a new collection of *ahadith* (sgl. *hadith*) incorporating all the Prophetic traditions unanimously agreed to by both Sunnis and Shi'ites.[29] After all, how could there be a cross-cultural dialogue when among themselves, Muslims are unable to have one. But then if the integrity of the Islamic space is not Arkoun's purpose or main concern, why should he attempt any of the above? What matters is the superimposition of a post-modern discourse of power on Islamic knowledge. In this case we may perceive secular and liberal tendencies. However, other than the fact that Arkoun talks about Islam using Islamic raw material to build up a post-modern discourse, one is entitled to ask what is Islamic about his liberalism.

In the same "liberal" vein, though perhaps more philosophically oriented, Soroush argues that while revelation is sacred, human interpretations are perceptual, and are socially and historically determined. They can thus be freely challenged in light of age-bound contextual requirements. Religious texts, like other non-religious ones, are theory-laden and based on contingent presuppositions, and therefore subject to expansion and contraction according to the assumptions preceding them. And since it is only through such presuppositions that one can hear the voice of revelation, "religion itself is silent" (Soroush 1998:244–5). Now that religion has been silenced and reduced to mere interpretations, enough space for the free reign of liberalism and reason is generated. All the while keeping those who want to hear that Islam is a revelation happy—provided of course that it is silent. This is not by any means to cast suspicion on Soroush's frame of reference or to attribute any ulterior motives to his approach. As a matter of fact his objective of reconciling revelation and reason through the union of Shari'ah, *irfan* (mysticism), and philosophy is laudable and insightful. However some methodological and consequential risks do pertain. If revelation is silent to what extent can the floodgates be opened to external systems of knowledge without undermining the integrity of Islam, the Islamic, and the Islamicate, or is it only to be opened for *irfan* and philosophy? Constituted and reinterpreted according to the principles of philosophy (Soroush 1998:246) how, when and where can the Shari'ah become a *constitutive* agent based on its own principles and derived presuppositions? And then of course there remains the important and conventional question as to how a universal revelation sent to all mankind could be commonly born, together with the hefty weight of philosophy and *irfan*. This would appear to be a specialized branch of knowledge attainable only by a small group of elites. With the claimed silence of revelation and with so much space available, what constraints are there to guard against contextual and external mechanisms of control and counter blocking narratives? The highly regarded Muhammad Iqbal was very supportive of Mustafa Kemal Ataturk's Turkey, which according to him had exercised "ijtihad" and consequently abolished the Caliphate in favor of modern secular parliamentary institutions (Kurzman 1998:260). Irrespective of the wisdom or otherwise of this Turkish "Islamic" interpretation, to what extent is Turkey today an inspirational model at any Islamic or secular level? What would Soroush make of the Turkish "model," and where would his silence of the Shari'ah thesis ostensibly lead to?

Like Soroush, Ahmad Moussalli in his book, *The Islamic Quest for Democracy, Pluralism, and Human Rights*, presents these values as a panacea, and clearly attributes the rise of the West to them. Yet were these values really *causes* of the West's ascendancy or *effects* of some other factors? After all, it could be argued that the dynamics of Western preeminence existed at times of absolute monarchs and sovereigns. And it was not until the twentieth century, according to Michael Saward, that democracy came to carry positive connotations on a wide scale (Saward 1998:1). By Moussalli's own admission, the very values of pluralism and tolerance had proven a disaster in the case of the Ottoman Empire (Moussalli 2001:142). It allowed the European powers to use and manipulate the *millet* system to undermine the Empire and to establish dominating footholds in it. When a Sultan chose to crack down on rebelling non-Muslim minorities in order to preserve the integrity of the Empire, he was accused of despotism and tyranny, accusations used to justify subsequent European intervention. In contrast, American president Abraham Lincoln, who defined democracy as the government of the people, by the people, for the people, did not particularly entertain such ideals when he ruled out the right of the "people" in the South to secede. The former was condemned as a reflection of "Oriental despotism," the latter lauded as part of the march toward progress and a harbinger of "manifest destiny"—a perhaps practical example as to how discourses of power and mechanisms of control serve to block one narrative in favor of another. They contest while affirming, mystify while de-mystifying, categorize while de-categorizing, de-legitimize all the while counter-legitimizing.

It has not been the purpose here to provide an extensive account of the works of different "liberal" scholars or to cast doubts on their intentions. The point has been to highlight some common themes which permeate their approaches, and some potential risks associated with their discourse. For either as conscious agents or as manipulated vehicles, their accomplishments do not appear to go beyond entrapping Muslims in the web of an alien historical and discursive experience. This in many cases serves to bestow upon them their rather dubious reputation, one sufficiently ambiguous as to seriously impact on their credibility. Without denying the possibility of gleaning some benefit from what thinkers who ascribe to this current may have to offer, it is important nevertheless to indicate that "liberals" fail to show how values of democracy and liberalism or pluralism may necessarily promise positive outcomes for Islam and Muslims. One should not lose sight of the fact that while Islam as a religion is capable of explaining away perceived and tangible worldly sufferings in terms of intangible otherworldly justifications, secular values do not enjoy this privilege. They are pragmatic, tangible non-theological values, and unless they are capable of delivering on what they claim or promise in this world, they are likely to lose much of their *raison d'être* in Muslim societies. "Liberal" Muslims will thus have to do a much better job at proving their case. The next chapter, which deals with human rights, will attempt to conceptualize and underscore some of the complexities they will need to tackle in the course of their efforts.

7
Human Rights:
A Double Discourse of Power

Like much of the paraphernalia of ideas and concepts emanating from social theory, "human rights" remains a controversial and contentious term. Its *content* and *use* arouses both unmitigated support on the one hand, and suspicion and ambivalence on the other. Much has been said about human rights and the professed concern for human "freedom" and "well-being" (Gewirth 1989:248). This view is corroborated by observation of the undeniably privileged condition of the individual agent in Europe and North America. Political, economic, and social relations in society, but particularly with respect to the state, are guarded by an array of protective legal and institutional structures providing for a good measure of stability as well as for an adequate feeling of security and welfare. Human rights from this perspective are seen diversely as progenitors, reflections or guarantors of such achievements. On the other side of the fence however, particularly though not solely in the Islamic world, the image is much more complex and hesitant. Inevitably there is a sense of admiration and yearning among many Muslims for enjoying the rewards linked, rightly or wrongly, with human rights principles. These feelings are exacerbated by the desolation of political life in much of the Muslim World and the prevailing tyranny undermining personal as well as collective dignity, self-respect, and self-esteem. Concomitantly however, there is a streak of suspicion, sometimes articulated, otherwise bordering on an instinctive reflex that a hidden agenda lurks in the sinews and contours of human rights. Colonial legacies and historical experiences continue to feed distrust of motives and intentions with "Western" sources, frequently leading to the 'baby' being thrown out with the dirty water. Such emotions hinder the possibilities of a constructive interaction of values and mutual learning. More significantly they aggravate the potential for stable relationships.

The best of intentions, nevertheless, fail to obscure problems and difficulties associated with "abuse" of the term and leads to questions about the real meaning, objectives, and agendas connected with and linked to "human rights." On the one hand, there is an argument which supports a universal, largely Eurocentric view of human rights, as applicable to all humanity and individuals irrespective of their cultures or values. On the other hand, an opposed view presents it as a product of European historical experience, representing values which they seek to impose on others, particularly on Muslim societies. This latter view does not just uphold the significance of cultural relativity, but is also cynical about the perceived dominative implications of the human rights agenda (Calder 2002:17). Moreover, while the Eurocentric view emphasized individual rights, to a large extent at the expense of obligations to religious as well as to communal values, the Islamic counterpart has done the opposite. It emphasized collective and individual obligations to Islam and to fellow mankind at the expense of rights, even those provided by the faith, and most significantly those rights due from the ruler and state. A perpetual "centrifugal" or *non-foundational* system of rights defined individuals in terms of increasingly autonomous and unconstrained capacities limited largely by the space occupied by other individuals. A cumulative "centripetal" or *foundational* order of obligations rendered individuals, as well as society, fettered, lacking even in relative autonomy, incapable of demanding due rights sequestrated or expropriated unjustly, and wanting in energy, initiative, and creativity. Both conceived a pathological human condition, sanctioning one side as the subject of a power discourse, divesting the other as its object.

Yet, each stance remains partial, wanting, and in conflict, essentially sustaining accusations leveled against both, with no clear resolution of their contradictions visible on the horizon. While there may be extra-contextual elements intrinsic to human dignity and rights, promoting a universalistic discourse exposes covert and overt external projects of domination. By the same token, while cultural differentials ought to be respected if homogeneity of human existence is to be avoided, taking refuge in cultural relativity or even Islamic values has frequently become a justification for a different set of domestic tyrannies, injustices, and corruption. Consequently, the universal translated into an external Eurocentric power discourse applied against Muslim states/regimes as well as their societies, and the relative, translated into a debased religious power discourse applied by domestic regimes against their own societies. Ironically, reflecting a condition of a *double discourse of power* assaulting and violating Muslim societies, both discourses, of human rights and tyranny, of the universal and the relative, in fact justified each other. Therein lay the roots of tension between Eurocentric interests and genuine Islamic values.

This chapter will attempt to examine inconsistencies of the human rights discourse especially where contradictions between *content* and *use* manifest themselves. It also attempts to underscore an Islamic *foundation* for "Rights," distinct from the ambiguities of human rights discourse and its double exertions on Muslim societies. A framework of *"rights and duties,"* understood in terms of a structure of *Justice* in the broadest sense of the term, may help reconcile the discrepancies between the *content* and *use* of human rights claims. These "Rights," as Gandhi once put it, in a manner consistent with many religious traditions and conceptions of Justice, "arose from duties well done" (Aziz 1999:45).

HUMAN RIGHTS AS A DISCOURSE OF POWER

Divergence between the *content* of human rights and their *use* reflects an *ideology* of sorts and a burgeoning *discourse* of power at the interface of which human rights tend to fall. This is the case because despite vehement denials and claims to universality, much of the talk about human rights does in fact and in practice "hinge on the conception of the human being which, 'simply' has those rights" (Calder 2002:19). This is further fortified by a claim to commensurate social and political institutions and structures, which provide viability to the protection of those proclaimed rights (Smith 1989:99). Liberalism, in its old and new variants, offered the principal ideological cover for those rights as well as for subsequent discursive justifications for repressing and blocking alternative narratives. This despite liberal claims to knowledge being separate and distinct from notions of power. Yet when the founding fathers of the United States inscribed in 1776 the "self-evident" truths that "all men are created equal, ... endowed by their Creator with certain unalienable Rights, ... among these are Life, Liberty and the pursuit of Happiness" (Hayden 2001:343), they did not have in mind as human beings the black slaves whom they treated like chattel, nor the native Indians whom they systematically decimated in a holocaust. Unabashedly, over two centuries later, in 2000, Theodore M. Heburgh re-cited the US Declaration of Independence as the most eloquent manifestation of all values that conform to the requirements of peace, justice, and the human right to "life, liberty, and the pursuit of happiness." Heburgh did not stop there; he further linked the Declaration to the *Pacem in Terris* document of Pope John XXIII, relating the Vatican's teachings to the Declaration of Independence as the new man-made secular religion of humanity (Appleby 2000:ix–x). If the history of the United States, while it currently upholds the banner of human rights, is an indication of what is yet to come when the *content* of such principles are translated into *use*, the future prospects do not seem bright. This has been particularly visible in the case of the Palestinians, their nation and society destroyed by Zionist Jews with the participation of the US, as well as in the invasion of Iraq by the US in March 2003. The atrocious behavior of high-ranking US officials and American forces in the notorious Abu Ghraib and similar prisons in Iraq, as well as in Afghanistan, and in the Guantanamo Bay prison on the island of Cuba, gives a clear indication of the American conception of *who* constitutes a human being. Such an attitude toward the *collective* "other," as falling short of the standards entitling them to consistent respect, is not a recent exception but apparently a well-established Eurocentric historical pattern and a credible projection indicator. In other words, these actions were not simply a matter of coincidence or a moment's lapse, judging by the recurrence of such an attitude, but of an epistemology of domination incorporating both the *prejudice* of ideology and the *discipline* of power, in the service of political preferences and strategic interests.

Political objectives and interests serve to *prejudice* the merits and significance of human rights in both political and moral discourse. Such prejudice is not simply "a matter of mistaken belief but of systematically distorted thought, a form of delusion or superstition, what today we might call an ideology" (Smith 1989:58), or to use a Marxist term, a "false consciousness." Ideology incorporates a "clearly understood political bias" that helps economize on the costs of knowledge by providing sources of belief systems consistent with political preferences (Goodin and Klingemann 1998:233–4). It is put in the service of a broader power relationship of legitimization and/or de-legitimization, integrating the political and the conceptual. The *political* defines the moral de-contextualizing of the latter in order to universalize what are essentially particular interests and privileges. Content and use diverge and conflict, as the particular justifies the universal. Both are put forth in support of schemes that, in their "motivations or effects, threaten the very aspects of human life which these rights were designed to protect or enhance" in the first place (Calder 2002:15). This holds true not only for those who raise the banner of human rights, but also for those who censure the concept for their own purposes and calculations. As an ideology, human rights lays the ground for the distortions which allow for demonizing an adversary, say Islam and Muslims, in terms of a good/evil dichotomy, so that any aggression against them can be worked out in its terms. We are talking here about an ironic situation in which ideology determines the stance for or against human rights, and where "human rights" becomes an ideology in its own capacity covering for "humanitarian intervention." Hence the destruction of Iraq, for instance, becomes an act of humane liberation, since if one party stands for the rights of humans, the "opposition" must, therefore, stand for something evil. Ideological distortions and dichotomies serve to set a conflict in a zero-sum game framework, immobilizing any structure of conversation, and reducing the conflict to an issue of *power*, based on prejudiced "knowledge" of the opponent.

At this level and stage it becomes easier to step into the sphere of *discourses* and discursive power formations and representations. This order of power, as Todd May has put it, depends less on the force of command and more on proliferating *disciplinary* norms empowering new ruling institutions, structures, and domains of knowledge associated with the rise of techno-industrial capitalism. Particular areas of knowledge combine with commensurate domains of power in order to produce other identifiable spheres of knowledge and of power in a continuous dialectic (May 1993:73). The truth of this knowledge is totally immaterial. What matters is that knowledge production and content are inseparably intertwined with the carrying out and use of this power. Both are linked in an elaborate web of mutual reinforcement, even when both are "heterogeneous" (May 1993:44, 51) or conflicting in content and use. Take for instance American self-perception as expressed in a memorandum presented to US President George Bush Jr. by the Chairman of the Joint Chiefs of Staff, advising on humanitarian intervention policy: "American leadership ... has established a new standard for the benevolent use of power. We are the nation to which other countries look first for assistance, for action, for support. To us often falls the task of mobilizing the power of other nations to leverage our own potential for good" (McChrystal 2000:59). Compare this with Bush's rather surprised reaction after the September 11, 2001 events, wondering why Muslims "hate us so much" and the United States' subsequent global rampaging. American shock and awe at this attack perhaps had less to do with the extent of the casualties, and more with the shattering of their own convictions of invulnerability, arising from the cracking of the knowledge/power structure which had sustained the American feeling of self-contentment. In order to restore the state of balance, human rights as a mode of knowledge, representing the supposedly "superior" way the US envisions and "knows" the human, a knowledge presumably lacking in the Islamic tradition, is intertwined with "humanitarian intervention" as the corresponding domain of power. The main objective is to overcome the limitations imposed by the "sovereign" state principle against outside intervention, the concept of the sovereign state itself being an historical outcome of an earlier sphere of knowledge and power. This is accompanied by parallel coercive pressure, violent and non-violent, aiming at changing Islamic educational curricula in order to refashion Muslims' identity in ways consistent with human rights discourse. This current repository of knowledge and power is no longer solely a conventional game of the *inside* against the *outside*, but is combined with "a network of small interlocking practices that are diffused across the social space" (May 1993:53).

The logic of human rights is simple and replicates that of the days of rising European fascism and the eruption of World War II (Sellars 2002:ix). It goes as follows: autocratic regimes, in their domestic environment, have created conditions conducive to the external attacks perpetrated in 2001. By taking up the cause of human rights these destabilizing conditions could be altered in a fashion consistent with US interests. This could be done without necessarily having to change or subvert "friendly" political systems, even if some figureheads at some point in time may be rendered dispensable. Pressure exerted on many regimes in the Arab World in the name of human rights, therefore, does not necessarily seek to undermine clients but to prod them in this specific interpretive direction. As those regimes bow to pressure in order to secure their survival, external knowledge and its corresponding domestic regime of power essentially become one, fortifying the dominative structure of the double discourse afflicting Muslim societies.

For if domination is no longer solely a matter of state totalitarianism or economic exploitation, if it is also a matter of how we know ourselves and the world we inhabit, then it is entirely possible to overturn state power or even economic relations without altering fundamentally the domination those institutions and practices were supposed to represent. (May 1993:53)

In other words, human rights discourse may help create a safer environment for power, and does not necessarily entail in any way challenging power's essential character.

This serves to perpetuate the contradictions of the content and use of human rights and of other similar discourses, and to give the impression of double standards. The problem however, may have less to do with duplicity, although this certainly always figures in the broader context, and more perhaps with epistemology and the distinct social and political space in which human rights are harnessed. In the *domestic* environment of *power*, human rights have been associated with Eurocentric moral and philosophical traditions, mainly liberalism, in more or less liberal societies, deduced from "a single overriding value or small clusters of [abstract] values" (Stone 2003:2). To question that, as Tom Campbell does, may obscure this reality but not necessarily negate it. Whatever might be said about the indeterminacy of human rights (Campbell 2003:18), as to what it means and whether it is universal or relative, there has in fact been an undeniable consistency between content and use, as well as the knowledge and the power that both mutually produced and sustained. In this respect human rights are *"premises"* leading to their logical conclusions manifested in the significant measure of freedom and welfare enjoyed by society. In the *external* space of *power*, or the domestic counterpart of Muslim societies, however, the epistemology of human rights is ordered differently, rather pragmatically and functionally. In this case, human rights are defined in terms of the *use* to which power wishes to put them, rather than in accordance with their moral *content*. This reverses the above order of human rights into being *"conclusions,"* rather than premises (Stone 2003:2; Campbell 2003:19), with the same system of *knowledge* in one context being a source and product of power, in the other being the source and product of weakness. Muslim regimes, committing themselves to human rights documents or principles, at least verbally and in accordance with the logic of power, do so largely at the bidding and command of a country like the US for instance. Adding an item or clause against prejudice to Islamic Law or values tends to be nothing more than window-dressing, since when contradictions do occur between human rights and Islam, the latter is in practice prejudiced. It is these inherent and structural contradictions that render human rights decisively partial, rather than the largely futile theoretical debate about whether it is a "Western" concept, a relative prerogative, or a universal endowment. "Data," wherever its source, is there for all to use, abuse, adopt, adapt, include or exclude. Knowledge, produced by a specific power order, could be genuinely universal if conveyed and received by some corresponding, even if asymmetrical, power capable of setting the parameters of the give-and-take structure, and of guarding its own autonomy and will. China and Iran come to mind in this respect, while the decay and collapse of the Ottoman and Soviet empires come to mind as exemplary outcomes of the failure to do so. The dialogical problem therefore, is not a matter of principle, but of the *how*.

Put to use, the entire human rights conceptual structure is established as a dominative power discourse over the tyrannical yet pitiful Arab regimes, and the evidently anguished Muslim societies, creating a high level of stress, anxiety, and confusion among both. Stressed regimes, unable to fathom what is really expected of them, in light of this indeterminate discourse, react erratically. Domestically they present themselves as opposing foreign intervention and as protectors of "authentic" values, employing a most incredulous nationalist and/or "Islamic" discourse. To external power, domestic rulers present themselves as the loyal servers of stability, and the guarantors of power's interests. To substantiate their case, they tend to argue that human rights would open the doors to chaotic, extremist, unpredictable, and undesirable alternatives, while targeting their own societies against which they level accusations of being the immature, unscrupulous, and irrational bearers of anti-power values. This helps explain why, for instance, the secular Egyptian State frequently seeks to weaken secular, so-called "opposition parties" while allowing for a measured display of strength by the Muslim Brotherhood in political or parliamentary showcases. The hollow religious and nationalistic discourse of the Egyptian ruling kleptocracy is, thus, no more credible than its American democratic counterpart, the former being nothing but the domestic mirror image of the latter. Mystified societies in turn, desperately seeking salvation in the discourse of human rights from the spectacle of regimes ruling them, fail to notice that they, as well as their governments, are merely the object of this discourse not its subject. The entire situation creates the illusion, at least to some, that an external humanitarian intervention may be the only hope if domestic change is to occur. Giving rise to internal dissenters sensitive to the idea of collaborating with external inter-ventionist actors, dissension tears at the fabric of society, increasing its vulnerability to power discourses, without necessarily making things any better. "Outside" power presents itself as the savior of human rights, the "inside" counterpart as the protector of Islamic and/or national values. The alternatives offered to society are between choosing human rights at the price of forsaking the "nation's" own values, or opting for the latter at the cost of having no human rights. This disciplinary choice structure has been propped up by the sacking and rape of Baghdad in the aftermath of the American invasion, in March 2003, conjuring up images of the Mongol invasion of 1258 CE, and providing breathing space for many of those regimes. The latter need only cite the Iraqi experience to their people as the alternative to their oppression to prod them to choose the better of two evils. A double power discourse is thus entrenched, ironically, around human rights, effectively consolidating domestic tyranny as well as external domination. Many Arab and Muslim societies are thus reduced to a state bordering on slavery. In this case it is not merely a matter of bondage, as was historically the case, or of being vanquished by a conqueror, although many would depict the submissive Arab condition as such. Slavery, as Vittorio Mathieu has observed, is also a state of *being* when entire societies, as a result of *material* and *value* needs, no longer have freedom of action or of thinking as their shared conduct is dominated by the "desire" to satisfy those needs (Mathieu 1986:39). Wendy Brown put it eloquently when she stated: "If rights are what historically subjugated peoples most need, rights may also be one of the cruelest social objects of desire dangled above those who lack them" (Douzinas 2000:371).

POLITICAL ILLUSIONS OF HUMAN RIGHTS

Human rights, as C.R. Beitz stated, "are meant for certain political purposes, and we cannot think intelligently about their content and reach without taking into account these purposes" (Campbell 2003:19). Skepticism about human rights, therefore, is not simply related to their value being "debased" as a result of their manipulation for narrow political purposes (Winston 1989:v), but more due to human rights essentially being *founded* and *embedded* in politics. Doubts concerning the concept reflect in reality the cynicism associated with the way many tend to feel and think about politics. As a political term couched in moral and legal language it is the means by which relative political principles are universalized ethically, and hegemonic ideological constructs and discursive formations are camouflaged. Human rights have become the foremost means in much of the political deliberation "determining the moral legitimacy of law…" (Stone 2003:1). The principles of human rights thus become useful as a polarizing instrument setting distinctions between the legitimate and the illegitimate, and in the most intense political sense determining the friend/enemy dichotomy. The full implications of such dichotomies and legitimizing tools tend to be blurred among Muslims. Demonized and denigrated, many in the Islamic world, particularly in official circles, tend to believe that it is mainly a problem of communication and public relations: If only Islam, or other Arab or Muslim causes, were presented better, or perhaps if an Arab lobby were built up in the corridors of US decision-making agencies, adept at competing with the Jewish lobby—a task that many self-deprecating Muslims tend to blame themselves for having failed to do—much antagonism would dissipate. The entire complexity of the problem is reduced to a matter of failing to impart a positive image in the media capable of rectifying the damage done by hostile interests. Yet a friend/enemy dichotomy set by, say, the US, goes beyond such limitations. A *"political enemy,"* as Carl Schmitt has indicated, notwithstanding religious overtones about Islam being the foe, need not be morally evil, visually repulsive or economically threatening. As a matter of fact it may even be gainful to engage in commercial dealings with such an adversary (Schmitt 1996:26–7). It suffices however, that he be the "other," foreign, or an outsider who does not ascribe to human rights values and morality, or is designated as such. The opposite also holds true. The friend, in the political sense, need not be of the finest moral caliber although it may suffice that he be "ours." One may recall that the same religio-political currents that had been manipulated by the US, through Muslim client regimes, against the communist bloc and Arab nationalist forces during the Cold War, are more or less the same currents that are now being demonized for the purposes of the same power. Human rights as a secular liberal legitimating principle, de-legitimizes Islam for discursive purposes related to calculations of knowledge, power, and politics. Accusations made by power about Muslims being evil, violent, disrespectful of human rights and dignity, controlling oil lifelines and thus a threat to civilization, support emotional distinctions made in favor of political categorizations. Defining the political enemy in other words, is *autonomous* of other economic, moral or aesthetic considerations, yet draws on distinctions they make mainly for verification (Schmitt 1996:27). What this means is that the entire project of portraying Islam in an appealing way will always founder on the rock of political dichotomies rather than resolve them. The subject matter concerned with the nature of the portrayal of Islam, therefore, does not really have much bearing, and is unlikely to influence adversarial political attitudes.

Instrumentalization of human rights serves to project the delegitimizing image of "barbarians" or a collective "public enemy"—in this case Muslim states and societies—who must be vanquished. The entire concept serves a double purpose. The enemy defined as the hostile *collectivity* does not incorporate *private* hostility as well, but applies solely to confrontations among collectivities (Schmitt 1996:28). *Individually* however, human rights adopt co-opting alternatives, separating private interests from their own collective environment, such separation itself being a hostile action to the extent that it fragments, atomizes, and undermines the targeted collectivity. At the individual level, human rights discourse conveys the promise, at least initially, if not of actual then at least of potential liberation, freedom, empowerment, and autonomy. When Islam is depicted as the enemy in the collective sense, the Muslim individual is approached differently as the object to be liberated, to become a full subject, that is, to be legitimized, by this very same discourse. Both individuals and the collectivity become the target of strategic deception or the "deliberate misrepresentation of reality constructed to gain competitive advantage" (Daniel and Herbig 1982:3).

The purpose of strategic deception is to shift the focus toward a misleading sub-target and to reduce its ambiguity "by building up [its] attractiveness [as a] wrong alternative." This causes the real target(s) "to concentrate his/[their] operational resources on a single contingency, thereby maximizing the deceiver's chances for prevailing in all others" (Daniel and Herbig 1982:6). The main goals of such deception, according to Daniel and Herbig, are threefold. The first and pressing objective is to condition a target's beliefs and structure his perceptions; the "process of constructing reality rather than recording it." The second and intermediate purpose is to influence the target's actions in a particular way. The third and ultimate aim is to benefit from the target's actions. And while almost all deceptions sooner or later are exposed as events unfold, "the trick for the deceiver is to ensure his lies are accepted long enough to benefit him" (Daniel and Herbig 1982:5, 34). To intensify the impact of the human rights discourse, an uneasy virtual alliance between power, internal and external, is formed against Muslim society. It becomes in the very interest of external power to buttress the sway of domestic regimes in order to render an individual yearning for breaking out of its shackles a prize to be attained at all costs, even that of giving up on collective identity and therefore autonomy. That is, to create an impossible situation or environment, out of which there is only one way to take or choice to make—the "right" choice, the "Western values" choice. For the Muslim individual to choose their own values is, therefore, to invite a condition of illegitimacy and non-recognition, separating the interest of the individual from his own belief structures in favor of human rights alternatives. Only gradually, and often too late, does the collective price that has been paid in terms of the shared loss of what individually had been cherished at the outset start to sink in—*slavery*. Feeling the pressure from strategic power and the prospects of domestic popular unrest, regimes choose to clamp down on the weaker party—*society*. This takes place at the expense of the professed principles of human rights, with power expressing its displeasure above the table, so to speak, yet simultaneously striking deals underneath—*invisibility*. Muslim society ends up at the receiving end of the worst of all worlds, suffering both collective and individual domination and tyranny, as human rights create a preferential gap between principles abstractly presented and concretely applied. This reflects new power realities and the dynamics of micro-politics which unlike more conventional power manifestations "do not so much *repress* ... inherent desires as *create* them" (May 1993:112; my emphasis). This changed nature of politics produces a culture of rights that does not recognize duties except to the very limited extent of responsibility toward other individual agents' autonomous space. Otherwise it would suffer the risk of being self-contradictory if it were to attempt to repress that which it has sought to create. Human rights, that is, constitute the "legal recognition of individual will" claiming to grant him his humanity and subjectivity (Douzinas 2000:11) in pursuit of self-chosen goals.

By creating desires rather than repressing them, human rights conceals the contradiction that autonomy, or the "self-rule of the individual" (Lindley 1986:6), is lost by the institutionalized determining of desired choices as well as by repressing them, giving the illusion of agent autonomy. Such illusion creates a feeling of freedom from external constraints of power, soft or hard, and presumably from manipulation by others. This is the major incongruity that Islam and Muslims have to wrestle with as they face a discourse which opens new horizons for individual *desires* opposed to a traditional authoritative system that frequently requires repressing or restraining them. Yet it is this claim to autonomy which reveals, if in a subtle fashion, the paradoxes of human rights, as only a well developed, rational, and purposeful self is entitled to their privileges. If it is contended that such characteristics are inapplicable to the worldwide Muslim community which, individually and collectively, may wish to live its own subjectivity, then this brings them under the rubric of "barbarians." Internal and/or external despotism, for barbarians, who by definition lack moral agency, "is a legitimate mode of government," to put it in the words of John Stuart Mill's treatise *On Liberty*, "provided the end be their improvement, and the means justified by actually effecting that end" (Chadwick 1975:28). Since pursuing that end may require anything from decimation in space, eternity in time, to the psychological alteration or subjugation of identity and subjectivity, human rights frequently resolve their contradictions by the destruction of the object, postponement into the future of promised salvation, or the dominative manipulation or engineering of the human state. This seeming self-negation is not necessarily just an outcome of sheer lies, inherent deviousness, double standards, or even cultural hegemony, but also has to do with the very structure of the concept, beyond pointless contentions about human rights' universalism or relativism.

What this means is that Muslims will have to recognize the transformations which have permeated the political landscape and develop the "epistemic" counter-tools that would allow them access to their micro-political world (May 1993:112). The required change in approach may be tactical rather than strategic, but failure at the level of tactics can very well lead to a commensurate strategic breakdown. This is what makes the challenge all the more formidable as long as Muslims continue to understand Islamic methodology in traditional terms, or even in the terms with which it had confronted modernity, in a post-modern world. Human rights discourse, described by Costas Douzinas as the "fate of postmodernity" and "the realized myth of postmodern society" (Douzinas 2000:1, 8), imposes its moral, legal, and micro-political claims in a disciplinary fashion through its institutional projections, be they publicity channels, education, psychological persuasion, or other forms of communication. Discursive knowledge, in other words, has changed the approach to politics from operating solely on the macro-ideological plane to the level of micro-politics as well. For when the secularist ideological order separating public politics from private belief is envisaged to be falling apart, most seriously by virtue of a resurgent Islamic religion, the new landscape is occupied by a discourse of human rights that can be taken as either "sacred" or "profane" (Asad 2003:155). Its purpose is to achieve the secular task of freeing religious belief, in the same fashion it has historically freed Church property for exchange, "as an object that can be negotiated and exchanged without any legal obstacles" (Asad 2003:147). Negotiations in this case reflect compromises made between unequal parties. With the increasingly perceived failure to maintain secular separation between the private and the public, both are to become the domain of market oriented negotiated identities and rights rather than committed beliefs. It is at this level of incommensurable "irreligiosity" that human rights and Islam will continue to be in conflict.

Knowledge creates awareness, perception, as well as self-understanding and self-discernment. It develops and constitutes *rituals* that establish a chain of "constraints as effective as they are 'natural'—flowing, seemingly from the exigencies of knowledge rather than the manipulations of power." The constraints of knowledge are more effective, if more dispersed and less controllable, than other constrictions imposed by power, because of a liberal ideology which proclaims the integrity of knowledge and its remoteness from affairs of power and hegemony (May 1993:112). What essentially is taking place here is the micro-political exercise of soft-power as opposed to hard-power. Soft command and knowledge propelled from "small practices of power" create new spaces and new constraints for power's action in the very attempt to carry out its venture (May 1993:112). Hence the discourse of human rights and its conceptual attachments of tolerance, freedom, liberalism, and their concomitant structures of NGOs, civil society, foreign aid, and other sources of soft as well as hard or coercive agencies. The claim that human rights are based on a liberal-individualist discourse which also ascribes to the notion that "true" knowledge is inherently "non-political" conceals "the highly if obscurely organized political circumstances obtaining when knowledge is produced" (Said 1979:10). Human rights discourse, in fact, is "as much a political weapon as the [disciplinary] walls of confinement or the guns of the police" (May 1993:112). Only when Muslims are able to conceptualize what is happening to them, in terms of the means by which they are being reconstituted, may they be able to ask the question of which among these variations they are willing to sanction and which they must discard (May 1993:112). Otherwise, inability to foresee the implications would allow such constitutive changes to operate without Muslims being able to impose the internalized limitations necessary to curb any potential or inherent malevolent underpinnings.

"Men's most opportune claims to humanity," as Clifford Geertz has stated, "are cast in the accents of group pride" (Rorty 1993:242). If this is true, at least on one level—the sociological—then one implication is that taking universal human rights as the representative structure of one humanity is inconsistent with human nature, unless of course one can claim to be able to eliminate group solidarity and cohesiveness.[1] This of course can happen, but with very destructive consequences. For in the age of human rights, "never before, in absolute figures, ... have so many men, women, and children been subjugated, starved, or exterminated on earth" (Derrida 1994:266). Former US ambassador to the UN and Secretary of State Madeleine Albright's retort in 1996, when it was brought to her attention that more than half a million Iraqi children had died because of American-led sanctions, that "it is worth it," fits this same "human rights" track record. By the same token, when Americans inflicted sadistic treatment on Iraqis in Abu Ghraib prison, they did not necessarily see themselves as violating human rights or the autonomy of fellow human beings, but Arabs and Muslims. They saw no contradiction between raising the banner of rights and committing such crimes. This by no stretch implies that those who perpetrated those acts, whether by ordering or executing them, were "morally ignorant," or exonerates them from guilt or justifies what they have done. Rather, it simply means that they were "preferentially wicked," guided by their sense of, and prejudice grounded in, "moral perspectivism." Such perspectivism asserts "there can *in principle* be no common measure between radically different 'takes' on the moral significance of a given set of actions"—meaning the absence of mutually recognizable moral frames of reference (Calder 2002:24, 25). To the barbarians, that is, moral precepts do not apply. Demonization provides the ripe grounds for applying the full brunt of racism.

From this it follows that denying moral agency to an opponent is to state that even in case his humanity is recognized, it does not entitle him to possess inalienable rights, and therefore, human rights. Jews may usurp Arab-Palestinian lands but if the latter choose to resist they are to be condemned, or, if shown condescending sympathy, are to be told how to resist, for they can not represent themselves but must be represented. Promises could be made to the "other" and *broken* without posing a challenge to the "cultured" ethical self-image. According to this logic, Palestinians, Arabs,

Muslims, and possibly others, cannot be "violated" unless those within the bounds of the human rights "culture" determine that they have been (Calder 2002:27). The presumably "civilized" culture stands as foe, judge, jury, and executioner. A state of unrivaled power discourse based on the disciplinary modes of morality, legality, media, and coercion, ensues.

Once power is engaged in manipulative relations with Muslims, the embodiment of an alternative and potentially threatening value system competing for the same universe, power exhibits a strong inclination to aggressively assert its values and, defensively, to protect its own autonomy. Seeking to uphold its cherished values, interests, and autonomy, power targets Muslims with the same scheming methods that undermine their autonomy, yet which it abhors for itself. A situation, that is, of doing unto others what one does not want done to oneself, with the added caveat that all is done *altruistically*. If power's domestic population is also suffering from different yet parallel aesthetic or bureaucratic modes of manipulation, such as to believe in such misguided altruism, then it becomes possible for a President Bush Jr. to wonder to his "constituency" with incredulity why Muslims "hate us so much." It also becomes possible for him to manipulate the *sentiments* of his own people to convince them that all counter lines of reasoning presented by Muslims are "morally irrelevant" (Rorty 1993:252). The difference in the exercise of power in either case is that while in the Muslim situation it seeks to produce *objects* who are *subjected* to power, rendering them the focus of a double layered power discourse, in the domestic case it seeks to produce *subjects* subjected to power. On both levels consistency between content and use, as well as self-image, is restored and preserved at the very moment when human rights are rendered a meaningless universal fiction. Illusion and reality thus coincide.

Another fallacy which carries the structural problems of human rights further concerns the concept's grounding. In the secular Eurocentric domain the human rights foundation–non-foundation debate bears its own complexities. There does not seem to be much contention about their morality, necessity, legitimating purpose, and basic inherent worth. It is a "given" which more or less grounds it on "*something*," despite inquiries raised as to whether it justifies itself, or needs to be justified from further premises. Even when losing its full force in its liberal-individualist form of legitimizing ideology, the concept of human rights tends to be reinvented by appealing to the social and economic needs of poorer societies. While the social and economic rights approach is frequently critical of the liberal variant, the fact that many of the basic needs of Muslim and other societies are couched in the language of human rights actually consolidates and re-enforces the entire edifice, including its ethnocentric individualistic components. Bringing material needs into the picture becomes a means to maintain the claim of human rights to universality. This becomes a tactic that weakens counter arguments. The point here is not that those who uphold concerns of equality are insincere, but that they could be easily manipulated as pawns in a larger chess game. Social and economic rights in fact add power and legitimacy to the beleaguered and increasingly doubted human rights discourse in much the same fashion that communism unwittingly justified liberal-democracy and capitalism. With the passing away of communism, the latter's rival ideological construct ran out of control, showing its true colors in the form of unreserved neo-liberalism, neo-conservatism, and globalism. The concern is that social and economic rights would serve the same justifying purposes until such time when human rights discourse could be totally self-justifying, non-foundationally and without disguise, in the form of brute force and unrestrained power. It helps to recall for instance that at one stage human rights served the purposes of rebellion against the state (for example in the former European Eastern bloc), only to end up in a different phase becoming an instrument of the state. The mere capacity of an ideology to incorporate new meanings actually prolongs its legitimacy, although by profusely multiplying meanings this could also lead to undermining its mobilizing potential and to a "semantic terminus" (Petrova 2004:203). This is where discourse takes over from ideology at the level of micro-politics in order to avoid such a fate.

A glimpse of this was hinted at in Richard Rorty's *pragmatic* "anti-foundationalist" project. "We see our task," he stated, "as a matter of making our own culture—the human rights culture—more self-conscious and more powerful, rather than of demonstrating its superiority to other cultures by an appeal to something transcultural" (Rorty 1993:246). In case anyone had any doubts where Rorty stands, he makes it quite clear that he does believe that "our" human rights culture is morally superior to those of others. Such superiority, he argues, does not necessarily count in favor of a "universal human nature" (Rorty 1993:245). Nothing is particularly problematic in someone believing his own culture to be superior, and in many ways it is commendable. What matters, however, are the practical implications of whatever Rorty may mean here. Repercussions could very well translate into a pragmatic, exploitative, interest-driven political dynamics of inclusion and exclusion of others, whenever and wherever it fits the purposes of power, based on pure self-justifications bearing moral claims.

An opposite view, in other words, may unintentionally exacerbate problems it was initially articulated to resolve or address. Contrary foundational claims are thus made to guard against human rights being construed pragmatically as a mere contingency or an unquestionable inevitability. According to this approach, if the very principle of human rights does indeed matter, as Gideon Calder has put it, then "the possibility of them being grounded" does make a difference, "both theoretically and practically" (Calder 2002:30). Yet, foundationalism is unlikely to ground human rights in other than conventional liberal ideology, or some form of social and economic considerations. The latter continue to face the dilemma of how to be embedded in some form of reinvented social discourse, or the thus far incoherent anti-global social movement. In either case, human rights seek a competing ideological base, a "persuading" discourse or controversial moral criteria. Take for instance the point made by Alan Gewirth regarding morality. First-order moral differentials manifest themselves in the works of philosophers such as "Kant, Kierkegaard, Nietzsche, Mill, and Marx, who hold, respectively, that the criteria for having rights consist in or are determined by reason, religion, power, utility, and economic class or history" (Gewirth 1989:182). For Muslims, at least at the primordial level, the attitude to the entire debate is much more straightforward. Rights, duties, and obligations, moral or otherwise, are grounded in Islamic revelation and the system of science and knowledge emanating from it represented by the Qur'an, Prophetic traditions (*Sunna*), and jurisprudence (*fiqh*/ijtihad). To Islam and Muslims this debate between foundationalism and its opposite makes little practical difference, beyond tactical maneuverings. If grounded, Muslims face an ideology, if non-foundational they face a discourse, in both cases politics and power are unlikely to be far behind, both being the real *grounds* of the entire project. Muslims who for one reason or the other get embroiled in this controversial debate of human rights, simply engage in it as its objects, subject to knowledge and power parameters for which they are simply its variables. Even when they call for respect for their own specificities, Muslims in fact have already accepted the governing limitations of the human rights command structure as a given, committing the fallacy of "misplaced absoluteness" (Aziz 1999:44). For even in cases where religion is presented as a moral criterion, it is Christianity, not Islam that is meant. In all other philosophical cases the criteria are related to knowledge-power of which Muslims are not a part, nor are they perceived as potentially such. It is not only Christianity that does not recognize Islam but also "reason, power, utility, economy, and history." The "mock rationality of the [foundational or non-foundational] debate conceals the arbitrariness of the will and power at work in its resolution" (MacIntyre 1989:179).

HUMAN RIGHTS: NESTING MECHANISMS OF DURABLE INEQUALITY

The Muslim community or the Umma has fallen victim to this illusion and mock outcome. Many so-called intellectuals among its members, as well as ruling figures, who constitute domestic *variables* with respect to power and domestic *parameters* with respect to their own society, aid and abet in the diffusion of this double layered power in both state and society. They have become the constituting elements of a "nested paradigm of ... transformation," according to which local actors already rooted or "nested" in a society or situation, team up in a broad array of activities and tasks in the service of such diffusion. Those actors include presumably "respected" mid-level educational, business, health, and religious leaders who control key complexes of groups and institutions—that is, supposedly leaders and representatives of a "civil society" subsumed in the human rights regime (Appleby 2000:18). Nesting ensures cooperation and compliance consistent with shifts in the "balance of forces," imposing a new assortment of interpretations which are designated to be the "truth" (May 1993:76). Through the disciplinary institutions of education, law, politics, economics, and culture as well as an external and internal coercive security apparatus, the entire social space is invaded, claiming that which is new as having always been. For instance, attempts to universalize and legitimize the idea of natural rights as *timeless*, as Karl Marx indicated, were nothing more than the expressions of a specific socio-historical context, itself the product of an earlier historical development and therefore far from being an "eternal truth" (Smith 1989:100; Douzinas 2000:9–10). To observe liberalism or human rights in historicist terms is to suggest that one *"knows"* them not only as heirs to and possessors of rights and freedoms, but also of structures of power, domination, exploitations, and contempt of "others" (Strong 1996:xix). Insights of the kind are the focus of blockage in the form of *strategic deception* grounded in the politics of knowledge and power superimposed on Muslim society and in the fabric of that society's intelligence structures. Short of spirited and informed resistance, or unqualified submission molded in power's own image, thus rendering application of direct force redundant, Muslim regimes and societies will continue to endure extremely foreboding and stressful states of affairs.

Deception is practiced in concealing differences between the concept of human rights and that of "Rights" (read Justice). The distinction is both ontological and epistemological. "Human rights" is a legal epistemology in which humans have rights. This signifies a state in which a general desire or interest constitutive of "humanity" serves the creation of a new right. Rights, that is, become reduced to "the disciplinary priorities of power and domination" expressed as "facts and agreements" in legislation, leading to the collapse of the "is" and the "ought" (Douzinas 2000:11). The right that *is*, becomes the moral demand of what *ought* to be. Rights and human rights, ontology and epistemology, collapse into being more or less one and the same—human rights and an epistemology. The latter knowledge *produced* by power becomes ontology and "rights" that *make, produce*, as well as *repress* the *"human"* in the Muslim domains. A legal epistemology based on human interest transforms into a determining ontology constitutive of Muslim identity, social and individual. In other words, an ontological right which constructs the "human" in Muslim societies is essentially grounded in the epistemological desire of power. The implication is that if Muslims wish to be considered as "human" or complete moral agents they have to adopt the values of power as givens. What we get is a subject/object, producer/consumer power hierarchy, set in a monopolistic discursive market where Muslims are nested in a value-taking paradigm. Anything they may competitively produce is blocked as a matter of interest and desire. Nesting promotes compliance among both intellectuals and the domestic ruling "variables" who take comfort in their inferior hierarchical status as *native informants*, to use Edward Said's designation, and as local clients. Conditions on the Muslim side reflect this paradigm on the level of ruling structures as well as on that of influential mirror-image domestic actors. Sensing the potential destabilizing impact of human rights, largely illegitimate regimes in the Arab and much of the Muslim world malign the principle. Since human rights are not distinguished from Rights/Justice, intentionally or otherwise, rejecting the former essentially constitutes denunciation of the latter. There are thus neither "rights" as such, nor a "human" subject or moral agent, and consequently tyranny and corruption.

The epistemological difference between the Eurocentric and the Muslim understanding of rights and of the "human" person, while evolving first from grounding values, is also based on different conceptions of human autonomy. In the Eurocentric view the human is autonomous, or in the Kantian formulation an *"end."* What follows from this reflects the continuous epistemological expansion of such autonomy. In the Islamic counterpart "Man" is *relatively autonomous*, for only in this case can there be a belief in afterlife reward and punishment based on freedom of choice, on the one hand, and predestination or belief in Divine will and command, on the other.[2] While man is honored and dignified, being created in the image of God and the receiver of His divine revelation, he is by no means an end. For to be an end is to conceive God in man's own image—man becomes the creator not the created, which is close to pseudo-idolatry from an Islamic perspective. The respective conceptions of law, rights, and humanity will therefore be fundamentally different, reflecting two worldviews, Islamic and secular.

It is not relative autonomy which leads to tyranny and corruption in Muslim societies, or undermines the value of humanity. Rather it is the fact that the "rights" prescribed by Islam are simply not enforced, autocratic rulers opting to rule arbitrarily and capriciously. In other words, it is not a "culture of human rights" that is needed, so much as a *culture of enforcement*[3] and its concomitant *mores of institution building*. For even when imported secular laws or institutions are adopted by many Muslim states, they frequently fail to produce purported outcomes. This is what may be expected with the absence of functional enforcing institutions, and when the real culture is one where laws, *any laws*, positive or divine, are stipulated to be broken or arbitrarily applied. Islamic thought after all, does incorporate a broad and well developed system of entitlements and Justice which include preservation of *religion, life, reason, progeny, property* and *honor* (Al-Raisouny 1992:41, 44).[4] These prerogatives underscore an entire domain of grounded rights capable of promoting human material and spiritual welfare if taken *seriously*, and justly and fairly implemented in letter as well as in spirit. This requires not only *bona fide* belief in these values—reflecting a structure of *legitimacy* as a major component of a just order and of Justice—but also the twin elements of *functional institutions* and *fair enforcement*, which together bring about and make viable a *system*. No Islamic order of any kind could be established, or be capable of upholding the above six entitlements, in the absence of one or both of those elements or structures.

Another source of tension between the Islamic and Eurocentric views of rights of humans at the most basic level is the transcendental grounding of the former, and the need for epistemic justification by the latter, not always forthcoming at least as far as Muslims are concerned. Put differently, breaking out of the limitations of the "external authority" of traditional morality has culminated in the "loss of any authoritative content from the would-be-moral utterances of the newly autonomous agent." For "why" as Alasdair MacIntyre has put it, "should anyone else now listen to him?" (MacIntyre 1989:177). The fact that there is no decisively convincing rationale has transposed the problem into the realm of constitutive power and discourse, for only in that context, so at least some would suggest, could such a fundamental conflict be settled. Establishing Eurocentric "authority" as well as a nested paradigm is the first step toward justifying the *invisible* hierarchy of *binary opposites* according to which structures of *durable inequality* are made to ferment and disseminate. The most effective form of power and domination, after all, is its invisible form.

In the Eurocentric liberal view, rights exist only if they are human rights. Accepting the Eurocentric premise, although in a perverse sense, Arab regimes adopt the view and practice that if there are no human rights then there are no Rights/Justice. Thus, instead of recognizing that in instances where there need not be human rights there may still be a separate ethical or moral system of rights, binary categorizations present this as a situation of opposites rather than of differences. This "imperialism of categories" (Aziz 1999:41) obscures any alternative ethical or moral system of rights, permitting a hierarchy of power categorized in terms of a superior/inferior and a corresponding human rights/human abuse dichotomy. Rules for some sort of a zero-sum game are set instead of a positive-sum game. This is the order of things if authority, knowledge, and power are to be monopolized. Any diversity accepted or consensus attained takes place only within the *nesting* parameters of the human rights discourse. In other words, to draw on human rights categorization is to draw on social and political institutions and practices that make the protection of such classifications possible. This develops a situation of dual peril, manifesting itself in a siege mentality in Muslim society with respect to external power, and domestically in a people–regime relationship of mutual contempt. Both conditions create a violence-prone psychological state, as insult is added to injury. This state of mind tends to be less than responsive to issues of rights or human rights. For everybody is guilty.

As a micro-political principle in the service of a macro-political regime of power, global and local, human rights adopts the same mechanisms of constitution and control, which function as sources of a durable hierarchy of inequality (*exploitation, opportunity hoarding, emulation,* and *adaptation*). Thus whereas micro-politics serve to manifest presumably positive aspects of human rights culture, this hides the real and bigger agenda based on macro-politics—the prize value larger than the sum of all its aspects. The US global campaign against so-called "terrorism" at the level of micro-politics, and its reduction of complexities to the mantra of either you are with "us" or with "the terrorists," is essentially a discursive "shock and awe" effort to block alternative discourses or narratives. Conversely, domestic regimes resort to exhibiting the negative aspects of human rights, concealing the larger agenda of tyrannical rule. In both cases subsequent actions are thus justified. In reality this translates into a worldwide macro-political "crusade" against Islam and its conceptions of the human, of rights, and of Justice. This further reflects the power of the supporting hegemonic institutions of control, both internal and external—law and military force. Both seek to establish a new colonial or imperial order, domestic and global, and based on legal institutions, with an organization such as the United Nations bestowing a façade of "legitimacy,"[5] the unrestrained use of local security and/or external military power providing for coercion, and human rights cultural discourse or the absence of it, imparting justifications. If human rights are designated to be the norm, then "terrorists" or "abusers," to varying degrees, are labels used to identify all those who challenge them. If characterized as "abnormal," then those demanding their rights are branded as rebels or instruments of external agencies. Together they construct a global disciplinary complex designed to punish those who choose to question the "norm." For the very production of "a normalized subject requires the production of its *other,* the 'abnormal,' whose abnormality has to be *repressed* and buried to reveal the normal as essence" (Massad 2001:3–4). All four mechanisms of durable inequality, and the two hegemonic institutions of repression and production, add up to being a most formidable means for such normalization. In the shadows of the murky boundaries between the internal and the external, the inside and the outside, humanity, let alone right, is lost.

HUMAN RIGHTS AND ISLAM:
THEORY AND PRAXIS OF A DISCURSIVE FORMATION

The opportunity hoarders

Like old wine in a new bottle, human rights represent a consistent pattern of hegemonic and imperial discursive formation. The conceptual edifice of human rights constituted a cross-referential unity with previous "texts" that had served the purposes of historical colonialism. It did not reflect a "sudden access to objective knowledge" about the legitimate rights that humans ought to enjoy. Rather, it perpetuated "a set of structures inherited from the past, secularized, redisposed, and re-formed by such disciplines as philology" as well as positive legal techniques, "which in turn were naturalized, modernized, and laicized" as new forms and ideas to be superimposed on the Muslim world (Said 1979:122). Human rights advocates who pursue, reflect, or come under the rubric of this trend actually project a sense of *déjà vu*. Most of their works gain significance less because of any profundity associated with what they say than because of the power structures which support them or the sphere within which they perform. Power, as the cliché goes, carries its own convictions.

This is by no means an attempt to deny the sincerity with which many scholars and intellectuals deal with the matter, in many cases out of genuine belief and concern. It is about those who tend to manipulate human rights discourse into a power posture with respect to Islam and Muslims. One class tends to fall within the category of *native informants* or opportunity hoarders, another within that of the exploiters. Both seek to underscore an Islamic adaptive and emulative attitude that would guarantee its location in an unprivileged power hierarchy. The structure of their arguments is such as to set *agendas* delineating constructed yet unrepresentative parameters and frameworks, advocating selective causes at the expense of the Islamic counterpart, confusing the contingent and the necessary, the procedural and the substantive, while ignoring issues of moral incommensurability. Agenda setting essentially controls the priority of *which* issues are to be raised or debased, *how* they are to be addressed, and *what* outcomes are to be desired, influenced, and if possible determined. This power artifact ascertains preconceived premises, as well as their foregone conclusions. In between, arguments tend to be nothing more than procedural exercises in letting off steam as far as the exploiters are concerned, and for opportunity hoarders a chance to manifest their nested fidelity to knowledge and power. Instead of emphasizing Islam's vocation in the search for the *godly* society and focusing on how to bring it about, social theory dismisses the entire domain as irrelevant or unfeasible, confining itself to "behavioral political science and the doctrinaire jurisprudence of rights." The latter simply being expressions of a moral poverty that denies transcendence on the grounds of clichéd perceptions of the extant (Douzinas 2000:6–7).

Abdullahi Ahmed An-Na'im's approach to Islam and the issue of human rights is a relevant sample of scholarly work that inspires controversy in terms of the above constraints and limitations. Essentially he is concerned with exploring cross-cultural techniques through which it may be possible to universalize the legitimacy of human rights particularly in Muslim societies. He advocates a course of "social engineering" through the manipulation of the processes of cultural dynamics and change from within Muslim culture itself (An-Na'im 1990:363–4). In this way cultural relativism can be accommodated in the broader universal context of human rights. He proceeds by suggesting *reciprocity* as the fundamental principle informing the principle. Human rights become *"those that a person would claim for herself or himself and must therefore be conceded to all other human beings"* (An-Na'im 1990:345, 366). Such a formula tends to simplify what is perhaps a much more complex matter. It is not uncommon that many who believe in this normative injunction would happen also to believe at the same time that it does not apply to those "outside the pale," so to speak. They may be able to understand why outsiders might wish very much to enjoy the same, but reject the notion that they are entitled to it as a matter of *right*, unless certain substantive and procedural alterations are undergone. In this case they may be able to *empathize* even when unable or unwilling to reciprocate. Religious conversion or citizenship acquisition, depending on the primary locus of identification, are examples of necessary transformations needed before a human being is entitled to full legal personhood. Yet if human rights are those claims due to all humans without discrimination based on "race, sex (gender), or religion," why does An-Na'im not include citizenship as well (An-Na'im 2003:3). A non-citizen in a foreign country is treated as a *human* though not necessarily as a full fledged legal *person*. Why should citizenship be accepted as a criterion of discrimination, and not religion or gender for instance? Or is this simply a case of one power discourse blocking another? Perhaps in the future, if the focus of identity and loyalty were to change away, say, from the nation-state, the concept of the citizen will be looked upon adversely as a feature of an "unpleasant" bygone era in favor of new discursive structures. But, can religion be treated in the same fashion?

Endowing human rights with a moral claim to "inalienable" rights due to persons by virtue of their being "human" does not veil, therefore, the self-contradictory ways in which they are frequently (ab)used. This begs distinctions which need to be made between a "human being" and a "person"; distinctions which human rights discourse, in its claim to universality, attempts to blur and to conceal, at least in appearance if not in reality. The designation "human being," on the one hand, relies on a biological classification whose membership is based on "medical" and "scientific" criteria. Designations of who constitutes a person, on the other hand, are founded on "moral" criteria, with the consequence that not every human being is by the same token a person (Husak 1989:236). One may credibly conceive of a common humanity in the biological sense, entitling all its members, in principle, to the same equal rights. In this case, An-Na'im's argument for reciprocity stands. Personhood, however, being a moral principle with legal implications, could very well challenge his claim. An-Na'im does not seem to make the analytical distinction between the two categories of humanity and personhood, and as a matter of fact tends to fuse both into one category. Children or the mentally incapacitated tend to be the most striking examples of distinctions made between humans and persons. Other cases however, are much more delicate and subtle, and may not be possible to determine by mere rational or procedural criteria due to complex substantive differentiations. One cardinal standard formative of such distinctions is *revelation* which imparts levels of moral agency, and thus full or partial personhood, or withholds them, along designated Islamic principles. Islam does recognize the oneness of humanity incorporating believers and unbelievers alike. However, substantive demarcations underscored as a result of differences in faith render humanity and "personhood," by the same token, mutually exclusive.

It may be asserted with a good measure of confidence that human nature and its constitution are universal—man being created in the image of God—with all humans enjoying more or less the same attributes of *instinct, rationality*, and *spirituality*.[6] However, the question is how these attributes are configured, be it the outcome of conscious choice or of existential circumstances that make for differentials. Simply put, someone of sound mind and judgment is unlike someone who acts solely on impulse informed by instinct. Again, at a higher level, a "believer" is on a different plane than someone who does not believe. Such abstract and substantive moral criteria bear concrete legal implications related to personhood as a matter of religious injunctions, not of cultural preferences—distinctions which An-Na'im tends to override and ignore. In all cases it does not suffice to concede to others what one wants for oneself, as he would argue. Jacob Neusner made a noteworthy point, that An-Nai'm might well have heeded, when he observed that it is not the purpose of religious texts to merely serve the rationales of philology, history, culture or even political contingencies or exigencies. A religious text is first and foremost a "statement of religion" which if read otherwise can only be misunderstood (Martin 2001:17). One must thus learn to appreciate the vital procedural and substantive differences between the two systems of Islam and human rights. Dealing with the spiritual aspects of human constitution, on the one hand, is to be informed by religious ontology. Organizational, rational attributes, on the other hand, tend to emphasize procedural epistemology. It should come as no surprise therefore that respective "rights" approaches frequently do not match or harmonize. Take for instance a case dear to Eurocentric hearts and associated with inheritance in Islamic Law: the fact that a female's inheritance is half that of a male member of the family.[7] When the Qur'anic revelation stipulates that this be the order of things, this is by *definition* equitable and just, reflecting how things *ought* to be and therefore *are* to be. It means that a woman's right to a share of the inheritance does not go beyond that. If she receives more, then justice will have been transgressed. This constitutes a statement of religious injunction not a matter of gender parity, for to each is his or her due. To rational or procedural conceptions, this substantive arrangement which impacts on an entire chain reaction of social and political structures, both tangible and intangible, makes little sense. Only an equal share inheritance can be designated equal and just, with gender equality opening the door for a whole array of social synthetic engineering procedures in order to render the different alike. Take also the example of dietary prohibitions in Islam. Muslims are strictly prohibited from eating pig meat.[8] A procedural mind-set may see the cause as related to the physical uncleanness of the animal, so that if conditions of raising pigs are such that the element of pollution is neutralized, the reason for prohibition disappears. Yet, even under purely hygienic conditions the prohibition stands as a substantive statement of religion not of hygiene. The very concept of dirt here becomes fundamentally different, even if both at one level are reconciled. On the religious plane it is related to the totality of human constitution, the instinctive, the rational, and the spiritual, and on the procedural counterpart to actual physical dirt.

Islam, as An-Na'im should perhaps well know, must be read and understood as a religious text not, as he strongly insinuates, as a relative appendage to a universal human rights discourse (An-Na'im 2003:1–2). In fact, the real nature of the incompatibility is not one between the relative and the universal but between a *false* claim *to universality* and a *universal* Islam. Human constructs or artifacts are time-bound, historical, and socially influenced. By their very nature they cannot be universal, constrained as they are by human finitude. Universality is the sole prerogative of the Divine, and only a divine revelation can make a true and "knowledgeable" claim to it. Arguments about human time-bound or historical interpretations do not disavow the reality of the ontological truth and universality of Islam. This means that any relative human artifacts, old or new, can only be made with reference to universal revelatory knowledge. This transforms the entire debate about the relative versus the universal from an either/or matter, to one about the symbiotic relationship *between* the two. Seeking universality in human constructs is an illusion and an exercise in futility even when endowed with pseudo-scientific respectability. The attempt at adapting Islamic universal referentiality to a relative human rights discourse therefore, is an epistemological error, and is as illogical as it is flawed.

Distinctions made between the human and the person, the relative and the universal, are essentially a problematic of *moral incommensurability*. This conundrum reflects a dichotomous state in which premises are set, choices are made, and hierarchies are privileged, rendering moral incommensurability itself a "product of a particular historical conjunction." This is especially the case when no rational approach could decisively justify claims or con-figurations of elements of a hierarchy, giving way to the arbitration of *power* and *utility*, rather than of *right* (MacIntyre 1989:179). In many cases the former two are confused with the latter as might makes right, and the desire or will that *is* becomes what *ought* to be. For example, when Alan Gewirth attempts to avoid an *"assertoric"* argument regarding the entitlement of humans to rights, in favor of what he calls a *"dialectically necessary method,"* he starts from the premise that entitlement to necessary goods is the prerequisite for the exercise of rational agency, the latter being the "common subject matter of all morality and practice." Agency demands that every agent or prospective agent have rights "to the necessary conditions of action"—freedom and well-being (Gewirth 1989:247–8). Yet "the claim that I have a right to do or have something is a quite different type of claim from the claim that I need or want or will be benefited by something." While the former is a matter of right, the latter is the province of utility (MacIntyre 1989:176). It is their equalization or fusion that provides power discourse with its potency, especially when utility is liberally invoked as the source of rights, even when both may in fact be morally incommensurable. It is one thing, for instance, to utilize un-owned dead land and from thereon claim ownership rights, it is another to deem Palestine a utilizable empty barren wasteland and make rights claims to it. After all, if human rights do not provide protection against the vagaries of utilitarian considerations, they would not be rights and certainly not universal. Any fictitious matching between utility and rights finds its parallel in the matching of the human and the person, the universal and the relative. Utility does not justify rights, humanity does not guarantee personhood, and a fallacious claim to universality does not mean that all comes therefrom. An undeniable potential link might very well exist between each pair, yet one is not the inevitable source of the other. Links must be justified from prior premises.

An-Na'im does not seem to take these factors into consideration when he proposes subjecting the Shari'ah, which he proclaims as "historical," to the judgment criteria of "universal" and therefore presumably "timeless" human rights (An-Na'im 1992:161). He ignores the moral incommensurability inherent in his choices, which themselves need to be justified, explained, and rationalized. MacIntyre, for instance, has indicated that no allusion to anything smacking of "human rights *qua* human rights" was made until near the end of the Middle Ages (MacIntyre 1989:178). Furthermore, if Divine revelation is historical while human knowledge is universal this suggests an "interesting" hierarchy which An-Na'im does not adequately account for except in utilitarian terms making a claim for rights. Yet a claim to universalism is an entitlement to some form of *determinism*. And if such universal determinism could be exposed to be nothing but a manifestation of a false consciousness, along

lines similar to earlier contentions made by communism, the end
of history thesis, secularism, the linear progression of history, and
other so-called "inevitabilities," then what we have here is nothing
but an ideology concealing its purposes and intents. This is evident
when An-Na'im takes recourse to the Islamic principle of abrogation
(*Naskh*).[9] Abrogation as had been practiced by Muslim jurists was
based on self-referential criteria, that is, the Qur'an or Prophetic *Sunna*
instating or abrogating itself. An-Na'im, in a rather libertarian fashion,
proposes applying the same principle but "other-referentially," in this
case in light of universal human rights laws and principles (An-Na'im
1992:57, 179–81). He suggests "abrogating" the Medinese stage,
during which many of the Islamic legal precepts were revealed, in
favor of the Makkan period. Only by setting aside "clear and definite
texts of the Qur'an and *Sunna*" of the Medina phase as having served
their "transitional purpose" could the Shari'ah be reconciled to the
requirements of human rights (An-Na'im 1992:179–80).

One can take An-Na'im's proposition further and ask why we
should not abrogate the Makkan phase as well. This may bring
Muslims even closer to human rights standards. An-Na'im may or
may not agree with such a suggestion on the grounds of maintaining
cultural specificities, but then is Islam primarily a religion or a
culture? Furthermore, what if future developments, as may very
well come to be, are such so as to bring human rights into direct
conflict with the Makkan stage? Would this be good enough reason
to abrogate it as well? An-Na'im's method certainly lends itself to
such an eventuality. Muslims consequently would be expected to
give up their right to live their faith in whole or in part, in deference
to pragmatic utilitarian exigencies, and above all to the imperatives
of the presumably "universal" human rights power discourse. An-
Na'im essentially adopts most if not all the mechanisms of durable
inequality, the outcome of which is that Islam might as well end up
abrogating itself.

An-Na'im however, is not the only one to call for indifference
and the shedding of what he calls "historical Shari'ah" (An-Na'im
1992:161). Bassam Tibi, a kindred spirit, calls upon Muslims to apply
the "method of historicism" to their religion otherwise they will
continue to feel "superior" to others, and consequently unwilling "to
speak the universal language of human rights in their own tongue."
There are three things, in other words, that Muslims are required
to do: 1—historicize their "Islamic revelation"; 2—give up on their
sense of pride in their faith; 3—speak some language "other" than

their own, with some concession made to their inability to speak it in the ways of its revealers (Tibi 1990b:131–2). Like An-Na'im, Tibi wishes to historicize Islam and universalize human rights. Again, nothing justifies this epistemological reversal nor is there any proof of its feasibility. The Shari'ah remains immutable while human rights discourse has a history. "Only things with a history, the human things, can come into conflict or contradiction with themselves" (Smith 1989:105). This can be observed in the incongruities of historicism. "If all historical movement is relentlessly progressive and all thought inescapably historical, in that it can only arise or acquire validity if it becomes generally accepted at a particularly historical period, no ideals or standards exist outside the historical process and no principle can judge history and its terror." Thus the eternal could never be comprehended (Douzinas 2000:9–10). As a result, as Luc Ferry and Alain Renaut have put it, "far from the historical having to be judged by the criteria of rights and of law, history itself ... becomes the 'tribunal of the world', and right itself must be thought of as based on its insertion in historicity" (Ferry and Renaut 1992:31; quoted in Douzinas 2000:11). "The symptom of the disease is ... declared to also be its cure but, like many less respected therapies, it leads to an even greater malady" (Douzinas 2000:11). It is not by chance that human rights have prevailed at the very moment of greatest "angst" about life's meaning and disquiet about the breakdown of moral convictions and political projects (Douzinas 2000:7, 374). And "if the value of human thought is relative to its context and all is doomed to pass with historical progress, human rights too are infected with transience and cannot be protected from change" (Douzinas 2000:10). The implication is clear. Human rights have no legitimate claim to universality or determinism and are liable therefore to be judged by something external to them, something perhaps immutable.

For Muslims to accept historicism is to undermine the revelatory essence of Islam in favor of human constructs. Supposedly benign calls for shedding superiority, presumably for the sake of human equality, are usually a subtle opening to re-engineering values, not to parity. It is not clear why, for instance, Tibi does not address his call to similar Eurocentric claims instead. As a matter of fact, in quite a crude way he advocates the values of the French Revolution and modern European culture as both a "global phenomenon and a universal frame of reference" (Tibi 1990b:113). He is not clear about whether, if Muslims were to shed the source of their "superiority," this would render them equals or inferiors. After all, who says if Muslims heed his call they would be accepted on a par by representatives of Eurocentric values? Where did the pathological inferiority with which Arab and Muslim regimes have dealt with the "West" leave them? Moreover, when Tibi calls for Muslims to talk the language of universal human rights in their own tongues, he sounds like someone suggesting everyone should speak, say, the English language, even if in their own accents. But where does this leave one's own language? In so many words, Tibi, going beyond An-Na'im, seems to be calling for the abrogation not only of the Medinese stage, but also of the Makkan period of Islam as well, and advocating that contemporary Muslims occupy a position of inferiority, more or less, by their own choice. Both "opportunity hoarders," in a rather vulgar fashion, constitute components of a common discursive formation.

The exploiters

Ann Elizabeth Mayer deals with the same issues, although as an "outsider" rather than as the insiders that An-Na'im and Tibi are supposed to be. This persuades her to be more cautious and less crude in her approach, even though she expresses the same disposition. As an exploiter she intimates; opportunity hoarders take the hint and put it to the praxis of abrogation, emulation, and adaptation. Where An-Na'im and Tibi refer to "universal" human rights, Mayer is more circumspect and uses the term "international" instead (Mayer 1990:134). More than a matter of semantics this harbors serious practical implications as native informants become more royal than royalty. In contrast to the "bad" Muslims who set up Islamic values as the controlling and defining measure, Mayer lauds An-Nai'm as an "enlightened" and "progressive" example of the "good" Muslim willing to reinterpret Islam in a way that would bring it in harmony with international human rights (Mayer 1990:134, 139). This is a rather typical approach, in which parameters are set, and the ranks are divided and categorized, allowing the targeting of those susceptible to being nested in the human rights discourse and willing to set its norms as the overarching standards (Mayer 1990:138–40). A dichotomy is constructed in which Eurocentric values are set to occupy the privileged position of power.

Mayer adopts a critical legalistic approach in which she advocates the standards of human rights laws as opposed to their "substandard" Islamic counterparts. Even though she recognizes that the conduct of actual governments carries no normative weight in Islamic law, she nevertheless uses the examples of regimes like those of Saudi Arabia and Pakistan, as well as Iran, to make her point (Mayer 1990:135, 154). In tandem, she advocates international human rights laws, and denies that they bear any of their previous imperialistic characteristics. Today, she states, "modern human rights theories are considered to be applicable to all humankind, and the rights of Muslims are given the same recognition of those of Westerners" (Mayer 1990:153). Yet it is statements of this kind that are problematic when they universalize that which is neither universal nor necessarily superior. Her claim that Muslims are given the same recognition, apart from strong doubts about its veracity, presupposes that Muslims should become like "us" or in "our image" in order to enjoy such a privilege. One cannot help but wonder how Mayer would react, for instance, to her statement being rephrased such that instead of human rights one were to affirm "Islam to be applicable to all humankind, and that the rights of non-Muslims are given the same recognition of those of Muslims." Islam as a matter of fact does define itself as universal and not as culturally relative knowledge. And Muslims also pride themselves that historically they did recognize the rights of religious or protected minorities to live their own faith.

One need only cite the example of Palestine and the blind support given to Israel's usurpation of Arab land, and its genocidal policies against the Palestinians, by the same upholders of the principles of human rights. Of course Mayer could argue that the US policy, for instance, does not always live up to the standards it professes but that this does not justify giving up on such values. But if she bestows upon herself the right to judge aspects of Islam and its application based on the performance of regimes like those of Saudi Arabia and Pakistan, the same could apply to contradictions inherent in how "Western" countries mal-practice what they preach. How for example they manipulate democracy and human rights to justify crimes against Afghanistan, Iraq, and Palestine, to contain Iran's legitimate rights to peaceful nuclear energy, while supporting Israel's nuclear ambitions as the only "democratic" state in the Middle East. President Bush has also indicated that the fact that the Palestinian government of Hamas has been democratically elected (February 2006) does not mean that the US must support it (*Al-Ahram*, March 31, 2006:1). Conversely, one may infer that the fact that most Arab client regimes are corrupt and tyrannical does not entail that the US must cease to shore them up. The lasting legacy of September 11, 2001, may not be the destruction of the World Trade Center and its aftermath, but the breakdown in the *invisible* hierarchy of binary opposites and the exposing of the US and the very values it claims to espouse. The US is no longer an "idea"—being reduced largely to a mere representative of brute force—as values of democracy and human rights come under increasing suspicion and are on the verge of being discredited in much of the Arab and Islamic World. Mayer's claim that these values and their legal and military manifestations have lost their ulterior motives does not stand up the scrutiny of empirical testing, judging by current events, as well as their historical antecedents. When she correctly observes that historical testimony demonstrates that religious scruples rarely dissuaded Muslim rulers from oppressing their subjects (Mayer 1999:39), she might as well have added that neither did Western values of freedom, democracy or human rights, in serving imperial purposes, fare much better.

In typical liberal fashion though, Mayer tends to stress individual concerns regarding state intrusiveness, downplaying collective Muslim grievances against imperialism as no longer being what it used to be and therefore irrelevant. Her argument, nevertheless, contributes to the development of a situation analogous to one where a nation, in this case Muslims, may at the level of the individual agent gain freedom from "constraints" by becoming a "colony of a wiser benevolent power." In each case, the individual agent can increase its freedom from constraint by relinquishing its power to govern itself (Feinberg 1973:16). By addressing different kinds of freedoms, liberal advocates attempt in an admirably subtle fashion to resolve the ideology's contradictions. They distinguish, not always in a visible fashion, between freedom from constraints and freedom of self-determination, the bargain being individual agency for collective domination. This helps explain why US allegations about bringing freedom and human rights usually end up in subjugation and human rights abuse, either directly or indirectly through the client regimes it sustains and supports. The problem here is thus not one of where ideas or laws may come from, for Islam and Muslims should be willing and capable of practicing the give-and-take necessary for the exchange of knowledge. Rather the problem is one of power, which must be neutralized as a prerequisite to any legitimate subsequent intercourse. The exploiters must, as a matter of principle, be kept from exploiting.

One example of where they should be curbed occurs when Mayer argues that authentic traditions impose themselves by their own authority, and that the fact that states like Iran need to enforce

Islamic attitudes in society by coercive or intimidating measures is a counter indication (Mayer 1999:13). Such flimsy logic ignores the fact that Islam is a religion not merely a tradition. In manipulating designations like "tradition" Mayer confuses religion with matters of culture and customs which can make no sacred claims to truth and are related more to force of habit. She thus purports that policies of Islamization are nothing more than "traditionalism" or the "ideology of tradition" (Mayer 1999:14). Human rights by implication are shielded from similar discursive and ideological accusations. It may be true that the more "authentic" a value system the less need there is for coercive measures; nevertheless, a law, any law, even if representative, requires a coercive support structure. Caliph Umar I (634–644 CE), at a time of the most intense commitment to Islam, could still recognize that what Allah restrains by the *Sultan* is more than what he restrains by the Qur'an.[10] Moral authority, that is, requires *moral power* beside it. Obscuring epistemological differences between a theory of human rights and a theory of rights embedded in the Islamic conception of Justice, as Mayer tends to do, is an example of crafty ideological concealment and discursive knowledge-power domination (Mayer 1999:26). Rights *per se*, emanating from revelation as a human understanding, can only be re-thought *self-referentially*, that is, through the method by which an epistemology continuously falls back on its ontological source. Islamic Justice or ontology in turn requires institutional structures that maintain its integrity including a structure of coercion. Human rights discourse is no such ontology.

Mayer's critique of Iran's use of "intimidating" measures such as "threats, beatings, jailing, torture, and executions" (Mayer 1999:13), does not elaborate on whether there might have been justifying circumstances. Capital punishment for instance, is an Islamic penalty for particular types of offences, yet human rightists seek to abolish it. Other than for reasons of discursive preference, why should the latter take precedence over the former? It is one thing to criticize capital punishment if applied unfairly, liberally, and as a means of terrorizing, with no just foundations or procedural consistency. It is another thing to oppose it as a matter of principle. In any case, Mayer should not have overlooked the fact that reintroducing Islam into the public sphere, after a long colonial period denying Islam access to public life, is an evolutionary process and not a simple affirmation, necessarily proceeding by trial and error. Nor should she have ignored the fact that the Islamic resurgence faces stiff resistance from powerful external actors, as well as domestic "post-colonial" alliances, perhaps small in number but certainly vociferous, organized, and resourceful.

Mayer most probably recognizes that regulative principles or the setting of limits *per se* is not a contradiction of freedom. Rather she seeks a freedom which reflects human agents' full right and ability to supply these principles and limits by themselves, as opposed to them being set by an Islamic authority. Such an understanding of freedom was reflected, though in a perverse form, in the following statement made by former US Defense Secretary Donald Rumsfeld, when the carnage in Iraq was brought to his attention: "freedom's untidy, and free people are free to make mistakes and commit crimes and do bad things ... Stuff happens" (CNN, April 11, 2003). Mayer, in the same frame of reference, cites Tunisia, under a figure such as Zain al-Abidine bin Aly—hardly a democrat or human rights advocate—as an acceptable reformist case in point, but not Iran, in which genuine popular participation does occur (Mayer 1990:156). In the name of secularism, even if in its autocratic and destructive forms, mistakes are justified and legitimized, and excuses are made when convenient. Islam however, cannot be allowed to enjoy the privilege. Mayer's conception of human rights and freedom does not fall a long way off Rumsfeld's. Both come at the expense of dominating and dehumanizing others.

Emphasizing full human agency as opposed to relative agency poses restrictions on Muslims' autonomy in living their faith, and renders it meaningless to try to understand the notion of freedom in Islam from the perspective of Western humanism (Nasr 1980:95). By the same token, Islam is not Christianity or Judaism either. Christianity makes claims to universality yet it has no divine law in its structure, rendering it a set of general moral exhortations. This background allows Mayer, in her secular version, to reduce the matter to one of mere choice, religion being simply a private not a public concern. Judaism has a law, but it is not universal and incorporates strong ethnic elements which would allow an atheist, for instance, to be a concomitant Jew. Islam cuts through both. It is a universal revelation that acquires its own legal structure and its own teleology. To anticipate that Islam will or should share the historical dynamics of both preceding thought and/or belief structures therefore has no justification. To demand that it does, constitutes a power discourse. To get domestic regimes and opportunity hoarders to oblige and participate in the same discourse intensifies its impact. Muslim society and the Umma at large are thus doubly victimized.

SOME REFLECTIONS ON RIGHTS IN THE ISLAMIC DOMAIN

To underscore the inconsistencies and cynical aspects of human rights discourse is not to say that all is well on the Muslim front. Nor does it mean that the corruption, tyranny, and injustices of regimes in that part of the world, as well as the abuse of their own people's rights, may be overlooked or allowed with impunity. "The vast majority of sensible criticisms of unjust political systems," as Husak has put it, "can be preserved as intelligible even if it is conceded that no human rights exist" (Husak 1989:243). Enjoining that which is good and forbidding that which is evil is an explicitly recognized Islamic right, allowing one to peacefully oppose transgressions, moral, social or political. When all else fails an "eye for an eye" is another principle of reciprocity and retribution against injustices perpetrated and committed by internal or external power structures. Both exemplary rights, however, require going beyond abstract exhortations to being organized and institutionalized if they are to be effective, long lasting, and systematic.

One sound critique of Muslim societies is their failure, with the possible exception of Iran, to reinstate faded Islamic institutions which on the one hand could protect individuals and their rights with respect to the state, and on the other consolidate it against external threats. The dynamic of institution building and enforcement appears to be distinctly lacking in dealing with the specificities of particular situations as opposed to abstract proclamations about Islam. Practical issues require concrete diagnostic and prognostic talents capable of bringing abstract principles and generalities to bear on context and realities (*praxis*). Otherwise, abstractions may not mean much in any practical sense, with lip-service respect paid, promoting the typical refrain of Muslims about their own failure to apply Islam as it should be applied, or their failure to be committed enough to their own faith. The real problem however may be both more complex and simpler than that. On the more complex level, on the one hand, faith may not be measured by material indices. Perhaps no community in modern times has had its faith so tested as Muslims have, and there are convincing indications they continue to be willing to sacrifice much in its cause. On the other hand, when the Makkan environment was such as not to permit Prophet Muhammad and the small coterie of believers to live their faith, they simply had to migrate to Medina. The best of faith could not do much about it, even during what may be called a "miraculous" period of revelation and utmost commitment. At the simplest level, it was a matter of cause and effect both then and now.

Playing on other than their own "turf," so to speak, can only lead to the current disenchanting situation that many Muslims take their lot to be. Until such a time when they are capable of creating their own propitious environment, continuing to dance to the tunes of human rights discourse can only lead to the same disappointing results. The Shari'ah stands above all other laws by virtue of its revelatory source.[11] To make allegations about its historicity is essentially to deny its divine origin, and to claim that the 'Divine' could not reveal a universal message for all times and places, or perhaps did not know that times and conditions would change. The fact that Islam explicitly states that it is the final revelation means its Law is permanent, for otherwise, a new revelation or Law for mankind would be needed or is possible, and structurally the faith would lend itself to indifference. Revelation cannot be superseded or abrogated except by another revelation (Al-Shafi'i 1987:125; Qur'an 16:103). Islam being the final revelation signifies it cannot be abrogated by any subsequent revelation and certainly not by any man-made or positive law, including human rights. This is a necessary and sufficient condition—an ontology. Whether the Shari'ah conforms to human rights discourse or not is, therefore, a matter of irrelevance. To make conformity, adaptability, and emulation its purpose would bring it under the epistemological spell of human rights politics, and down the road, its ontology. The political agenda of this discourse will simply dominate Muslim affairs, their identity formation and political existence.

The essence of political existence, as Carl Schmitt has put it, consists in a community being able to determine its own identity boundaries and hierarchies. Only then can it uphold its existence in the political sphere. "When it no longer possesses the capacity or the will to make this distinction, it ceases to exist politically. If it permits this decision to be made by another, then it is no longer a politically free people and is absorbed into another political system" (Schmitt 1976:49). When a community, as a collectivity or as individuals, is dispossessed of its own hierarchical structures of identification, goals, and ideals, and with no clear conception of where such hierarchies stand within the community's internal landscape, such a community can only become a theatre of war for all its constituent elements. This could very easily turn into an *anomic* condition (Feinberg 1973:14). When this happens, as when some Muslims tend to compromise in order to reconcile Islam with human rights, Mayer sure enough, and rightly so, describes the outcome of such *acrobatics* as a "very awkward ... melange" (Mayer 1999:24). Even when doing the bidding of power, it turns out to be a thankless task. Short of a total transformation the Muslim "other" cannot be accepted.[12]

Muslim claims or arguments that Islam has always incorporated human rights principles contribute to discrediting Islamic thought rather than adding to it. Islam's mandate is undermined when Muslims attempt to prove it consistent with human rights in order to render it legitimized, or seek to discredit the human rights discourse as the only means to build up the credibility of the Shari'ah. Islam justifies itself on its own authority not on the authority of any human rights discourse. It acquires its own system of rights, duties, and obligations, as well as its own dichotomies and hierarchies.[13] A so-called "Universal Islamic Declaration of Human Rights" (UIDHR, 1981; Mayer 1999) for instance, can only invite cynicism not only because of its attempt to model itself on the Universal Declaration of Human Rights, but also because the real problem remains primarily one of enforcement. In the modeling case Islam is both manipulated and misrepresented to conform to external patterns, undermining the Shari'ah's autonomy and setting it in an unprivileged hierarchy. In the case of enforcement, if it is plainly visible that Arab and most Muslim states are not bound or restrained by any concept of law, and are ruled arbitrarily and corruptly, then any UIDHR is not worth the ink.

Contrasting the Islamic understanding of rights with human rights is a first step toward claiming the religious domain's autonomy, and determining constraints and parameters; what in jurisprudential language is called *usul*—the foundations. Search for commonalities constitutes the *varying* aspects which follow, subject to former constraints. Eurocentric approaches attempt to maximize human rights while minimizing corresponding, presumed fettering, duties and obligations, providing maximum autonomous space to the human agent. The Islamic approach is based more on a dialectical relationship between rights and duties consistent with mankind's relative autonomy. Rights beget duties and duties beget rights. This applies to rulers and ruled alike, or at least ought to. One is therefore inclined to disagree with Seyyed H. Nasr when he arranges rights and duties as consequents and antecedents respectively (Nasr 1980:97). Both must go hand in hand, duties begetting rights and rights begetting duties. Otherwise a highly skewed situation is very likely to ensue as people tend naturally toward acquiring that which they perceive as their "dutiful" rights while shirking that which is their "rightful" duty. This is self-evident in the highly distorted relationship of rights and duties between rulers and ruled in the Muslim world, courtesy of a long tradition of *fiqh sultani*.

Human rights discourse has been associated with calls, currently in vogue among some Arab rulers as well as in the United Sates, for the "renewal" of Islamic religious thought, or to use Arkoun's terminology, for *re-thinking Islam*. "Renewal" is a euphemism for altering Islamic values as well as identity-forming educational curricula away from notions of resistance, will, and jihad, in a fashion consistent with power's desires, wishes, and interests. A historical colonial convention in the Muslim experience has been to invoke *passive* Sufism or some form of sheer spiritualism whenever Islam invited Muslims to resist domination, internal or external. Jihad as the exertion of *will* power in worship and in fighting, in spirituality and in materiality, is redefined in passive terms as solely confined to spiritual development or as the "greater jihad." Something along those lines is implicit in the call for abrogating the Medinese State period while maintaining only the Makkan spiritual experience. When regimes or pseudo-intellectuals claim that "renewal" is what is needed, they are in fact collaborating with external discourses aiming at blocking Islamic narratives. For with such proclamations they endeavor to undermine Islam as a protest movement in demand of rights/Justice, while external forces seek to emasculate it as a resistance current demanding autonomy/ Justice from power. Essentially it is not simply the thought that both are after but the commensurate deconstruction and reconstitution of Islamic identity in power's own image, domestic and/or foreign.

Accepted Islamic wisdom in general, therefore, is not the priority that needs to be re-thought, but *al-fiqh al-sultani* in specific. This aspect of *fiqh* needs to be deconstructed and then reconstructed self-referentially. For it is from there that Islamic history has gone wrong. A thorough critique of *al-fiqh al-sultani* can help contribute to rectification. Political reform, the *enforcing* prerequisite for other social and legal changes, may then take place from within Islam's own frame of reference. A first and essential step is to break the vicious circle which set *pseudo-ulama* and the rulers together in collusion, taking a *mazhabi/fiqhi* pretense, in order to justify and weave such a partnership into the faith. This process of de/reconstruction in other words, is a prerequisite for the necessary step of *re-conceptualizing* human rights as only a facet of the more comprehensive Islamic understanding of *Justice*. Justice incorporates the multidimensional aspects of rights, duties, obligations, responsibilities, fairness, and dignity embedded in Islamic values. It *appropriates* human rights into a corresponding Islamic conceptual framework, within which knowledge/power linked with the discourse could be "de-associated" and deconstructed. Particularly as this discourse continues to conceal and obscure, on the one hand, and reflect and manifest on the other, dominative *strategic* interests.

Re-conceptualization in terms of Islamic Justice is of crucial importance in undermining the logic of outside imperial power that wishes to "*sell*" human rights "knowledge" to Muslim societies, as well as inside tyrannical powers that wish to *sell* them "ignorance" of their rights. A mirror-image situation in which both *knowledge* and *ignorance* reflect each other, rendering the very concept and discourse of human rights *essentially* problematic. As Ignacio Ramonet has insightfully observed, "[m]arketing has become so sophisticated that it aims to sell not just a brand name or social sign, but an identity. It's all based on the principle that *having is being*" (Asad 2003:152; my emphasis). This dynamic process is part of a conceptual policy framework that can come in many packages; as Gerald Segal has put it: "trading with the enemy (in non-strategic goods)," encouraging capitalism's secret weapon—an apolitical middle class unwilling to make sacrifices for a radical ideology; and empowering business leaders through trade, thus creating alternative centers of power (Segal 1998:2). In a world of scarcity, inequality and uncertainty, creating desires through human rights discourse (read *having* in order to *be*) is conducive to, and helps explain why, corruption, the tearing apart of the fabric of human relations, and the degradation of moral values in the global market, are being normalized as a way of life. This *violating* and *violent* outcome is rendered more sinister as more collective and individual agents adopt a commensurate identity, and as opposing religio-moral forces fall back on an escalating counter violence.

Another factor in Islamic history which influenced Muslim attitudes toward the Shari'ah, and from thereon constituted their culture of enforcement or lack of it, was the tragic events on the battlefield of Karbala' in Iraq (61 Hijri/680 CE). It was ironic that a presumably Muslim state army would say its obligatory prayers supplicating God to bless and have mercy on the Prophet and his household, only to embark, having ended their prayers, on massacring the Prophet's grandson Imam Hussain and members of his family. Apart of being a tragic crime of the first order which lies at the root of Islamic schisms, Sunni and Shi'ite, it also had less tangible yet as troubling consequences. It created an insidious mental and psychological break between work and faith, between what *ought* to be and what *is*; a condition which many Muslims have come to make their peace with. The plains of Karbala', in other words, witnessed not only the massacre of many of the house of the Prophet, but also the destruction of the unity of *Word, Faith*, and *Action*, not to mention that of the Umma. Nothing was sacred anymore, and no one was safe. In the game of power all is fair, and therefore, no human mattered, no rights, only duties to power, and for that matter, no faith, religion, Shari'ah or Law. Only the whim and caprice of the ruler mattered, as one whom, according to *al-fiqh al-sultani*, everybody had to obey and "never" rebel against however un-Just (*fasiq*) he may be, lest they err in the sight of God or bring about sedition (*fitnah*). Hence, from Karbala' down to the present day when Arab governments can cast their votes in the Arab League against providing any military assistance to aid the American war against Iraq in 2003, only to make available all their assets to invading American forces (Bennis 2006:165), saying or claiming to believe in one thing, doing another, has become the Arab lot.[14] Hence, appeals to enemies or for any remaining friends to respect Arab culture, traditions, religion, or interests are unlikely to go heeded due to the lack of worthiness in such pleas. Observing the character and performance of Arab rulers and elites on all fronts, it is extremely difficult for any party to take them seriously or credibly. They talk about Arab and Islamic unity but work for divisiveness, call on the name of Islam but act according to whatever their caprice imposes, curse the US and Israel but carry out their commands and bidding. The price is clear for all to see, and has touched upon all levels of Muslim society, affecting individuals' mental and psychological states of mind, including the so-called *ulama* and their *mazaheb*. Mourning the death of Hussain, therefore, is not the mere grieving of a human death that is an everyday occurrence—for those who invoke Prophetic traditions prohibiting such expressions—but that of a faith seriously ruptured. For the trickle-down effect over the centuries has come to manifest itself, religiously, socially, and politically, as a norm of corruption rather than as an exception. Yet, traditions of *al-fiqh al-sultani* continued to exacerbate this pathological state as increasing numbers of people came to take their cue from the rulers and their religious functionaries. As in the case of rights and duties, such an attitude and culture espoused a dialectical relationship, attitude shaping culture, culture molding attitude. By reordering a religious/political hierarchy which reflected the historical and moral distinction between the Caliphate/ Imamite, on the one hand, and *kingship* on the other, ritualism, instrumentalism, tyranny, and hypocrisy had their day, and still do. They operated as mutually enforcing manifestations, covering for each other, at the expense of the letter and spirit of the faith. Sunnis, in their self-contentment, continue to ridicule and object to the Shi'ites' recurring lamentation of Karbala' and its ensuing repercussions. Yet, the insidious impact of the Umma's gradual shift toward corruption must have been so serious and insightfully clear to Imam Hussain back then to render it worth the horrific sacrifice of his person together with most members of his household. If this is not a good cause for lamentation by all Muslims, Sunnis and Shi'ites alike, what is? It remains an invaluable service to Islam, after all, that Shi'ites have kept the memory of this tragic occurrence alive awaiting such a time when Sunnis may come to recognize and acknowledge its full impact on the faith and on themselves.

The point here is not to rehash grievances which have arisen in the past, even if they continue to vividly impinge on the Muslim Umma in its present. Rather, and essentially, it is to challenge the self-righteous pride which shirks responsibility and accountability, and simply engages in finger pointing rather than self-reflection. A good measure of *modesty* is the prerequisite for a forward looking Islamic project of unity. Arrogance, as all Muslims know, even if couched in religious pretensions, is in hell.[15] For when the Prophet said to the effect that, "I have left among you what if you hold fast to you shall never go astray, the book of God and members of my household," and the latter are then treated the way they have been, then *somebody* or some group must certainly have gone astray.[16] Shi'ite lamentations serve as a perpetual reminder of the corruption and tyranny of power, of the fact that something had gone fundamentally wrong in Islamic history. *Sultani* and *mazhabi* hostility toward such demonstrations of grievance, displayed or hidden, was the Sunni ruling establishment's ploy to channel Sunni Muslims' attention away from opposition, eliciting at the same time their unconscious *de facto* support for the corrupt power structure which they themselves were suffering from. A vicious circle of divide and rule that *al-fiqh al-sultani* has brilliantly devised.[17]

CONCLUSION

Human rights discourse reflects a particular worldview that aims at reordering the world in conformity with global power and strategic interests. Its influence is far reaching both in the external and internal environments of Muslims, and is likely to extend to their identity-structures and social fabric. Like earlier discourses it carries a hidden political agenda concealed in subtle details and cryptic double meanings. It is pursued through an alliance of interests incorporating domestic rulers, regimes and classes contemptuous of their own and equally despised, and foreign representations of power. As with earlier experiences of colonialism, although unabashed and on a much broader scale, these domestic forces have turned their backs on their own societies, joining ranks with an unprecedented wave of alien hegemony. The hostility of domestic regimes to human rights as well as foreign support for their dissemination do not necessarily signal opposing forces but, ironically, two sides of the same coin, victimizing the Muslim community.

Attempting to expose a power discourse, however, is not, or ought not be, a means to obfuscate the debilitating condition of Muslim, and particularly Arab, societies. Their state of social and political pathology allows such a discourse of knowledge and power to exercise domination with impunity. Prophet Muhammad is reported to have said: "a believer is not bitten from the same pit twice." Nevertheless, the long experience of most Arab and Muslim countries with colonialism has not served to deepen their insights into colonial tactics, strategies, and deceptions. In an anarchic, merciless, power striving world where for better or for worse only the fittest survive, Arab and Muslim societies fail to exhibit acute survival instincts. They continue to be bitten incessantly in a tragic recurrence of events bordering on the absurd, without showing any inclination to learn their lessons. Thus, while it has been common for both Euro-culture and its Muslim counterpart to point fingers of blame and condemnation at each other, possibly for justifiable reasons, it would help if each were to look at hard realities in their own mirrors and then try to change them.

Exiled from their righteous past, lost in their chaotic present and weary of their uncertain future, return from exile is Muslims' only hope for the future and what it may bring—when they will find recourse in their own values, rather than in doubting them. It is futile therefore, to call for a conversation or dialogue between different upholders of distinct worldviews—one that is conducted on the totally different conceptual planes of Justice and of human rights—without a recognition and grasp of the nature of the problematic. This is especially the case when the same vocabulary or language is frequently used to project an image of commonality or overlapping meanings in order to reach some agreement at all costs. Yet, agreement at all costs

is possible only as agreement at the cost of the meaning of human life; for agreement at all costs is possible only if man has relinquished asking the question of what is right; and if man relinquishes that question he relinquishes being a man. But if he seriously asks the question of what is right, the quarrel will be ignited ... the life-and-death quarrel: the political—the grouping of humanity into friends and enemies—owes its legitimacy to the seriousness of the question of what is right. (Schmitt 1996:103)

Interview

Conducted by Cemalettin Hashimi (Johns Hopkins University), Shehla Khan, (Manchester University), and Nuh Yilmaz (George Mason University).

"Islam is one, a religion, and a transcendent revelation." Isn't this the case for religion in general? Why have you focused on this point recurrently? What are the methodological, ontological, and epistemological consequences of this argument?

Well, it depends on how you look at the concept or "category" of "religion." I am not using the term here in an anthropological sense, at least not solely so, or in a sociological structural-functional framework. When I talk about religion, more specifically about Islam, I am talking primarily about revelation—how the Islamic faith defines itself—and, secondarily, about theological, and socio-political organization. This is the arena where one tends to find significant contradictions between social theory's approaches to religion versus a religious understanding of the faith, or as I have argued in one of this book's chapters [see Chapter 6 above] the historical understanding of religion versus the religious understanding of history. When for instance social theory says that all religions basically serve the same purpose and function and that therefore it is possible to situate them all in a common generalizing framework, this may be the case *procedurally* speaking. All religions, it may be claimed, derive from a sacred source or illumination, sanctify reality, and proffer meaning to life and consolation to suffering, their visible manifestations being expressed through certain prescribed collective rituals and obligations. In this sense one can speak about religion "in general." There would be no fundamental differences between strictly monotheistic Islam, Trinitarian Christianity, the tribal God of Judaism, or caste Hinduism with its numerous deities.

Substantively speaking, however, the situation may be totally different. It matters in this case what each and every religion says about itself, how it justifies its core beliefs, what meanings it projects on reality, and what is the ultimate Truth it claims to uphold. Here the above distinctions make a world of difference. Much of these considerations are ignored by social theory, rendered beyond its purview, or at best perceived reductively as a cultural phenomenon.

I am seeking, therefore, and this is an ongoing process, to develop a methodology which integrates "substantive" religion with social theory, so that the former recognizes the utility of the latter, while the latter acknowledges the former as a legitimate source of knowledge. This is why I have stressed Islam as one, a religion, and a transcendent revelation, especially when social theory tends to offer a different portrait of many Islams—Iranian Islam, Moroccan Islam, Indonesian Islam, etc.—confusing the cultural for the religious and, basically, constructing a fragmenting conceptual structure in the Islamic community. I have sought to do so in this book by making a clear distinction between Islam, the Islamic, and the Islamicate. It is in terms of the second and third categories that it may be possible to deal with "religion," and then only partially so since there will always be an interplay between all three, as an anthropological or sociological manifestation of Islamic revelation and an unfolding Divine plan in history.

Isn't the use of religion as an anthropological category Eurocentric as Talal Asad argues? How do you, then, solve the methodological problems of studying religion when the category itself is "Western"?

Talal Asad attempts to trace how the notion of religion has been constructed historically, thus privileging social theory in the hierarchy of meaning. Taking this into consideration, my ambition is to open the way for a concomitant religious understanding of history, reversing the hierarchy but not ignoring theoretical accomplishments. As I read Asad, he argues that the very category of religion was a European *historical* construction, which allowed for secularization to take place. Secular power then set the boundaries between the religious and the secular. However, in historical Islam, the delineation of such boundaries was never really an issue. So what applies in one historical case does not necessarily apply to the other, and from thereon, or to its conceptual constructions.

Do not you think that that is exactly what Asad claims in his critique of religion as a universal category that relies on European anthropology?

If religion is simply a European anthropological construct which allowed secularization, how then can we explain, in those very terms, religious revival not only in Islam but also in Christianity? One should not forget that a basic presupposition of social theory, bordering on determinism, has been that as humanity modernizes, it moves toward secularization and away from religion. However, it failed to explain or predict what one may term the "return of the sacred," even in the secular world, and in this sense it has suffered a major blow.

I am attempting to argue, thus, that conceptual Eurocentrism of this kind should not be allowed to dominate the understanding of religion in the same fashion for instance that the category of "democracy" should not be allowed to monopolize the definition of "freedom." Otherwise how can "religion" and/or "freedom" become endowed with different meanings from the perspective of a different, say, Islamic discourse? Reconnecting theory with the sacred, far from weakening it may actually help strengthen it as well as help empower and re-energize an Islamic discourse, not in a hostile relationship with theory, but in one of symbiotic give and take. Concepts after all are dynamic and fluid categories, and how one defines a particular category, and what assumptions one makes, largely determine one's path of ontological and epistemological inquiry.

Yet irrespective of how one may define or redefine religion within social and historical contexts (i.e. anthropologically as Asad would argue) there always is an essence which sets the boundaries of possibilities, and as far as the revealed Abrahamic religions are concerned, manifests perpetual Divine intervention in history beyond human schemes or constructs. In many ways therefore, what I am purporting to do is opposite to what Asad has been trying to carry out, although not necessarily in opposition to it. Admittedly, the role of mankind in historical religious formation is undeniable, and the same should obtain for that of the "Divine" in history. This is where Ibn Khaldun's methodology proves insightful and of particular relevance and significance. Hopefully at some point of insight both roles may re-converge and we can pick up where Ibn Khaldun has stopped.

What makes one political strategy or conceptualization more Islamic than another one? Is it the association with the historical-political experience of Muslims (such as Khilafat and Wilayat al-Faqih) or the consonance with the Book (Qur'an) and *Sunna*? Or is it something more contingent which is related to content and context, as for instance, the representation of Muslims'

interests, the articulation of their demands, the solving of their
problems?

Conceptualization is an attempt to understand and to bring together
the different elements of a phenomenon into a coherent whole and in
the religious or Islamic domain one uses terms such as stem (*asl*) and
branch (*far'*). The former is the conceptual and necessary the latter is
the concrete and contingent. Political strategy in those terms is the
means toward an Islamic end. The question therefore is not what
makes a political strategy more Islamic than another, but rather which
political strategy serves Islam more than the other, subject to Islamic
constraints. The comparison here is between political strategies as
being the contingent elements serving the necessary values, not
between the latter and Islam. This is the prerequisite of what one
may term Islamic politics. Now if you mean by your question how
to choose among political strategies and according to which Islamic
criteria, the answer will have to lie in knowledge and commitment to
goals and ends (religious as well as social, political and economic), as
well as a host of factors such as prudence, competence, capabilities,
foresight, which would be the hallmarks of any effective leadership
and/or viable strategy. The distinction between the religious and the
political is not necessarily procedural but substantive, namely what
values constitute your highest terms of reference and how do you
apply the political/procedural to further the Islamic/substantive?

The Islamic of course is *defined* principally by its primary sources
the Qur'an and *Sunna*, and to a lesser extent *advised* by its cumulative
heritage and historical experience. This constitutes the conceptual
"stem" if you will. On the level of the contingent or the "branch"
an Islamic system is responsible for representing Muslims' interests,
articulating their demands, and solving their problems. Together
the stem and the branch constitute a unity and the structure of
Islamic system and the twin sources of its legitimacy. This is not an
either/or matter in which one seeks the interests of the faith to the
detriment of Muslims' welfare, or pragmatic interests at the expense
of principles. Granted, it is not easy, but this is the challenge that
Muslims worldwide will have to face, and in any case, there are no
easy solutions.

Now of course what constitutes Muslims' interests is defined,
articulated, and aggregated differently than in, say, non-Muslim
democracies. Despite overlapping universal human needs, there
remains a distinct space which makes for fundamental differences,

be it in belief, consciousness, worldview, as well as ontology and epistemologies.

Why would you then consider democracy as a non-Islamic form of governance?

In many instances democracy is confused as a rather neutral mechanism of elections and free choice. Now it is important to stress that mechanisms cannot be separated from the values they uphold, and which they themselves are supportive of. Democracy requires a liberal secular system or something of that order. If democracy is imported into an Islamic value structure we are likely to face two possibilities. If democracy dominates as the necessary parameter, while Islam is subjugated as the contingent variable, then the imported ontology and epistemology will govern. If the opposite takes place and Islam actually and genuinely dominates then we face a situation in which democracy embedded in an Islamic value system inevitably tends to metamorphose into *shura*. From thereon we face ontological and epistemological divergences between the two mechanisms. Any apparent procedural commonalities are likely to give rise to serious substantive discord. An Islamic *shura* system is more than a mere democratic or American counterpart. Moreover, Muslims tend almost always to mystify themselves with the details of democracy, elections, and the supposed freedoms associated with it, losing sight of the big picture. Writ large, democratic discourse aims at creating "open" societies, which can be easily infiltrated and permeated by the imperial system in a way that allows for perceived personal liberties to obscure collective domination of the Umma. Now since the Umma is a collective Islamic principle, one may imagine what is at stake.

Thus, when for instance Arabs complain about the atrocities that Israel commits against the Palestinians, frequently the retort is that Israel is the only democracy in the Middle East. Falling into the discursive trap, Arabs fret trying to prove that Israel is not a democratic state, as if democracy is the issue, instead of citing it as an example of the organic bond between democracy, on the one hand, and power and colonial discourses on the other.

Also comes to mind the systematic "democratic" decimation of millions of Indians in America, the Algerian parliamentary electoral experience in the early 1990s, and the demonization of Hamas by the US and the EU. These illustrations, among others, do not merely constitute double standards or hypocrisy, but rather illustrate elements of a democratic power discourse that is consistent with itself. The more Muslims demand "democracy" be applied to them the more the imperial discourse becomes enshrined, the *details* of democratic process and mechanisms serving to obscure its foundations and *discursive content and substance.* In fact, we come very close to the same situation in which the Orient *orientalizes* itself, or rather, *democratizes* itself.

However, as a revelation and a "living essence" constituent of Muslims' self, Islam leads them to resist such a discourse instinctively, even if not by design. This is also why the US global campaign against what it euphemistically calls "terrorism," aims in reality at this *essence.* In the magician's sleight of hand, if Muslims defend the essence of Islam they can always be accused of defending terrorism. One should be aware, therefore, of *strategic deceptions* of the kind incorporated in concepts, labels, or mechanisms such as terrorism, democracy, freedom, equality, and others yet to come. For they reflect discursive agendas of power, frequently saying what they do not mean, nor meaning what they say, yet in all cases they are determinate of a subject/object hierarchical order.

How do you evaluate what has been described as the rise of "liberal/moderate Islam"? In Turkey, for example, we find pro-Islamic groups who likewise strive to avoid being labeled anti-Western. How would you respond to the claims of political groups who are neither in radical opposition to the values of their society nor in opposition to the language of Westernity?

I find it important not to engage in the vicious circle of categorizing who is moderate or radical depending on the position of any particular Islamic group with respect to the "West" or to Western values (I use the term "West" here cautiously as I believe there is an important distinction to be made between Europe and the US). This is to construct a subject/object hierarchy in which all Muslims, and not just politicized Islamic groups, are placed in an unprivileged relationship. It is not the point here to say whether Islamic currents should or should not be hostile or friendly to the "West." This is a contingent not a necessary matter. There is no reason whatsoever for Muslim hostility towards countries or states which do not adopt hostile attitudes toward the Muslim world, their values, or their political and national aspirations and interests. The opposite also holds true. Categories such as radical or moderate do not have much meaning except as euphemisms, which conceal other intents and purposes—an ideology of sorts. In this sense they are suspect.

My main concern however is that many of the same mistakes which allowed Islam to be hijacked and Muslims to be manipulated to their own detriment during the Cold War are being repeated even if in the context of a different global environment. You mention Turkey, and if I understand you correctly, you seem to associate that country, under the leadership of the Justice and Development Party (AKP), with what you call "liberal/moderate Islam." There are a couple of points I wish to make here. First, despite the Party's presumed Islamic background, it remains too early to judge the Turkish experience or to claim that it represents any model or stands for something. At best, one can only say that it deserves the benefit of the doubt. The Party has a long way to go to reestablish an Islamic institutional infrastructure, which would then reflect on the country's domestic and external policies and attitudes. In other words, it still has to establish its credibility and Islamic credentials, a process made all the more difficult by having to do so under the sword of Damocles—the army. Prodded by the US, the military institution could still move against the government. Constraining the army's power is perhaps one important reason why Prime Minister Recep Tayyip Erdogan's government seeks to move closer to the European Union. Secondly, there are important questions regarding what is demanded of Turkey under the AKP. What is required of it, what is expected of it, and what is to be made of it? Do we have a situation here in which Turkey is expected to represent an approved of secular so-called "Islamic" state? Is it supposed to be a counter model put forward to compete with Iran and to provoke a Sunni–Shi'ite rivalry between two major Muslim countries so that they may end up neutralizing each other? Is Turkey to be the instrument used for the re-hijacking and manipulation of Islam in the same fashion as this was done through client states such as Saudi Arabia and Pakistan against Arab nationalist regimes and the communist bloc during the Cold War? Having served their purposes, is Turkey now to step into their shoes instead? And if the goal of the purported Turkish "model" is to be neither in radical opposition to the values of their society nor in opposition to the "language of Westernity," as you put it, to what extent can such a balancing act be maintained, or do we have here a dancing on the stairs situation? Furthermore, it will not help the Party much to claim to be a representative of a liberal Islam. "Liberal" is both a loaded and ambiguous term unto itself whose meaning is not clear and must be clarified before one can determine what a so-called "liberal Islam" actually means. After all, it may simply mean a secular liberal system which carries nothing of Islam but its name, or for that matter, it may actually refer to an "American Islam" *à la* Saudi Arabia, although in its Turkish variant. These are the type of questions which the AKP will have to address in order to establish its credibility and Islamic legitimacy.

In your approach, is being a Muslim a phenomenological, cultural, legal, political or historical category as you assert a radical difference between a Muslim and a non-Muslim in terms of solving the problems of Umma? In such a context, when many "Muslim" thinkers adopt a secular or liberal position, how do you distinguish between a Muslim and a non-Muslim in their respective approaches to Islam?

First I wish to clarify that by a non-Muslim I mean an individual who does not ascribe to the Islamic faith—someone who is perhaps a Christian, a Jew, a Hindu, a Buddhist, or belongs to any other faith system. Short of a clear renunciation of the Islamic faith or a categorical act or statement to the effect, I do not condone those who liberally accuse others in their faith even if they have presumably "erred" in their ways: this is a matter best left solely to Allah. Having said that I do believe that it is legitimate to argue that a particular individual, a politician, an intellectual, a scholar, even a presumed *'alim*, or whoever it may be, is in "error," and that this error is in contradiction with clear stipulations of Islam, its spirit, or its interests. I might even go as far as saying that secularism may be an option, even as a *transient* phenomenon, when religious thought goes into stagnation, suffers corruption or is incapacitated for one reason or another including the lack of the knowledgeable, the sincere, and the pious bearers of the faith's responsibilities, that is, suffers an absence of leadership. Failure has its price and those who failed in upholding the real spirit of their faith must be held accountable, starting with those most responsible, the "*ulama,*" particularly among them who constituted "fuqaha' al-Sultan." The "secular" response could be perceived as their chastisement, and therefore may have not been necessarily a totally negative historical experience. However, I do stress its transience. I am under the impression that this transient secular period is coming close to an end with a clear, tangible, and, yes, religious sign—the Iranian Islamic revolution; an opinion I believe to be corroborated by the Prophetic tradition related to men from Persia bringing back the faith. It has not been the intention of my work, therefore, to label anybody, but rather to call upon *all* members of the Umma, of all persuasions, to see "the signs," and not to continue to be driven by inertia.

This brings us to your question about who is a Muslim—whether a Muslim constitutes a phenomenological, cultural, legal, political, or historical category. I believe the answer to this question is more amenable if contextualized in an inclusive order, not addressed simply as a matter of a fluid and continuously changeable identity. This would make it almost impossible to determine the *essence* of who constitutes a Muslim. A Muslim, in the broadest terms, is a multi-dimensional perhaps even a civilizational category at the apex and foundation of which comes revelation and religion respectively, yet including all other categories—the phenomenological, the cultural, the legal, the political, and the historical. S/he is the embodiment of the *universality* that is Islam, not an either/or category. Faith and "believing" is the essence of Islam and what constitutes a "Muslim." Separated from the other categories s/he is like a fish taken out of its water environment. In essence it remains a fish, but its health and welfare are in jeopardy. Such is also the case with Islam and Muslims. The Prophet's migration from Makka to Madina as the former place came to constitute an "impossible" milieu perhaps reflects this problematic.

In the light of these comments, do you think that a liberal Muslim thinker can issue a fatwa?

Briefly, I believe the answer to this question can only be conditional. It depends on the necessary and contingent, that is, on whether to that "thinker" Islam is the necessary parameter while liberalism is the contingent variable, or the opposite, liberalism being necessary and Islam contingent. In the former case, one can talk about a Muslim who happens to be of a "liberal" orientation still defined by the faith (i.e. Muslim Liberal), and provided s/he meets the knowledge qualifications, s/he may by all means issue a fatwa. In the latter case, however, we are talking about a liberal who happens to be a Muslim and who simply tailors Islamic knowledge to the mandates of a secular liberal ideology (i.e. Liberal Muslim). Such a person is unlikely to meet the requirements of Islamic knowledge which demands Islam be *necessary* before a fatwa could be issued. A discourse about Islam is not the same as an Islamic discourse. This is both a methodological as well as a commitment requirement.

A specific success of European International law and its configuration of the theory of International Relations (IR) is to make its European-ness, its particularity, invisible. Taking your insistence on methodology into account, we wonder why you specifically, as in your chapter title, speak of an *Islamic* International Law or paradigm of nations instead of referring to an ordering of the world? Do you think the clear and visible declaration of a "particularity" simultaneously re-locates the challenge posed by Muslims to the present ordering of the world as a sub-set within the emerging critiques of International Relations/International Law?

I am not sure that European International law and its configuration of the theory of IR has made its European-ness invisible. It may be true that it attempts to insert a chain of equivalences to buttress its "invisibility" but it also seems to me that this process is increasingly losing its effectiveness. Accusations, increasingly made, about the exercise of "double standards" in the conducting of IR and the implementation of international law are essentially statements made about the *particularity* of the Eurocentric historical experience and not a reference made to its universalism or humanism. Perhaps at one time this type of discourse had gained some ground, but it is my impression that these grounds are now eroding. Ironically, this appears to be the case at the very high moment of perceived "Western" triumph associated with the collapse of the communist bloc, with the freeing again of the forces of wild and inhumane capitalism and domination. Neoliberalism and American imperialism which instrumentalize discourses of democracy, human rights, freedom, among other terms, are in effect exposing not obscuring the false claims of power discourse.

Such is the case that the "Islamic" International Law or paradigm of nations can make a credible claim that historically it has, and continues to provide a true reflection of reality, notwithstanding concealing appearances. When I use the term "Islamic" I am not referring therefore to the particular, the specific, or to a sub-set within the emerging critiques of International Relations/International Law. Rather I point to a universal theoretical alternative that, through historical stages and changing times, has not lost its potency, logic or inherent "truth." I am proposing an alternative model, a theory, within the context of Islamic thought, which could be modified, added to, and built upon. Islam, including its principled theoretical constructs, should not be presented as just the province of Muslims, but as a universal liberating discourse for the downtrodden worldwide, Muslims and non-Muslims alike, as a matter of fact, for humanity as a whole. After all, if Islam clearly defines itself to be universal as indicated both in the Qur'an and the *Sunna*, the main challenge of the Islamic paradigm will therefore be to show itself relevant to the emancipatory interaction of humanity. For that purpose it does not need to render itself invisible or try to hide anything.

You propose the theory of Wilayat al-Faqih as a "crisis solving principle" to resolve political problems of Muslims. Nonetheless we know that alongside similarities there are several differences between traditions and *mazhabs* (such as Sunni–Shi'ite or Hanafi, Shafi'i, Ja'fari, Zaydi, etc) in Muslim societies. Taking these differences in mind, to what extent can the theory of Wilayat al-Faqih be generalized and applied to the Muslim World?

Yes, there are differences in the structure of *ulama* relationships in the Sunni and Shi'ite *mazhabs*. I would also add that there are qualitative and knowledge differences between the Sunni and Shi'ite *ulama*, in favor of the latter. It is both those differences that work against theoretical generalization. I do not believe either that Sunnis could develop their own theory and praxis of Wilayat al-Faqih, as neither the structure of their *mazhab*, their historical experience, nor the authority, competence or vested interests of their clerics and rulers would allow for such an eventuality. However, by a "crisis solving principle" I really had leadership praxis in mind. I claim that the Islamic world has a leadership structure in the praxis of the Iranian revolution. The "head" is there, and it needs the rest of the Islamic body behind it. Call it *allegiance* if you will. A striking example is the overwhelming "bipartisan," "non-sectarian" popular support that the Lebanese Hizbollah enjoys, particularly after having successfully bloodied the Israeli army in the July 2006 war. What theory cannot resolve, praxis may be able to transcend.

Do you think this qualitative difference arises from their historical and political development and experiences in the last decades, or

there is a substantial difference which arises from their theological positions related to their notion of political theory?

Perhaps it is not simply a matter of one aspect or the other being the source of such a qualitative difference as what I think has more to do with the dialectics of both, the historical and the contemporary. The Shi'ite notion of political theory, their historical experience as an oppositional group, as well as the evolutionary triumph of a line of thought which maintained the dynamics of ijtihad (the *Usuli* school) over the more emulative tendencies of the *Akhbari* counterpart in the eighteenth and nineteenth centuries, the ensuing respected authority invested in imams and religious figures based on *ilm* (erudition), *adala* (Justice), and *taqwa* (piety), the autonomy of the *mazhab*, and finally the Islamic revolution in 1979, have all together in my opinion allowed for a unique dialectical outcome.

Let's talk a bit about a specific example then. The invasion of Iraq and its fragmentation has been catalytic in the proliferation of a sectarian discourse such as rise of a Shi'a Crescent, fall of a major Sunni State, sectarian strife, etc. Given the dissemination of this sectarian discourse in light of the imperialist policies of global powers, how do you define and explain the conflict in Iraq and its consequences? How might we reinterpret the conflict with a view to opening up spaces for Muslims to cultivate emancipatory politics?

This is a complex question, which requires much more space than would be possible here. At any rate, I believe that in order to understand what is happening in Iraq we need to look at the conflict there within the framework of two overlapping conceptualizations. In the first, it is important to recognize that the US invasion of Iraq was not simply a goal in itself but a means toward a much more ambitious end. Iraq was to be the springboard from which to break out into Central Asia and beyond in order to take over the "World Island" or the Eurasian landmass. The purpose was and continues to be the breaking-up of Russia, but more importantly to control and besiege China, especially as the latter continues to become more dependent on imported oil. Former US national security advisor Zbigniew Brzezinski made it clear in his book *The Grand Chess Board*, that he "who controls Eurasia controls the world." Iraq was also to be the prize with which to finance this strategic project, given its abundant oil reserves. The so-called "war on terrorism" in other words, does not have Iraq or Islam as its ultimate target, but China, the former being the means toward the latter end—a classical case of strategic deception, confusing an adversary about means and ends, tactics and strategies. By controlling the sources of energy supplies, which stretch from the Middle East into the Caucasus and Central Asia, the US basically positions itself in an extremely advantageous geo-strategic location. The "politics of terrorism"—the euphemism for Islam and revisionist states—is a sort of intimidating rallying cry for all to join ranks in some form of global coalition, in order to reduce and tilt the costs of constructing the New Order in favor of the United States. This leads us to the second conceptual framework pertaining to what is actually happening in Iraq. It seems to me that six overlapping wars are taking place there concurrently: a world war, a regional war, a proxy war, a national war, an internal war, and an intelligence or dirty war. All these wars, including any "sectarian" noises, are linked to the above project. By examining and analyzing their dynamic interplay I believe this would help explain much of the seeming confusion regarding what is actually taking place in this country. Without going into the details of each war, suffice it to say that the outcome and consequences of these wars will determine the fate of Iraq, and from Iraq, the fate of the Muslim world as well as the world at large, will be decided. Opening spaces for Muslims to be able to cultivate emancipatory politics fundamentally hinges, as a necessary (though not sufficient) condition, on the failure and defeat of this American project at all those war levels. Other conditions will depend on Muslims' ability to undertake collective projects—away from their tribal ways, to clean up their act internally, and to break out of the actual and conceptual confines of the bounded state and *mazhabi* prejudices, both of which I believe have reached a dead end in that part of the world.

Lately, we witnessed several discussions about what is defined as European Islam. How do you understand the emergence of that category? Do you view this category as productive of a distinct subject position for European Muslims or as one which, while empowering them socially-politically at the European level, nevertheless reduces their relationship to Muslims elsewhere to a cultural-sociological level? If the latter is the case, what kinds of strategies do you propose with regard to the relationship between the *Muslims in Europe* and those elsewhere?

To respond to your question here, I wish to make a couple of propositions, which could then be translated into purported strategies. First, and as I have argued in this book, there is only one Islam anywhere. There is no European Islam, no Arab Islam, no Iranian Islam or any other Islam. This is a very important point that should always be clear to all Muslims everywhere. However, one may concede something like "the *mazhab* of the Muslims of Europe." As, for example, when Imam Shafi'i re-viewed and revised his own *mazhab* after he moved from Iraq to Egypt and noticed a different set of issues there. Then of course there are the Islamicate considerations where second and following Muslim generations would tend to form their own indigenous "European Muslim" culture. Secondly, I would argue that the strength and influence of European Muslim communities is to a large extent a function of the power and strength of their Muslim brethren in the Islamic heartland. The more powerful the latter the more support they could give to the former to improve their communal situation. The implication here is that Muslims in Europe could provide two major services to their faith while being "good citizens" in their hosting countries. They may be able to transcend *mazhabi* differences by contributing to new *mazhabi* thought capable of synthesizing and benefiting from both Sunni and Shi'ite contributions, as well as reconciling a "novel" *mazhab* to their very different conditions. This of course would require that the Muslim community be able to restrain elements coming from the Muslim world carrying the baggage and problems of where they come from. This is at the thought and intellectual levels. On the level of praxis and based on the second proposition, European Muslims should attempt to channel their acquired resources from their new home countries to bring about the necessary political and social changes in the abode of Islam or in one of its key countries. For by bringing about a transformation there, European Muslim communities would, as a matter of fact, be rendering a great service to themselves by opening new dimensions of support. Concentrating resources on bringing about change in the Muslim "center of gravity" rather than dispersing them is in my opinion a key strategic and tactical decision. Ironic as it may sound, the real challenge of the Muslim communities is in Muslim lands not in Europe, and in this sense, the fate of European Muslims and others in the abode of Islam is intertwined. To recognize this is to be both a good Muslim and a good citizen. Alternatively, engaging in anti-Western diatribes and going around shooting and blowing up people in the streets at random, while it may let out some steam, does not serve any of those purposes. It further brings that part of the world and the corrupt rulers in Muslim countries closer together.

In the present global political context, various projects—often articulated through liberal visions in opposition to "extremism," "terrorism," and so on, with empirical references citing the Turkish model, European Islam, Liberal Islam—have arisen that both aspire and claim to represent Muslims through differential strategies. What are the key points of difference between these liberal-leaning representational projects and your approach? How would you claim that the latter is more representative of the interests of Muslims?

Your question suggests that I am making contentions of representation. In fact I am not making any such grand claims. Whether my work is representative or not is something that will have to be decided by the readers and the Muslim people rather than by myself. While I hope it may turn out to be so I cannot be the judge. In the meantime, my ambition at this stage is to suggest alternative routes of thought and methodologies, which attempt to avoid both praxis and methodological errors in the type of projects you have mentioned in your question. Successful representation in my opinion is an inclusive not an exclusive project. It calls for collective efforts, provided those efforts serve a common goal instead of opposite, contradictory, and hostile ones. Differential strategies of the various projects you mention, while all claiming representation and the good of the Umma, in fact consume much of their energies turning against each other and undermining what they claim to uphold. They seem to suffer from some form of inherent contradiction emanating from all being more or less *other-referential* rather than *self-referential*. My approach attempts to address the risks associated with the former and which reduces the "Muslim" to being a mere *object*, and emphasize the importance of the latter as a necessary condition of subjectivity. If my project could play even a small part in unveiling these risks and suggesting possible alternatives, then I believe I will have contributed something.

Can you elaborate more on other-referential and self-referential? Does self-referential refer to a position that cultivates a political position in the interest of Muslim Umma and communities in different places or does it have to do more with the sources of thinking and acting in the production of these projects?

By self-referentiality I mean essentially a method and way of thinking and investigation by which epistemology always falls back on its own ontology. This is a necessary condition of subjectivity. Conversely if epistemology falls back on an "other's" ontology, this inevitably reduces a person or a community to an object. That person or community consequently ceases to think for itself and is thus rendered incapable of defining its own interests autonomously and independently. When Muslims attempted to study the reasons behind and sources of European power, due to a methodological failure in referentiality, they ended up in fact objectifying themselves. What was to be studied became instead the standard according to which Muslims ended up seeing and judging themselves, based on whatever criteria the "other" set. Muslims in fact never really "studied the 'West,'" they were instead overwhelmed by it. To be overwhelmed is essentially to allow for a breakdown in the unity of ontology and epistemology. The latter then becomes un-grounded, or re-grounded in a separate or alien ontology.

Political fragmentation amongst Muslims on the one hand provides a global flexibility for Muslim political subjectivity while on the other hand it prevents Muslims from forming globally representative political positions. In this context, how do you regard the dialectic between the formation of a global Muslim power requiring a degree of homogenization and unification on the one hand, while maintaining space for diversity and difference on the other?

The dialectics of diversity and unity have always been a social and political concern. I believe it is better addressed at the level of praxis rather than theory. There are all sorts of different theories out there providing for all types of arguments, counter-arguments and polemics that may go on for ever, particularly when differences are essential. Those who claim that democracy is the ideal system for dealing with such complexities actually engage in wishful thinking, for even democracy is exclusive. In America it started by wiping out the Indians and enslaving the blacks, in the modern state it came after a good measure of "human" and religious homogenization that involved wars, massacre, and atrocities; in Palestine, "the only democracy" evicted and excluded the Palestinians. The problem is that many tend to ignore history and look at the "democratic West" as it stands today, after it had settled its own contradictions through violent exclusions. They think they can simply start from where the "West" has ended only to face the hard reality that they must undergo their own exclusionary process. It may or may not be violent, but is in any case costly, with the added burden that "exclusion" carries a bad name. Yet the fact remains that ultimately a choice has to be made and a decision acted out, meaning that managing dialectics falls in the realm of praxis and the *political*. A time must come when some one, some force, some current has to undertake the political act of enforcement. Historical empires as well as modern states were brought into existence by such acts of decisiveness and determination. How long they survive, are able to unify diverse people, societies or cultures, and protect their high interests in a conflictive environment, is a reflection of competency and adept leadership, be it of individuals, a class, a dynasty, or community. Such competency in fact involves managing both unity and diversity—praxis. The challenge is to maximize inclusion and minimize exclusion, yet in any case there is no escaping a measure of exclusivism. Rebuilding and reconstituting the disintegrated Muslim Umma will inevitably have to face this kind of challenge. Usually a common external threat is a powerful catalyst for unity despite diversity. Given the colonial and imperial wave that is overshadowing the entire Muslim world, a self-respecting nation would have, strategically speaking, already come together by now. Yet in the very abode of Islam, Muslims cannot decide their faith to be the homogenizing factor within the context of which diversity is managed. The same attitudes that had sealed the fate of Muslims in Spain are again at play, as self-destructive bickering among contemporary Muslims drives them toward the same fate. The ship is sinking and well on its way down. Yet instead of joining hands in order to avert disaster, all seem to be more interested in pointing fingers of blame at each other. If attitudes do not change, soon enough who is to blame will matter no more. It is within this conceptualization of the situation that I propose Iran for Islamic world leadership, casting aside "tribal" prejudices, ideological conflicts, and *mazhabi* sophistry.

Do you, then, propose some kind of political hegemony that encompasses any possible Muslim political subjectivity to create a political front on the one hand, but leaves diverse theological or cultural Muslim experiences of Islam open to other articulations? In short, does your vision suggest politically united, but culturally, socially, and theologically diverse experiences of Islam?

A quick response to your question would be yes. Some form of religio-political hegemony, based on a measure of political centralization as well as on consent and concession, is necessary if the Muslim Umma is to be able to counter opposing global homogenizing forces and values. In this respect I wish to add, also, that universality is that which is capable of providing unity among diversity rather than of eliminating multiplicity. This is why Islam in its respect for differentiation and diversity is universal, while the homogenizing pressures of globalization or Americanization, whichever way you may want to put it, ironically render a supposedly all-encompassing phenomenon parochial, doctrinaire, and relative. In this sense, this is an appeal to some Islamist groups which appear to seek to homogenize Islamic and Islamicate manifestations and understandings to reconsider their ways, as they may end up doing a disservice to Islam. Perhaps this is what could be understood from Prophet Muhammad's tradition to the effect that differentiation within the Muslim community, and/or among its *ulama*, is a mercy and blessing.

Notes

1. For instance: "Thus, have We made of you an Ummat justly balanced, that ye might be witnesses over the nations, and the Messenger a witness over yourselves" (Qur'an 2:143; www.IslamiCity.com).
2. Yehoshafat Harkabi was a former Chief of Israeli Military intelligence (1955–59), and an advisor on intelligence to former Israeli Prime Minister Menachem Begin.
3. Parts of the following analysis have been borrowed from Sabet (2000).
4. One of course has to distinguish here between being a Muslim society and being Islamic in the sense that the structure and process of the state coincide and are congruent with the totality of Islamic values rather than merely with their appearance, that is, *ritualism*.
5. "And did not Allah check one set of people by means of another, the earth would indeed be full of mischief: But Allah is full of bounty to all the worlds" (Qur'an 2:251).
6. The "Islamic" justification for the choice of Iran and Wilayat al-Faqih here as a most relevant leadership principle is based on the Prophetic Tradition narrated by Abu-Huraira, the companion of the Prophet. When the Qur'anic verse "if ye turn back (from the path), He will substitute in your stead another people [non-Arab?]; then they would not be like you," was revealed (47:39), the Prophet was asked who those substituting people may be. He put his hand on Salman al Farisi's (the only Persian Muslim at the time) shoulder and said "this man and his people. By him in whose hands my soul is, if the faith were to be as far as Pleiades (*al-Thurayya*) [secular epoch?] it shall be brought back by men from Persia [The Islamic Revolution?]" (Al-Tabari 1980; v. 26:42). See also Al-Qurtobi (1967; v. 16:258). This does not preclude further rational justifications based on the theory and practice of the Iranian leadership.
7. The Prophet is reported to have said: "I have been commanded to fight until people profess that there is no God but Allah...." The Christians in the southern part of Arabia were also asked by the second Caliph of Islam to choose any place outside of the Arabian Peninsula to inhabit. Though done with full dignity and honor, it was based on the command of the Prophet that there is to be only one religion in Arabia.
8. For example believers vs. unbelievers (4:142); the deaf and the hearing (11:25); those who see vs. those who are blind (40:59); party of God vs. party of Satan (58:19 and 22), among many other binary opposites.
9. "They say, 'If we return to Medina, surely the more honourable (element) will expel therefrom the meaner.' But *honour belongs to Allah and His Messenger, and to the Believers*; but the Hypocrites know not" (Qur'an 63:8; Translation by Yusuf Ali).

10. "Verily, this community of yours is one community and I am your Lord, so worship ME" (Qur'an 21:92; Translation by Yusuf Ali); "And know that this community of yours is one community, and I am your Lord. So take ME as your Protector" (Qur'an 23:52; Translation by Yusuf Ali).

11. The Islamic theory of nations and Ibn Khaldun's theory together with the empirical experience of the Iranian Islamic revolution provide ample opportunity for broadening Muslims' intellectual horizons of research (ijtihad).

12. The al-Azhar Theological school in Egypt, one of the main centers of Sunni scholarship in the world, announced the following on July 6, 1959: *"The Shi'a is a school of thought that is religiously correct to follow in worship as are other Sunni schools of thought."* On the same date, Shaikh Mahmoud Shaltout, the head of the al-Azhar Theological school, announced the al-Azhar Shia Fatwa: "1) Islam does not require a Muslim to follow a particular Madh'hab [school of thought]. Rather, we say: every Muslim has the right to follow one of the schools of thought which has been correctly narrated and its verdicts have been compiled in its books. And, everyone who is following such Madhahib [schools of thought] can transfer to another school, and there shall be no crime on him for doing so. 2) The Ja'fari school of thought, which is also known as *"al-Shia al-Imamiyyah al-Ithna Ashariyyah"* [i.e. The Twelver Imami Shi'ites] is a school of thought that is religiously correct to follow in worship as are other Sunni schools of thought. Muslims must know this, and ought to refrain from unjust prejudice to any particular school of thought, since the religion of Allah and His Divine Law (*Shari'ah*) was never restricted to a particular school of thought. Their jurists (*Mujtahidoon*) are accepted by Almighty Allah, and it is permissible to the 'non-Mujtahid' to follow them and to accord with their teaching whether in worship (*Ibadaat*) or transactions (*Mu'amilaat*)" (http://shiite-muslim.anime.co.za/anime/Shiite_Muslim).

13. "When We decide to destroy a population, We (first) send a definite order to those among them who are given the good things of this life and yet transgress; so that the word is proved true against them: then (it is) We destroy them utterly" (Qur'an 17:16). Whether possibly being offensive about some companions of the Prophet, for reasons which go back to historical conflicts in early Islamic history, is worse or less so than undermining the principle of Justice, is moot. However, the following Qur'anic verse may provide a hint: "Allah loveth not that evil should be noised abroad in public speech, except where injustice hath been done; for Allah is He who heareth and knoweth all things" (Qur'an 4:148). If the Shi'a feel they had been subjected to historical injustices they have a right to voice their grievances as well as to identify who they believe to have inflicted such injustices on them. It may serve presenting their case better, however, if they avoid any impropriety in this respect. By the same token, Sunnis in turn should quit pretensions that no historical errors have been committed and that it was all a matter of ijtihad, especially that much of the Muslim world today is still living the consequences of this erroneous "ijtihad." As Imam Ali has said, "know men by righteousness not righteousness by men." In any case, given the

challenges that the Muslim world is facing, it may be best to manifest an ability to transcend such problems, in word as well as in deed, particularly when they are being rehashed and manipulated by both domestic and external enemies.

14. Joseph Braude, who worked for the CIA, observed that "politically ambivalent" and "liberal" Sunni *ulama* in the Gulf states of Bahrain, the UAE and Kuwait, not to mention Egypt, "tend to be hard pressed for cash" (Braude 2003:71). The implication is there for all to read.

15. Such a condition borders on a form of pathological *xenophilia* where any and everything coming from the "other," in this case mostly the West, is better, even if this may not be the case. Muslims have been strictly forewarned about such a state in the *hadith* where Prophet Muhammad says to the effect: "you shall follow the ways [*sunan*] of those before you [Jews and Christians] foot step by foot step, were they to enter a lizard's pit you shall follow in" (author's translation). This does not in any way indicate that there is nothing of value to learn from other nations or people. After all, the Prophet is also reported to have said "seek knowledge even in China [read end of the world]." Rather, the former *hadith* refers to the collapse in the faculty of discernment, and the failure of distinguishing and differentiating capacities, that many Muslims will come to suffer from. Essentially it refers to lack of good judgment. One may add that such shortcomings of judgment could be a product of xenophilia, as well as its opposite extreme, xenophobia.

16. Islam upholds this position, and the following discussion is based on such an Islamic belief and understanding of events. It is important to note that no nation is given a "blank check" so to speak. In this respect the Prophet is reported to have said to the effect: Let people not come [on the Day of Judgment] with their works and you [the Arabs] come with kinship and status (author's translation).

17. Qur'anic narrations (*qasas*) are not merely a recounting of religiously significant events which transpired, but are at the same time "prophecies" and "news" as to what is to occur in the future, in analogical equivalences. This is perhaps why Prophet Muhammad, describing the Qur'an, is reported to have said "... in it are recounts about those before you, and the 'news/prophecies' of that which is after you ... (*fihi khabar man qablakum wa naba'a ma ba'dakum* ...)." Thus for instance, where Jews are condemned by the Qur'an for killing the Prophets of God, the Qur'an in effect was also stating that Muslims, though on a reduced "analogical" dimension, being a *blessed* nation (Umma *marhouma*), and therefore immune from committing a "capital" sin, will perpetrate a *parallel* crime and kill the Prophet's grandson (for example Imam Hussain) and other members of the Prophet's household. Or, when the *people of the book* are accused of corrupting their *revealed* scriptures, Muslims again, on a reduced scale, commit parallel corruption *interpreting* their Qur'anic and/or *hadith* scriptures (as manifested for example in *fiqh sultani*)—the Qur'an itself, being immune from corruption, and many *ulama*, though by no means all, being not much different from the condemned rabbis of the children of Israel. Such proposed "prophetic" dimensions of *qasas*

call perhaps for further investigation. See also the *hadith* of the *sunan* above (note 15).

18. Issam No'man indicated in *Al-Quds Al-Arabi* newspaper, published in the UK, that, based on information from high level American officials, the US has been arming Sunni radical groups in Lebanon, in order to instigate a Sunni–Shi'ite conflict and to attack Hezbollah, while blaming al-Qaida for the violence (April 18, 2007). It seems that the US together with some Arab states and parties are following the same manipulative tactics with these groups as they did earlier during the Afghan War (1979–89). The final targets, no doubt, are Iran and Syria, against which the US has been working hard to build an Arab–Israeli alliance.

CHAPTER 1

1. A distinction should be made between "modernization" and "modernity." Bendix (1967:329) for example has argued that "many attributes of modernization, like widespread literacy or modern medicine, have appeared, or have been adopted, in isolation from other attributes of modern society. Hence, modernization in some sphere of life may occur without resulting in 'modernity'."

2. For a critique of Weber's thesis see Tawney (1962); Hudson (1949); and Means (1966:372–81). An excellent critique by Samuelson (1964) suggests that the emergence of the Protestant ethic may have been due to the rise of capitalism rather than vice versa.

3. For a compromise position between Weber and his critics see Demerath III and Hammond (1969:104–5). They propose that "instead of arguing that Protestantism helped pave the way for capitalism by spinning out a legitimating ethic of its own, it may be more accurate to indicate that Protestantism was crucial in simply breaking the yoke of traditional Catholic dominance allowing for the autonomous evolution of alternative forms of political and economic production of which capitalism was one manifestation."

4. Since several modes of production can be available and possible at any one historical stage, human will inevitably plays a role in choosing among the different alternatives. Of course the choice will be influenced and conditioned by the objective and concrete social circumstances determined by the consensual (voluntary or coercive) arrangement of available material resources. See Maduro (1982:45).

5. Although the interaction between the social context and the religio-political/secular movements may be either conflictive or harmonious, this study will henceforth apply the model to conflictive social settings.

6. Thermidor—the name of the month in the French revolutionary calendar in which Robespierre was ousted from power and eventually executed—refers to the return of society to its normal conditions of institutional functioning. See Brinton (1959).

7. Characterizing a regime as conservative on the national level does not necessarily imply anything about the foreign policy of that particular regime. A politically conservative system may promote and support

revolutionary movements in other parts of the world. It is therefore not inconsistent to adopt a pro-status quo national policy while encouraging anti-status quo movements abroad. See Oakeshott (1962:168–96).

8. Epistemology aims "to clarify the origin, structure, and methods of knowledge formation and, most importantly, to construct ideal standards of objectivity and ideal criteria of validation which can guide investigators as they seek to test their knowledge claims" (Connolly 1967:69–70).

9. This work set the foundation for the Marxist paradigm that religion was simply a superstructural component of the economic substructure. In his sixth thesis on Feuerbach, for example, Marx (1981) stated that "human essence," of which religion is an intrinsic subjective component, was in reality "the ensemble of the social relations" (122). In contrast Weber (1958) perceived religion as a potential determinant of social relations. It is worthy of note, however, that Engels (1956), recognizing the problems associated with religious reductionism, in his later works admitted a positive and autonomous role for religion.

10. The functional role of religion has been studied under the strong influence of the functionalist school. Among its pioneers see: Parsons (1951); Morton (1957); Malinowski (1954).

11. According to Bultmann, demythologizing refers to the "method of interpretation ... which tries to recover the deeper meaning behind the mythological conceptions" (1958:13). He defines mythology as a "mode of representation in consequence of which cult is understood as action in which non-material forces are mediated by material means" (1984:42).

12. According to Shi'ism "the Qur'an contained crude religious notions for the masses (exoteric), and at the same time had deliberate obscurities and ambiguities which would lead the philosophically minded to contemplate and to achieve a true rational understanding of religion (esoteric)" (Keddie 1963:53).

13. One of the revolutionary posters for example depicted Ayatollah Khomeini defeating a defunct Shah on which was inscribed "For every Pharaoh there is a Moses" (Fischer 1986).

14. Imam Hussain was the grandson of the Prophet Muhammad and the third imam for Shi'ite Muslims. He was killed at Karbala' in Iraq with many of his family and companions by the Umayyad army of King Yazid in 680 CE.

15. Ayatollah Khomeini's usage of the term "satanic" underscores the extent of the contradictory relationship between the two polar groups, and is to be understood as a reference to any condition that subverts the natural harmony between man and God. In the same vein as René Guénon, he used this term independently of any personalized idea that conformed with some theological outlook. As Guénon puts it: "What has to be taken into account is, on the one hand, the spirit of negation and of subversion into which 'Satan' is resolved metaphysically, whatever may be the special forms that may be assumed by that spirit in order to be manifested in one domain or another, and, on the other hand, the thing that can properly be held to represent it and so to speak 'incarnate' it

in the terrestrial world in which its action is being studied ..." (Guénon 1953:291).

16. Shari'ati makes a distinction here between an intellectual and a free thinker. To him every free thinker is an intellectual but not every intellectual is a free thinker; the intellectual at times being merely one who does mental work without necessarily being conscious of his society's culture or needs. (See Shari'ati 1980a:8.)

CHAPTER 2

1. Regarding such non-linear circular laws see the Tradition by Prophet Muhammad in which he identifies the unfolding stages of Islamic history as follows: Prophethood and Caliphate (= Government of God); Biting Kingship (= hereditary); Government by Force (= up for grabs dictatorships); and finally the Government of God (Al-Albani 1958:8–9; 1). Muslims have tended to understand this and other similar traditions simply as prophecies of events which are to take place sometime in the future. However, a deeper look may help bring forth laws of sufficiency. In those terms the tradition identifies "sufficiency" to be the historical epoch when the end of Islamic history both (re)connects and (re)establishes continuity with its past. How to establish this normatively sufficient condition (stem) is a necessary cognitive exercise (branch) (for example *Wilayat al-Faqih* and the Iranian Islamic revolution?). Ernst Bloch's circular aphorism that "the true genesis is not in the beginning but in the end," may be of relevance in this context (Carr 1986:xxxix).

2. Qur'anic narrations (*qassas*), for instance, do not merely reflect bygone accounts, but circular frameworks of reference through which past, present, and future meanings of events meet and connect. While events may be indeterminable, they are by no means chaotic. In this sense they are very contemporary and very real. See Qur'an 22:45; 28:58; 6:6; 15:4; 38:30 among many others.

3. Al-Shafi'i is the founder of one of the four major Sunni schools of jurisprudence. The choice of Al-Shafi'i in this chapter is mainly for purposes of illustration and does not exclude contributions from other Sunni or Shi'ite schools of jurisprudence. The precision of his methodology however remains insightful and is stressed.

4. In reproducing its own elements by the interaction of its own elements, the Shari'ah not only creates an autonomous order, but further produces its own very elements as well. This process goes beyond mere autonomy to reflect a condition of autopoiesis, or "self-production" (Zeleny 1981:6). To Niklas Luhmann, an autopoietic system "constitutes the elements of which it consists through the elements of which it consists. In so doing it sets limits which do not exist in the substructure complexity of the environment of the system" (Teubner 1988:14).

5. Perturbation refers to "self-reproducing" law that is dependent on its "inner states" and "on the past," but that "cannot be predicted." In this sense, "the indeterminate nature of [the Shari'ah] is inextricably bound up with its autonomy. ... Inputs which appear identical to the outside

observer do not necessarily have the same internal effect" (Teubner 1993:2).

6. The Islamic methodology proposed here is a stem–branch (Tree) methodology. This means that any rational effort "stems from a (juridical) foundation (*asl*)," "ends with a foundation," or is "guided by a foundation." See Al-Jabri (1996:113). On the complementary relationship between reason and revelation, see Al-Jabri (1996:72–4).

7. Qur'anic source: 16:103. Compare this circular and procedural reasoning, made in the ninth century with what Teubner says in the twentieth century: "Even if it can be proven with scientific evidence that a factual statement in a legal procedure is blatantly wrong, that factual statement of the court ... will not be reversed (apart from very few, narrowly defined exceptions) unless the procedural requirements are fulfilled" (Teubner 1989:744).

8. On the divisive potential of such tensions between intellectuals and the *Fuqaha'* and Ayatollah Khomeini's reference to it see Khaled Tawfiq (*Kayhan Al-Arabi*, August 10, 1995; supplement: 5). See also Tawfiq's insightful discourse regarding Ulama-intellectuals' cooperation in "Al-Fiqh Al-Siaysi" [Political Jurisprudence], (*Kayhan Al-Arabi*, February 20, 1995; supplement: 5).

9. The importance of reinstating the full dimensions of Islamic methodology may be underscored by Luhmann's perceptive observation that normative structures (isolated from a cognitive shield) are highly vulnerable since "[t]hey are sensitive to open defiance and unenforceability because doubts have a spillover effect and spread over the system. Cognitive structures, on the other hand, may be specified and remain relatively isolated" (Luhmann 1990:230). This argument, in less sophisticated form, underlies Islamists' claims to the necessity of an Islamic state as a normative-cognitive structure.

10. For an excellent and lucid exposition of such historical developments see the adeptly titled book by Tarnas, *The Passion of the Western Mind*, New York: Ballantine Books (1991:333ff).

11. See Qur'an 29:43; 21:67; 2:73 and 67:10, among many other verses. Regarding the autonomous individual see Qur'an 25:43: "Seest thou such a one as taketh for his God his own passion (hawah)...?" Man being his own God (i.e. master; setting his own criteria—rational or otherwise) is largely what secular humanism is all about. See also 45:23 among others. Qur'an further makes a strong link between conjecture and passion: "They follow nothing but conjecture and what their own souls desire (*ma tahwa al-anfus*)."

12. Compare this understanding with the Social Science Encyclopedia's definition of reason as "the name of an *alleged* human faculty capable of discerning, recognizing, formulating and criticizing truths" (my emphasis). The uncertainty incorporated in this definition of reason is substantively similar to the definition of passion, in the Arabic *Al-Mu'jam al-Wasit* [The Intermediate Lexicon], as an opinion based on uncertain proof (i.e. alleged), related to an internalized human desire/autonomy (human faculty), and which could be for good and evil (results of fallible attempts at discerning, recognizing, formulating, and criticizing

truths). By this very definition, reason and truth (religion) diverge; a truth criticized is a truth no more. This centrifugal dynamic consequently reflects a condition of passion. The latter does not refer to an emotional condition but to a rational autonomy. See Kuper and Kuper (1985:687); and Anis, Muntasser, Al-Sawalhi, and Ahmed (1973: 2:1001).

13. Compare Weber's "nullity" observation with what Brzezinski, in the later part of the twentieth century, identified as a pervasive Western problem: "permissive cornucopia." Brzezinski applies the term to a society in which "everything is permitted and everything can be had" (Brzezinski 1993: xii, 65). The term appears to be synonymous with hedonistic values.

14. According to Tarnas (1991:402) "the one postmodern absolute is critical consciousness, which by deconstructing all, seems compelled by its own logic to do so to itself as well. This is the unstable paradox that permeates the postmodern mind."

15. By "explicative mode of knowledge" or *al-bayan*, Al-Jabri (1996:13ff) refers to the system of knowledge produced by the Islamic civilization based on pure Arab and Islamic linguistic discourses.

16. One should stress here that reason and revelation can only converge at a narrowest point but never merge. Were they to do so then the former may be claimed as a substitute. The philosophical implications of this matter remain beyond the scope of this chapter. Suffice it to see the revelation–reason relationship in terms of stem and branch.

17. See for instance Ziauddin Sardar who states that "the pursuit of the Islamic state has itself become an ideology"; that this is a "form of secularization"; and that "the Iranian state is clearly based on this assumption" (in Anees, Abedin, and Sardar 1991:70). That ideology and *mazhab* are based on two different discursive relations and therefore subject to different modes of analyses eludes him. By implication, any Islamic *mazhab* with activist political connotations may then be accused of such ideological trappings. Sardar appears to be making an ideological statement himself, separating the necessity of pursuing an Islamic state from the interests of Islam and Muslims. The logical conclusion of such discursive statements would take us full circle back to the separation of religion and politics—i.e. secularization, or some form of de-politicized passive traditional order.

18. Perhaps it may be suitable at the end of this chapter to provide a working definition for the concept of appropriation as it has been developed and applied: Appropriation as a reconstructive tool envisages a centripetal, symbiotic, and valid process of "dialysis" which Islamizes, neutralizes, and/or preempts social theory while incorporating and maintaining its elements of precision. It establishes cognitive circularity and structural identity with Islamic normativity, and by capitalizing on existing "knowledge" is time parsimonious insofar as it reconstructs as it deconstructs, builds as it demolishes, transforms as it incorporates.

CHAPTER 3

1. Assabiyya comes from the root Arabic word "ASB" which means the nerve or the command center of something. The closest English meaning of the word as used by Ibn Khaldun is solidarity. *Al-Khawass* comes from

the root Arabic word "Khss" which implies the designative nature of a special thing or quality. The closest English meaning of the word as used in this chapter is the special groups or elites who occupy their position due to their incorporation of Islamic moral values.

2. See for example the Islamic polemical discourses on leadership by Al-Mawardi (1982); Ibish (1966); see also Sobhi (1969).

3. Ibn Khaldun's *assabiyya*, Gramsci's *hegemony*, and Ayatollah Khomeini's *Wilayat al-Faqih* have been chosen due to their common superstructural approach to society and government. Situating society in the superstructure eventually transforms the latter into a total structure.

4. The point that Ibn Khaldun makes is particularly insightful to warrant citing here. As he put it: "Now it is rare to find gentleness in men who have keen intelligence and awareness; rather is it to be found among the duller people. ... It has thus been shown that intelligence and foresight are defects in a politician, for they represent an excess of thought, just as stupidity is an excess in stolidity. Now in all human qualities both extremes are reprehensible, the mean alone being commendable: thus generosity is the mean between extravagance and niggardliness, and courage between rashness and cowardice, and so on for other qualities. And that is why those who are extremely intelligent are described as 'devils' or 'devilish' or something analogous" (Issawi 1958:130).

5. According to Samuel Huntington, "there is a failure to distinguish between what is modern and what is Western. The one thing which modernization theory has not produced is a model of Western society ... which could be compared with, or even contrasted with, the model of modern society. Modern society has been Western society writ abstractly and polysyllabically. But to a non-modern, non-Western society, the processes of modernization and Westernization may appear to be different indeed. This difficulty has been glossed over...." (Huntington 1988:365).

6. See also Sharabi's comparison of Arab societies with that of Japan. The fact, according to Sharabi, that Japanese people adhered to official ideology resolved the society's tension between tradition and modernization, at least on the political level. In Arab society, this tension remained an open social and political problem without social or political resolution (Sharabi 1989:158). Unfortunately, except for a very brief reference on page 13, Sharabi does not discuss the Iranian experience and whether it may offer insights toward resolving this dilemma. It is important to note, however, that in his brief reference he does not exclude such a potential.

7. It is insightful here to note the exceptional historical case of President Gamal Abdel Nasser of Egypt (1954–70). Despite the secular nature of his regime, it was his *charisma* which situated his leadership in the superstructure where he came to symbolize the people's belief systems, including Islam. His charisma largely resolved the inherent contradictions between Islamic and secular legitimacies, though during Nasser's regime the only Islamic model available was one condemned later by Grand Ayatollah Khomeini as *American Islam*. However, one should add that since charismatic authority is the most unstable form of authorities, as Max Weber has observed, contradictions were inevitably bound to re-

emerge once Nasser had disappeared from the national scene. Regarding "American Islam," it is important to recall that former US Secretary of State John Foster Dulles had explicitly proposed to Nasser in the early 1950s that Islam be used as an instrument against the communist tide. Nasser's rejection of the idea did not mean that the Americans did not pursue this course of action on their own, finding willing so-called "Islamist" collaborators in the process. Such collaboration reached its peak during the Afghanistan war (1979–88) and the collapse of the Soviet Union in its aftermath. Also in 1990 after the Iraqi invasion of Kuwait, Shaikh Yusuf al-Qaradawi, in an interview with the Saudi *National Guard Magazine*, expressed the opinion that seeking the help of foreigners (Americans) is permissible (Haddad 1991:260). Effectively, Qaradawi was sanctioning American colonial hegemony over the *abode of Islam* and rendering lessons from Muslims' experience with the West over a period of close to 200 years irrelevant. The unpersuasive logic that Iraq was the immediate and actual threat while the US was a distant and potential one simply reflects simplicity of thought at best, and complicity at worst. Such attitudes and sympathies help explain Nasser's harsh policies toward Islamic currents during his time. After all, Islam was one of Nasser's three strategic circles (the other two being the Arab world and Africa), but when dealing with it he came to the *same* "American Islam" conclusion that Imam Khomeini arrived at later. Figures such as Qaradawi, as well as other Islamic currents, may need to reassess and reflect on their own performance and transcend their own hatreds. This may be a much more constructive process instead of being obsessed with settling scores against Nasser and/or Arab nationalism. Such is a battle in which everybody can only lose. The same applies to pan-Arab forces. Their lukewarm position regarding the Islamic movement of Hamas, after its taking over of the Gaza strip in June 2007, was quite noticeable. This despite their awareness of the extreme corruption of Fatah movement leadership and its virtual collaboration with Israel. Grudges on both sides continue to blind sight and insight.

8. Structural and sociological analysis of Islamic history and events can be irrelevant insofar as such analysis imposes a secular Western/Islamic hierarchy of understanding. Consequently Muslims using those methods as independent explanatory tools end up, consciously or otherwise, losing their sense of self-understanding as well as a sense of their past, present and future. As the *Economist* has rightly observed, "Religions have a way of getting to parts of the human psyche that secular ideologies no longer reach" (27 March–2 April 1993:46). It is at the heart of this matter that the problem of *Orientalism* lies. See Said (1979) and Hanafi (1991).

9. The feasibility of such an approach may be underscored by the following remarks of a Jewish Iranian woman: "It's much better than it was in the days of the Shah. It's much freer for me than it was. Nobody bothers me if I bother nobody. And they let me drink my vodka at home." *Manchester Guardian Weekly* (February 21, 1993:10). See also *The New Yorker* (June 22, 1992:41, 70, 76), and "In Ahmadinejad's Iran, Jews still find a space" (April 2007), *The Christian Science Monitor* (csmonitor.com).

10. See for example Cross (1958:1338). The Dictionary labeled Theocracy as "intrinsic" to the "Mohammedan" (sic) religion.

11. Generally speaking, Theocracy came to refer to religio-political systems where God is recognized as the immediate ruler, or where the temporal ruler is constrained by the final direction of the theological head. See Bogdanor (1987:610). Max Weber on the other hand, labeled the fusion of temporal and spiritual powers in the hands of one ruling person as "Caesaropapism." Arjomand (1988:123) applied this term to the Safavid Dynasty of Iran (1501–1722). For other definitions see M'Clintock and Strong (1880:317); Fern (1945:775); and MacIvar (1947:153).

12. In Twelver Shi'ism commitment to the rulings of a dead *mujtahid* is prohibited as long as a living one exists. If however, no *mujtahid* was available, people were allowed to follow the teachings and writings of a dead *marja'i-taqlid*. See Algar (1969:10).

13. See the interesting discussion by Khaled Tawfiq, "Readings on the Role of the Umma in the Islamic Political System," (*Kayhan Al-Arabi*, December 7, 1992:6).

CHAPTER 4

1. It is true that the Hanafi school of thought recognized that territorial implications affected religious rulings, as opposed to a purely non-territorial personal obligation to follow such rulings. However, this hinged on a non-Islamic territorial law not contradicting any Islamic injunction (such as eating pork or drinking wine). The latter always had precedence even though a Muslim in non-Muslim territory was expected to obey local rules and laws.

2. Al-Shaybani was called the Hugo Grotius of the Muslims by Joseph Hammer von Purgstall (Khadduri 1966:56). His works are described by Weeramantary as "the world's earliest treatise on international law as a separate topic" (Weeramantary 1988:130). As a matter of fact, Weeramantary argues persuasively that it was the influence of Islamic international law that served as the triggering factor in the development of the Western counterpart. Western scholars in the fifteenth and sixteenth centuries were well aware of Arab/Islamic literature and sciences through Spain and Italy. Weeramantary also provides a host of circumstantial evidence indicating that Grotius was influenced by Islamic scholarship even though he never acknowledged it (Weeramantary 1988:149–58). Appreciative references to the Qur'an and to Islamic law pertinent to international relations can also be found in the writings of Montesquieu (Weeramantary 1988:108–9).

3. Al-Ghunaimi has indicated that "it is not accurate to include the doctrines of the various Islamic schools of thought [paradigms] in the *Shari'ah stricto sensu*. These schools, in fact represent different processes of speculation on what the divine law, *the Shari'ah* might be" (Al-Ghunaimi 1969:133).

4. An epistemic community consists of knowledge-based experts who share both cause-effect conceptions and sets of normative and principled beliefs (Goldstein and Keohane 1993:11). This does not mean that members of such a community have to agree on every detail. By the same token *ijma* does not necessarily mean the absence of differences, but rather their

existence within a common Islamic normative structure. In this sense, differences between, for instance, Hanafis and Shafiis regarding details of conducting relations with non-Muslim nations need not be understood or translated into discontinuity or an absence of *ijma*, at least as far as the Islamic theory is concerned. In the Islamic religious field, this also applies to the Sunni–Shi'ite divide.

5. In what follows in this section I draw on work by Charles Tilly. However, I expand his organizational and intra-state focus to the international and global context.

6. *Dar al-ahd* or the abode of the covenant is used here to refer to peaceful relations of a more or less enduring kind (non-imperialists). *Dar al-sulh*, or the abode of peaceful arrangements, connotes temporality and contingency determined by less enduring, more tense relations (semi-imperialists). *Dar al-baghy*, or the abode of aggression, refers to imperialist and hostile actors.

CHAPTER 5

1. "This day have I perfected your religion for you, completed my favor upon you, and have chosen for you Islam as your religion" (Qur'an 5:3); and "The religion before God is Islam" (Qur'an 3:19).

2. "Verily this Umma of yours is a *single* Umma" (Qur'an 21:92; 23:52).

3. "Ye are the best of Peoples evolved for mankind" (Qur'an 3:110).

4. "Never will the Jews or the Christians be satisfied with thee unless thou follow their form of religion. Say 'the guidance of God; that is the (only) guidance'" (Qur'an 2:120). Quoting Huntington in this context is instructive: "A world of clashing civilizations ... is inevitably a world of double standards: people apply one standard to their kin-countries and a different standard to others" (1993:36).

5. It comes as no surprise for instance, that Mahmoud Hafez (March 25, 2007), the president of the *Arabic Language Complex* in Egypt, has expressed serious concerns that the violent aggression underway against the Arabic language will produce, in the period of a generation or two, an entire social class that does not belong to Egypt or to the Arabic language, and instead to other languages and the countries which speak them (www.middle-east-online.com). Shaikh Yusuf al-Qaradawi (February 25, 2007) also dedicated an entire program to such threats in *al-shari'ah wa al-hayat* [Shari'ah and Life], a weekly program on the Qatari *al-Jazeera* network (www.aljazeera.net) (both networks in Arabic).

6. "But those who ... give ... preference over themselves, even though poverty was their (own lot). And those saved from the covetousness of their own souls—they are the ones that achieve prosperity" (Qur'an 59:9).

CHAPTER 6

1. This chapter is a revised version of the study "Liberalism and the Contestation of Islamic Sovereignty," by Amr Sabet, originally published

in 2003 in The Emirates Occasional Papers No. 52 in English (ISSN: 1682–1246 and ISBN: 9948–00–513–9) by the Emirates Center for Strategic Studies and Research (ECSSR), P.O. Box 4567, Abu Dhabi, UAE. The Arabic version of this study has been published by the ECSSR in 2004 in the International Studies Series No. 55 (Dirasat 'alamiyyat, ISSN 1682–1211; ISBN 9948–00–693–3). This chapter has been published with special permission from the ECSSR. Copyright © in the above-mentioned publications belongs to The Emirates Center for Strategic Studies and Research. All rights are reserved. Except for brief quotations in a review, this material, or any part thereof may not be reproduced in any form without permission in writing from the publisher.

2. One instructive historical example of significance occurred during the reign of the Ottoman Sultan Suleyman I (1520–66), known in the West as "the Magnificent," but cherished by the Ottomans as "the Law-giver" (*al-Qanuni*). While the empire was Islamic, the Shari'ah as the law of the religious community coexisted with *qanun* as law of the empire—one body of laws being sacred, the other imperial. Their distinctive characters nevertheless were brought into conformity by an outstanding jurist of the time Ebu's-su'ud (1490–1574). In Ottoman historical annals, Ebu's-su'ud was the most prominent representative of this legal order, and through the medium of fatwas, was able to harmonize the secular law with the Shari'ah, "creating, in effect," what came to be perceived as "the ideal Islamic legal system" (Imber 1997:x, 24). This historical period, while offering a potentially insightful experience particularly relevant to contemporary conditions, has unfortunately not been sufficiently examined, Muslim scholars being more preoccupied with Western history rather than their own.

3. "This is the Book; in it is guidance sure, without doubt, to those who fear Allah" (Qur'an 2:1).

4. See for instance (Soroush 2000:16).

5. The relationship between faith and knowledge is clear in the Qur'anic verse 2:282: "fear God and God will teach you" (author's translation; *wattaqu Allah wa yu'allimukum Allah*).

6. The following quotes by Hans Morgenthau, a founder of the realist school of international relations, depict such a policy objective and condition very clearly: "What we suggest calling cultural imperialism is the most subtle and, if it were ever to succeed by itself alone, the most successful of imperialistic policies. It aims not at the conquest of territory or at the control of economic life, but at the conquest and control of the minds of men as an instrument for changing the power relations between two nations. If one could imagine the culture and, more particularly, the political ideology, with all its concrete imperialistic objectives, of State A conquering the minds of all citizens determining the policies of State B, State A would have won a more complete victory and would have founded its supremacy on more stable grounds than any military conqueror or economic master. State A would not need to threaten or employ military force or use economic pressure in order to achieve its ends; for that end, the subservience of State B to its will would have

already been realized by the persuasiveness of a superior culture and a more attractive political philosophy.

"This is, however, a hypothetical case. Cultural imperialism generally falls short of a victory so complete as to make other methods of imperialism superfluous. The typical role cultural imperialism plays in modern times is subsidiary to other methods. It softens up the enemy, it prepares the ground for military conquest or economic penetration. Its typical modern manifestation is the fifth column ... While the technique of cultural imperialism has been perfected by the totalitarians and has been forged into the effective political weapon of the fifth column, the use of cultural sympathy and political affinities as weapons of imperialism is almost as old as imperialism itself" (Morgenthau 1993:72–3).

7. "After (the excitement) of the distress, He sent down calm on a band of you overcome with slumber, while another band was stirred to anxiety by their own feelings, Moved by wrong suspicions of Allah—suspicions due to ignorance. They said: 'What affair is this of ours?' Say thou: 'Indeed, this affair is wholly Allah's.' They hide in their minds what they dare not reveal to thee. They say (to themselves): 'If we had had anything to do with this affair, We should not have been in the slaughter here.' Say: 'Even if you had remained in your homes, those for whom death was decreed would certainly have gone forth to the place of their death'; but (all this was) that Allah might test what is in your breasts and purge what is in your hearts. For Allah knoweth well the secrets of your hearts" (Qur'an 3:154). Could this verse form a basis for comprehending the underlying motivations and psychological construction of both groups under the pressure of "crisis" and "distress"?

8. "Say: 'O Allah. Lord of Power (And Rule), Thou givest power to whom Thou pleasest, and Thou strippest off power from whom Thou pleasest: Thou enduest with honour whom Thou pleasest, and Thou bringest low whom Thou pleasest: In Thy hand is all good. Verily, over all things Thou hast power'" (Qur'an 3:26); "To every people is a term appointed: when their term is reached, not an hour can they cause delay, nor (an hour) can they advance (it in anticipation)" (Qur'an 7:34); "There is not a population but We shall destroy it before the Day of Judgment or punish it with a dreadful Penalty: that is written in the (eternal) Record" (Qur'an 17:58).

9. Religious dialectics may be seen implied in the following Qur'anic verse referring to Pharaoh (thesis?) and Moses (anti-thesis?), the latter loved by and raised in the bosom of Pharaoh who unknowingly nurtures his own destroyer, leading ultimately to the liberation of the children of Israel from bondage (synthesis?): "'Throw (the child) into the chest, and throw (the chest) into the river: the river will cast him up on the bank, and he will be taken up by one who is an enemy to Me and an enemy to him': But I cast (the garment of) love over thee from Me: and (this) in order that thou mayest be reared under Mine eye" (Qur'an 20:39). This gives substance to claims that many social theory concepts are merely reduced theological principles.

10. "This day have those who reject faith given up all hope of your religion: yet fear them not but fear Me. This day have I perfected your religion

for you, completed My favor upon you, *and have chosen for you Islam as your religion*" (Qur'an 5:3; my emphasis).

11. "But ye shall not will except as Allah wills, the Cherisher of the Worlds" (Qur'an 81:29); "But ye will not, except as Allah wills; for Allah is full of Knowledge and Wisdom" (Qur'an 76:30).

12. Hence for example the statement "all roads lead to Rome," or the Caliph of Baghdad (Harun al-Rashid, ruled 786–809 CE), on observing a cloud, stating "rain where ever you wish your tax is to me," or the British Empire "upon which the sun never set," or the statement of President Ronald Reagan, "you can run but you can't hide." In so many words, all appear to be saying what Qarun had said before meeting his fate: "This has been given to me because of a certain knowledge which I have. Did he not know that Allah had destroyed, before him, (whole) generations, which were superior to him in strength and greater in the amount (of riches) they had collected? But the wicked are not called (immediately) to account for their sins" (Qur'an 28:78).

13. "If a wound hath touched you, be sure a similar wound hath touched the others. Such days (of varying fortunes) We give to men and men by turns (*nudawiluha bayna annas*): that Allah may know those that believe, and that He may take to Himself from your ranks Martyr-witnesses (to Truth). And Allah loveth not those that do wrong" (Qur'an 3:140).

14. "And We wished to be Gracious to those who were being depressed in the land, to make them leaders (in Faith) and make them heirs" (Qur'an 28:5); "How many were the gardens and springs they left behind, And corn-fields and noble buildings, And wealth (and conveniences of life), wherein they had taken such delight! Thus (was their end)! And We made other people inherit (those things)! And neither heaven nor earth shed a tear over them: nor were they given a respite (again)" (Qur'an 44:25–9).

15. See for instance sura *al-Kahf* in the Qur'an (the Cave; chapter 18) especially verses 61–82 where Moses meets a man, to whom knowledge is given by God, who commits certain inexplicable acts that Moses cannot fathom or approve of until their future wisdom is explained to him.

16. "And those who had envied [Qarun's] position the day before began to say on the morrow: 'Ah! it is indeed Allah Who enlarges the provision or restricts it, to any of His servants He pleases! had it not been that Allah was gracious to us, He could have caused the earth to swallow us up! Ah! those who reject Allah will assuredly never prosper'" (Qur'an 28:82).

17. Perhaps this is the moral of the Qur'anic narration (*qasas*) of Pharaoh and the Israelites. Despite the wretched condition of the Israelites they would probably have suffered Pharaoh's fate had they followed his ways. Divine punishment was actually visited upon them when, still influenced by Egyptian religious culture, they chose to worship the Golden Calf.

18. "So he went forth among his people in the (pride of his worldly) glitter. Said those whose aim is the Life of this World: 'Oh! that we had the like of what *QARUN* has got! for he is truly a lord of mighty good fortune!'" (Qur'an 28:79); "That Home of the Hereafter We shall give to those who intend not high-handedness or mischief on earth: and the end is (best) for the righteous" (Qur'an 28:83).

19. "But those who had been granted (true) knowledge said: 'Alas for you! The reward of Allah (in the Hereafter) is best for those who believe and work righteousness: but this none shall attain, save those who steadfastly persevere (in good)'" (Qur'an 28:80). See also the Qur'anic reference to Saul as he moved toward battle, and the prior disciplining and weeding out of his troops (2:249).

20. As a matter of fact, there is scriptural evidence which lends preference to positive optimism over negative feelings of pessimism: "So lose not heart, nor fall into despair: For ye must gain mastery if ye are true in Faith" (Qur'an 3:139).

21. "Behold! they came on you from above you and from below you, and behold, the eyes became dim and the hearts gaped up to the throats, and ye imagined various (vain) thoughts about Allah" (Qur'an 33:10).

22. "'O my People! Yours is the dominion this day: Ye have the upper hand in the land: but who will help us from the Punishment of Allah, should it befall us?' Pharaoh said: 'I but point out to you that which I see (myself); Nor do I guide you but to the Path of Right!'" (Qur'an 40:29).

23. "Behold, thy Lord said to the angels: 'I will create a vicegerent on earth'" (Qur'an 2:30); "O David! We did indeed make thee a vicegerent on earth: so judge thou between men in truth (and justice): Nor follow thou the lusts (of thy heart), for they will mislead thee from the Path of Allah" (Qur'an 38:26). The following verse bestows the conditions and right to vicegerency and representation: "Ye are the best of peoples, evolved for mankind, enjoining what is right, forbidding what is wrong, and believing in Allah. If only the People of the Book had faith, it were best for them: among them are some who have faith, but most of them are perverted transgressors" (Qur'an 3:110). The Prophet is also reported to have mentioned that the Qur'an is the linking thread between God and the Muslim Umma.

24. The Prophet is reported to have said: "We the Prophets have been instructed to address people in accordance with the level of their understanding" (quoted by Taha; in Kurzman 1998: 271).

25. The Islamic methods of ijtihad and procedural cognition are clearly stated in the following Qur'anic verse: "O ye who believe! Obey Allah [first Principle], and obey the Messenger [application(s)], and those charged with authority [uli al-amr] among you [those qualified: interpreters/theoreticians/empiricists = mazhab]. If ye differ in anything among yourselves [as a result of the latest category], refer it to Allah and His Messenger [back to first Principle and applications], if ye do believe in Allah and the Last Day: That is best, and most suitable for final determination" (4:59). The above are very similar to methodologies applied in scientific research, starting from first principles, to applications, to *theories*, *approaches* or *paradigms*, to presenting a new insight or discovery involving the latter (= ijtihad). Procedural similarities, however, should not obscure substantive differences (see Al-Shafi'i 1987:125). Also, *uli al-amr* is understood here to refer to those *qualified* (read charged with authority) in their field not, courtesy of *fiqh sultani*, to the ruler/sultan as such or for that matter to *pseudo-ulama*, particularly when *unqualified*, whether in terms of piety, sincerity, justice or competence.

26. The Prophet is reported to have said: "The differences of opinion among the *learned* within my community are [a sign of] God's grace" (my emphasis). The *hadith* clearly refers to learned not free market opinions.

27. Taha was executed in 1985 by the Sudanese military regime of Ja'far Numeiri (1969–85).

28. "And thou (standest) on an exalted standard of character" (Qur'an 68:4); "We sent thee not, but as a mercy for all creatures" (Qur'an 21:107).

29. The Egyptian Mufti Ali Jum'a (March 21, 2007) indicated that the 25 volumes of common Sunni–Shi'ite *ahadith* have been compiled by the *Complex for Narrowing Differences between Mazaheb* in Iran. However he indicated that both Sunnis and Shi'ites have failed to deliver their accomplishments in this respect to the Muslim public (http://arab.moheet. com/asp/subject.asp?ch=1).

CHAPTER 7

1. The Qur'an makes it clear that a universal humanity is practically impossible, given the different levels of consciousness and beliefs: "Mankind was one single nation, and Allah sent Messengers with glad tidings and warnings; and with them He sent the Book in truth, to judge between people in matters wherein they differed" (2:213). See also Qur'an, 5:48; 10:19; 11:118; 16:93; 42:8; 43:33. The Muslim Umma is defined as one, unique, and separate from all others (21:92; 23:52).

2. "I have only created jinns and men that they may serve Me [worship Me; follow My ways]" (Qur'an 51:56). Only God is the "End."

3. Prophet Muhammad is reported to have said: "Those [that is nations, communities] before you perished because, when their honorable [read the rich and powerful] stole they were let go, and when their poor stole they were punished. By Him in whose hands my soul lies, if Fatima the daughter of Muhammad were to steal, Muhammad would cut off her hand" (author's translation). The problem of "Law," as the Prophetic *hadith* (tradition) indicates, is not in its severity but in its arbitrary and unjust implementation. If the Law is too harsh to be applied fairly, injustice should not be added to its harshness. The typical juridical refrain, that what cannot be applied in its totality is not to be left in its entirety, does not apply here. In fact it becomes nothing more than an additional discredit to *al-fiqh al-sultani*. This is particularly so when a law capriciously applied or only applied to the weak turns out to be nothing but an act of *injustice* committed in the name of God, consequently bringing about Divine wrath, as the *Hadith* indicates.

4. Those rights were classified by Al-Juwaini (d. 478 AH/1085 CE; the Imam of the Two Sanctuaries), and later by his student Al-Ghazali (d. 505 AH/1111 CE), and adopted with minor variations by Fakhruddin Al-Razi (d. 606 AH/1209 CE). See Al-Raisouny (1992:38–46).

5. In 1995 US Ambassador to the UN Madeleine Albright described the organization as a "tool of American foreign policy" (Bennis 2006:24).

6. In the Qur'an, it is common to equate those who give up on belief with debasement ("Seest thou such a one as taketh his God his own passion (or

impulse)? ... Thinkst thou that most of them listen or understand? They are only like cattle;—Nay, they are worse astray in path" (Qur'an 25:44); see also Qur'an 7:179). Rationality is the mid-level attribute qualified to lead an individual to the highest level, that of spirituality, or to arrogance and hubris confining him to where he stands ("By the soul and the proportion and order given to it ... Truly he succeeds that purifies it and he fails that corrupts it" (Qur'an 91:9)), or to utter and instinctive debasement, that is regression and fall ("For the worst of beasts in the sight of God are the deaf and dumb,—those who understand not" (Qur'an 8:22); see also: "For the worst of beasts in the sight of God are those who reject Him: They will not believe" (Qur'an 8:55)). Islam constitutes the minimum level of moral configuration accepted in the sight of God; minimal because an individual may be a Muslim, thus within the "pale," yet still in need of much to improve his ethical standing, this as opposed to an ethical person whose work may be in vain ("Hast thou not turned thy vision to those who claim sanctity for themselves? Nay—but God doth sanctify whom He pleaseth ..." (Qur'an 4:49)); see also 24:21; see Qur'an 3:19: "The Religion before God is Islam (submission to His Will). Nor did the People of the Book dissent therefrom except through envy..."; see also Qur'an 3:85: "If anyone desires a religion other than Islam (submission to God) Never will it be accepted of him."

7. "God (thus) directs you as regards your children's (Inheritance): to the male, a portion equal to that of two females" (Qur'an 4:11); see also: "and nowise is the male like the female" (Qur'an 3:36).

8. "He hath only forbidden you dead meat, and blood, and the flesh of swine" (Qur'an 2:173); see also: Qur'an 16:115.

9. See An-Na'im (1992:57–60), where he explains this principle.

10. *Sultan* in Arabic literally means power, with the connotation of authority. However, it also refers to the figure of the ruler. The message of the statement is that morality cannot survive without power and authority. Honesty for example can be claimed to be an "authentic" human value. This does not mean that there should be no laws or coercive measures in place in case the code is broken. The fact that "dishonest" people may resist such measures is not an argument against "authentic" values or those measures, but rather one against those who transgress such a value.

11. "It is He who hath sent His Apostle with Guidance and the Religion of Truth, to proclaim it *over all religion*, even though the pagans may detest (it)" (Qur'an 9:33; my emphasis); see also Qur'an 48:28; 61:9. See: "This day have those who reject the faith given up all hope of your religion; Yet fear them not but fear Me. This day have I perfected your religion for you, completed My favour upon you, and have chosen for you Islam as your religion" (Qur'an 5:3).

12. This epistemology is clear in the following Qur'anic verse: "Never will the Jews or the Christians be *satisfied* with thee *unless thou follow their form of religion*. Say 'the guidance of God;—that is the (only) guidance'" (Qur'an 2:120; my emphasis). Only doing the bidding of power would restrain its exercise, yet resistance is called for at the end of the verse. Such belief is what renders the Muslim community a community of

will despite visible setbacks. To break Muslims' *will* inevitably calls for undermining their *ground* belief structure—Islam.

13. "Can the blind be held equal to the seeing?" (Qur'an 6:50). "These two kinds (of men) may be compared to the blind and deaf, and those who can see and hear well. Are they equal when compared?" (Qur'an 11:24). See also Qur'an 16:75; 39:9.

14. "And remember [children of Israel] We took your covenant (to this effect): Shed no blood amongst you, nor turn out your own people from your homes: and this ye solemnly ratified, and to this ye can bear witness. After this it is ye, the same people, who slay among yourselves, and banish a party of you from their homes; assist (Their enemies) against them, in guilt and rancour; and if they come to you as captives, ye ransom them, though it was not lawful for you to banish them. Then is it only a part of the Book that ye believe in, and do ye reject the rest? But what is the reward for those among you who behave like this but disgrace in this life?—and on the Day of Judgment they shall be consigned to the most grievous penalty. For Allah is not unmindful of what ye do. These are the people who buy the life of this world at the price of the Hereafter: their penalty shall not be lightened nor shall they be helped" (Qur'an 2:84–6).

15. "Muhammad is the apostle of Allah. And those who are with him are strong against Unbelievers, (but) compassionate amongst each other" (Qur'an 48:29).

16. While all Muslims, both Sunni and Shi'ite, acknowledge this *hadith*, the Sunnis also state another *hadith* which replaces "members of my household" with "my *sunna*" instead. The latter is also designated as *sounder* than the former. In any case, such casuistry misses the point. Holding fast to members of the Prophetic household is part and parcel of holding fast to the *sunna*. To treat members of the family of the Prophet the way they were historically dealt with is to transgress the latter. *Hadith* translation is by the author.

17. A recent, though by no means unique, case in Islamic history occurred when the Egyptian Mufti Ali Jum'a stated in *Al-Ahram* newspaper that "separation of religious institutions from the State is hateful deceit (*dajal mamqut*)" (July 6, 2007:40). If the Egyptian State is widely acknowledged to be ruled by a virtual kleptocracy, which despite all its failings has perfected the art of divesting values from their meaning, the nature of the *nested* relationship between the two can only be imagined. Thus at a time when the Islamic world is being attacked, invaded, and targeted by external forces and evangelist groups, the Mufti issued a fatwa that Muslims are free to choose any faith they wish. While human rights groups may rejoice at such a proclamation, for Muslims this appears to be the harbinger of what is yet to come. The Mufti qualified his fatwa by stating that a Muslim's conversion is conditional on not disturbing public peace or threatening society, or he could otherwise be punished (Middle East Online July 26, 2007; www.middle-east-online.com/?id=50675). If the Mufti's fatwa could be argued to pose a threat to both, especially given what the Muslim world is facing, the Mufti, irrespective of his juristic justifications, could, ironically by his own fatwa, be held legally liable for what he has said.

Bibliography

Abu-Sulayman, A.H.A. (1993) *Towards an Islamic Theory of International Relations* (Herndon: The International Institute of Islamic Thought).

Adams, Charles J. (2001) "Foreword," in Martin, Richard C., ed., *Approaches to Islam in Religious Studies* (Oxford: Oneworld).

Adamson, Walter L. (1980) *Hegemony and Revolution* (Berkeley: University of California Press).

Adorno, Theodor (1951) *Minima Moralia: Reflections from a Damaged Life*, trans. E.F.N. Jephcott (London: New Left Books).

Afshar, Haleh (1985) *Iran: A Revolution in Turmoil* (London: Macmillan).

Ahmed, Akbar (1992) *Postmodernism and Islam* (London: Routledge).

——(2002) *Discovering Islam*, rev. ed. (London: Routledge).

Ahmed, Akbar and Donnan, Hastings (1994) *Islam, Globalization and Postmodernity* (London: Routledge).

Akhavi, Shahrough (1980) *Religion and Politics in Contemporary Iran* (Albany: State University of New York Press).

——(1983) "The Ideology and Praxis of Shi'ism in the Iranian Revolution," *Comparative Studies in Society and History*, Vol. 25, No. 2 (April).

Al-Albani, Muhammad N. (1958) *Silsilat al-Ahadith al-Sahiha* (The Chain of Authentic Traditions) (Beirut: Al-Maktab Al-Islami).

Al-Attas, Syed Mohammad Naquib (1985) *Islam, Secularism and the Philosophy of the Future* (London: Mansell Publishing Ltd).

Algar, Hamid (1969) *Religion and State in Iran 1785–1906* (Berkeley: University of California Press).

Al-Ghunaimi, M.T. (1969) *The Muslim Conception of International Law and the Western Approach* (The Hague: Martinus Nijhoff).

Al-Jabri, Muhammad Abed (1990) *Al-Aql Al-Siyassi Al-Arabi* (The Arab Political Mind) (Beirut: Markaz Derasat al-Wihda al-Arabiyya).

——(1996) *Bunyat Al-Aql Al-Arabi* (The Structure of the Arab Mind), 2nd edn (Beirut: Markaz Derasat al-Wihda al-Arabiyya).

Allardt, Erik and Rokkan, Stein, eds (1970) *Mass Politics* (New York: The Free Press).

Al-Mawardi, Abu al-Hassan bin Habib (1982) *Al-Ahkam al-Sultaniya* (The Ordinances of Government) (Beirut: Dar Al-Kutub al-Ilmiya).

Al-Qurtobi, Muhammad bin Ahmed al-Ansari (1967) *Al-Jami' li-Ahkam al-Quran* (The Collection to the Ordinances of the Qur'an) (Beirut: Dar Ihya' al-Turath al-Arabi).

Al-Raisouny, Ahmad (1992) *Nazariyat al-Maqased* (The Theory of Purposes) (Al-Mu'assassa al-Jamii'ya lil-Dirasat wa al-Nashr wa al-Tawzi').

Al-Shafi'i, Muhammad bin Idris (1987) *Al-Risala fi Usul al-Fiqh* (Treatise on the Foundation of Islamic Jurisprudence), trans. and ed. by Majid Khadduri, 2nd edn (Cambridge: The Islamic Texts Society).

Al-Tabari, Muhammad bin Jarir (1980) *Jami' al-Bayan fi Tafsir al-Quran* (The Collection of Explication in Interpreting the Qur'an), 4th edn (Beirut: Dar al-Ma'rifa).

Anees, Munawar Ahmed, Abedin, Syed Z. and Sardar, Ziauddin (1991) *Christian–Muslim Relations: Yesterday, Today, Tomorrow* (London Gray Seal).

Anis, Ibrahim, Muntasser, Abdel-Halim, Al-Sawalhi, Attia and Ahmed, Muhammad Khalafallah (1973) *Al-Mu'jam al-Wasit* (The Intermediate Lexicon) 2nd edn (Cairo: Mujamma' al-Lugha al-Arabiyya).

An-Na'im, Abdullahi Ahmed (1990) "Problems of Universal Cultural Legitimacy for Human Rights," in An-Na'im, Abdullahi Ahmed and Deng, Francis M., eds (1990) *Human Rights in Africa* (Washington, D.C.: The Brookings Institution).

——(1992) *Toward an Islamic Reformation* (Cairo: The American University in Cairo Press).

——(2003) "Introduction: 'Area Expressions' and the Universality of Human Rights," in Forsythe, David P. and McMahon, Patrice C., eds (2003) *Human Rights and Diversity* (Lincoln: University of Nebraska Press).

An-Na'im, Abdullahi Ahmed and Deng, Francis M., eds (1990) *Human Rights in Africa* (Washington, D.C.: The Brookings Institution).

Appelbaum, Richard (1970) *Theories of Social Change* (Chicago: Markham Publishing Company).

Appleby, Scott (2000) *The Ambivalence of the Sacred* (Boulder: Rowman & Littlefield Publishers, Inc).

Arjomand, Said A. (1988) *The Turban for the Crown* (New York: Oxford University Press).

Arkoun, Mohamed (1994) *Rethinking Islam*, trans. by Robert D. Lee, (Boulder: Westview Press).

——(1998) "Rethinking Islam," in Kurzman, Charles, ed., *Liberal Islam* (Oxford: Oxford University Press).

Arthur, C.J. (1981) *The German Ideology* (New York: International Publishers).

Asad, Talal (2003) *Formations of the Secular* (Stanford: Stanford University Press).

Ashby, William R. (1956) *An Introduction to Cybernetics* (London: Methuen).

Aziz, Nikhil (1999) "Human Rights in an Era of Globalization," in Ness, Peter van, ed., *Debating Human Rights* (London: Routledge).

Azodanloo, Heidar G. (1992) "Formalization of Friday Sermons and Consolidation of the Islamic Republic of Iran," *Critique*, Vol. 1 (Fall).

Ball, Terence, Farr, James, and Hanson, Russell L., eds (1989) *Political Innovation and Conceptual Change* (New York: Cambridge University Press).

Barnes, T. and Duncan, J. (1992) "Introduction: Writing Worlds," in Barnes, T. and Duncan, J., eds, *Writing Worlds* (London: Routledge).

Bayat-Phillip, Mangol (1980) "Shi'ism in Contemporary Iranian Politics: the Case of Ali Shari'ati," in Kedourie, Elie and Haim, Sylvia, *Towards a Modern Iran* (London: Frank Cass).

Beeman, William O. (1983a) "Patterns of Religion and Economic Development in Iran from the Qajar Era to the Islamic Revolution of 1978–79," in Finn, James, ed., *Global Economics and Religion* (London: Transaction Books).

——(1983b) "Images of the Great Satan: Symbolic Representations of the U.S. in the Iranian Revolution," in Keddie, Nikkie, ed., *Religion and Politics in Iran* (New Haven: Yale University Press).

Bendix, Reinhard (1967) "Tradition and Modernity Reconsidered," *Comparative Studies in Society and History* (April).

Benjamin, Andrew, ed. (1989) *The Lyotard Reader* (Oxford: Basil Blackwell).

Bennis, Phyllis (2006) *Challenging Empire* (Massachusetts: Olive Branch Press).

——and Moushabeck, Michel, eds (1991) *Beyond the Storm* (New York: Olive Branch Press).

——and Moushabeck, Michel, eds (1993) *Altered States* (New York: Olive Branch Press).

Bereano, Philip L., ed. (1976) *Technology as a Social and Political Phenomenon* (New York: John Wiley).

Berger, Peter (1967) *The Sacred Canopy* (New York: Doubleday & Company Inc).

Beteille, A. (1983) *The Idea of Natural Inequality* (Delhi: Oxford University Press).

Binder, Leonard (1988) *Islamic Liberalism* (Chicago: The University of Chicago Press).

Black, Cyril E. (1966) *The Dynamics of Modernization* (New York: Harper & Row Publishers).

Bocock, Robert (1986) *Hegemony* (London: Tavistock Publications).

Bogdanor, Vernon, ed. (1987) *The Blackwell Encyclopedia of Political Institutions* (Oxford: Basil Blackwell).

Booth, K. (1997) "Security and Self: Reflections of a Fallen Realist," in Krause, K. and Williams, M.C., eds, *Critical Security Studies: Concepts and Cases* (London: UCL Press).

Braude, Joseph (2003) *The New Iraq* (New York: Basic Books).

Brinton, Crane (1959) *Anatomy of Revolution* (New York: Vintage Books).

Brown, Michael E., Lynn-Jones, Sean M., and Miller, Steven E., eds (1995), *The Perils of Anarchy* (Cambridge, Massachusetts: The MIT Press).

Brown, Robert McAffee (1978) *Theology in a New Key* (Philadelphia: The Westminster Press).

Brzezinski, Zbigniew (1993) *Out of Control* (New York: Macmillan Publishing Company).

——(1997) *The Grand Chess Board* (New York: Basic Books).

Buci-Glucksman, Christine (1982) "Hegemony and Consent: A Political Strategy," in Sassoon, Anne Showstack, ed. (1982) *Approaches to Gramsci* (London: Writers and Readers Publishing Cooperative Society Ltd).

Bultmann, Rudolf (1958) *Jesus Christ and Mythology* (New York: Charles Scribner's Sons).

——(1984) *New Testament and Mythology* (Philadelphia: Fortress Press).

Burchill, S. and Linklater, A. (1996) *Theories of International Relations* (New York: St Martin's Press).

Burns, James McGregor (1978) *Leadership* (New York: Harper & Row Publishers).

Buzan, B. (1991) *People, States and Fear*, 2nd edn (Boulder: Lynne Rienner).

Calder, Gideon (2002) "Grounding Human Rights: What Differences Does it Make?," in Moseley, Alexander and Norman, Richard, eds, *Human Rights and Military Intervention* (Aldershot: Ashgate).

Calder, Norman (1982) "Accommodation and Revolution in Imami Shi'i Jurisprudence: Ayatollah Khomayni and the Classical Tradition," *Middle Eastern Studies*,Vol. 18, No. 1 (January).

Campbell, Tom (2003) "Human Rights: The Shifting Boundaries," in Campbell, Tom, Goldsworthy, Jeffrey and Stone, Adrienne, eds, *Protecting Human Rights* (Oxford: Oxford University Press).

Cantori, Louis J. and Ziegler Jr., Andrew H., eds (1988) *Comparative Politics* (Colorado: Boulder).

Carmines, Edward G. and Robert Huckfeldt (1998) "Political Behavior: An Overview," in Goodin, Robert E. and Klingemann, Hans-Dieter, eds, *A New Handbook of Political Science* (Oxford: Oxford University Press).

Carr, Edward H. (1986) *What is History?* ed. by Davies, R.W. 2nd edn (London: Macmillan Press Ltd).

Chadwick, Owen (1975) *The Secularization of the European Mind in the Nineteenth Century* (Cambridge: Cambridge University Press).

Chehabi, H.E. (1991) "Religion and Politics in Iran: How Theocratic is the Islamic Republic?" *Daedalus*, 120 (3).

Christian Science Monitor (April 27, 2007) (csmonitor.com).

Clark, I. (1999) *Globalization and International Relations Theory* (Oxford: Oxford University Press).

Clausewitz, Carl von (1976) *On War*, trans. and eds, Michael Howard and Peter Paret (Princeton, NJ: Princeton University Press, 1976).

CNN (April 11, 2003) (www.cnn.com/2003/US/04/11/sprj.irg.pentagon/).

Collin, Finn (1985) *Theory and Understanding* (New York: Basil Blackwell).

Comte, Auguste (1957) *A General View of Positivism* (New York: Robert Speller & Sons).

Connolly, William E. (1967) *Practical Science and Ideology* (New York: Atherton Press).

Coullson, N.J. (1964) *A History of Islamic Law* (Edinburgh: Edinburgh University Press).

Cross, F.L., ed. (1958) *The Oxford Dictionary of the Christian Church* (London: Oxford University Press).

Curtis, James E. and Petras, John W., eds (1970) *The Sociology of Knowledge* (London: Gerald Duckworth & Co. Ltd).

Dahl, Robert (1956) *A Preface to Democratic Theory* (Chicago: The University of Chicago Press).

Daniel, Donald C. and Herbig, Katherine L., eds (1982) *Strategic Military Deception* (New York: Pergamon Press).

Darwish, Hamid, *Kayhan Al-Arabi*, December 29, 1994.

Davidson, Lawrence (1998) *Islamic Fundamentalism* (London: Greenwood Press).

Davis, James (1979) "Towards a Theory of Revolution," in Kelly, George and Brown Jr, Clifford, eds, *Struggles in the State* (New York: John Wiley).

Davis, Kingsley (1961) *Human Society* (New York: Macmillan).

Demerath III, N. J. and Hammond, Phillip E. (1969) *Religion in Social Context* (New York: Random House).

Demko, George and Wood, William B. (1994), eds, *Reordering the World: Geopolitical Perspectives on the Twenty-First Century* (Boulder, CO: Westview).

Der Derian, J. (1989) "The Boundaries of Knowledge and Power in International Relations," in J. Der Derian and M.J. Shapiro, eds, *International/Intertextual Relations* (Toronto: Lexington Books).

——ed. (1995) *International Theory* (New York: New York University Press).

Derrida, Jacques (1976) *Of Grammatology*, trans. Gayatri C. Spivak (Baltimore: The Johns Hopkins University Press).

——(1978) *Writing and Difference* (London: Routledge and Kegan Paul).

——(1994) "Wears and Tears (Tableau of an Ageless World)," in Hayden, Patrick, ed. (2001) *The Philosophy of Human Rights* (St. Paul, MN: Paragon House).

Deutsch, Karl (1971) "Social Mobilization and Political Development," in Finkle, Jason and Gable, Richard, eds, *Political Development and Social Change* (New York: John Wiley).

Donnan, Hastings, ed. (2002) *Interpreting Islam* (London: Sage Publications).

Doran, C.F. (1991) *Systems in Crisis* (Cambridge: Cambridge University Press).

Douglass, Jack, ed. (1970) *Understanding Everyday Life* (Chicago: Aldine).

Douzinas, Costas (2000) *The End of Human Rights* (Oxford: Hart Publishing).

Dwyer, Kevin (1991) *Arab Voices* (Berkeley: University of California Press).

Eagleton, Terry (1983) *Literary Theory* (Oxford: Basil Blackwell).

Eckstein, Harry (1970) "On the Etiology of War," in Kelly, George and Brown Jr., Clifford, eds, (1979) *Struggles in the State* (New York: John Wiley).

Eco, Umberto (1990) *The Limits of Interpretation* (Bloomington: University of Indiana Press).

El Fadl, Khaled Abou (2001) *Speaking in God's Name* (Oxford: Oneworld).

Ellul, Jacques (1972) "The Technological Society," in Teich, Albert H., ed., *Technology and Man's Future* (New York: St. Martin's Press).

Engels, Friedrich (1956) *The Peasant War in Germany* (Moscow: Foreign Languages Publishing House).

Engineer, Asghar Ali (1980) *The Islamic State* (Delhi: Vikas Publishing House PVT Ltd).

Esposito, John L., ed. (1990) *The Iranian Revolution* (Miami: Florida International University Press).

Esposito, John L. and John O. Voll (2001) *Makers of Contemporary Islam* (New York: Oxford University Press).

Fadlallah, Sayyed Muhammad Hussain (1991) *Kayhan Al-Arabi*, July 1.

——(1992) *Kayhan Al-Arabi*, December 14.

——(1996) *Kitab al-Jihad* (*The Book of Jihad*) (Beirut: Dar al-Malak).

Fanon, F. (1963) *The Wretched of the Earth* (New York: Grove).

Farhang, Mansour (1985/86) "Revolution and Regression in Iran," *Comparative Politics*.

Feinberg, Joel (1973) *Social Philosophy* (New Jersey: Prentice-Hall, Inc.).

Femia, Joseph V. (1981) *Gramsci's Political Thought* (Oxford: Clarendon Press).

Ferguson, Y.H. and Mansback, R.W. (1989) *The State, Conceptual Chaos, and the Future of International Relations Theory* (Boulder, CO: The University of Denver).

Fern, Vergilius, ed. (1945), *An Encyclopedia of Religion* (New York: The Philosophical Library).

Ferry, Luc and Renaut, Alain (1992) *From the Rights of Man to the Republican Idea*, trans. F. Philip (Chicago: Chicago University Press).

Feuerbach, Ludwig (1957) *The Essence of Christianity*, trans. George Eliot (New York: Harper and Row).

Field, G. Lowell and Higley, John (1980) *Elitism* (London: Routledge and Kegan Paul).

Fierro, Alfredo (1977) *The Militant Gospel* (Maryknoll, New York: Orbis Books).

Finkle, Jason and Gable, Richard, eds (1963) *Political Development and Social Change* (New York: John Wiley).

Finn, James, ed. (1983) *Global Economics and Religion* (London: Transaction Books).

Fischer, Michael M.J. (1986) *Iran: From Religious Dispute to Revolution* (Cambridge: Harvard University Press).

Forsythe, David P. and McMahon, Patrice C., eds (2003) *Human Rights and Diversity* (Lincoln: University of Nebraska Press).

Foucault, Michel (1970) *The Order of Things*, trans. A. Sheridan (New York: Random House).

——(1972) *The Archeology of Knowledge*, trans. A. Sheridan (New York: Pantheon).

——(1977) *Language, Counter-Memory, Practice: Selected Essays and Interviews*, trans. Donald F. Bouchard, and Sherry Simon (New York: Cornell University Press).

Frye, Alton, ed. (2000) *Humanitarian Intervention: Crafting a Workable Doctrine* (New York: Council of Foreign Relations).

Fukuyama, Francis (1992a) *The End of History and the Last Man* (New York: Avon Books).

——(1992b) "The End of History?," in Rourke, John T., ed., *Taking Sides* (Connecticut: The Dushkin Publishing Group).

Furtado, Celso (1967) *Development and Underdevelopment*, trans. by Ricardo W. De Aguiar and Eric Charles Drysdale (Berkeley: University of California Press).

Geertz, Clifford (1973) *The Interpretation of Cultures* (New York: Basic Books).

Gellner, Ernest (1992) *Postmodernism, Reason and Religion* (London: Routledge).

——(1994) "Foreword," in Ahmed, Akbar S. and Donnan, Hastings, *Islam, Globalization and Postmodernity* (London: Routledge).

Gerth, H.H. and Mills, C. Wright (1958) *From Max Weber* (New York: Oxford University Press).

Gewirth, Alan (1989) "Why There are Human Rights," in Winston, Morton E., ed., *The Philosophy of Human Rights* (Belmont California: Wadsworth Publishing Company).

Ghulyun, Burhan (1990) *Ightial Al-Aql* (The Assassination of the Mind), 3rd edn (Cairo: Madbouli).

——(1994) *Al-Mihna al-Arabiyya: al-Dawla didh al-Umma* (The Arab Malaise: The State against the Nation) (trans. from the French), 2nd edn (Beirut: Markaz Dirasat al-Wihda al-Arabiyya).

Gill, S.R. (1991) "Reflections on Global Order and Sociohistorical Time," *Alternatives*, Vol. 16.

Gill, S. and Mittelman, J.H., eds (1997) *Innovation and Transformation in International Studies* (Cambridge: Cambridge University Press).

Gilpin, R. (1981) *War and Change in World Politics* (Cambridge: Cambridge University Press).

Goldgeier, J.M. and McFaul, M. (1992) "A Tale of Two Worlds: Core and Periphery in the Post-Cold War Era," *International Organization*, Vol. 46, No. 2 (Spring).

Goldstein, J. and Keohane, R.O. (1993), "Ideas and Foreign Policy: an Analytical Framework," in Goldstein, J. and Keohane, R.O., eds, *Ideas and Foreign Policy* (Ithaca, NY: Cornell University Press).

Goodin, Robert E. and Klingemann, Hans-Dieter, eds (1998) *A New Handbook of Political Science* (Oxford: Oxford University Press).

Gould, Julius and Kolb, William L., eds (1964) *A Dictionary of the Social Sciences* (New York: The Free Press).

Graham Jr, George (1984) "Consensus," in Sartori, Giovanni, ed., *Social Science Concepts* (London: Sage Publications).

Gramsci, Antonio (1978) *Political Writings 1921–1926* (London: Lawrence and Wishart).

——(1980) *Selections From the Prison Notes* (New York: International Publishers).

Green, Jerrold D. (1982) *Revolution in Iran* (New York: Praeger Publishers).

Guénon, René (1953) *The Reign of Quantity* (London: Luzac).

——(1962) *The Crisis of the Modern World* (London: Luzac and Company Ltd).

Gurr, Ted (1971) *Why Men Rebel* (Princeton, New Jersey: Princeton University Press).

Gutting, Gary (1989) *Archeology of Scientific Reason* (Cambridge: Cambridge University Press).

Habermas, Jürgen (1976) *Legitimation Crisis*, trans. Thomas McCarthy (London: Heinemann).

——(1987) *The Philosophical Discourse of Modernity* (Cambridge, MA: MIT Press).

——(1989) *The Theory of Communicative Action*, Vol. 2, trans. Thomas McCarthy (Boston: Beacon Press).

Haddad, Yvonne Yazbeck (1991) "Operation Desert Shield/Desert Storm: The Islamic Perspective," in Bennis, Phyllis and Moushabeck, Michel, eds, *Beyond the Storm* (New York: Olive Branch Press).

——(1993) "The 'New Enemy'? Islam and Islamists After the Cold War," in Bennis, Phyllis and Moushabeck, Michel, eds, *Altered States* (New York: Olive Branch Press).

Hafez, Mahmoud (March 25, 2007) (www.middle-east-online.com).

Hall, Catherine (2002) *Civilizing Subjects* (Cambridge: Polity Press).

Hall, J.A., ed. (1994) *The State: Critical Concepts* (London: Routledge).

Hallowell, John (1973) *The Moral Foundation of Democracy* (Chicago: Chicago University Press).

Hanafi, Hassan (1991) *Muqaddimah fi Ilm al-Istighrab* (An Introduction to the Science of Occidentalism) (Cairo: al-Dar al-Fanniyyah).

Harkabi, Yehoshafat (1977) *Arab Strategies and Israel's Response* (New York: The Free Press).

Hayden, Patrick, ed. (2001) *The Philosophy of Human Rights* (St. Paul, MN: Paragon House).

Heikal, M. (1996) *Secret Channels* (London: HarperCollins).

——(April 26, 2007) *aljazeera TV network* (www.aljazeera.net).

Heisenberg, W. (1971) *Physics and Beyond*, trans. Arnold J. Pomerans (New York, Harper and Row).

Hodgson, Marshall G.S. (1977) *The Venture of Islam* (Chicago: Chicago University Press).

Holden, Barry (1988) *Understanding Liberal Democracy* (London: Phillip Allan).

Holsti, K.J. (1985) *The Dividing Discipline* (Boston, MA: Allen and Unwin).

Hudson, Winthrop S. (1949) "Puritanism and the Spirit of Capitalism," *Church History*, Vol. 15, No. 1.

Hourani, Albert (1967) "Islam and the Philosophers of History," *Middle Eastern Studies*, Vol. 3, No. 3 (April).

Huntington, Samuel (1968) *Political Order and Changing Societies* (New Haven: Yale University Press).

——(1988) "The Change to Change," in Cantori, Louis J. and Ziegler Jr., Andrew H., eds, *Comparative Politics* (Colorado: Boulder).

——(1992) "No Exit: The Errors of Endism," in Rourke, John T., ed. *Taking Sides* (Connecticut: The Dushkin Publishing Group).

——(1993) "The Clash of Civilizations?" *Foreign Affairs* (Summer).

Hurrell, A. and Woods, N. (1995) "Globalisation and Inequality," *Millennium*, Vol. 24, No. 3 (Winter).

——eds (1999) *Inequality, Globalization, and World Politics* (Oxford: Oxford University Press).

Husak, Douglas (1989) "Why there are no Human Rights," in Winston, Morton E., ed., *The Philosophy of Human Rights* (Belmont California: Wadsworth Publishing Company).

Hussain, Asaf (1985) *Islamic Iran* (London: Frances Pinter).

Ibish, Yusuf, ed. (1966) *Nusus al-Fikr al-Siyasi al-Islami* (Readings in Islamic Political Theory) (Beirut: Dar al-Tali'ah).

Ibn Khaldun, Abd al-Rahman (1958) *The Muqaddimah* (An Introduction to History), trans. Franz Rosenthal (Princeton: Princeton University Press).

Ikenberry, G.J. (1996) "The Myth of Post-Cold War Chaos," *Foreign Affairs*, Vol. 75, No. 3 (May/June).

——(1999) "Liberal hegemony and the Future of American Postwar Order," in Paul, T.V. and Hall, J.A., eds, *International Order and the Future of World Politics* (Cambridge: Cambridge University Press).

Imber, Collin (1997) *Ebu's-su'ud: The Islamic Legal Tradition* (Edinburgh: Edinburgh University Press).

Irfani, Suroosh (1983) *Revolutionary Islam in Iran* (London: Zed Books).

Issawi, Charles (1958) *An Arab Philosophy of History* (London: John Murray).

Jackson, R.H. (1993) "The Weight of Ideas in Decolonization: Normative Change in International Relations," in Goldstein, J. and Keohane, R.O., eds, *Ideas and Foreign Policy* (Ithaca, NY: Cornell University Press).

Johnson, Chalmers (1968) *Revolutionary Change* (London: University of London Press).

Jouvenal, Bertrand de (1948) *Power: The Natural History of its Growth*, rev edn (London: Batchworth).

——(1957) *Sovereignty: An Inquiry into the Political Good*, trans. J.F. Huntington (Chicago: University of Chicago Press).

Juergensmeyer, M. (1993) *The New Cold War?* (Berkeley, CA: University of California Press).

Jum'a, Ali (March 21, 2007) (http://arab.moheet.com/asp/subject.asp?ch=1).

——*Al-Ahram*, July 6, 2007.

Keddie, Nikkie, ed. (1983) *Religion and Politics in Iran* (New Haven: Yale University Press).

——(1963) "Symbol and Sincerity in Islam," *Studia Islamica*, No. 19.

Kedourie, Elie and Haim, Sylvia G. (1980) *Towards a Modern Iran* (London: Frank Cass).

Kelly, George and Brown Jr, Clifford, eds (1979) *Struggles in the State* (New York: John Wiley).

Khadduri, M. (1955) *War and Peace in the Law of Islam* (Baltimore, MD: The Johns Hopkins Press).

——(1966) *The Islamic Law of Nations* (Baltimore, MD: The Johns Hopkins Press).

Khomeini, Imam [Rouhullah] (1985), *Islam and Revolution*, trans. Hamid Algar (London: KPI).

Kingsbury, B. (1999) "Sovereignty and Inequality," in Hurrell, A. and Woods, N., eds, *Inequality, Globalization, and World Politics* (Oxford: Oxford University Press).

Kleindorfer, Paul R., Kunreuther, Howard C. and Schoemaker, Paul J.H. (1993) *Decision Sciences* (New York: Cambridge University Press).

Knox, MacGregor (1996) "Conclusion: Continuity and Revolution in the Making of Strategy," in Murray, Williamson, Knox, MacGregor and Bernstein, Alvin, eds, *The Making of Strategy: Rulers, States and War* (Cambridge USA: Cambridge University Press).

Kohanski, Alexander S. (1977) *Philosophy and Technology* (New York: Philosophical Library).

Kolb, David (1986) *The Critique of Pure Modernity* (Chicago: The University of Chicago Press).

Krasner, Stephen (1982) "Structural Causes and Regime Consequences," *International Organization*, 36 (Spring).

——(1985) *Structural Conflict* (Berkeley, CA: University of California Press).

Krause, K. and Williams, M.C., eds (1997) *Critical Security Studies: Concepts and Cases* (London: UCL Press).

Kuper, Adam and Kuper, Jessica, eds (1985) *The Social Science Encyclopedia* (London: Routledge & Kegan Paul).

Kurzman, Charles, ed. (1998) *Liberal Islam* (Oxford: Oxford University Press).

Landau, Martin (1972) *Political Theory and Political Science* (New York: Macmillan).

Larijani, Muhammad Javad (1995) "Islamic Society and Modernism," *The Iranian Journal of International Affairs*, VII (1).

Laswell, Harold D. (1976) *Power and Personality* (New York: W.W. Norton).

Layne, Christopher (1995) "The Unipolar Illusion," in Brown, Michael E., Lynn-Jones, Sean M., and Miller, Steven E., eds, *The Perils of Anarchy* (Cambridge, Massachusetts: The MIT Press).

Lazlo, Ervin (1991) *The Age of Bifurcation* (Reading: Gordon and Breach).

Levine, Daniel H. (1981) *Religion and Politics in Latin America* (Princeton, New Jersey: Princeton University Press).

——(1986) "Religion and Politics in Comparative Historical Perspective," *Comparative Politics*, Vol. 19 (October).

Lewis, Bernard (1990) "The Roots of Muslim Rage," *The Atlantic Monthly* (September).

Liddell Hart, B.H. (1967) *Strategy* (London: Faber and Faber).

Lindley, Richard (1986) *Autonomy* (London: MacMillan).

Linz, Juan (1970) "An Authoritarian Regime: Spain," in Allardt, Erik and Rokkan, Stein, eds, *Mass Politics* (New York: The Free Press).

Luhmann, Niklas (1988) "The Unity of the Legal System," in Teubner, Gunther, ed., *Autopoietic Law* (Berlin: Walter de Gruyter).

——(1989) *Ecological Communication*, trans. John Bednarz Jr. (Oxford: Polity Press).

——(1990) *Essays on Self-Reference* (New York: Columbia University Press).

Lyotard, Jean-Francois (1988) *The Differend: Phrases in Dispute* (Minneapolis: University of Minnesota Press).

——(1984) *The Postmodern Condition: A Report on Knowledge*, trans. G. Bennington and B. Massumi, (Minneapolis: Minneapolis University Press).

MacIntyre, Alasdair (1966) *A Short History of Ethics* (New York: Macmillan).

——(1989) "Some Consequences of the Failure of the Enlightenment Project," in Winston, Morton E., ed., *The Philosophy of Human Rights* (Belmont California: Wadsworth Publishing Company).

MacIvar, R.M. (1947) *The Web of Government* (New York: The Macmillan Company).

Maduro, Otto (1977) "New Marxist Approaches to the Relative Autonomy of Religion," *Sociological Analysis*, Vol. 38, No. 4.

——(1982) *Religion and Social Conflict*, trans. Robert R. Barr (Maryknoll, New York: Orbis Books).

Mahdi, Muhsin (1964) *Ibn Khaldun's Philosophy of History* (Chicago: University of Chicago Press).

Malinowski, Bronislaw (1954) *Magic, Science and Religion and Other Essays* (New York: Doubleday).

Manchester Guardian Weekly, February 21, 1993, Vol. 148, No. 8.

Mannheim, Karl (1970) "The Sociology of Knowledge," in Curtis, James E. and Petras, John W., eds, *The Sociology of Knowledge* (London: Gerald Duckworth & Co. Ltd).

Martin, Richard C. (2001) "Islam and Religious Studies: An Introductory Essay," in Martin, Richard C., ed., *Approaches to Islam in Religious Studies* (Oxford: Oneworld).

Marx, Karl and Engels, Friedrich (1964) *On Religion* (New York: Schocken).

——(1981) Arthur, C.J., ed., *The German Ideology* (New York: International Publishers).

Massad, Joseph (2001) *Colonial Effects* (New York: Columbia University Press).

Mastanduno, M. (1999) "A Realist View: Three Images of the Coming International Order," in Paul, T.V. and Hall, J.A., eds, *International Order and the Future of World Politics* (Cambridge: Cambridge University Press).

Mathieu, Vittorio (1986) "Prolegomena to a Study of Human Rights," in UNESCO, ed., *Philosophical Foundations of Human Rights* (Paris: UNESCO).

May, Todd (1993) *Between Geneology and Epistemology* (Pennsylvania: The Pennsylvania State University Press).

Mayer, Ann Elizabeth (1990) "Current Muslim Thinking on Human Rights," in An-Na'im, Abdullahi Ahmed and Deng, Francis M., eds, *Human Rights in Africa* (Washington, D.C.: The Brookings Institution).

——(1999) *Islam and Human Rights* (Boulder: Westview Press).

McChrystal, Stanley A. (2000) "Memorandum to the President," in Frye, Alton, ed., *Humanitarian Intervention: Crafting a Workable Doctrine* (New York: Council of Foreign Relations).

McGuire, Meredith B. (1981) *Religion: The Social Context* (California: Wadsworth, Belmont).

M'Clintock, Rev. John, and Strong, James (1880) *CYCLOPAEDIA of Biblical, Theological, and Ecclesiastical Literature* (New York: Harper and Brothers Publishers).

McSweeney, B. (1999) *Security, Identity and Interests* (Cambridge: Cambridge University Press).

Means, Richard L. (1966) "Protestantism and Economic Institutions: Auxiliary Theories to Weber's Protestant Ethic," *Social Forces*, No. 44 (March).

Middle East Online, July 26, 2007 (www.middle-east-online.com/?id=50675).

Migdal, Joel (1988) *Strong Societies and Weak States* (New Jersey: Princeton University Press).

Mill, John Stuart (1985) *On Liberty* (Indianapolis: Bobbs-Merrill).

Moltmann, Jürgen (1967) *Theology of Hope*, trans. James W. Leitch (New York: Harper and Row).

Moore Jr, Barrington (1967) *The Social Origins of Dictatorship and Democracy* (Boston: Beacon Press).

Morgenhau, Hans J. (1993) *Politics Among Nations*, revised by Kenneth W. Thompson (New York: McGraw Hill).

Morton, Robert K. (1957) *Social Theory and Social Structures*, rev. edn (Glencoe: Illinois Free Press).

Mosca, Gaetano (1965) *The Ruling Class*, trans. Hannah D. Kahn (New York: McGraw-Hill Book Company).

Moseley, Alexander and Norman, Richard, eds (2002) *Human Rights and Military Intervention* (Aldershot: Ashgate).

Motahhari, Ayatollah Mortaza (1985) "The Nature of the Islamic Revolution," in Afshar, Haleh, *Iran: A Revolution in Turmoil* (London: Macmillan).

——*Kayhan International*, May 20, 1989.

Moussalli, Ahmad S., ed. (1998) *Islamic Fundamentalism: Myths and Realities* (UK: Ithaca Press).

——(2001) *The Islamic Quest for Democracy, Pluralism, and Human Rights* (Gainesville: University Press of Florida).

Mumford, Lewis (1976) "The Automation of Knowledge," in Bereano, Philip L., ed., *Technology as a Social and Political Phenomenon* (New York: John Wiley).

Murray, Williamson, Knox, MacGregor and Bernstein, Alvin, eds (1996) *The Making of Strategy: Rulers, States and War* (Cambridge: Cambridge University Press).

Nabi, Malek bin (1961) *Shurut al-Nahda* (The Conditions of Renaissance) (Cairo: Dar al-Uruba).

Najmabadi, Afsaneh (1987) "Iran's Turn to Islam: From Modernism to a Moral Order," *The Middle East Journal*, Vol. 41, No. 2 (Spring).

Nasr, Seyyed Hossein (1980) "The Concept and Reality of Freedom in Islam and Islamic Civilization," in Rosenbaum, Alan S., ed., *The Philosophy of Human Rights* (Westport: GreenWood Press).

Nehme, Michel (1998) "The Islamic–Capitalist State of Saudi Arabia: Surfacing of Fundamentalism," in Moussalli, Ahmad S., ed., *Islamic Fundamentalism: Myths and Realities* (UK: Ithaca Press).

Nerhot, Patrick (1988) "The Fact of Law," in Teubner, Gunther, ed., *Autopoietic Law* (Berlin: Walter de Gruyter).

Ness, Peter van, ed. (1999) *Debating Human Rights* (London: Routledge).

Nettl, J.P. (1994) "The State as a Conceptual Variable," in Hall, J.A., ed., *The State: Critical Concepts, Vol. 1* (London: Routledge).

Nixon, Richard (1994) *Beyond Peace* (New York: Random House).

No'man, Issam (2007) *Al-Quds Al-Arabi*, April 18 (www.alquds.co.uk).

Norris, Christopher and Benjamin, Andrew (1988) *What is Deconstruction?* (New York: St. Martin's Press).

Oakeshott, Michael (1962) "On Being Conservative," *Rationalism in Politics and Other Essays* (London: Methuen).

Olson, Mancur (1971) "Rapid Growth as a Destabilizing Force," in Finkle, Jason and Gable, Richard, eds, *Political Development and Social Change* (New York: John Wiley).

Pareto, Vilfredo (1968) *The Rise and Fall of Elites* (New Jersey: The Bedminster Press).

Parsons, Talcott (1951) *The Social System* (Glencoe, Illinois: Free Press).

——(1954) *Essays in Sociological Theory*, rev. edn (London: Collins-Macmillan Ltd.).

Pasha, M.K. (1997) "Ibn Khaldun and World Order," in Gill, S. and Mittelman, J.H., eds, *Innovation and Transformation in International Studies* (Cambridge: Cambridge University Press).

Paul, T.V. and Hall, J.A., eds (1999) *International Order and the Future of World Politics* (Cambridge: Cambridge University Press).

Pellicani, Luciano (1981) *Gramsci* (Stanford, CA: Hoover Institution Press).

Petrova, Dimitrina (2004) "Social and Economic Dimensions of Universal Rights," in Sajo, Andras, ed., *Human Rights with Modesty* (Leiden: Martinus Nijhoff Publishers Corp).

Pipes, Daniel and Clawson, Patrick (1993) "Ambitious Iran, Troubled Neighbors," *Foreign Affairs*, Vol. 2, No. 1.

Qaradawi, Yusuf (2007) *Al-shari'ah wa Al-hayat* (Shari'ah and Life), February 25, *al-Jazeera* network (www.aljazeera.net).

Qur'an: The meaning of the glorious Qur'an: text (1980), translation and commentary by Abdullah Yusuf Ali (Cairo, Egypt: Dar al-Kitab al-Masri).

Rahman, Fazlur (1981) "Roots of Islamic Neo-Fundamentalism," in Soddard Phillip H., Cuthell, David C. and Sullivan, Margaret W., eds, *Change and the Muslim World* (New York: Syracuse University Press).

——(1982) *Islam and Modernity* (Chicago: The University of Chicago Press).

——(2001) "Approaches to Islam in Religious Studies," in Martin, Richard C., ed., *Approaches to Islam in Religious Studies* (Oxford: Oneworld).

Rajaee, Farhang (1990) "Iranian Ideology and Worldview: The Cultural Export of Revolution," in Esposito, John L., ed., *The Iranian Revolution* (Miami: Florida International University Press).

Ramonet, Ignacio (2000) "The Control of Pleasure," *Le Monde Diplomatique*, May.

Randall, Vicky and Theobold, Robin (1985) *Political Change and Underdevelopment* (London: Macmillan).

Rauf, Muhammad Abdul (2001) "Outsiders' Interpretations of Islam: A Muslim's Point of View," in Martin, Richard C., ed., *Approaches to Islam in Religious Studies* (Oxford: Oneworld).

Reisman, W.M. (1990) "International Law After the Cold War," *The American Journal of International Law*, Vol. 84, No. 4.

Reynolds, Charles (1989) *The Politics of War* (New York: St. Martin's Press).

Richards, Alan and Waterbury, John (1990) *A Political Economy of the Middle East* (Boulder: Westview Press).

Rorty, Richard (1979) *Philosophy and the Mirror of Nature* (Princeton: Princeton University Press).

——(1993) "Human Rights, Rationality and Sentimentality," in Hayden, Patrick, ed. (2001) *The Philosophy of Human Rights* (St. Paul, MN: Paragon House).

Rosenbaum, Alan S., ed. (1980) *The Philosophy of Human Rights* (Westport: Green Wood Press).

Rourke, John T., ed. (1992) *Taking Sides* (Connecticut: The Dushkin Publishing Group).

Ruggie, J. (1998) *Constructing the World Polity* (London: Routledge).

Rustow, Dankwart A. (1968) "Introduction to the Issue Philosophers and Kings: Studies in Leadership," *Daedalus*, 97 (Summer).

Sabet, Amr (2000) "The End of Fundamentalism?," *Third World Quarterly*, Vol. 21, No. 5.

Said, Edward (1979) *Orientalism* (New York: Vintage Books).

——(1981) *Covering Islam* (New York: Pantheon Books).

——(1993) *Culture and Imperialism* (London: Chatto and Windus).

——(1994) *Representations of the Intellectual* (New York: Pantheon Books).

Saint Simon, Henri de (1964) *Social Organization, The Science of Man and Other Writings*, trans. Felix Markham (New York: Harper and Row).

Samuelson, Kurt (1964) *Religion and Economic Action: A Critique of Max Weber* (New York: Harper and Row).

Sanks, T. Howland and Smith, Brian H. (1977) "Liberation Ecclesiology: Praxis, Theory, Praxis," *Theological Studies*, No. 38.

Sardar, Ziauddin (1987) *The Future of Muslim Civilization* (London: Mansell Publishing Ltd).

Sartori, Giovanni (1968) "Democracy," in Sills, David L., ed., *International Encyclopedia of the Social Sciences* (New York: Macmillan).

——(1984) "Guidelines for Concept Analysis," in Sartori, Giovanni, ed., *Social Science Concepts* (London: Sage).

Sassoon, Anne Showstack, ed. (1982) *Approaches to Gramsci* (London: Writers and Readers Publishing Cooperative Society Ltd).

Saward, Michael (1998) *The Terms of Democracy* (Cambridge: Polity Press).

Sayyid, B.S. (1997) *A Fundamental Fear* (New York: Zed Books).

Schmitt, Carl (1976) *The Concept of the Political*, trans. George Schwab (New Jersey: Rutgers University Press).

——(1996) *The Concept of the Political*, trans. George Schwab (Chicago: University of Chicago Press).

Segal, Gerald (1998) "Not Bombs But Baywatch," *Newsweek*, March 8.

Sellars, Kirsten (2002) *The Rise and Rise of Human Rights* (Gloucestershire: Sutton Publishing).

Shaltout, Mahmoud (July 6, 1959) (http://Shiite-muslim.anime.co.za/anime/Shiite_Muslim).

Sharaby, Hisham (1989) *NeoPatriarchy* (New York: Oxford University Press).

Shari'ati, Ali (1978) *Hajj*, trans. Somayyah and Yasser (Ohio: Free Islamic Literatures).

——(1979) *On the Sociology of Islam*, trans. Hamid Algar (Berkeley: Mizan Press).

——(1980a) *From Where Shall We Begin*, trans. Fatollah Marjani (Houston: Free Islamic Literature).

——(1980b) *Fatima is Fatima*, trans. Laleh Bakhtiar (Tehran: Shariati Foundation).

——(1980c) *Marxism and Other Western Fallacies* (Berkeley: Mizan Press).

Sheikh, Naveed S. (2003) *The New Politics of Islam: Pan-Islamic Foreign Policy in a World of States* (London: Routledge Curzon).

Sheridan, Alan (1980) *Michel Foucault* (London: Tavistock Publications).

Shils, Edward (1981) *Tradition* (London: Faber & Faber).

Sills, David L., ed. (1968) *International Encyclopedia of the Social Sciences* (New York: Macmillan).

Singer, M. and Wildavsky, A. (1993) *The Real World Order: Zones of Peace, Zones of Turmoil* (Chatham, NJ: Chatham House).

Skocpol, Theda (1982) "Rentier State and Shi'a Islam in the Iranian Revolution," *Theory and Society*, Vol. 11, No. 3.

Smith, Steven B. (1989) *Hegel's Critique of Liberalism* (Chicago: University of Chicago Press).

Sobhi, Ahmad Mahmoud (1969) *Nazariat al-Imamah ladha al-Shi'a al-Ithna Ashriya* (The Theory of the Imamite among the Twelve Shi'ites) (Egypt: Dar al-Ma'aref).

Soddard, Phillip H., Cuthell, David C. and Sullivan, Margaret W., eds (1981) *Change and the Muslim World* (New York: Syracuse University Press).

Spencer, Herbert (1961) *The Study of Sociology* (Ann Arbor: University of Michigan Press).

Soroush, Abdel Karim (1998) "The Evolution and Devolution of Religious Knowledge," in Kurzman, Charles, ed., *Liberal Islam* (Oxford: Oxford University Press).

——(2000) *Reason, Freedom and Democracy in Islam*, trans. and ed. Mahmoud Sadri and Ahmad Sadri (Oxford: Oxford University Press).

Stanley, Manfred (1976) "Technology and its Critics," in Bereano, Philip L., ed., *Technology as a Social and Political Phenomenon* (New York: John Wiley).

Stempel, John (1981) *Inside the Iranian Revolution* (Bloomington: Indiana University Press).

Stone, Adrienne (2003) "Introduction," in Campbell, Tom, Goldsworthy, Jeffrey and Stone, Adrienne, eds, *Protecting Human Rights* (Oxford: Oxford University Press).

Strong, Tracy B. (1996) "Foreword," in Schmitt, Carl, *The Concept of the Political*, trans. George Schwab (Chicago: The University of Chicago Press).

Suganami, H. (1989) *The Domestic Analogy and World Order Proposals* (Cambridge: Cambridge University Press).

Taha, Mahmoud Mohammed (1998) "The Second Message of Islam," in Kurzman, Charles, ed., *Liberal Islam* (Oxford: Oxford University Press).

Tamadonfar, Mehran (1989) *The Islamic Polity and Political Leadership* (Boulder: Westview Press).

Tarnas, Richard (1991) *The Passion of the Western Mind* (New York: Ballantine Books).

Tawfiq, Khaled (1992) *Kayhan al-Arabi*, December 7.

——(1995) *Kayhan Al-Arabi*, August 10.

——(1995) *Kayhan Al-Arabi*, February 20.

Tawney, R.H. (1962) *Religion and the Rise of Capitalism* (Gloucester, MA: Peter Smith)

Tehranian, Majid (1995) "Where is the New World Order: At the End of History or Clash of Civilizations?," *Iranian Journal of International Relations*, VII (2).

Teich, Albert H., ed. (1972) *Technology and Man's Future* (New York: St. Martin's Press).

Teubner, Gunther, ed. (1988) *Autopoietic Law* (Berlin: Walter de Gruyter).

——(1989) "How the Law Thinks: Towards a Constructivist Epistemology of Law," *Law and Society Review*, Vol. 23, No. 5.

——(1993) *Law as an Autopoietic System*, trans. Anne Bankowska and Ruth Adles, ed. Zenon Bankowski (Oxford: Blackwell Publications).

Thompson, Sir G. (1961) *The Inspiration of Science* (London: Oxford University Press).

Tibi, Bassam (1990a) *Islam and the Cultural Accommodation of Social Change* (Boulder: Westview Press).

——(1990b) "The European Tradition of Human Rights and the Culture of Islam," in An-Na'im, Abdullahi Ahmed and Deng, Francis M., eds, *Human Rights in Africa* (Washington, D.C.: The Brookings Institution).

Tilly, C. (1975) "Reflections on the History of European State-making," in Tilly, C., ed., *The Formation of National States in Europe* (Princeton, NJ: Princeton University Press).

——(1999) *Durable Inequality* (Berkeley, CA: University of California Press).

Tucker, Robert C. (1981) *Politics as Leadership* (Columbia: University of Missouri Press).

Turner, Bryan S. (2002) "Orientalism, or the Politics of the Text," in Donnan, Hastings, ed., *Interpreting Islam* (London: Sage Publications).

Toynbee, Arnold (1972) *A Study of History*, revised and abridged by Toynbee, Arnold and Caplan, Jane (New York: Weathervane Books).

UNESCO, ed. (1986) *Philosophical Foundations of Human Rights* (Paris: UNESCO).

Viaud, Gaston (1960) *Intelligence: Its Evolution and Form*, trans. A.J. Pomerans (New York: Harper & Row Publishers).

Voeglin, Eric (1974) *The New Science of Politics* (Chicago: The University of Chicago Press).

Walker, R.B.J. (1993) *Inside/Outside: International Relations as Political Theory* (Cambridge: Cambridge University Press).

Walton, K.L. (1973) "Linguistic Relativity," in Pearce, G. and Maynard, P., eds, *Conceptual Change* (Boston, MA: D. Reidel).

Waltz, K.N. (1979) *Theory of International Politics* (Reading, MA: Addison-Wesley).

Walzer, M. (1967) "On the Role of Symbolism in Political Thought," *Political Science Quarterly*, Vol. 82, No. 2.

Weaver, Marry Anne (1993) "The Egyptian Connection: Inside the World of Omar Abdel-Rahman," *The New Yorker*, April 12.

Weber, Max (1958) *The Protestant Ethic and the Spirit of Capitalism*, trans. Talcott Parsons, (New York: Charles Scribner's Sons).

Weeramantary, C.G. (1988) *Islamic Jurisprudence* (London: Macmillan).

Weiner, Myron (1966) *Modernization: The Dynamics of Growth* (New York: Basic Books).

Wellmer, Albrecht (1985) "On the Dialectic of Modernism and Postmodernism," *Praxis International*, Vol. 4.

Wendt, A. (1992) "Anarchy is What States Make of it: the Social Construction of Power Politics," *International Organization*, Vol. 46, No. 2 (Spring).

Wiarda, Howard (1985a) "Toward a Nonethnocentric Theory of Development: Alternative Conceptions from the Third World," in Wiarda, Howard, *New Directions in Comparative Politics* (Boulder: Westview Press).

——(1985b) *New Directions in Comparative Politics* (Boulder: Westview Press).

Wight, M. (1966) "Why is There no International Theory?," in Der Derian, J., ed., *International Theory* (New York: New York University Press, 1995).

Wildavsky, Aaron (1980) *New York Times Book Review*, April 27.

Williams, H., Wright, M. and Evans, T. (1993) *International Relations and Political Theory* (Buckingham: Open University Press).

Wilson, Thomas (1970) "Normative and Interpretive Paradigms in Sociology," in Douglass, Jack, ed., *Understanding Everyday Life* (Chicago: Aldine).

Winston, Morton E. (1989) "Preface," in Winston, Morton E., ed., *The Philosophy of Human Rights* (Belmont, CA: Wadsworth Publishing Company).

Wuthnow, Robert (1991) "Understanding Religion and Politics," *Daedalus*, Vol. 120, No. 3 (Summer).

Zakaria, F. (1998) *From Wealth to Power* (Princeton, NJ: Princeton University Press).

Zartman, I.W. (1995) "Putting Things Back Together," in Zartman, I.W., ed., *Collapsed States: The Disintegration and Restoration of Legitimate Authority* (Boulder, CO: Lynne Rienner).

Zeleny, Milan, ed. (1981) *Autopoiesis: A Theory of Living Organization* (New York: North Holland).

Index